A CENTURY OF SPORTS

A CENTURY OF

SPORTS

by THE ASSOCIATED PRESS SPORTS STAFF

Supervising Editor: Will Grimsley

Photo Editor: Thomas V. diLustro

Project Director: Keith Fuller

Editor-In-Chief: Dan Perkes

Authors: Hal Bock, Bob Green, Will Grimsley, Dick Joyce, Ted Meier, Charles Morey, Sid Moody, Herschel Nissenson, Ken Rappoport, Mike Rathet, Mike Recht, Ed Schuyler Jr., Tom Saladino, Karol Stonger and Ben Thomas, New York; Jerry Liska, Chicago; Bloys Britt, Charlotte, N.C.; Hubert Mizell, Miami; Denne H. Freeman, Dallas; John Farrow and Geoffrey Miller, London; Kay K. Tateishi, Tokyo; Harvey Hudson, Paris; and Fenton Wheeler and Alejandro Torres Victoria, Madrid.

Copy Editor: Norman Goldstein

Book Design: SOHO Studio

Pictures were made by staff photographers of The Associated Press and its member newspapers. Additional photographs provided by The Baseball Hall of Fame, U.S. Trotting Association, Hall of Fame of The Trotter, Harness Racing Institute, Hockey Hall of Fame, U.S. Handball Association, National Cowboy Hall of Fame, Basketball Hall of Fame, Ford Motor Co., Football Hall of Fame, and the U.S. Golf Association.

Produced in the U.S.A. by The Plimpton Press.

CONTENTS

FOREWORD

To trace a century of sports, as *The Associated Press* has done on these pages, is a singular achievement and a remarkable chronicling of the growth, popularity, and, yes, even relevancy of sports in modern society. One needs only to focus on the decade of the '60s to illustrate what a phenomenal explosion has taken place.

In 1959, for instance, there were 16 major league baseball teams. Today, there are 24.

In 1959, there were six National Hockey League teams. Today, there are 14.

In 1959, there were eight major league basketball teams. Today, there are 17 teams in the NBA and 11 in the ABA.

In 1959, there were 10 National Football League teams. Today, there are 26 and we are talking in terms of 32 by 1980.

In 1959, professional golfers played a schedule of 43 tournaments worth $1,187,340 in prize money. This year, the PGA tour has 63 stops, total worth $7,100,000.

Add to those examples the growth of automobile racing, harness racing, skiing —just about every phase of sports you can examine.

During the 1960s, multimillion-dollar stadiums were built in Los Angeles, San Francisco, Washington, Atlanta, St. Louis, New York, Pittsburgh, San Diego, and in Houston, where baseball and football games were played inside in controlled comfort while outside a driving rain splashed heat-baked pavements, and also where a college basketball game was played before more than 52,000 spectators. Work and planning went on for like structures in Philadelphia, Dallas, Foxboro, New Orleans and Detroit.

Today, more people attend each 13-game single weekend schedule of National Football League games than attended the league's entire season of play in any year prior to 1936. Attendance at our pre-season games in 1970 was higher than any regular season NFL total before 1961.

The *AP* newsmen and editors who put this book together well understand the point I'm making because it has been their job and the job of others like them to provide the detailed coverage of each of these events—from the pre-season game at Tampa to the Super Bowl, from the baseball exhibition at Daytona Beach to the World Series, from the Wednesday pro-am before the Los Angeles Open to the U.S. Open and the Masters, from the 6-furlong sprint at Charlestown to the Kentucky Derby, from the Penn-Columbia boat race to the Henley Regatta, from the Sherbrooke, Ont., training camp to the Stanley Cup, from the first Stanford scrimmage to the Rose Bowl.

The growth in sports is attributable to many factors, not the least of which is the telling of the story by newsmen such as those who make up *The Associated Press* sports staff. They are as much a part of sports as the players and the administrators and the fans. It is my privilege to introduce you to their *Century of Sports*.

Pete Rozelle
Commissioner
National Football League

PREFACE

Sports have an international language all their own. The various countries differ in customs and ideologies—and frequently go to war to defend them—but all find a common ground on the athletic field. There are few nations that do not have respect for the stronger, the faster and the more skillful man.

Sports have been with us almost from the first day of man's appearance on earth. In an era of increasing leisure time, the fastest growing community interest—both in the United States and around the world—has been sports. We are now in an age of the greatest expansion both in spectator and participant sports.

No one seems better qualified to examine this sports explosion than the Sports Staff of *The Associated Press.* They are specialists in their respective fields. Alejandro Torres Victoria, who collaborated with John Fenton Wheeler of the *AP*'s Madrid Bureau in writing about bullfighting, estimates that he has witnessed 2,400 corridas. Kay Tateishi, of the Tokyo Bureau, is an expert on judo, the subject on which he writes. Bob Green follows the tour with the professional golfers and Bloys Britt is *The AP*'s man with the barnstorming auto racers. Other authors are equally knowledgeable of their subjects.

This is not intended to be an encyclopedia. It is the story of sports—more than 40 of them, from the obscure ones such as rugby and rodeo to the commercial giants such as football and baseball. *A Century of Sports* tells not only of their birth and phenomenal growth, but brings them alive with anecdotes and personalities.

Wes Gallagher
General Manager
The Associated Press

INTRODUCTION

This is a book that's mostly about fun—and written to be read for fun.

But it's a serious book, too, because it covers the Sports Explosion—one of the sociological and economic wonders of our time.

The Sports Explosion is not really an explosion at all, of course. The term is simply the current, handy phrase for the steady—and, sure enough, sometimes wild—growth in sports activity and interest of all kinds.

Each generation, starting with the time a man first decided to see how far he could throw a rock, undoubtedly has paid attention to sports and watched it grow.

But never before has there been anything to match what we are going through now.

Many of you will remember when the sports writers of the 1920s and '30s wrote about the Golden Age of Sports. World War II brought that to an end—or at least to an interruption. Now, since the early 1950s, we've had the Sports Explosion.

The drive for more and better teams has played a part in many things, including the Civil Rights movement. It was in sports that the black man showed most dramatically and most publicly that he is the equal of any man.

But more than anything else, the Sports Explosion has meant a kind of benevolent, continuing madness that impels people to the stadium, to the diamond, to the rink, to the outdoors for skiing, sailing, hunting, tennis and golf.

Remember when we had baseball in the summer, football in the fall, basketball in the winter and track in the spring? Of course there were boxing, golf, tennis, hockey and swimming—but mostly these things seemed to sort of fill in the chinks between seasons.

Now all of these sports overlap. The seasons merge.

Football season is nearly half over by the time the World Series begins. Before the World Series ends, basketball and hockey seasons have begun. You can go on watching football until late January. And you can still see basketball and hockey games after the baseball season resumes in April.

Only a few years ago, it seems, the winter months were the quietest time in sports. To fill space we even used to write at length about something called the Hot Stove League—and that was just a cliché for gossipy stuff about baseball when you didn't have anything else to write about.

Now there are about 1,000 four-year colleges playing basketball. There are two major professional basketball leagues with a total of 28 teams. And major professional hockey has more than doubled in size to 14 teams stretching from coast to coast and as far south as St. Louis.

It used to be that only a handful of golf tournaments really claimed much attention—the Masters, the British Open, the U.S. Open, the PGA and a few others. Now there is a major tournament nearly every week except for a brief respite in December and early January.

Not so long ago, for most people, auto racing was just a once-a-year burst of hysteria in Indianapolis, except for a few nuts running around red clay tracks in the South. Now there is so much auto racing, there are so many big tracks and so many people packing into them that fans can claim to have the fastest-growing sport in the world.

That's the Sports Explosion.

There is so much sports news now that in 1970 *The Associated Press* devised a new system for transmitting it by wire to its member newspapers at 1,050 words a minute in both printed form and perforated paper tape used to run automatic typesetting machines. That speed, 1,050 words a minute, is about 16 times as fast as anybody ever transmitted news mechanically before.

In keeping with the tenor of the times, we call it Super Speed Sports Service. The Sports Explosion demands no less.

Do you doubt that sports ranks in interest with the Indochina War, the environment, drugs and other issues that are vital to our well-being—even our survival?

Not likely if you remember that in recession years when night club, restaurant, theater and other kinds of recreation businesses decline—and some go broke—only sports maintains its patronage and continues to grow.

In 1969, the Associated Press Managing Editors Association—an organization of news executives whose newspapers are members of *The AP* and receive its services—sponsored a professional survey of sports readership.

The survey showed that 31 per cent of the men and 9 per cent of the women questioned turn first to sports news. In contrast, 3 per cent of the men and 6 per cent of the women said they turn first to national news, and 7 per cent of both men and women read local news first. Women even turn to sports before they turn to women's news.

Why?

Maybe the answer is that in times when just about everything else in life often seems a little sour, in the performance of highly skilled athletes, people can see moments of excellence they haven't been able to attain in their own lives. It's the kind of excellence that is easy to see, understand and share in vicariously, the excellence of mastery of the body.

Former Chief Justice Warren said it this way: "I always turn to the sports page first. The sports page records people's accomplishments; the front page has nothing but man's failures."

Richard M. Nixon, who has admitted he was never much of an athlete, also has said that what he really would like to be is a sports reporter. Instead he settled for being President of the United States. But he has spent a lot of time as President telephoning athletes to urge them on to great performances and to congratulate them afterward. The President has accorded athletes almost the same treatment he gave the astronauts who walked on the moon. He flew to the Pacific to congratulate the Apollo 11 astronauts; he flew to Fayetteville, Ark., to hand his personal national championship plaque to the University of Texas when it beat Arkansas in football.

The next year, Nixon waited until the final *AP* poll determined the national championship, then went to Lincoln to present a plaque to the University of Nebraska. Nebraskans liked that—even while giving coach Bob Devaney a bigger ovation than they did the President.

Less than a week later, when the *AP* trophy was presented, 1,600 persons bought dinner tickets—and the banquet had to be moved from a ballroom to the municipal auditorium. Then another 400 persons bought tickets just to sit in the bleachers and watch.

So it does seem to be true that the search for vicarious excellence is the basic drive that sends people to the stadium or the sports section or the TV set. And it is also true that this search makes them want much more than the score of the game. They want to know about the athletes, what makes them the way they are, about the athletes' wives and children and parents, what kind of people they all are, what makes a winner, what makes a loser, and what sports is all about, anyway.

What sports is all about is what this book is all about—the games people play that are for fun.

Robert H. Johnson
General Sports Editor
The Associated Press

George Halas' name is synonymous with the origins of the National Football League. He is shown here during his playing days at Illinois and exhorting his players during the Bears-Giants Championship Game in Chicago in 1963.

chapter 1

FOOTBALL

From the Walls of Ivy to Weekend Madness

THE PROS by Mike Rathet

Mike Rathet, 36, is *The AP's* specialist in pro football and baseball, but football is where his heart lies. He once quit the profession to nurse the American Football League through its growing years in 1967 and 1968. He is author of a book, *The Other League*, tracing the birth, growth and death of the AFL. A graduate of New York University, he first joined *The AP* in 1956.

The year was 1920, the war to end all wars was over, and all the Johnnys had come marching home again.

America was ready to follow the beat of another drum.

Responding to the sounds trumpeting an era of prosperity, postwar merchants of boom sought new ways to capitalize on the situation. In the small Illinois town of Decatur, corn starch magnate A. E. Staley pondered the problem, hit upon a solution and unwittingly made the decision that changed the living patterns of millions of Americans.

Staley decided that corn starch and football could be linked in a successful marriage.

The man Staley chose to perform the ceremony was George Halas, a former University of Illinois star who was working for the Burlington Railroad calculating the stresses and strains on railroad bridges. Staley convinced him the stresses and strains of playing football for money would be more rewarding.

"He indicated he would be willing to pay me $100 a game, which I thought was a pretty good deal," Halas remembers. "It was over twice as much as I was making working all week for the Burlington."

And so Halas, young, vibrant, imaginative, but tempered by a businessman's respect for a hard-earned dollar, went to work for Staley, organizing a group of men who would make corn starch during the week and play for the greater glory of the product on Sundays.

Until the Staley-Halas marriage was formed, professional football existed as a semipro sport, company teams and town teams getting together on short notice, agreeing to a set of rules and playing a game on any open field.

"It was all haphazard," Halas recalls. "You often didn't know whom you were playing the next Sunday. We had to make sure the teams would show up on the dates scheduled."

The need for organization resulted in a meeting on Sept. 17, 1920, in the Canton, Ohio, Hupmobile Agency of Ralph Hays. There, at 8:15 P.M., the forerunners of today's millionaire owners squatted on the running boards of the cars, sipped beer and agreed to form the first organized professional football league.

In the minutes of the meeting, kept by A. F. Ranney of the Akron Professional Football Team, the historic moment is noted in just 21 words: "It was moved and seconded that a permanent organization be formed to be known as American Professional Football Association. Motion carried."

Halas voted for the motion as did representatives of 10 other teams. They also agreed that the legendary Jim Thorpe be president, that a fee of $100 be charged for membership and that all members should have the name of the league printed on their stationery.

The honor roll of charter members includes Halas' Staleys, now the Chicago Bears, and such tongue-tickling names as Canton Bulldogs, Hammond Pros, Dayton Triangles, Rochester Jeffersons and Rock Island Independents.

But from those humble beginnings more than half-a-century ago stems an evolutionary process that has taken the sport from tiny town to major metropolis, from $100 franchise to $20 million property, from virtual obscurity in the face of baseball and college football to a dominant position as America's No. 1 glamor attraction.

Now the National Football League stretches from coast to coast with 26 teams in 25 cities. More than 12 million people annually fill stadiums to 95 per cent of capacity. Some 65 million people sit glued to television sets to watch the culminating event of the season—the Super Bowl.

Wives become virtual widows on Sundays when hubby's favorite team plays. Movie theaters close down on Monday nights in the face of a nationally televised game. Court decisions have to be rendered when season tickets, passed along in wills, are fought for by members of the same family.

In Wauwatosa, Wis., two fifth-grade classes at the Methodist church school are asked to select their No. 1 hero, the suggested names including Jesus, Queen Elizabeth and Albert Schweitzer. When the votes are tabulated there is a tie for first place between Jesus and a write-in candidate—Green Bay quarterback Bart Starr.

At Miami, site of the Super Bowl, Apollo 8 astronauts Frank Borman, Jim Lovell and Bill Anders and their families are guests of NFL Commissioner Pete Rozelle. Eddie Borman, the astronaut's son, spies the red-and-yellow tickets in Rozelle's hands and can't restrain his emotions.

"Boy, dad," says Eddie, "that trip around the moon was worth it. We get to go to the Super Bowl game."

The reasons for those responses to the form of entertainment that professional football provides have been discussed by fans, analyzed by leaders of the sport and psychoanalyzed by doctors trained to understand the idiosyncrasies of a nation.

The theory most advanced, and most accepted, is that professional football —mixing the sophistication inherent in a complicated play precisely executed with the brute nature of bodies colliding in a tangle of arms and legs—strikes a responsive chord in today's society.

Both players and coaches have tried to put that idea in focus. Sonny Jurgensen, the quarterback for the Washington Redskins, explains it this way:

"I've always considered myself a group therapist for 60,000 people. Every Sunday I hold group therapy and the people come and take out their frustrations on me. If I fail, it magnifies their failures, and if I succeed it minimizes them. The fans actually add to the game itself, because if you are playing at home, they are pulling for you, and if you are on the road, you are fighting 60,000 people."

Another player who tried to explain the unique response to the sport was Bill Glass, a one-time defensive end with Cleveland who went on to the ministry.

Truly a great athlete, Jim Thorpe, the Carlisle Indian, was named in 1950 the greatest football star of the half-century in The Associated Press **mid-century poll of the nation's sportswriters and sportscasters. He's shown in the early 1900s.**

Above, in an early pro game between Canton and Massillon, Wilbur (Fats) Henry, who is in pro football's Hall of Fame as a tackle, carries the ball for Canton on a tackle around play.

Below, the Canton Bulldogs play the Columbus Panhandlers as spectators stand on the sidelines to catch the action.

"In this century, people in ordinary jobs are cut off from what they are doing," Glass said. "They sit behind their desks and don't have any real relationship to what else is going on. They are struggling against things they can't see. There is a day-to-day routine but never any crisis situation. But in football it all builds up to a peak performance for $2\frac{1}{2}$ hours on Sunday.

"There is a clearly defined objective, an obvious opponent. You have to be emotionally and physically and psychologically ready for that $2\frac{1}{2}$-hour crisis. And if you triumph, it's clear right away. Football is so exciting because it's an intensified slice of life."

There also is agreement that the 60-minute wars fought every Sunday are violent—and that that violence begets fans. Two of the most respected coaches in the business—the late Vince Lombardi and Paul Brown—have tried to put that in their perspective through words.

"I think the nature of man is to be aggressive and football is a violent game," Lombardi explained. "But I think the very violence is one of the great things about the game, because a man has to learn control. He is going to go in to knock somebody's block off, and yet he must keep a rein on it. I can't think of any other place that demands such discipline."

"I've known women who thought football was worthless and brutal," Brown acknowledges. "But they just don't understand the sport and they don't understand the nature of the male. Most of those big collisions don't really hurt. The players are dressed and protected. They are young and strong. Anyway, the fact is that young men enjoy it. Nothing is going to stop it.

"If we could just have a Super Bowl between Russia and the United States, instead of all those tanks and ballistic missiles, things would be a lot better."

The male of the species, who now gets as much or more than $100,000 a year to perform for an adoring public, first began playing for pay in 1892 when the famed Pudge Heffelfinger of Yale collected $500 to play a game for the Allegheny Athletic Association.

Heffelfinger brought three other players with him who were paid "twice railroad fare" for a game against another Pittsburgh team. And the Allegheny club felt well rewarded when Heffelfinger produced the only points in a 6–0 victory.

It wasn't until another three years had passed that the first game involving a team of professionals was played, at Latrobe, Pa., sponsored by the YMCA. Latrobe beat Jeannette, Pa., 12–0. In the ensuing years, pro teams began to spring up and disappear with amazing regularity and there is only one entity that has lasted from infancy to maturity—the Cardinals, now representing St. Louis but originally taking shape in 1898 on Chicago's South Side.

Until 1920, the biggest events, in retrospect, were the appearance on the scene in 1915 of the Sac and Fox Indian, Thorpe, and the growth of company teams that accompanied the end of World War I in 1919. One of those formed at that time was organized by George Calhoun and Earl (Curly) Lambeau, who talked the employers of the Indian Packing Company into putting up $500 for uniforms and equipment for the team that became the Green Bay Packers.

Despite the fact that Thorpe's skills had been eroded somewhat by the time the American Professional Football Association changed its name to National Football League in 1922, he still was one of its main attractions. And though time had stripped away some of the luster from the bronzed body, 1923 came and went with still another story adding to the legend.

It was in that year that Thorpe, then with the Toledo Maroons, played against the Oklahoma All-Stars, who had just taken on a young rookie who eventually would play an important role in the sport's growth—Steve Owen. On the first play from scrimmage, Owen stormed in from his tackle position and found himself face to face with Thorpe, who was blocking for the runner.

Some wore helmets, others didn't, in this 1916 pro football game between the Columbus Panhandlers and the Cleveland Indians.

Without hesitating, Owen smashed into Thorpe, sent a hand flying into his face and knocked him down. The next play ended similarly, Thorpe on the ground and Owen smiling triumphantly. Owen couldn't help beating his breast to a teammate: "Old Jim has slowed up, I guess. He doesn't care for this blocking business anymore."

The ball was snapped for the third time and Owen, secure in his assessment of the situation, came crashing through again. Only this time he ignored Thorpe and went straight for the ball carrier. The next thing he remembers is being on the ground in a heap, sledge hammers thumping in his head.

Stunned and shaken, Owen wobbled to his feet and, as he did, someone patted him gently on the back and whispered in his ear: "Always keep an eye on the old Indian."

Despite Thorpe and the new league, pro football remained a risky operation in its formative years, so much so that there were times when a team had to worry about getting out of town with the money it had been guaranteed. Halas recalls that one such incident occurred in a game between his Staley Starchmakers and the Rock Island Independents. During the game, one of Halas' players, George Trafton, tackled a Rock Island halfback by the name of Joe Chicken so hard that he suffered a broken leg.

That, naturally, incurred the wrath of the Rock Island fans, who made menacing gestures at Trafton after the game. Seeing that, Halas handed Trafton an envelope containing $3,500—the club's split of the receipts—and told him to run back to the hotel where the team was staying.

"Those Rock Island fans were in an ugly mood," Halas recalls. "I figured if they started something, I'd have nothing to run for except the $3,500. Trafton would be running for his life."

That the sport survived is a tribute to the pioneers like Halas, whose vision anticipated the future, ignored the ignoble present and pressed onward while teams appeared and disappeared in startling numbers. Detroit, for example, had a team in 1920 and 1921. It folded after that, but came back in 1925. In 1927, Detroit was out again. A year later, Detroit entered again. In 1929, Detroit made another hasty exit. It wasn't until five years later, when the Portsmouth, Ohio, franchise was shifted to Detroit, that the city became a permanent member.

The 26-team structure that exists today, as a matter of fact, did not take final shape until 1968—the year the Cincinnati Bengals joined. In the intervening time, the NFL had passed through 92 different team entities in 52 different locales.

But while Detroit couldn't make up its mind, New York did in 1925 when Tim Mara and Will Gibson were awarded a franchise. The exact figure paid by Mara and Gibson is a matter of dispute, but it was either $500 or $2,500. Whatever it was, Mara is remembered as saying he didn't know much about football but "I figure an exclusive franchise for anything in New York is worth what I paid."

The NFL now had the team that would eventually become its flagship franchise—the anchor for its empire—and that was accompanied by the signing by the Chicago Bears of Harold (Red) Grange, the "Galloping Ghost" of Illinois fame. While the entry of the New York franchise would pay dividends in the future, Grange's signing had more immediate rewards. For his signing brought pro football its first major headlines.

"We used to hopefully look for some mention of the Bears in the newspapers each day," Halas remembers, "even one of those little two-inch items which get in just to fill out a column. But most times our advance stories were tossed into the waste basket. But, boy, did we cheer when we found one. We even thought we had arrived when we landed two of those pieces in a Chicago foreign language newspaper in the same week."

Grange, maintaining his hold on the public despite relinquishing his amateur status, translated his signing into headlines that enabled the Bears to take advantage by arranging a cross-country tour of 18 exhibition games, eight in one 12-day stretch. The tour reached its peak in New York and Los Angeles, where crowds of 70,000 bought tickets.

While the Bears' barnstorming tour was long by comparison with today's 14-game schedule spread over 14 weeks, the all-time endurance record was set a year later by the Duluth Eskimos. The club's owner put together the tour after placing a call to Ernie Nevers, the Stanford great, and asking him if he would play for the Eskimos for $15,000 plus a share of the gate receipts.

Nevers said he would, but "I should have asked how long the season was going to be." The season lasted 112 days, and in that time the Eskimos covered 17,000 miles in a 29-game tour that began in Portland, Maine, and ended in San Francisco. The most amazing statistic is not the mileage, however, but the 19–7–3 record the team compiled playing with only a 13-man squad.

But professional football was about to enter a new era as it turned into a new decade. The major impetus, oddly enough, came from one of the most unusual games ever played—the 1932 playoff between Halas' Bears and the Portsmouth Spartans.

"The streets of Chicago were frozen solid and covered with ice and snow so we played indoors in Chicago Stadium," Halas recalls. "There were no out of bounds. The sidelines were the two-by-ten boards that lined the stadium floor. There was dirt on the floor because the Barnum and Bailey circus had been there."

Ernie Nevers played in the early days of pro football for the Duluth Eskimos. The team, playing with only a 13-man squad, compiled a 19–7–3 record in one 112-day season.

During the game, the Bears' great runner Bronko Nagurski faked a line plunge, then retreated to pass and hit Grange with the only touchdown of the game in a 9–0 victory. The Portsmouth coach was enraged, claiming Nagurski was not five yards behind the line of scrimmage when he threw the pass—which was the rule at the time.

At the league meeting in 1933, Halas moved to amend that rule, making it legal to throw a forward pass from anywhere behind the line of scrimmage. Halas also forced through a rule that the ball be moved in 10 yards from the sidelines, rather than five, after going out on the previous play—a rule that had to be used by necessity in the Chicago Stadium game.

Joining Halas as a force for change was George Preston Marshall, who had joined the league in 1932 as the owner of the Boston Redskins, forerunners of the Washington team. Outspoken, tough, irreverent, Marshall proposed that the goal posts be moved to the goal line and that the league be divided into two divisions, the winners meeting in a championship game.

The net result was movement, scoring and excitement. In the 1920s and early 1930s, professional football was a game of brute force, the Single Wing used almost universally and the off-tackle slant used almost every play. Passes were rare, and often cause for derision. But the new rules enabled sophistication to be added to brute force, the pass and the field goal becoming important weapons.

Without those rules changes, the game we now witness—the game of Joe Namath and Roman Gabriel, the game of Tom Dempsey and Jan Stenerud—might never have reached the pinnacle it has. At the same time that Marshall contributed his thoughts to the rules that created more wide open play, he became the first owner to envision the sport as a spectacle.

"Football is a game of pageantry," Marshall said. "It derives from the gladiator shows of the Romans. It is strictly amphitheater. Its great success is due to

Among the best of the football players in the early days of the game was Bronko Nagurski (3) shown here running interference for Beattie Feathers.

the color surrounding it. It needs music and bands. Football without a band is like a musical without an orchestra."

So Marshall instituted a marching band for the Redskins, 110 musicians decked out in $25,000 worth of Indian costumes. Although most teams have copied Marshall's theories on exploiting pageantry, there were those at the time who suspected that the band was as dear to Marshall's heart as his players.

One who might have thought so was Jack Mara, president of the Giants, who was witness to Marshall's antics one year when a blizzard struck Washington before a Giants-Redskins game. Marshall immediately began a frantic search to get equipment to clear the field before game time. Two hours before kickoff, however, snow still blanketed the field, and Mara admittedly was worried.

Suddenly Marshall appeared, a smile on his face. "They're coming," he told Mara. "They'll be here in plenty of time."

"The snowplows?" Mara asked.

"No," said Marshall, his brow furrowing at Mara's lack of understanding. "The overshoes for the band."

Halas' eye for rules changes and Marshall's penchant for pageantry were accompanied in rapid order by four other significant developments—the slimming down of the ball in 1934 to present-day specifications that allowed for gripping it easier; the arrival on the scene in 1935 of Don Hutson; the initiation of the player draft in 1936, and the signing in 1937 of Sammy Baugh.

Hutson and Baugh showed what could be done with the slimmer ball and the new rules. Both Hutson, who joined Green Bay, and Baugh, who joined Washington, were tall and slender, unlikely models for the players of the day. But brute force was not their message. They proved that physical power was far from being the total scope of football. Their message was finesse.

Hutson was a receiver, fast and with sure hands. But his major contribution was the discovery of faking, shifting shoulders, swaying hips and false steps to throw the defender off the trail. Until Hutson perfected deception, receivers merely ran on a straight line. But, with first Arnie Herber and then Cecil Isbell as his passer, Hutson showed that a receiver could take a devious route and frequently arrive at a predetermined spot on the field without a defender trailing him.

Baugh was a passer, a sidearm slinger with quickness, a superior sense of timing and unerring accuracy. He was totally confident in the latter. When he first reported to the Redskins, coach Ray Flaherty sent him through a blackboard drill, outlining a play in chalk and throwing questions at the rookie quarterback. As he outlined one particular play, Flaherty indicated a spot on the blackboard and said, "When the receiver reaches this point, I want you to hit him in the eye."

Baugh looked up and, without the trace of a smile, said:

"Which eye?"

Because of his ability, Baugh did not have to wait for a receiver to get open before risking a pass. Knowing where the receiver would wind up on the pass route, he threw as the receiver made his break, the trajectory of the pass bringing it to the predetermined spot at the same time as the receiver. It was as revolutionary as Hutson's faking.

In that manner, Hutson and Baugh had brought to professional football the precision passing game that exists today. But there was one more step in the of-

Green Bay receiver Don Hutson starred in the mid and late '30s. He is credited with being the first man to make use of faking and false steps to deceive defenders.

fensive evolution, the changeover from the Single Wing to the T formation, which opened the door to additional gambits and enhanced the skills displayed by players such as Baugh and Hutson.

Halas had used the T formation since the day he helped found the league, the center handing the ball directly back to the quarterback between his legs rather than throwing it back through the air as he did to the tailback in the Single Wing. But the early T was a tightly aligned formation and offered no more chance to get around the ends than any other alignment.

In 1930, Halas lured Ralph Jones from Illinois to be his coach and Jones spread the ends and the halfbacks a couple of yards to loosen up the T formation. He also had one of his halfbacks trot out to the side of the formation before the play started, becoming a "man-in-motion" and pulling defenders with him. That further spread both offensive and defensive alignments.

There still appeared to be a piece of the puzzle missing, for the T formation as modified by Jones wasn't any more noticeably successful than the Single

Wing. Jones left the Bears in 1933 and Halas resumed coaching, striking up a friendship with Clark Shaughnessy, then coaching at the University of Chicago.

A man who delighted in the detailed study of the game, Shaughnessy pondered the T formation day in and day out, compiled endless stacks of reference material and made a number of suggestions to Halas concerning play design and the use of precise terminology to control the movement of the players.

The culmination of their partnership came in 1940 when the two collaborated on the plan that would send the Bears, armed with talent such as quarterback Sid Luckman, halfback George McAfee and linemen Danny Fortmann and Joe Stydahar, against the Baugh-led Redskins in the championship game. Suddenly, the T flowered, the Redskins faltered and the Bears held a 73–0 victory—and a nation's imagination.

Conversion to the formation was made over the next several years by every team and there was more excitement about professional football than ever before. Names like Baugh, Luckman, Bob Waterfield, Bill Dudley, Charley Trippi, Steve Van Buren and Marion Motley would become familiar during the period. But it wasn't until the end of the decade, after World War II and the introduction of unlimited substitution, that the flowering T formation provided the sweet smell of success for club owners who had invested in the sport.

The war, of course, spelled disaster. Cleveland halted operations. Philadelphia and Pittsburgh combined forces and played as the Phil-Pitt Eagles. And Pittsburgh later joined with the Chicago Cardinals to play as Card-Pitt. In all, 638 players served in the war. But the NFL survived, and in 1945 attendance surpassed one million again. A year later, there was news on all fronts, on both sides of the ledger.

Bert Bell, the man generally credited with a number of key decisions that spawned an era of unmatched growth, was elected commissioner and, despite resistance from several colleagues, Dan Reeves moved his Cleveland Rams to Los Angeles, creating a truly national league by stretching it from coast to coast.

On the debit side of the ledger, two members of the New York Giants—Frank Filchock and Merle Hapes—were suspended. There had been a bribe offer. Neither reported it, and the sport's image was damaged. At the same time, the league was attacked on another front by the formation of a rival league, the All-American Football Conference. A war for players ensued, not at the prices that would be thrown at players during a later inter-league battle, but one just as bitter and just as much of a threat to survival.

It took only three years for owners in both leagues to realize that peaceful coexistence without bankruptcy was impossible in the face of nosediving attendance. Commissioner Bell and AAFC representative Arthur Friedlund finally announced a merger of the two, the NFL absorbing the Cleveland Browns, the San Francisco 49ers and the Baltimore Colts.

But for the game that professional football was yet to become there were two developments of even greater significance—the first the introduction by Shaughnessy, now coaching the Los Angeles Rams, of the flanker or third end when he placed halfback Elroy (Crazy Legs) Hirsch out wide.

The other development eventually would overshadow all the others. In 1938 the NFL had hired Hugh (Shorty) Ray to overhaul its rules and make suggestions that would enhance the game. Ray had done such a thorough job in an attempt to make professional football a faster, more exciting game that by 1949 there were 150 differences between the college and pro variety. Ray now made one more suggestion—free substitution—and it was adopted.

Free substitution gave birth to the era of specialization, enabling those with unique offensive skills to employ all their energies in that direction and creating defensive specialists whose task it was to seek out and destroy the purveyors of offensive fireworks. It added that final dimension—the defensive player whose skills were as appreciated by fans as those of the offensive player.

It made room in the 1950s for people like Gino Marchetti, Art Donovan, Bill George, Joe Schmidt, Dick (Night Train) Lane and Emlen Tunnell and words such as violence, mayhem, intimidation—words that began to awaken a nation to the response psychologists still are analyzing. And it spawned behemoths of the size of 6-foot-6, 288-pound Big Daddy Lipscomb who, when asked how he made a tackle, replied:

"I pick 'em up one by one, and I throw 'em away till I come to the one with the ball. Then I keep him."

And it put the spotlight on confrontation—between precision offenses and brutal defenses, between offensive stars such as fullback Jimmy Brown of Cleveland and defenders such as linebacker Sam Huff of the New York Giants. Their one-on-one battles always made headlines and always left one another technicolored from head to toe in silent tribute to the intensity with which they battled.

"I remember one game in particular," Huff recalls. "The first time Jimmy carried the ball, he rammed into the middle of our line. I came up fast, hit him hard and stopped him for no gain. As the pile untangled, I sneered at him, 'Brown, you stink.' Jimmy didn't say anything. He just got up slowly, as he always did, and walked back to the huddle.

"The second time Jimmy carried, the same thing happened. He rammed into the middle, I dived into the hole and stopped him for no gain. I sneered harder and said louder, 'Brown, you stink.' Again Jimmy didn't say anything. He just got up slowly and walked back to the huddle.

"The third time Jimmy carried the ball he drove in the middle. But nobody stopped him. He got a couple of key blocks, exploded past me and the secondary and raced 65 yards for a touchdown. Trotting back to the Browns' bench, he turned to me and grinned. Then he shouted:

" 'Hey, Huff, how do I smell from here?' "

It was magic. But that magic had its base in free substitution and the elements that were going into making the game the one we now know. As offenses became more explosive, defenses had to adjust to keep up. Power was the first answer for finesse. Free substitution, allowing as it did for specialists, enabled finesse to be met with finesse.

The defense that finally began to catch up with the offenses was first put together in 1950 by that same Steve Owen who used to tangle with Jim Thorpe. By then the coach of the New York Giants, Owen employed a six-man defensive line with one linebacker and four defensive backs. But the secret to his success with the formation was that the two ends in the line often dropped back like modern linebackers. Because the two ends and four backs fanned out, the formation reminded people of an open umbrella and was called "The Umbrella Defense."

More importantly, that defense was the forerunner of the modern 4 linemen-3 linebackers-4 backs alignment. To handle that, however, required a new breed of defender. Since there were only four linemen, they had to be mobile as well as big. The linebackers had to be nearly as big as linemen to stop the run and nearly as fast as backs to cover passes. And the backs had to be quick, agile and intelligent.

Parallel with that development came an innovation as important to defense as the T formation was to offense—the theory of "reading" offenses. "The offensive play is a total design," explains defensive tackle Merlin Olsen of the Los Angeles Rams. "Each player has a part. So if we on the defense watch the parts and react accordingly, we should all act together to stop the play. We all listen to different music, but we come out together."

Professional football now had the elements to capture a nation's imagination. But the nation had not been entirely sold. Several teams still were having problems and in 1951, Baltimore folded. A year later, the New York Yankees franchise had to be transferred to Dallas, where it met with a similar lack of success. The league then decided to offer the club as a road attraction. At Akron, Ohio, one of the stops for the team that was dubbed the Dallas Orphans, the situation bordered on the ludicrous. Gino Marchetti remembers the scene vividly.

"There were fewer than 1,000 people in the stands," says Marchetti. "Jimmy Phelan, our coach, said to us in the dressing room, 'We are going to dispense with the usual introductions as you come on the field. Instead of that, you will go into the stands and meet each of the customers individually.' "

So professional football, which now had the necessary ingredients for the success that would startle everyone before the decade ran its course, needed some way to get its message across. It found that method in television and it found the instrument in a crew-cut quarterback named Johnny Unitas, who cost the Baltimore Colts an 80-cent phone call.

Professional football and television made their way to the altar for the first time in 1949 when the NFL championship game was telecast on a special network. Prior to that there had been only sporadic experiments with the medium. But following the 1949 marriage, the future began to take shape, and the man who gave it substance was Dan Reeves of the Los Angeles Rams. In 1950 the Rams signed a contract for the telecasting of all Los Angeles games. In 1949 the Rams had drawn 205,109. They suffered almost a 50 per cent cut in 1950, attendance dropping to 110,162. The cause was obvious, and the following year home games were blacked out. Attendance immediately climbed to 234,110.

The lesson learned was not lost upon Bert Bell. As more and more teams flirted with television, the NFL commissioner reflected on the experience gained in the Rams' experiment and in 1956 made it mandatory that only road games be televised—or home games be blacked out. Television provided more and more fans with an opportunity to see the game and its stars—Otto Graham, Bobby Layne, Norm Van Brocklin, Ollie Matson, Lou Groza, Ray Berry and Unitas.

At the same time, television techniques provided the opportunity for fans to learn the game that seemed so complicated without explanation. At home, the fan received his explanation or, as one newly fascinated viewer explained: "You watched a game on television and, suddenly, the wool was stripped from your eyes. What had appeared to be an incomprehensible tangle of milling bodies from the grandstand, made sense. It was the first real triumph of educational television. It created a nation of instant experts in no time."

Unitas then gave professional football that last kick in the pants it needed—drama. In one single game, the 1958 championship, a nation became enthralled with the sport as the Colts and New York Giants battled over a mere 100 yards of green grass, paying the ultimate price of bloodied and bruised bodies in exchange for being recognized for their achievements.

The city of Baltimore had climbed back into the professional football arena in 1953 when it was awarded the floating Dallas franchise. Weeb Ewbank became the coach and announced a five-year plan aimed at bringing the city a championship. It took exactly that length of time and the 80-cent phone call to get Unitas. Unitas joined the Pittsburgh Steelers in 1955 after finishing his college career at the University of Louisville, but without fanfare he was released by the club. He proceeded to hook up with the Bloomfield, Pa., Rams and wait. Ewbank called in 1956.

In the years since he joined the Colts, Unitas has become the prototype for the professional quarterback, possessor of the ability to drop back and set rapidly, blessed with a quick release, able to launch a pass with pinpoint precision. The talent in the Golden Arm is further embellished by the mind of the man and driven by the impression left by that first rejection slip.

"The great ones never forget what it means to come up the hard way," says Norm Van Brocklin, a former great passer, now the Atlanta coach. "Unitas knows what it is to eat potato soup without the potatoes in it."

But Dec. 28, 1958, was a champagne day for Johnny Unitas, the Baltimore Colts, even the losing New York Giants, and all of professional football. For the drama played out at Yankee Stadium indelibly etched the picture of the sport on the American sports mind. The sports public had read and heard of great games before, but television enabled them to see this one. Professional football was about to pass into its current phase as part of the culture of the nation.

And it was Unitas who was the focal point of the drama, after a 20-yard field goal by Colts' placekicker Steve Myhra with 20 seconds remaining tied the score 17–17 and sent the game into sudden death overtime—the first in NFL history. At Yankee Stadium, and throughout the country in front of living room TV sets, fans hunched forward to await the tense struggle for supremacy that would be decided by the first team scoring.

Unitas, crafty, seemingly under no pressure, immediately drove the Colts for the winning touchdown, sending Alan Ameche crashing through the line after eight minutes and 15 seconds had elapsed for the score that gave Baltimore a 23–17 victory and exploded the mind of almost every fan watching.

Against that backdrop, and certain that there were fans throughout the country with money to pay to see professional football outside the 12-city NFL, Lamar Hunt, Dallas millionaire and football fan, announced the formation of the American Football League just a year later. Hunt, along with K. S. (Bud) Adams of Houston, had been rebuffed in bids to have the NFL expand to include their cities, and had decided to buck the establishment. The date was Aug. 14. In retrospect it would be circled as another turning point in professional football's growth. But at the moment there was nothing but yawns.

The NFL was solidly entrenched in Baltimore, Cleveland, Chicago, Detroit,

Green Bay, Los Angeles, New York, Philadelphia, Pittsburgh, St. Louis, San Francisco and Washington. And, in its first move to wipe out the AFL, the NFL placed a rival team in Dallas.

Hunt, however, moved ahead, and the AFL began play in 1960 with eight teams, in Boston, Buffalo, Dallas, Denver, Houston, Los Angeles, New York and Oakland, which took over when a Minneapolis group pulled out at the last minute. Not surprisingly, the NFL again expanded the following year with the formation of the Minnesota Vikings.

The battle lines were drawn, but Hunt looked past the inevitable clash. "I was encouraged because pro football had become so tremendously popular," he said, "and because I knew there were many cities interested in backing a competitive league. I felt that an American League, side by side with the National Football League, could be a success."

While the AFL was getting off the ground, two other events of consequence took place—Vince Lombardi left his job as an assistant with the New York Giants and became head coach at Green Bay and Pete Rozelle became commissioner of the NFL following the death of Bert Bell.

The job faced by the AFL in trying to survive was underscored as soon as the training camp season began in 1960. "I remember that first tryout camp we had," recalls Sid Gillman of the San Diego (originally Los Angeles) Chargers. "Every bartender in Los Angeles thought he could play football. These gorillas would be outside every day standing in their cleats, lined up for inspection."

But the AFL did begin play on schedule—and proceeded to total losses in the neighborhood of $3.5 million. The NFL, meanwhile, was showered with success, attendance climbing steadily upward and surpassing four million for the first time in 1962. The stars were there—Paul Hornung and Bart Starr, leaders of the Lombardi legions who began winning NFL titles with startling regularity in 1961,

A quarterback's life has never been an easy one. Here, the Jets' Joe Namath despondently leaves the field during a dust storm in a game against Kansas City and the Giants' Charley Conerly is about to be thrown for a 20-yard loss by Gino Marchetti of the Colts in a 1959 game.

and possibly the greatest runner of all time, Jimmy Brown, who in 1963 rushed for 1,863 yards.

The AFL also had headline-makers, but the biggest one was Harry Wismer, the owner of the New York Titans, who had driven the club to the brink of bankruptcy. The Titans' offices were in Wismer's Park Avenue apartment, where ticket buyers often were ushered in by a Swedish maid. The living room was Wismer's office. The coaches used the dining room. The publicity department was housed in the butler's pantry, and the mimeograph they used for press releases was stored in the bathroom.

The Titans' games might as well have been played in Wismer's apartment too for attendance was poor, although it was padded. But everyone was aware of that, including the players. Before one game, linebacker Larry Grantham even suggested that the spectators should be introduced before the start of the game instead of the players. "After all," Grantham explained, "we outnumber them."

But while Wismer's house was crumbling, and threatening to bring down the entire AFL with it, he did get the league to join together and sell its television rights on a league-wide basis—the step that would ultimately save the league. Until then, all teams had negotiated their television contracts separately. At the same time, the NFL, which also realized that bargaining collectively very likely

New York Giants forward wall holds the charging Baltimore Colts line, enabling teammate Pat Summerall (88) to kick field goal in title game in Baltimore in 1959.

would return more money, sent Rozelle to Congress for approval of such action. He secured it, and with it the future of professional football.

While television would be the weapon that ultimately enabled the AFL to survive, the first step was to salvage the situation in New York. The man who did that was David (Sonny) Werblin, stepping forward in January 1963, at the head of a five-man syndicate that purchased the Titans and rechristened them the Jets. There also were several other developments that helped stabilize the situation—Hunt moved his Dallas team to Kansas City, Al Davis took over as managing general partner of the Oakland Raiders and eight No. 1 choices signed with AFL clubs as the bidding for talent continued to escalate.

"The first three years the NFL didn't pay that much attention to us," AFL Commissioner Joe Foss pointed out. "But this year it locked horns with us."

The checkbook battle for players had escalated to the point where money was only one of the weapons being used. Fringe benefits, including honeymoons, convertibles, cattle and gas stations, also were promised. Notre Dame end Jack Snow was offered a honeymoon in Hawaii by the Chargers. Pittsburgh linebacker Marty Schottenheimer accepted a deal with Buffalo because it included a rear window defroster for his new car.

Such special attention, however, surprised some players, and halfback Gale

Paul Hornung, a premier quarterback at Notre Dame, went on to more fame as runner and kicker for the Green Bay Packers. Here, in a 1961 game against the Baltimore Colts, he broke for daylight, literally carrying would-be tacklers with him.

Sayers of Kansas said he signed with the NFL's Chicago Bears rather than Hunt's Kansas City Chiefs because "it made me uncomfortable having a millionaire (Hunt) holding doors for me."

The major ploy used by both leagues was to try and keep a player from being reached by the other league, and at times a comic-opera situation was created. Such was the case involving Harry Schuh, a Memphis State tackle.

Schuh became the object of a manhunt when the Oakland Raiders whisked him away from Jackson, Miss., where he played his final college game, to keep him out of the hands of the Los Angeles Rams. His first stop was New Orleans, where the entourage keeping him from the outside world stopped just long enough to add his wife. Then it was on to Las Vegas. The Rams, however, picked up the trail there.

The Raiders reacted as quickly as a quarterback to a blitz, grabbed Schuh and put him on a plane to Los Angeles. But they forgot about the slumbering Mrs. Schuh. Awakening to find her husband gone, Mrs. Schuh was at first concerned, but eventually calmed by the Raider representatives. They suggested she become a decoy, flying to Los Angeles and stopping there rather than continuing on to Hawaii to meet her husband.

Mrs. Schuh agreed, but the Rams ignored her and flew East to meet instead with Schuh's parents at their New Jersey home. After a long discussion, the Ram representatives convinced Schuh's parents, in the interest of their son, to ask the police to issue a missing-persons bulletin.

But they were too late. Schuh had signed with the Raiders in Hawaii.

Into that atmosphere stepped television and Werblin. The battle of checkbooks weighed heaviest on the AFL, and only money could keep the fight going. On Jan. 29, 1964, that was provided by the National Broadcasting Company, which announced a $36 million television pact with the AFL.

"What saved the AFL obviously was the NBC television contract," said Cleveland owner Art Modell after the battle between the leagues had ended. "It gave them recognition, gave them financial support, gave them a competitive weapon in bidding for players."

Armed with that weapon and his own theory that the price to be paid for a player should encompass not only talent but also any charismatic quality that might translate into box-office success, Werblin went after a slope-shouldered Alabama quarterback, Joe Namath.

"When Joe walks into a room, you know he's there," explained Werblin. "When another rookie walks in, he's just another nice looking kid. Namath's like Babe Ruth or Lou Gehrig."

And so Werblin offered Namath a contract for $427,000, Namath signed it, and the final step in the escalation process had been taken. Tommy Nobis went with Atlanta for $500,000. Donny Anderson went with Green Bay for $600,000. And more fan interest was centered on the size of contracts than what was happening on the playing field.

Even in outer space attention was riveted on the signing of players. While the AFL's Houston club and the NFL's Falcons were bidding for Nobis, Gemini 7 hurtled high above the earth. Inside the space capsule, astronaut Frank Borman radioed earth, receiving the biggest news of the day. Borman digested the news and then radioed NASA: "Tell Nobis to sign with Houston."

Owners finally became concerned and peace talks were initiated, the main figures being Hunt and Tex Schramm of the Dallas Cowboys. As they closed in on an agreement, the entire future of professional football was placed in jeopardy by two other figures—Al Davis and Pete Gogolak. Davis was named to succeed Joe Foss as AFL commissioner while Gogolak, a place kicker, played out his option with the AFL's Buffalo Bills and signed with the New York Giants.

The latter development threatened to open a Pandora's box in which there would be wholesale raids. And what that would mean was underscored when Davis initiated a plan to raid the NFL for veteran players by paying them exorbitant bonuses to sign contracts that would be effective as soon as they played out their option. Almost immediately, the Oakland Raiders announced they had signed Los Angeles quarterback Roman Gabriel and, over a three-week period, Davis began negotiations with more than a dozen other NFL veterans, including San Francisco quarterback John Brodie.

The potentially dangerous situation was made somewhat less explosive by the peace talks, rapidly coming to fruition. Finally, on June 8, 1966, Rozelle, Hunt and Schramm entered the Warwick Hotel in New York at 6:15 P.M. to announce the merger of the two leagues.

There were seven major points to the agreement: Pete Rozelle would be the commissioner. The leagues would play a championship game. All existing franchises would remain at their present sites. A combined draft would be held. Two franchises would be added, one in each league, with the money from both being paid to the NFL. AFL clubs would pay indemnity of $18 million to the NFL over a 20-year period. Inter-league pre-season games would be played beginning in 1967 and a single league schedule would commence in 1970.

"The two big things we wanted we got—the championship game and the preseason games," Hunt said.

All that remained was to play that first championship game—the Super Bowl. Arguments that had raged for six years about the merits of the two leagues would be settled, and they were on Jan. 10, 1967, when Vince Lombardi's Green Bay Packers humbled the Chiefs owned by Hunt, 35–10. Asked after the game for an evaluation of the Chiefs, Lombardi said: "I do not think they are as good as the top teams in the NFL. I'd have to say NFL football is tougher."

Whether it was NFL football or just the Packers remained a moot question the following January because the Packers won it again, beating Oakland 33–14. But for Super Bowl III there were new faces—the Baltimore Colts representing the NFL and the New York Jets representing the AFL. On the eve of the game, Jets' quarterback Joe Namath put his pride where his mouth was and predicted openly: "We'll win. I guarantee it." On Sunday, Jan. 12, 1969, the Jets did, beating Baltimore 16–7 in a major upset that established AFL parity with the NFL on the playing field.

Next the AFL sought to establish that parity at the conference table, where the owners proceeded to fight out the problem of how to structure the expanded league for the future. The NFL had grown to 16 teams with the addition of Atlanta and New Orleans while the AFL had expanded to a 10-team league following the addition of Miami and Cincinnati. Majority sentiment was for keeping the 16–10 lineup. Minority sentiment was for realigning into two 13-team conferences for the 1970 season. Minority sentiment eventually became majority sentiment.

On May 17, following two previous meetings and a nonstop, 35-hour, 45-minute marathon session in New York City, Baltimore, Cleveland and Pittsburgh agreed to join the 10 AFL teams and form the American Conference. The 13 remaining NFL teams would form the National Conference.

There remained one more date for confrontation before the American Football League passed into legal extinction and under the National Football League banner, the Jan. 4, 1970, Super Bowl at New Orleans. And, as fate dictated, that final test of inter-league strength sent Hunt's Chiefs against the Minnesota Vikings. The Chiefs won 23–7, putting a Hollywood ending on the AFL's decade.

But that also set the stage for the future—a future oddly enough jeopardized by the very nature of professional football's role in a society growing ever more sophisticated and aware. And nothing underscored that as much as the fingers that pointed at Kansas City quarterback Len Dawson during the week before the Super Bowl.

On the Tuesday night before the Chiefs met the Vikings, it was reported that Dawson would be subpoenaed to testify in a nationwide gambling probe. There were no direct accusations, but the linking of Dawson's name with gambling was a jolt to a professional football hierarchy extremely sensitive and wary about even the hint of scandal.

That professional football would move quickly and decisively at the slightest hint of trouble had been shown in two previous instances—one involving Paul Hornung of the Green Bay Packers and Alex Karras of the Detroit Lions and the other involving Joe Namath of the New York Jets. In 1963, Commissioner Rozelle suspended Hornung and Karras for betting on their own teams. And, in 1969, following Namath's greatest triumph, Rozelle ordered him to sell his interest in an East Side New York night spot allegedly frequented by undesirable elements.

Dawson, however, had not been guilty of any wrongdoing. He said so, Rozelle said so, and even President Richard Nixon said so when he called the Kansas City dressing room after the Super Bowl victory, offered his congratulations and his assurance of Dawson's innocence. And Dawson never was subpoenaed.

But the incident did emphasize the fact that, by attaining a singular position atop the sports world, professional football would be constantly subjected to microscopic examination by the very society that had raised it to its exalted level.

History dictates that. It had, as a matter of fact, dictated it from the very moment that the sport's pioneers started up that long road at Canton, Ohio, in 1920. But no one, not even the visionary George Halas, could peek that far into the future.

On the occasion of the 50th anniversary of that historic founding, Halas frankly admitted as much, saying:

"I never even allowed myself to dream about such success."

Football is a war. Ask Y. A. Tittle. With blood streaming down his face, he watches in anguish as the Steelers score a touchdown on his intercepted pass.

THE COLLEGIANS by Herschel Nissenson

Herschel Nissenson, 37, has been a member of the sports department since February 1968 and took over as college football specialist in 1969. He joined *The AP* in Newark, N.J., in November 1960, becoming New Jersey state sports editor in 1961. A native New Yorker, he attended CCNY and was a member of the 1954 Metropolitan Intercollegiate soccer champions. His early newspaper experience came as newsman for *International News Service* and telegraph editor for the *Middletown* (N.Y.) *Daily Record*.

Darrell Royal, head coach at the University of Texas, once said nothing is ever new in college football.

The ground-gobbling Wishbone-T attack which he installed in the 1960s was nothing more than a variation of the Triple Option popularized earlier by Bill Yeoman at the University of Houston. The Triple Option is an offshoot of the Split-T inaugurated by Don Faurot at Missouri in 1941.

The Split-T called for a ball-carrying quarterback sliding along the line of scrimmage with the option of keeping the ball or pitching it out to a trailing back, depending on the reaction of the defensive end.

While the Mirrored Wishbone defense Notre Dame threw at Texas in snapping the Longhorns' 30-game winning streak by 24–11 in the 1971 Cotton Bowl may have been unique in the way the players lined up, it was in reality a nine-man defensive line and only two players had their basic field position altered.

Football inventiveness began as far back as the first intercollegiate game on Nov. 6, 1869, at New Brunswick, N. J. Rutgers defeated Princeton 6–4 in a game that was primarily soccer, rather than football.

But that game gave birth to the sleeper play, the wrong-way player, coaching strategy . . . even tradition.

The contest was played 25 to a side. Two members of each team—they were called captains—were stationed near the opponent's goal, hoping to slip over a score from their unguarded positions. Thus was the sleeper play conceived.

At one point, a Rutgers player mistakenly kicked the ball toward his own goal. The kick was blocked, but Princeton took advantage of the opportunity and soon scored.

The Rutgers leader noticed that Princeton gained an advantage from its taller players and ordered his men to keep the ball close to the ground, a piece of strategy that paid off.

A big trophy, in those days, was an old Revolutionary War cannon, which enterprising students kept lugging back and forth the 20 miles or so between the campuses. Not long before the game, the Princetonians settled this competition in their favor by sinking the cannon in several feet of concrete. If Princeton's Tigers had a tiger mascot, Rutgers would have kidnapped it.

The challenge for that first game was issued by Rutgers, eager to avenge a humiliating 40–2 baseball defeat at Princeton's hands in 1866.

Besides the captains, the remaining 23 players were divided into groups of 11 "fielders," who lined up in their own territory as defenders, and 12 "bulldogs," who carried the offensive burden. It was sort of instant two-platoon football. The ball could be advanced only by kicking or batting it with the feet, hands, head or sides and the teams changed direction after each goal.

Two weeks later, Princeton evened the series 8–0, but a third match was canceled by the respective college administrations on grounds that football was interfering with studies. However, Columbia took up the sport in 1870 and the cries of overemphasis died down.

Millions of fans turn out to see college football today, but that first match attracted a gathering of a hundred or so, including an umbrella-waving Rutgers professor, who shouted at the participants:

"You men will come to no Christian end!"

He was wrong. No fewer than seven of the original 25 Rutgers players later became ministers of the gospel.

The actual ancestry of intercollegiate football dates back to 1875 when Harvard defeated McGill University of Canada 4–0 in a game combining rugby and Boston soccer at Hamilton Park in New Haven, Conn. Since Harvard's rules were different from those of other football-playing colleges, they were forced to look to Canadian teams for opposition.

The following year, Harvard met Yale in a 30-man game in which running with the ball and tackling were permitted. That was the forerunner of the hard, physical contact that became an integral part of the game.

One reason Harvard, Princeton and Yale are known as the Big Three is that each played an important role in the development of football. Harvard took up rugby and played it consistently in the mid-1870s. Princeton initiated the calling of a convention in 1876 which resulted in the formation of the first Intercollegiate Football Association. In 1880, Yale succeeded in getting the number of players reduced from 15 to 11.

Meanwhile, the game continued to progress. In the late 1870s came the introduction of scrimmage downs instead of the rugby scrum. In 1884, the wedge appeared and interference (i.e., blocking) became a feature of the game.

Tackling below the waist was legalized in 1888 and that forced a change in offensive deployment to protect the ball carrier. The line contracted and the backs moved in closer to bring about a formation pretty much as it is today. The game changed from wide pitchouts to mass momentum plays—and things really got rough.

In 1894 came the most sweeping rules revisions in 10 years. The dangerous wedge was outlawed, game time was reduced from 90 to 70 minutes, tackling of an opponent who didn't have the ball was prohibited, a kickoff had to travel 10 yards to be in play and a third official—a linesman—was added to the referee and umpire.

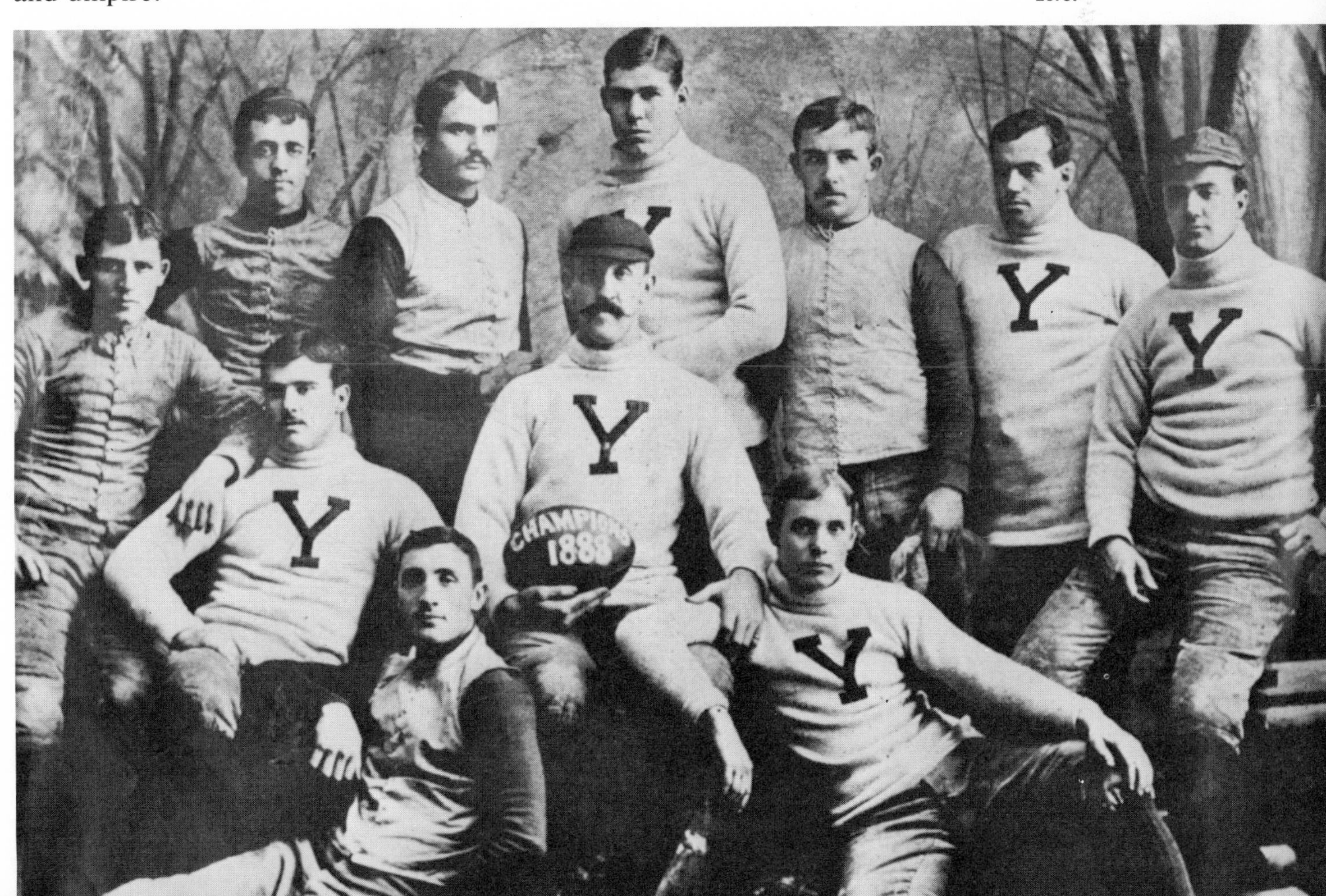

Yale, with the famed Amos Alonzo Stagg, extreme left, Tom McClung, on whose shoulder he rests his arm, and Pudge Heffelfinger, rear, directly behind player with football, among members of the team, posed in 1888. In that year they scored 698 points while their 13 opponents scored a total of zero.

Despite attempts to eliminate some of the roughness, football continued under fire as the public demanded an end to the brutality. In 1896, new rules made at least five men mandatory on the offensive line and prohibited more than one step towards the opponents' goal before the snap of the ball.

Still, football remained in the elemental stage at the turn of the century. The storm broke in 1905 as a survey by the *Chicago Tribune* showed 18 dead and 159 serious injuries. President Theodore Roosevelt called representatives of the Big Three to the White House and told them it was up to them to save the sport by removing every objectionable feature.

"Brutality and foul play should receive the same summary punishment given to a man who cheats at cards," he said.

California, Columbia, Northwestern, Stanford and Union were among those who suspended football for a while.

In December of that year, the Intercollegiate Athletic Association was organized, a group that five years later was to become the National Collegiate Athletic Association. The IFA and the IAA met in January of 1906 and merged as the American Intercollegiate Football Rules Committee. They adopted a program to open play and reduce the hazards, a plan that saved the game.

Out of that 1906 meeting came the legalization of the forward pass, the biggest single development since the introduction of scrimmage plays and a system of downs. The game evolved from a mass brute force attack to a quick-striking offense.

Although Gus Dorais and Knute Rockne of Notre Dame brought the forward pass from obscurity to national fame with a 35–13 victory over Army in 1913, St. Louis University—which, ironically, no longer fields a football team—was the first to exploit the new offensive weapon.

In 1906, coach Eddie Cochems developed the first passing combination—Bradbury Robinson to Jack Schneider.

The 1906 meeting also produced several other important rules changes. They included reduction of game time from 70 minutes to two 30-minute halves, establishment of the neutral zone, increase of the down distance from five to 10 yards and the outlawing of hurdling.

The objectives of the new rules were: (1) to make the game safer and more interesting, (2) to produce a more open game, (3) to remove the premium on mere weight and develop a greater opportunity for speed, agility and brains, and (4) to improve the standards and develop better officiating.

Year by year, more changes were made. In 1909, the value of a field goal was reduced from four to three points. A year later, seven men were required on the offensive line and in 1912 came five more significant rules.

These were addition of a fourth down, reduction in field length from 110 to 100 yards, kickoff from the 40-yard line instead of midfield, making a touchdown six points instead of five and removal of the 20-yard limit on forward passes. Rules changes since 1912 have been comparatively minor and modern football can be said to date from the 1913 season.

To that point, the sport had been dominated by Yale, Princeton and Harvard, with an occasional sally from Penn, Lafayette, Sewanee, Washington, Navy, the Carlisle Indians and Michigan's famed point-a-minute teams under Fielding "Hurry Up" Yost, which won 55 of 57 games from 1901 through 1905 and outscored the opposition 2,821–42.

Amos Alonzo Stagg, left, sits with Knute Rockne during a track and field meet in Chicago in 1930. Theirs are among the greatest names in football history.

Organized coaching was introduced at Harvard in 1890 and the Yale eleven of 1891 was generally considered the first really good college team, although the 1888 Elis under the legendary Walter Camp included some of the most famous names the game was ever to know—Amos Alonzo Stagg, Pudge Heffelfinger and George Woodruff.

Heffelfinger was an all-time great player. Stagg, Woodruff and Glenn "Pop" Warner were among the game's most inventive minds.

Camp, of course, was the so-called "Father of American Football." From 1876 to 1910 he was the outstanding figure in the development of playing technique and strategy. From 1879 to 1925 he was a member of every rules convention and rules committee. Until his death, he was the acknowledged leader in the evolution of the game through the framing of its playing rules. He also started the All-America teams.

But there were others. Pop Warner unveiled the Single Wing and Double Wing formations, although the dates are unclear. Until the Double Wing came into existence, the Notre Dame box and shift and the Single Wing were the most popular styles of attack.

But perhaps the greatest name in football history was that of Amos Alonzo Stagg. For 41 years he coached at the University of Chicago. In his 70s, he took over at the College of the Pacific and still later joined his son, Amos Alonzo Jr., at Susquehanna University. He finally retired in 1953 because of his wife's illness but he still helped out at Pacific in 1954.

As a player at Yale and later coach, his career spanned almost the entire first 70 years or so that football differed from rugby and soccer.

He was the most prolific of inventors, in the way of plays, formations, techniques and playing and field equipment.

He was a leader in the formation of what is now the Big Ten, the last surviving member of the original Intercollegiate Football Rules Committee, a member of five Olympic committees, an ingenious strategist.

The Notre Dame shift can be traced back to Stagg. In 1906, the year the for-

ward pass was legalized, Stagg had 64 pass plays. He is credited with being the first to use the center snap. He used an onside kick in 1894 and a quick kick in 1896. He probably was the first to use a huddle. He contributed four fundamental principles to the modern T formation.

Notre Dame became a power in 1913, when the Dorais-Rockne passing demonstration against Army was followed by a general awakening to the possibilities of the aerial game.

In 1914, Illinois, in Bob Zuppke's second year at the helm, rose to the top. It was Cornell and Nebraska in 1915, the same year that Pop Warner took over at Pitt and began a string of four unbeaten seasons.

Football, often described as a war, survived the real thing. In 1919, thousands of players returned from World War I and the sport entered upon its biggest and most exciting period yet. That year, tiny Centre College, the famed Praying Colonels, upset mighty Harvard 6–0 and Knute Rockne had the first of five unbeaten teams at Notre Dame. A year earlier, Rockne took over as coach and George Gipp arrived on the Notre Dame campus.

Then came the 1920s—The Golden Twenties, they were called—and the Golden Dome of Notre Dame rose above all under the brilliant Rockne.

California, under Andy Smith, and Cornell, under Gil Dobie, were among the elite, but the Fighting Irish rolled on.

Then, in October of 1924, two of the most memorable events in football history occurred. Red Grange, Illinois' "Galloping Ghost" from Wheaton, Ill., scored five touchdowns in a sensational performance against Michigan and Grantland Rice penned his lines christening the Notre Dame backfield of Harry Stuhldreher, Jim Crowley, Elmer Layden and Don Miller as "The Four Horsemen." Between Grange and the Horsemen, the nation went football-mad.

The year 1925 saw Dartmouth, Alabama and Michigan in the limelight and in 1926 it was Army, Navy and Brown's Iron Men. Illinois, Yale, Pitt, Texas A&M and Tennessee in its second year under Bob Neyland were the powers in 1927.

The 1924 Notre Dame football team produced the famed Four Horsemen. They were Harry Stuhldreher, quarterback, behind the center; halfback Don Miller, left in backfield; Elmer Layden, fullback, behind Stuhldreher, and Jim Crowley, halfback, right in backfield.

Tennessee, which had a 76–6–5 record in Neyland's first nine seasons, was strong again in 1928, along with Georgia Tech, Southern California, Detroit and Boston College. Notre Dame had an off-year, but managed to win one for the "Gipper," George Gipp, beating Army.

Notre Dame bounced back in 1929 and 1930 before a tragedy that stunned the football world. Knute Rockne died in a plane crash in Kansas in March of 1931, leaving behind memories that live to this day.

Warner, Stagg, Zuppke, Yost, Percy Haughton of Harvard, Dr. Harry Williams of Minnesota. They were among the great coaches of the first 60 years. But Rockne stood above all.

Said Warner: "No one ever asked me to pick the greatest football coach of all time, but if I were asked I would unhesitatingly name Rockne. No man ever

Red Grange, Illinois' Galloping Ghost, tucks the ball firmly in his hands and follows the interference of a teammate. Grange, in October of 1924, scored five touchdowns in a sensational performance against Michigan.

had a stronger or more magnetic personality. No man ever had a greater ability to transform that magnetism into football results."

In 13 years of coaching, Rockne compiled a majestic 105–12–5 record.

The 1920s also brought about several more rules changes. The point after touchdown was introduced in 1922 and, in 1927, the goal posts were set at the rear of the end zone and a one-second pause was required after a shift. The shift lost its appeal and waned.

The shift went back to Stagg, although Notre Dame publicized it. The primary shifts were the Notre Dame shift, the Minnesota shift of Doc Williams and the Heisman shift at Georgia Tech.

Besides Rockne's death, 1931 saw more casualties on the football field and another outcry against the roughness inherent in the game. In 1932, the most far-reaching changes in two decades set up further safeguards and eliminated some of the dangers.

These included making the ball dead when any portion of the ball carrier except the hands or feet touched the ground. Also, padding was required over hard and dangerous equipment. Helmets became mandatory in 1939.

With Rockne's death, other teams jumped into the fray. Southern California, under Howard Jones, became a power and, in 1932, Colgate boasted Andy Kerr's famous "unbeaten, untied, unscored on . . . and uninvited" eleven.

The following season was highlighted by Columbia's dramatic 7–0 victory over Stanford in the Rose Bowl thanks to a tricky play labeled KF79. Princeton

Chicago's Jay Berwanger, wearing the football gear of the day, posed this running action. In 1935 he won the first Heisman Trophy.

was a titan in the mid-1930s and, in 1935, Notre Dame defeated Ohio State 18–13 in one of football's greatest games. That year, Chicago's Jay Berwanger won the first Heisman Trophy.

It was Minnesota and Louisiana State in 1936 and Pitt had its best team under Jock Sutherland in 1937, a year that also spotlighted Fordham's "Seven Blocks of Granite."

It was Texas Christian and the passing of Davey O'Brien in 1938 and Texas A&M in 1939. Minnesota won national championships in 1940 and 1941 and then football had to survive another war.

In 1941, the substitution rule was radically changed to permit practically free use of players, but in 1942 the rules were frozen as some 250 colleges dropped football for the duration.

Still, the war years had their share of great teams. Ohio State, under Paul Brown, was king in 1942 and Notre Dame, under Frank Leahy, the following year. Then came three great Army teams featuring Doc Blanchard and Glenn Davis, Mr. Inside and Mr. Outside. The Army coach was Col. Earl "Red" Blaik.

Notre Dame and Army battled to a scoreless tie in 1946 and also tied for national honors.

In 1940, just before America's involvement in World War II, came the most far-reaching development since the 1912 rules changes. The modern T formation was devised.

Actually, football's original formation—the so-called "regular formation"—was an old form of the T, but the quarterback wasn't directly under the center. Then, George Halas of the professional Chicago Bears spread his left end wide with a man-in-motion to the right. Stanford, under Clark Shaughnessy, went to the Rose Bowl using the same style of attack. The respective quarterbacks were two of the best, Sid Luckman of the Bears and Stanford's Frankie Albert.

The offense had now evolved from the original T of mass momentum plays to the punt formation of Yost's early-1900 Michigan teams . . . to the more open style introduced by the forward pass . . . to the power and deception of Warner's wingback attack with an overshifted line and linemen pulling out as blockers . . . to the shifts of Stagg, Minnesota's Williams, Heisman and Jesse Harper and Rockne at Notre Dame . . . and finally back to the T, with modern, streamlined embellishments.

Don Faurot's Split-T in 1941 was termed the most original and significant contribution to offensive football in 10 years. In 1943, Notre Dame, under Leahy, and with Johnny Lujack at quarterback, abandoned the shift and all opposition to the T collapsed.

Notre Dame and Michigan dominated in 1947, Michigan and Notre Dame in 1948. Notre Dame and Oklahoma ruled the roost in 1949 and the Sooners captured the national championship in 1950. That was prophetic, because the 1950s was to be the decade of the Oklahoma Sooners under coach Bud Wilkinson. From 1953 to 1957, they established modern football's longest winning streak, 47 games, until a 7–0 loss to Notre Dame.

As the 1950s drew to a close, Auburn, Louisiana State and Syracuse made the headlines.

Significant changes on the field marked the 1960s—the Soaring Sixties, as they

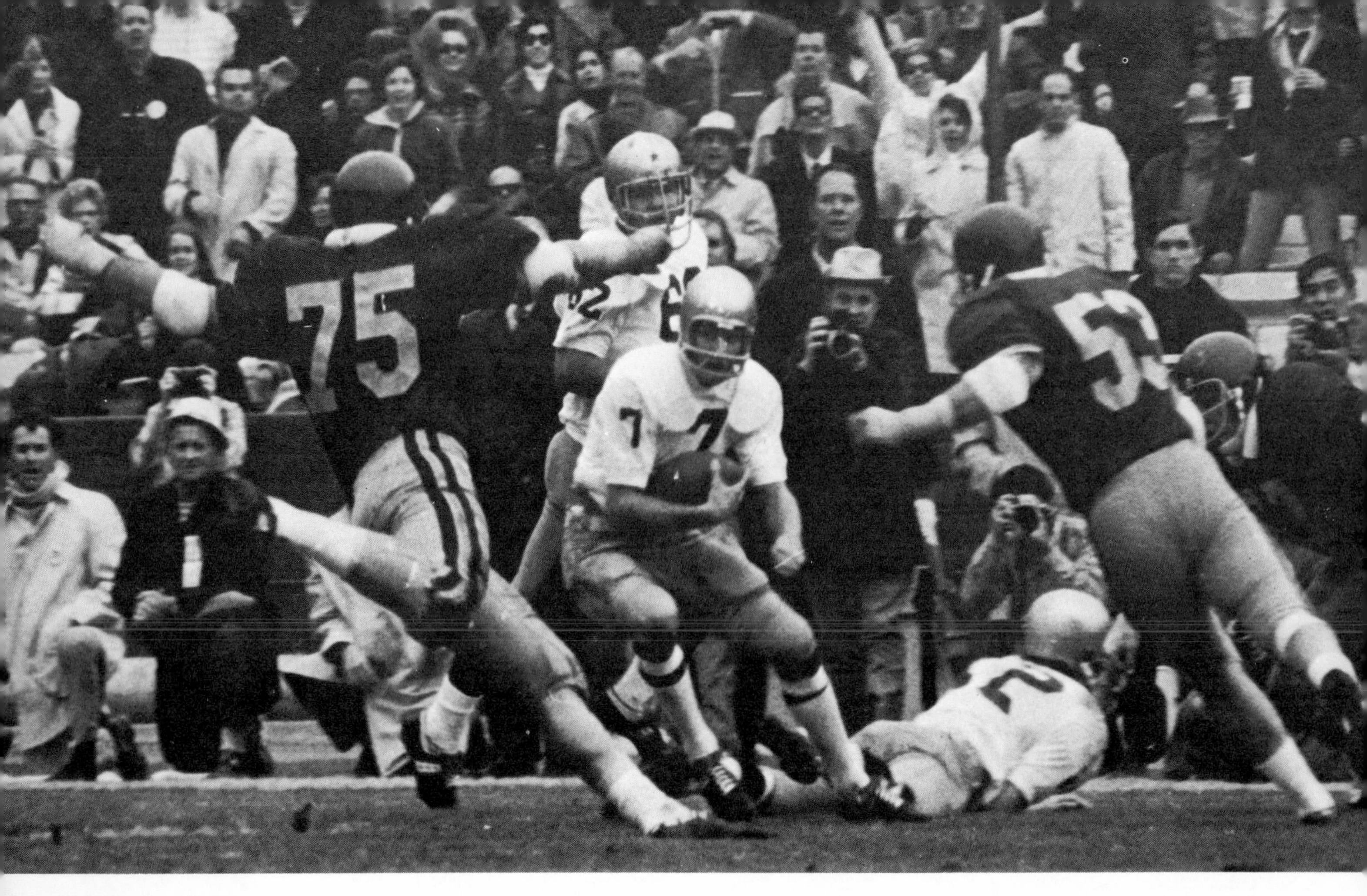

Southern California's John Vella (75) and Greg Slough (53) converge on Notre Dame quarterback Joe Theismann during game in 1970 at Los Angeles.

became known. Alabama, Texas and Arkansas were the winningest teams, but that doesn't really tell the story.

The decade produced record highs in scoring, rushing, passing, receiving and kicking. It was the most exciting decade in the history of football.

While the young set switched to maxi-hair and miniskirts, the old game also took on a new look. College football ended the 1950s as a game played on grass by two-way players with all-around talents. It ended the 1960s as a game played increasingly on artificial turf by specialized members of platoons.

After the "wild card" substitution rule of 1960, substitution was increasingly liberalized until it became completely two-platoon in 1965. Clock-stopping rules changes brought an increase of 27 plays per game between 1964 and 1968.

Though it normally drops with more plays, efficiency actually increased, resulting in a more explosive game. Everybody opened up. Seventy passes in a game was nothing any more. Coaches with fleet split ends and flankers went for the bomb.

Quarterbacks became runners as well as passers. Triple options made the rushing game even more dangerous and defensive coaches had nightmares. A 21-point lead—or more—no longer was safe. Houston scored 100 points in a game. Pitt and Cincinnati each scored 48 . . . and lost.

Greatest of the Decade polls chose Southern Cal's O. J. Simpson as the top player, Ohio State of 1968 as the best team, Alabama's Paul "Bear" Bryant as the outstanding coach and Texas' dramatic 15–14 victory over Arkansas in 1969 as the top game.

In 1970—actually on New Year's Day, 1971—Texas' 30-game winning streak came to an end at the hands of Notre Dame in the Cotton Bowl and Nebraska supplanted the Longhorns as national champions.

What's ahead?

"The 1970s seem to be the decade of great opportunity for intercollegiate football," said Joe Paterno of Penn State. "Our high school athletes are better. Furthermore, there is more emphasis on intelligence, ambition and character, and the general quality of our people playing is superior.

"I, for one, don't believe that the fact that we have to explain 'why' should be a problem. In fact, it should be an added benefit derived from the game for the players. However, along with the fact that the coaches will have to give up arbitrary discipline, will come, I believe, more college coaches achieving faculty rank and academic tenure—in order to give them the same protection that our classroom colleagues have.

"Perhaps another development in this area will be the elimination of football dorms. More and more football players resent being herded together and would prefer to be in the mainstream of college life and a normal member of a student body—which member is fortunate enough to be able to participate in a great extracurricular activity such as football.

"I think we will see tighter administration of recruiting. I believe the NCAA will pass rules which will limit the number of trips a prospect can make, not only to an individual school, but as to the number of schools in which he may be interested. I think before the '70s are over we will have a limit as to the number of grants-in-aid a university can offer."

The game itself?

"The same basic qualities that made for winning football a few years back still hold up today," said Darrell Royal. "It is still a game of hit or be hit and those with a strong heart and quick afoot and who can mash down the scales are the ones that seem to take care of our side the best. We do not have the same iron-clad control over the student-athlete that we had 15 years ago and this is something that all coaches must adjust to as the game progresses."

Johnny Gardner of Texas A&M goes head over heels after snagging pass in game against Texas in 1970. Defender is Rick Nabors (41) of the Longhorns.

This is Abner Doubleday, the man credited with starting the national pastime—the game of baseball.

President Kennedy was among those chief executives who have tossed out the first ball to open a baseball season. He's shown in Washington at start of the 1963 season.

chapter 2

BASEBALL

The National Pastime—Rich in Fact and Fable

by Dick Joyce

Dick Joyce, a Brooklyn native and graduate of St. Bonaventure, has had a varied journalism career. He was on the sports staff of *United Press International* for five years, did stints with the *New York World-Telegram and Sun*, the *New York Post* and *NBC News* before joining *The AP* in July 1968. He worked on the radio desk before moving into sports, where he now serves as day supervisor of the New York desk.

Rising from his box seat at the Washington, D.C., ball park, the president of the United States rears back and throws out the first baseball of the new season. In no other professional sport does the president attempt to make it his duty to add his prestige and presence to the opening day. As the oldest of professional sports in the United States, baseball is rich in legend—both fact and fable.

But baseball is more than Babe Ruth belting a prodigious homer, Ty Cobb flashing his spikes, Bob Feller humming his fastball or Willie Mays making a basket catch. It is a lucrative business and, to some, a kind of religion.

One hundred years old in 1969, pro baseball entered the 1970s being threatened as the national game. Professional football was making giant inroads, the reserve clause scare popped up again and baseball was suffering growing pains caused by expansion.

In addition, the players' union, through the efforts of its director, Marvin Miller, was making major gains in obtaining higher salaries and more benefits. So much so that the players threatened to strike if the club owners failed to loosen their purse strings.

But organized baseball has survived the Federal League, the 1919 Black Sox scandal, the old Mexican League, television, court cases testing the constitutionality of the reserve clause, the reduction of its minor leagues, and hopscotching of franchises by its owners.

The Giants, a name etched in baseball history, posed for this team picture in 1888. It was known then as the New York Base-ball club.

Albert Spalding, left, and Tim Keefe display the look of 19th century baseball.

Despite the nation's population growth, it has become apparent that baseball had diluted its talent by the rapid addition of eight new clubs in the 1960s. Pro football and pro basketball have vastly increased in popularity since the 1950s and also have expanded, drawing young talent that had been virtually all baseball's.

Baseball, in a not too different form, burst upon the American scene some time in the 1830s.

Baseball rulers stand by the myth that the game is of purely American origin, a brainstorm which came to one Abner Doubleday during the spring of 1839 in the sleepy central New York State village of Cooperstown.

Yet, historians have presented enough evidence to ascertain that baseball had its origin in the English game of rounders. In fact, there is evidence that rounders at one time actually was called "base-ball" in certain parts of England as early as 1744.

In America, the game was variously known as roundball, townball and even baseball as it grew in popularity in the 1830s and 1840s, especially in the East. Around the turn of the century when English-born Henry Chadwick, regarded as the first prominent sports writer, claimed that baseball was a derivative of rounders, the National League, led by A. G. Spalding, set up a national commission to delve into the origin of baseball, stating, in fact, that Chadwick's claim was unpatriotic.

In 1907, one year after its formation, the special commission decided, despite sketchy information, that Doubleday, a Civil War hero, had indeed founded base-

These two men are members of baseball's Hall of Fame. The painting on the left is of Cy Young, winner of 511 games between 1890 and 1911. On the right is Wee Willie Keeler, who coined the phrase, "Hit 'em where they ain't."

ball at Cooperstown. One present-day historian contends that if Doubleday was in Cooperstown at the time, he would have been AWOL from West Point.

Years later, in 1934, baseball's rulers, apparently in an effort to set up a centennial celebration to boost baseball's interest, again went on record as saying that the game was purely of American origin. Funds were appropriated to build a shrine at Cooperstown as a lasting tribute to the heroes of the game.

The first known set of rules, surprisingly many of which still stand today, was laid down by the Knickerbocker Baseball Club of New York on Sept. 13, 1845. Although similar to the English game of rounders, the rules stipulated that the infield be diamond-shaped instead of oblong and that there be four bases instead of five. In another change from rounders and townball, the new rules stated that a player could be put "out" by touching him with the ball rather than hitting him with it.

Alexander J. Cartwright, considered the "Father of Baseball," formulated the playing rules and adopted a standard field of play. He reduced the number of players on a side from 11 to nine. Runs were known as aces then, and the game ended when one side scored 21 aces, in any number of even innings for both sides.

Cartwright established the bases 90 feet apart and the pitching distance as 45 feet. In that time, the catcher—with no mask, glove or other protection—stood far enough in back of the hitter so as to catch the ball on the first bounce, and the shortstop played in front of the baseline.

The first recorded game in which these rules were put into effect took place at the Elysian Fields in Hoboken, N.J., June 19, 1846. The Knickerbockers lost, 23–1. The game caught on quickly in the New York City area where, within a few years, every empty lot was filled with young men playing baseball.

As the game grew by the late 1850s, the first league was formed—the National Association of Baseball Players, in 1857. Then, by the time the Civil War ended, the game had spread throughout the states. By 1868, 18 states and territories had a total of 400 baseball clubs—mostly amateur—but with some clubs paying small sums to star players.

The Cincinnati Red Stockings were the first pro club, frankly admitting in 1869 that all of its players were salaried. Highest paid were two brothers, Harry and George Wright, $1,400 and $1,200, respectively. The Red Stockings traveled throughout the country and finished the season with an incredible record of 65 victories and one tie without a loss. They extended their streak to 130 victories the next season before losing 8–7 in extra innings to the Atlantics of Brooklyn.

In 1870, Chicago formed a rival professional organization with its object to beat the champions. The White Stockings, as they were known, accomplished their task, beating Cincinnati two straight. It was such a blow to the Red Stockings' prestige that the club disbanded the next year.

Meanwhile, George Wright and A. G. Spalding joined the Boston club which was to become the champion for five straight years, 1871 to 1875.

The game began to flourish with one drawback—gambling. Gamblers brazenly waved their bankrolls at the ball park, bookies set up special booths beneath the stands, and business was plentiful. Naturally, bribery of players occurred. The public began to lose faith in the players and the game itself. Dishonesty and rowdiness were prevalent.

In 1876, the National League of Professional Baseball Clubs, forerunner of the National League, was formed. Its object was to make the game a clean, popular sport free from gambling. There were eight cities as charter members: Boston, Chicago, Cincinnati, Louisville, Hartford, St. Louis, Philadelphia and New York. Some 31 NL franchises were held during the 25 years up to and including 1900.

It was a major step toward baseball establishing itself permanently as organized business. The National League champion Baltimore Orioles became one of the most colorful teams in history during their 1894–96 reign, with such stars as John McGraw, Wee Willie Keeler, Hughie Jennings, Wilbert Robinson, Kid Gleason, Joe Kelley and Jack Doyle.

The National League produced other great stars in its early years, including Hugh Duffy of Boston, who hit .438 in 1894, highest ever in the majors; Cap Anson, who played 27 seasons, mostly with the Chicago White Stockings; Mike (King) Kelly; Kid Nichols; Bobby Lowe (first to hit four homers in one game); Tim Keefe; John Montgomery Ward; Jess Burkett; Roger Connor, and Dan Brouthers.

Cy Young, the only pitcher to win more than 500 games, made his debut with Cleveland in 1890. Honus Wagner broke in with Louisville in 1897. Nap Lajoie started with Philadelphia in 1896 and Old Hoss Charles Radbourne with Providence in 1881.

Except for brief periods in its early years before 1900 the National League was an eight-team circuit. In the beginning it was challenged five times, but withstood each attack. It warred with the American Association in 1882, the Union Association in 1884, the Brotherhood of Players League in 1890, the American League in 1901–02 and the Federal League in 1914–15. The Union and Players League lasted one year, the Federal two and the American Association 10. The National League's biggest war was with the American League and this resulted in the formation of two major leagues.

Judge Kenesaw Mountain Landis was baseball's commissioner in the tough years of the game.

The Chicago Cubs' famous double-play combination, Tinker to Evers to Chance, began with Joe Tinker and Johnny Evers, above, and ended with Frank Chance shown at bat in the right-hand photo.

The American League came about 25 years after the National, achieving major league status in 1901. Its prime movers were Ban Johnson, former Midwest newspaperman, and Charles A. Comiskey, former player, manager and club owner. It began as an expansion of the old Western League and rose swiftly, mainly on the efforts of Johnson, who became the AL president, and raided the NL of many of its stars, including Lajoie, Ed Delahanty, Cy Young, Willie Keeler, Jimmy Collins, Sam Crawford and Jack Chesbro.

The original cities in the junior circuit were Detroit, Buffalo, Philadelphia, Minneapolis, Indianapolis, Milwaukee, St. Paul and Kansas City. In 1901 Boston, Chicago, Baltimore and Washington replaced Minneapolis, Indianapolis, Kansas City and Buffalo. In 1902, St. Louis replaced Milwaukee. In 1903 New York took over from Baltimore.

The American and National leagues established peace in 1902 and a national commission was formed to rule baseball. It was made up of Ban Johnson, Harry C. Pulliam, NL president, and August Herrmann, Cincinnati owner. They ruled baseball until Feb. 20, 1920, when Judge Kenesaw Mountain Landis was chosen commissioner. He ruled the sport with a strong hand until his death in 1944.

In 1915, Judge Landis handled the Federal League's antitrust suit against the majors and helped bring about a settlement whereby players who jumped, such as Hal Chase, Mordecai (Three-Finger) Brown and Joe Tinker, were reinstated and the Federal League disbanded.

After the National and American leagues joined hands, the first modern World Series was played in 1903, with Boston surprising Pittsburgh, five games to three. In 1906 the first intracity series was held as the Chicago White Sox, known as the "Hitless Wonders," upset the Chicago Cubs.

Fred Merkle became famous on Sept. 23, 1908, a day the Giants and Cubs were battling for the NL pennant. In the ninth inning, Merkle, a New York base runner, failed to touch second base, thus preventing the Giants from winning the game. The game ended in a 1–1 tie and had to be replayed from the start at the conclusion of the season. The Cubs won it, giving Merkle a dubious but permanent niche in history despite an otherwise good career.

The Cubs were among the standout teams of this era with a double play combination of Joe Tinker, Johnny Evers and Frank Chance. Many argued that Connie Mack's Philadelphia A's infield of Stuffy McInnis, Eddie Collins, Jack Barry and Frank Baker—known as the $100,000 infield—was better, but Franklin P. Adams of the *New York Evening Mail* made the Cub combination immortal through a poem which said in part:

"These are the saddest of possible words:
" 'Tinker to Evers to Chance'
"Trio of bear cubs, and fleeter than birds, Tinker, Evers and Chance."

It was during this time, too, that "Take Me Out to the Ball Game" became a popular song and "Casey at the Bat" was oft recited.

The early years of the NL also produced such heroes as Christy Mathewson, who compiled a 313–188 lifetime pitching mark; Pittsburgh's Flying Dutchman, Honus Wagner, a .329 hitter for 17 seasons and an outstanding shortstop; six-time 20-game winner Mordecai (Three-Finger) Brown of the Cubs, and Iron Man Joe McGinnity, who rang up a 35–8 record in 1904 and 247–142 in his career with the Giants and Dodgers.

McGinnity is best remembered for his endurance—the ability to pitch, and win, both ends of a doubleheader.

Years later, after Lefty Gomez, an eccentric Yankee left-handed pitcher, first became married, his new bride saw him pitch one day. After the game, Lefty's wife, knowing next to nothing about baseball, said, "You did well. Are you pitching again tomorrow?" Lefty gave her a startled look, then barked: "Who in hell do you think I am—Iron Man Joe McGinnity?"

The first two decades in 1900, which spanned the era of the dead ball and the lively ball (cork-cushioned), also produced Ty Cobb, who ranks with Ruth among the game's premier stars. Statistics tell much of the story. Cobb, who played with the Detroit Tigers and Philadelphia A's from 1905–1928, led the AL in batting 12 times. He holds the all-time major league career batting mark of .367 and rapped out 4,191 hits, a record unlikely to be topped. Stan Musial, for example, a .337 hitter for 22 seasons with the St. Louis Cardinals, fell 500 hits short.

Behind Cobb's glowing figures stood a fierce competitor who was a savage base runner. The Georgia Peach batted over .300 for 23 straight years; he scored more runs, stole more bases and made more hits than anyone in history. Three times he topped .400 in batting average—.420 and .410 in 1911 and 1912 and .401 in 1922 at the age of 37.

Grover Cleveland Alexander, with Philadelphia and Chicago of the NL, Walter Johnson of Washington and Eddie Plank of the Athletics, also were the great pitching stars of the time.

They pitched in the era of the spitball when saliva, licorice and other foreign substances were put on the ball in order to make it do tricks. The spitball was outlawed in 1920, except for those whose living depended on it. Burleigh Grimes was one such hurler who threw it until 1934 in his career with Brooklyn and Pittsburgh.

Although outlawed, pitchers continued to throw the spitter. After he retired, Preacher Roe admitted throwing it. Whitey Ford, Lew Burdette and Don Drysdale

Lou Gehrig, Babe Ruth and Tony Lazzeri, from left, were three members of the famed New York Yankees "Murderers Row."

were other prime suspects in later years. But it's something umpires had a tough time proving.

A few years back, Norm Larker complained to umpire Frank Secory that Burdette had just thrown a spitter. Secory denied it, saying: "Naw, those were sinkers." Larker snapped back: "Sinkers! One of them 'sinkers' just splashed me in the eye!"

George Herman "Babe" Ruth probably will remain the greatest hero the game has ever known. His booming bat turned the game of speed and skill into one of power. Before his homers began electrifying the country, most hitters choked up on the bat, willing to settle for singles and doubles.

From the time he broke in with the Boston Red Sox as a pitcher late in 1914 until he bowed out as a pinch-hitter for the Boston Braves in 1935, Ruth slammed 714 homers, a feat which may never be beaten.

Ruth was a man of considerable baseball talent, as well as being a fun-lover, drinker and carouser off the field. Before being sold to the Yankees in 1920, Ruth compiled an 87–44 won-lost pitching record, including 23 victories in both 1916 and 1917. He also held a World Series record of consecutive scoreless innings pitched until 1962.

As a fielder, Ruth was a ball hawk and he had a rifle arm. In 1919 while still with Boston, Ruth set a major league record by hitting 29 homers. He was to follow with 54 and 59 homers the next two seasons. He helped make the Yankees a dominant power. The 1927 Yankees are regarded as probably baseball's best team ever. Ruth, who hit his record 60 homers that year, Lou Gehrig, Bob Meusel and Tony Lazzeri were the most feared batsmen in the game and were known as "Murderer's Row." Each had more than 100 runs batted in for a 544 total. Gehrig knocked in 175 runs while Earle Combs weighed in with a .356 batting average. Ruth was as flamboyant as he was good. In the era of colorful nicknames, Babe also was known as the "Sultan of Swat."

One of his most famous homers was his called-shot off Charlie Root in the third game of the 1932 World Series against the Chicago Cubs. After Root got two quick strikes on him, Ruth held up two fingers and pointed with his bat to the center field stands. He ripped the next pitch into the spot where he had pointed.

Once, after a night on the town, the Babe showed up sleepy-eyed. A teammate remarked, "You look a little beat, Babe." Ruth then bet his mate $100 that he would hit a homer. On the first time at bat Babe did just that. Later, he tripled, tripled and homered again.

The Bambino, on several occasions, drew the wrath of manager Miller Huggins. After Ruth stayed out all night, Huggins fined the Babe $1,000 but later refunded it when Ruth promised to reform. But in 1925, Ruth showed up late one afternoon and Huggins hit him with a $5,000 fine and suspended him. "The fine's a joke," said Ruth. "They don't fine bootleggers that much."

Babe said he would never play for Huggins again and he asked that owner Jake Ruppert fire Huggins. But Ruppert stood his ground and backed his manager. Ruth apologized.

Ruth eventually commanded an $80,000-a-year salary—before the advent

Two of the greatest Yankees of all time had their days at Yankee Stadium. Babe Ruth, left, in 1948, and Lou Gehrig in 1939 said good-bye to the fans who had thrilled to their many accomplishments.

of income taxes. During World War II the Japanese troops had no greater insult to hurl at U.S. Marines in the Pacific than: "To hell with Babe Ruth," indicating how renowned an American the Yankee slugger was. Many believe that Ruth's feats helped save the game which had been rocked by the 1919 Black Sox scandal.

Seven members of the Chicago White Sox admitted to conspiring to throw the World Series to Cincinnati. Barred from baseball for life despite having been cleared by a federal jury and repudiating their confessions later were: Shoeless Joe Jackson, considered one of the game's great natural hitters, Eddie Cicotte, Chick Gandil, Lefty Williams, Swede Risberg, Fred McMullin, and Happy Felsch. Buck Weaver, although said not to be actually involved in the conspiracy, knew about it and failed to report it. He, too, was barred.

There also was a furore in the 1920s when Ray Chapman was struck in the head by one of Yankee pitcher Carl Mays' submarine balls and died in the hospital that night.

The 1914 Boston Braves are a memorable team from the early years. On July 19, the Braves were buried in the National League basement, 11 games behind the front-running Giants, winners of three straight pennants.

Late in July the Braves took nine of 12 on a western trip while the Giants slumped badly. With fiery manager George Stallings juggling his shaky group of rookies and old pros (Johnny Evers and Rabbit Maranville among them), the Braves pulled into a tie with the Giants on Labor Day. Boston was a team with only three dependable pitchers and one .300 hitter.

Before almost 75,000 fans at Boston on Sept. 7, the Braves met the Giants in a double-header. The Braves beat Christy Mathewson by scoring twice in the last of the ninth. But the Giants came back to win the second game, 10–1. However, the next day the Braves won and were on their way. They steamrolled to the pennant, winning by 10½ games, a feat that looked impossible in July.

Connie Mack was a familiar figure in the dugout in mufti as he used scorecard in directing play of his Philadelphia Athletics.

In the World Series, the Braves met Connie Mack's world champion Philadelphia Athletics, regarded as one of the greatest teams in baseball at the time. Boston knocked out Chief Bender in the opening game and went on to win four straight, the first time in history any team swept the Series in four games.

Baseball was to wait 37 years for another miracle team—the 1951 New York Giants.

In the early part of the century, baseball had many other standouts. There was Nap Lajoie, who batted .339 over 20 years with Cleveland and Philadelphia in the AL; Eddie Collins, a .333 hitter over 24 AL campaigns; the Waner brothers, Paul (Big Poison) and Lloyd (Little Poison), both .300 hitters for over 15 seasons, mostly at Pittsburgh; Rogers Hornsby, who hit .400 three times, including the modern mark of .424 in 1924 for the Cardinals and Detroit's Harry Heilmann, who won the AL batting title four straight times.

There also were George Sisler of the St. Louis Browns, a .340 hitter for 15 seasons, topped by a .420 average with an all-time record of 257 hits in one season; Tris Speaker, outstanding center fielder for Cleveland and Boston in the AL with a .344 lifetime batting average; slugging Lou Gehrig, who was overshadowed by Ruth and set the record of playing in 2,130 consecutive games before illness felled him; Al Simmons, a .334 hitter for 21 seasons, mostly with the A's, and Jimmy Foxx, who clubbed 534 homers in his career.

Meantime, John McGraw, known as Little Napoleon for his stern ways, managed the Giants to four straight pennants between 1921 and 1925.

In 1930, the beginning of the Depression, many stars of the 1920s, including Ruth and Gehrig, continued their slugging, and Foxx developed into a home run hitter, second only to Ruth. And new heroes emerged.

The A's, with Lefty Grove, Mickey Cochrane and Simmons, and the Cardinals, led by Pepper Martin, battled in the 1930 and 1931 World Series. Martin hit Grove, an eventual 300-game winner in the majors, as if he owned him in both seasons. And in 1931, Martin collected a record-tying 12 hits, ran the bases with abandon and turned in sparkling fielding plays.

But New York teams dominated baseball thereafter up to the start of World War II. The Giants, managed by Bill Terry, won pennants in 1933-36-37 and came close three other times. The Yankees, managed by Joe McCarthy, won AL titles in 1932-36-37-38-39-41 and captured the World Series each time.

Detroit, led by slugging Hank Greenberg, Charlie Gehringer and pitcher Schoolboy Rowe, broke the Yankee dominance in 1934 and 1935, but was beaten by the Cards (1934) in the World Series. It was in 1934 that Terry, a .341 hitter through 14 seasons, uttered his famous putdown of the lowly Dodgers. "Are the Dodgers still in the league?" he asked. On the last day of the season he found out. The Dodgers beat the Giants and the Cards clinched the pennant.

The St. Louis Gas House Gang of the 1930s was the sport's most exciting team, with enough characters to last most teams a lifetime. They were a rough, tough, brawling crew, managed by Frankie Frisch, who played under John McGraw with the Giants. In addition to Pepper Martin, there were the Dean brothers, Dizzy and Paul, also known as Daffy; Joe Medwick, Leo Durocher and Rip Collins.

They battled fans, umpires, the opposition, as well as themselves. They also

The Dean brothers, Jerome Herman (Dizzy) at left, and Paul flanked Grover Cleveland Alexander at Hot Springs, Ark., in 1935. Alexander then was an ace moundsman of earlier times. The Deans earned their spurs with the St. Louis Cardinals, whom they helped win the pennant in 1934.

had their own band, called the Mississippi Mudcats. In 1934 Dizzy won 30 games and Daffy 19, and the Cards won 33 of their last 45 games to capture the NL flag. In game seven of the World Series, Medwick caused an uproar when he slid hard into Detroit third baseman Marv Owens. There were no fists thrown, only angry looks. But when Medwick went out to his left field position, the Detroit crowd cascaded bottles and garbage toward him. Judge Landis, who was in the stands, ordered Medwick removed from the game for his own protection. The Cards won the series.

The 1930s also meant the blossoming of left-handed pitcher Carl Hubbell of the Giants into stardom. A baffling screwball artist, Hubbell won 253 and lost 154, including a victory string of 24.

The All-Star Game, the dream of *Chicago Tribune* sports editor Arch Ward, was instituted in 1933 and one year later Hubbell turned in the memorable feat of striking out five of the AL's most feared hitters in a row. They were Ruth, Gehrig, Foxx, Simmons and Joe Cronin.

Mel Ott joined the Giants as a 16-year-old under John McGraw and, with his unorthodox batting style of lifting his right leg, crashed 511 career homers, good for No. 3 on the all-time homer list until surpassed in recent years by Willie Mays, Mickey Mantle and Hank Aaron.

Johnny Vander Meer, Cincinnati left-hander, made his mark in 1938, pitching back-to-back no-hitters, a feat which never has been matched.

Two years earlier marked the arrival of Joe DiMaggio to the Yankees and Bob Feller to the Cleveland Indians. Another future Hall of Famer arrived in 1939, Ted Williams of the Boston Red Sox. And a couple of years later, Stan Musial, a one-time sore-armed pitcher, was brought up by the Cardinals.

In DiMaggio's first season he hit .323, an omen of what was to come; Gehrig hit .354 and Bill Dickey, one of baseball's foremost catchers, .362 to lead the Yankees to their first of four straight pennants.

Seventeen-year-old Feller was a strong-armed right-hander out of Van Meter, Iowa, who blazed fastballs. He struck out 15 and 17 men in two rookie appearances and in 1946 set a major league season strikeout mark of 348, which was to stand until 1965 when Sandy Koufax of the Los Angeles Dodgers fanned 382. Rapid Robert pitched three no-hitters, in 1940, 1946, and 1951.

Like DiMaggio, Williams and so many others, Feller's career was interrupted by military service. After four years in the Navy, Feller returned with a lot missing off his fastball but he developed a good curve and excellent control to make him a key member of the strong Cleveland staff until the 1950s.

Baseball suffered through the lean years during World War II. Night baseball, which was introduced on May 23, 1935, by Cincinnati owner Larry MacPhail for a game against the Phillies, greatly increased by 1944. It was to become the rule rather than the exception. The only major league owner who refused to install lights was Phil Wrigley of the Chicago Cubs.

During the war years, baseball was hard-pressed for talent. In 1944, Cincinnati put 15-year-old Joe Nuxhall, a left-handed pitcher, in uniform, and shortstop Tommy Brown, 16, was plucked off the Brooklyn sandlots to play for the Dodgers. Veterans who had seen better days were given a reprieve. The Browns signed a one-armed semipro outfielder, Pete Gray. It was the same Browns' owner, controversial Bill Veeck, who a few years later, shocked baseball by using a midget, Eddie Gaedel, as a pinch-hitter.

Baseball was given a slight scare in 1946 when Jorge Pasquel and his brothers began flashing big bankrolls in front of major leaguers in an effort to make them jump to the outlawed Mexican League. Eighteen players jumped, including Sal Maglie, Max Lanier, Mickey Owen (famous for his missed third strike as Dodger catcher in the 1941 World Series) and Luis Olmo.

Commissioner A. B. "Happy" Chandler leveled a five-year ban on the players, who returned after a short period when the league folded. The ban eventually was lifted after three years, with only Maglie, of the Giants, making a major contribution.

Johnny Vander Meer, Cincinnati Reds southpaw, hurled successive no-hitters in 1938. His first was against the Boston Braves. He repeated the feat four days later against the Brooklyn Dodgers.

In the '30s, Carl Hubbell, left, was baffling hitters with his screwball and in the '60s it was Sandy Koufax and his fastball that had hitters dragging their bats back to the dugout.

After the war, Musial, Williams, DiMaggio and Feller returned for many productive seasons, although Williams' career again was interrupted during the Korean War. With these stars emerged such others as Warren Spahn, Whitey Ford, Mickey Mantle, Willie Mays, Jackie Robinson, Roy Campanella and Yogi Berra.

Williams, controversial and slipshod as a left fielder, was regarded as the game's keenest student of the art of hitting.

Williams was the last major leaguer to hit the magic .400 mark—.406 in 1941. After his World War II service, Williams captured four more batting crowns (1947-48-57-58) and was 40 years old when he won his sixth title. He batted .344 lifetime with 521 homers.

Another consistent performer was Musial, who topped .300 18 times in 22 seasons, was a six-time NL batting king and slugged 475 homers.

The time after the war was one of rapid growth, record World Series purses and high salaries. A major flow of talent came when baseball lifted its barrier against Negroes. Actually a few blacks had played in the American Association, then a major league, in the 1880s, before the league folded.

Branch Rickey, who as general manager of the St. Louis Cardinals set up baseball's farm system, startled everyone when he signed the first Negro, Jackie Robinson, to a contract with the Brooklyn organization in 1946. After an outstanding year at Montreal, Robinson was brought up to the Dodgers at the age of 28 and proved to be a big cog until his retirement after the 1956 season.

A daring base runner, capable second baseman and a .300 hitter, Robinson quietly took racial abuse in 1947, but he paved the way for other Negroes. Join-

Joe DiMaggio's record of hitting safely in 56 consecutive games still stands as one of baseball's outstanding achievements.

For more than 20 years, Stan Musial, right, and Ted Williams, below, ravaged pitchers with their heavy hitting. Williams, in 1941, batted .406, the last man to bat over .400 for a season.

Bobby Thomson of the New York Giants hits one of the most famous home runs in baseball history, against the Brooklyn Dodgers at the Polo Grounds in New York. This home run in the last of the ninth inning not only won the game, but also the pennant for the Giants in this third and final pennant playoff game of the season.

ing him on the Dodgers later were such standouts as Roy Campanella and Don Newcombe. In 1948 Larry Doby signed with Cleveland to become the AL's first black. The door was even opened for Satchel Paige, legendary pitcher in the Negro leagues, who helped Cleveland win a pennant in 1948 even though he was well past his prime and somewhere near 50 years old.

Baseball saw fit in 1971 to enroll Paige in the Hall of Fame. Through the 1960s major league rosters were filled with Negroes, many American and Latin blacks turning into the standout players in both leagues.

During Robinson's prime he helped the Dodgers become a dominant power as they won pennants in 1947-49-52-53-55-56. Other big contributors to the Dodger cause were Gil Hodges, Duke Snider, Carl Furillo, Pee Wee Reese, Johnny Podres, Campanella and Newcombe.

Their play helped wipe out the reputation Brooklyn had for producing poor ball teams and zany players. Babe Herman was one of those, once becoming one of three runners winding up at third base at the same time.

The only team more dominant than the Dodgers in the late 1940s and on were the Yankees. From 1947 through 1964, they won five straight pennants, 1949–53, and then four in a row, 1955–58, and finally another five straight, 1960–64. With these 15 AL flags came 10 world championships.

The Yankees met the Dodgers in six "Subway Series" during this time and lost only once, in 1955. Big guns at one time or another were Charlie Keller, Vic Raschi, Allie Reynolds, Tommy Henrich, Ford, Berra and switch-hitting Mickey Mantle, who crashed 536 homers before he retired, hampered much of his career by injuries.

While the Yankees enjoyed staying power as a dominant force, the life span of miracle teams again proved to be short. Next was the 1951 New York Giants, led by manager Leo Durocher, a sharp-tongued, clever manipulator. Leo the Lip fought with fans, umpires, sports writers, club owners and commissioners. He was banned for the 1947 season because Commissioner Chandler didn't like the company he kept. Leo had been Dodger manager at the time.

In the middle of the 1948 season—in one of baseball's most stunning managerial switches—Durocher took over as manager of the Giants, considered a traitorous move by rabid Dodger fans. In a short time, Durocher cleaned house of his lead-footed, poor-fielding sluggers, declaring: "I want fast men who can hit and run. I want a tight infield." In 1950 the Giants hustled their way to third place. But in 1951 the Giants went into a tailspin at the start and lost 11 in a row. Durocher shuffled his players and called up 19-year-old Willie Mays, destined to become one of the game's greats, from the minors. But the Giants still faltered and trailed the first-place Dodgers by 13½ games on Aug. 11.

The next day they bounced back, sweeping a double-header from Philadelphia. Then they beat the Dodgers three in a row and took three more from the Phillies, the 1950 pennant winners. The Giants racked up 16 victories in a row, reducing the Dodgers' lead to five games. Then they hit another 10-game win streak. On Sept. 20, they still were 4½ games out.

The red-hot Giants won their last four while the Dodgers could only win three of their last seven, throwing the bitter rivals into a best-of-three playoff. The teams split the first two games and the Giants were six outs away from losing the pennant. The Dodgers led 4–1 going into the last of the ninth when the Giants erupted. After Whitey Lockman's double made the score 4–2 and put Don Mueller on third base, Dodger ace Don Newcombe was replaced. Ralph Branca took over and threw a strike past Bobby Thomson. But Thomson socked the next pitch for a homer, giving the Giants a 5–4 victory and the pennant. Bedlam broke loose.

Baseball, which operated under two eight club setups for 50 years, underwent its first change in 1953 when the Boston Braves were moved to Milwaukee. A year later the St. Louis Browns shifted to Baltimore, and the Athletics were transferred from Philadelphia to Kansas City in 1955. In 1958 the first teams moved to the West Coast, the Brooklyn Dodgers to Los Angeles, and the New York Giants to San Francisco in a stunning shift of teams which drew well and were bitter rivals with a colorful history.

In the World Series, both great plays and major errors are magnified. Above, Mickey Owen chases his dropped third strike with two out in the ninth inning of the fourth game of the 1941 series. Tommy Henrich reached first base as the Yankees went on to win the game and the series. Left, Willie Mays makes what is considered by many as the greatest catch in baseball history. Mays not only caught Vic Wertz's long drive here in the eighth inning of the first game of the 1954 series, but whirled to make the throw back to the infield.

The scoreboard at Yankee Stadium on Oct. 8, 1956, tells the whole story—a string of zeros for the Brooklyn Dodgers. Don Larsen, being hugged by Yogi Berra, pitched the first perfect game in World Series competition.

	1	2	3	4	5	6	7	8	9	10	R	H	E
BROOKLYN	0	0	0	0	0	0	0	0	0		0	0	0
YANKEES	0	0	0	1	0	1	0	0			2	5	0

But the Braves and A's weren't through moving yet. In 1966 the Braves, who earlier had set attendance records in Milwaukee, switched to Atlanta, and in 1968 the A's packed up and left for Oakland.

In 1960 a congressional investigation and the formation of a proposed third major league, the Continental League, led to both leagues announcing expansion to 10-team leagues. The AL jumped the gun by moving into Los Angeles and Minneapolis-St. Paul for the 1961 season. Minnesota obtained the Washington franchise, while a new club was put in the nation's capital.

The Continental League, with Branch Rickey as president, never got off the ground, but it did help put another team back in New York—the Mets—and a club in Houston for the 1962 NL season. Baseball had its first domed stadium with Houston's Astrodome that season.

Generally the expansion clubs fared poorly, with the Mets the laughing stock of the nation because of their ineptness and manager Casey Stengel asking: "Can't anybody here play this game?"

Baseball made another expansion move for the 1969 season, adding Montreal and San Diego in the NL and Seattle and Kansas City in the AL. Failure to draw fans, among other factors, caused the AL to withdraw from Seattle after one season and shift the franchise to Milwaukee, thus silencing the court suits filed ever since the Braves pulled out of Milwaukee.

Through all this change, Warren Spahn had hung up his spikes after pitching 363 victories, mainly with the Braves, and Sandy Koufax of the Dodgers and Bob Gibson of the Cardinals emerged as two of the game's best pitchers. Koufax threw four no-hitters, more than anyone in history, before elbow trouble cut short his career at age 30. From 1962 to 1966 Koufax compiled the league's lowest ERA and set a World Series mark of 15 strikeouts in a single game—until Gibson broke it with two more.

Entering the 1960s three individual season records were considered unreachable: Babe Ruth's 60 homers, Ty Cobb's 96 stolen bases and Joe DiMaggio's 56 consecutive game hitting streak. But in 1961 Roger Maris of the Yankees hit 61 homers. The pressure was almost too much for Maris as patches of hair fell out of his head. Playing in an extended 162-game season, Maris matched Ruth's 60-homer output on Sept. 25 and five days later, on the final day of the season, homered into the Yankee Stadium stands off Boston's Tracy Stallard for No. 61.

Since Ruth had played during a 154-game schedule when he hit 60, Commissioner Ford Frick ruled that the Bambino's mark was not broken, but that each feat was to stand separately. In no other record-breaking incident did the commissioner, a former ghost writer for the Babe, make such a ruling. In 1962 Maury Wills of the Dodgers stole 104 bases, breaking Cobb's record. But DiMaggio's hitting streak stood.

He did it in 1941, batting .408 over two months, also scoring 56 runs and driving in 55. He was stopped July 17 at Cleveland, being held hitless in three official at-bats by Al Smith and Jim Bagby Jr., with the help of some sparkling fielding by the Indians' third baseman, Kenny Keltner.

Another Yankee with a permanent niche in baseball history is Don Larsen, who pitched the first and only perfect game in World Series history. It came

Hank Aaron of the Atlanta Braves is shown driving the 3,000th hit of his major league career against Cincinnati in Cincinnati on May 17, 1970.

Mickey Mantle and Roger Maris terrorized pitchers as one of the most devastating 1-2 punches in baseball history. Switch-hitter Mantle, top, blasts a home run in 1968. Below, Maris connects for his record-setting 61st home run in 1961. In that same year, Mantle hit 54 home runs.

against the Dodgers at Yankee Stadium Oct. 8, 1956. Not a runner reached first base against the big right-hander who had an undistinguished career beforehand and it remained so afterward.

Baseball's third miracle team was the 1969 Mets, tabbed as amazing in 1962 when they were born of expansion because of the amazing way they booted away ball games. A collection of has-beens, never-wases and raw rookies, the early Mets were managed by a garrulous old geezer named Casey Stengel, who had been let go by the Yankees after the 1960 season, after winning 10 AL titles in 12 seasons.

In their first season the Mets won 40 games and lost 120. They lost 100 or more games for five of their first six seasons. In 1968 they finished ninth in a 10-team league.

Early in 1969, the Mets began to show some promise. By August the young pitching arms of Tom Seaver and Jerry Koosman were mowing down batters; Cleon Jones, Donn Clendenon, Ron Swoboda and Tommie Agee were doing some timely hitting, and their infield stopped letting everything go through their legs.

Yet, even late in the season, only the staunchest of Mets fans would suggest

Tom Seaver reflected the determination of the New York Mets as he hurled in the fourth World Series game against the Baltimore Orioles in the 1969 World Series, won by the Mets in five games.

their heroes could go all the way. But the Mets began getting the good breaks. They bumped off the Cubs in several crucial series and won the division flag by eight games after moving into first place on Sept. 10.

Next came the league playoff under the new setup and the Mets topped Atlanta in three straight. In the World Series the Mets took on the mighty Baltimore Orioles, runaway winners in their division. The Orioles possessed proven sluggers such as Boog Powell and Frank Robinson and had a proven pitching staff. The Orioles won the opener, but the Mets won the next four with some amazing fielding plays and some good fortune. New York gave the Mets a celebration unmatched since World War II.

While such powerful hitters as Roberto Clemente, Ernie Banks, Harmon Killebrew and Carl Yastrzemski held forth during the 1960s, pitching got the upper hand and batting averages dipped to an all-time low. In 1930 the majors had 66 players with 400 or more at-bats hitting .300 or better. By contrast, Yastrzemski won the AL batting title with a .301 mark, the only player in that league to top .300. Only five players in the NL hit .300 that season.

The reasons are many, but mostly because of the development of relief pitching as a specialty and the fact that most hitters swing for the fences. Ralph Kiner, the Pittsburgh slugger who shared or won seven NL homer crowns, said it all years ago: "Home run hitters drive Cadillacs; singles hitters don't."

Other reasons given include bigger and better gloves; bigger, more symmetrical ball parks; lighter, thinner bats, and night games and coast-to-coast travel by air.

Baseball legislated against the pitchers for the 1969 season when it lowered the pitching mound from 15 inches to 10 and reduced the strike zone. There has been a marked upturn in batting averages since.

Baseball also has met the challenge of a drastic reduction of its minor leagues since the coming of television, which prompted minor league fans to sit home and watch the big leaguers rather than seeing the minors in person. Television has come through with some fat contracts while baseball has set up winter instructional leagues and rookie leagues, starting in June, for their new talent.

The reserve clause scare, which has come up off-and-on for the last 60 years, was brought up again when Curt Flood was traded by the Cardinals to the Phillies after the 1969 season, but refused to report. Instead he filed a $4.1 million antitrust suit against baseball, charging the clause is a form of slavery that violates his constitutional rights.

The reserve clause is a bit of fine print in every player's contract which binds him to the club for life until the club trades, sells or releases him. The Supreme Court, in 1922 and 1953, ruled in baseball's favor. Other such cases have been settled out of court, but Flood's case was still being battled in the courts as 1971 began, even though Flood, who sat out the 1970 season, agreed to a trade for the 1971 season to Washington.

The Flood case, dwindling attendances in some cities, the rise of pro football and the dilution of major league talent are some of the key problems baseball faced as it moved into the downhill side of the 20th century.

The first World Series game of 1970 between Cincinnati and Baltimore got off with a bang. Exciting sequence recorded the action as Reds' Bernie Carbo tried to score in sixth inning of game. Umpire Ken Burkhart was caught between Carbo and O's catcher Ellie Hendricks who made tag with glove, though ball was in his right hand. The umpire called Carbo out and a beef ensued. O's won, 4–3, and went on to take the series.

Early golf belonged to the Scots. Above, golfers play St. Andrews in the late 1800s. The gent below is Tom Morris Sr., a pioneer of the game of golf. He's seen again at the right with his son, Tom Morris Jr.

chapter 3

GOLF

The Scots Started it but the Millionaires Took Over

by Bob Green

Bob Green, 39, has one of the most enviable assignments in sports. As golf writer of *The Associated Press*, he follows the sun with the pro tour. He was sports editor of the *Roswell (N.M.) Record* before joining *The AP* in 1954. He worked in the Albuquerque, Santa Fe, Dallas and Boston bureaus and was night editor of the New York sports desk before taking his current assignment.

One prominent pundit has described golf as a game played by hitting a small, stationary object with an implement ill-conceived for that purpose. The sport was born out of the boredom of shepherds, tending their flocks on the hillsides of the Holy Land. It was nurtured among the sand and rabbit burrows of the wind-swept Scottish sea coasts. It was transplanted to the cow pastures of America and elsewhere.

Some observers, oriented to more active and more brutal pastimes, have scorned golf as no sport at all. "How can you call golf a sport?" asked one commentator. "A man walks down a fairway at about one mile an hour, a small tyke carrying his bag of clubs. Occasionally, he will stop and take a swing—once about every 15 minutes. I gag when I hear television announcers say, 'Here comes Arnold Palmer burning up the fairways . . .' Burning up the fairways at a mile an hour?"

Yet golf has caught the imagination of the world and developed into one of the major participant and spectator sports of the age.

At last reports, there were said to be nine million golfers in the United States alone—of various descriptions and skills—and around 7,000 golf courses, with new layouts being built every day.

The king of Morocco had a private course built around his castle. The former King Edward VII, who abdicated his throne to marry a commoner, was an avid golfer—player and watcher. Political writers once said the state of the union revolved around the extent of President Dwight D. Eisenhower's slice. President Richard Nixon kept in trim on the golf course, although he was a poor player, and his vice president, Spiro Agnew, became notorious for the people he wounded with his hooks and slices off the first tee.

Captain Alan B. Shepard, the astronaut who walked on the moon on Feb. 6, 1971, gave golf a universal dimension when he used an improvised 6-iron and stroked a ball he had brought aboard Apollo 14 and, in his words, saw it fly for "miles and miles."

By 1971, players on the pro tour were playing for purses totaling $7 million and more. There were times that as much as $60,000 hung on a single putt. Arnold Palmer, Jack Nicklaus and Bill Casper became golfing millionaires—the first three men to reach $1 million in prize money alone.

The men who made the pro golf tour were a breed within themselves. Their equipment was precision-honed. Their attire was colorful, fancy and expensive. Sporting goods concerns made billions keeping the good golfers and the duffers equipped with clubs, balls, gloves, tees, bags and carts. It was a booming business.

A scrawny New England caddie, Francis Ouimet, took the game out of the stuffy country club sphere and brought it to the masses by beating Britain's two great stars, Harry Vardon and Ted Ray, for the U.S. Open crown in 1913. The immortal Bob Jones, cocky Gene Sarazen, flashy Walter Hagen, dour and methodical Ben Hogan, flawless Byron Nelson, all contributed to the momentum in the 1920s, 1930s, 1940s and 1950s.

Then came the new age. The age of Arnold Palmer, Jack Nicklaus and Bill Casper.

Palmer, a magnetic, dynamic individual who had a faculty for pulling out last minute victories in major championships, intrigued the world. It was he who gave impetus to television and the big networks soon began battling for the chance to give the golfers exposure at the rate of $50,000 to $75,000 a minute to commercial sponsors.

Then Palmer's throne was rocked by Nicklaus, a burly bear of a man who faced Arnie head-to-head and won. Almost unnoticed, Casper, the mild-mannered Mormon with allergies enough to stock an infirmary, moved in to take the spotlight from both Palmer and Nicklaus, winning the Player of the Year Award both in 1969 and 1970.

It was personalities such as these who turned golf into a multibillion-dollar sport and spectator attraction. But much of the credit must be given to the pioneers.

It was men such as Hagen, Long Jim Barnes and MacDonald Smith, playing for peanuts, who got the tour started back in the late 1920s. Fred Corcoran, a bull-necked Irishman with a sharp promotional mind, built the tour into its first $1 million circuit, making the public conscious of men such as Hogan, Nelson and Sam Snead. Joseph C. Dey Jr. became a leveling influence as the first commissioner in the 1960s when a players' strike threatened to break up the Professional Golfers Association.

Golf cannot point to a legal father as in the case of Abner Doubleday in baseball and Dr. James Naismith in basketball. There is considerable doubt that the game was born at all. It just happened.

There are those who suggest, with tongue firmly placed in cheek, that it may have originated before the invention of the wheel with a caveman idly thumping away at a pebble with a knobby stick.

More likely is the explanation of the U.S. Golf Association. Historians have discovered that Roman legions in the days of Caesar played a game called paganica, which involved hitting a ball stuffed with feathers with a bent stick. In the first century before Christ, Romans overran Europe, crossed the English Channel and occupied parts of England and Scotland. Historians assume the invaders continued to bat the ball around and that the sport infected the natives.

Although Scotland generally is credited with being the cradle of the game, there are some researchers who insist that a similar game was played on a large scale in the Low Countries. They point to drawings from Holland supposedly antedating the 15th century when first references to the game were made in Scotland. One of these drawings shows an old man leaning on a curved stick which bears a remarkable likeness to one of the earlier golf clubs. Another shows a little girl with several heavy-headed clubs under her arm.

It is certain that the Dutch played a game called "kolf." And the Belgians had a game called "choulle" which is mentioned in legal documents dating back to the 1350s. And they are, perhaps, distant cousins of the game, involving hitting a ball with a stick. But, as far as is known, none of these involved a hole in the ground with the players attempting to climax their round with a putt—golf's one distinguishing feature.

But it is to Scotland that most turn for golf's origins.

There are indications it was played as early as the 1300s. The first mention of the game, however, occurred in the reign of King James II in 1457. This was the period before firearms. The bow and arrow was the chief weapon of warfare. The neighboring English, always at odds with the Scots, were supposed to be superior archers. So there was a royal decree that all male citizens should spend a certain amount of time brushing up on their marksmanship. When the citizens showed interest in other forms of recreation, the king clamped down. Thus it was that on March 6, an act of Parliament sternly warned Scotsmen "that fut ball and golfe must be utterly cryit dune."

Most of the early mentions of the game, in fact, dealt with decrees discouraging the game. There were laws against playing on the Sabbath. Tariffs were established on golf balls imported from Holland. The hardy Scots paid little attention, continuing to hack away at feather-stuffed balls with knobby sticks. In 1491 Parliament passed a law fixing a fine and imprisonment for anyone caught playing the game and also imposed a fine and jail sentence for anyone on whose property the game was played.

The story goes that some of the nobility partial to the game invited the king out to try it for himself. James reluctantly agreed. He took a few royal swings and the bug had bitten. The law was not rescinded immediately, but, with royalty playing the game, it soon became meaningless. The gentry and tradesmen alike took up the game.

James V found time from his war with Henry VIII of England to play at Gosford in East Lothian, where he set up a private links.

His daughter, Mary Queen of Scots, was reared in the tradition. She learned to play at an early age and continued when she went to school in France.

It was during her reign, in 1552, that the famous St. Andrews course in Scotland—recognized as the birthplace of golf—came into being. The queen played openly, drawing criticism from her enemies. She played at St. Andrews and the fields beside Seton. Her critics accused her of stepping outside the castle door and taking a few practice swings shortly after her husband was murdered.

Royal devotion to the game remained intact for centuries. But the game still encountered opposition. Through pressure from the clergy, the Town Council of Edinburgh passed a resolution in 1593 forbidding play on Sunday. Town records show that John Henrie and Pat Rogie were prosecuted for playing on the Leith Links "during sumonses."

The game, however, endured. It became primarily a sport for club members. The Royal Blackheath Club was started in 1608. The Honourable Company of Edinburgh Golfers began in 1744, playing on the Leith Links. It's apparent many of those early members were much like their present-day counterparts in that they considered the game a shortcut to the 19th hole. One account says they often closed the day with "copious libations of pure and unadulterated claret."

Ten years later, in 1754, the Society of St. Andrews Golfers, later known as the Honourable Company of the Royal and Ancient Club, came into being. The members adopted 13 articles for the game's first rules, and these rules still form the nucleus of standards accepted throughout the world today. One rule said the golfer must play honestly for the hole and not for the opponent's ball.

There were greats even in those early days. There was Old Alick, a professional in the early 19th century. There was Allan Robertson, a ball-maker and outstanding player who had a long and intense rivalry with Old Tom Morris. It was Robertson, incidentally, who was the first man to break 80 at the Old Course at St. Andrews. There was Willie Park and the Dunn brothers, Willie and Jamie. And there was Young Tom Morris, son of Old Tom. He was a prodigy, winning three consecutive British Open championships, 1868–70, by the time he was 21. He won again in 1872. He was a bold, aggressive player who disdained style for power. His first three championships were won by an average of nine strokes. He was a legend in his time and golf lovers still make pilgrimages to his grave.

The game, played with such passion in Scotland, began to spread, to Ireland, to England. Ships' officers took it to Canada as early as 1850. Shortly afterward, small, three-hole courses were established in Montreal.

Scot professionals became in demand everywhere. The game was on its way to becoming a multimillion-dollar business.

But it was slow to catch on in pioneer America, the nation that eventually was to dominate the game.

The man who brought the game to America was John Reid, who was born in Scotland, first saw the game played there, then moved to the United States. He was an executive in an iron foundry in Yonkers, N.Y., when, in 1887, he found that a friend and fellow Scot, Robert Lockhart, was returning to Scotland on business. Lockhart made a trip to St. Andrews and the shop of Old Tom Morris and ordered six clubs and a couple of dozen balls to be delivered in the United States.

Reid had planned to wait until spring to surprise his select group of friends with the new game but became so excited with the arrival of the clubs he couldn't wait. On Feb. 22, 1888, Reid gathered some of his cronies and took them to a Yonkers cow pasture. Three short holes were laid out and the cups dug with the head of one of the irons. It was the first course in the United States.

Later that year, Reid and his buddies formed a club, built a six-hole course and the game was on its way. In 1892 they moved to a new course, a short distance away, that featured among other things a large tree by the home green. It was a favorite place for depositing jackets, picnic lunches and liquid refreshments. As their ranks and good times grew, they became known as the "Apple Tree Gang." They dubbed the course St. Andrews.

While the "Apple Tree Gang" laid the cornerstone for golf in America, they didn't have it to themselves very long. Theodore A. Havemeyer, a prominent member of Newport, R.I., society, fell in love with golf, constructed a nine-hole course in Newport and founded the Newport Golf Club. Duncan Cryder, another transplanted Scotsman, is credited with taking the game out of its cow pasture stage. In 1889 he and two Long Island friends commissioned Willie Dunn, a Scottish architect and professional, to lay out a 12-hole course on the eastern end of Long Island. It was unveiled in 1891, shares were sold at $100 each and Shinnecock Hills became the country's first duly incorporated golf club.

The country's first 18-hole course was built in Chicago. Big, stubborn Charles Blair Macdonald was the driving force behind it. He built a small course and introduced his friends at the Chicago Club to the game after he returned from schooling at St. Andrews University in Scotland. Macdonald, a headstrong man of great determination, developed into an excellent player and figured prominently in the first competitions held in the United States.

In the summer of 1894, the Newport Golf Club sent out invitations to amateurs and professionals to compete in September for the championship of the country. Twenty players competed in the 36-hole, medal play event. Macdonald was favored, but lost to W. G. Lawrence, a Newport player. Macdonald fumed, protesting it should have been match play. A month later the St. Andrews Club of Yonkers, the "Apple Tree Gang," announced plans for a match play tournament. Macdonald won his way to the finals, played Laurence Stoddard even through 18 holes, then lost on the first extra hole. This time he said he was ill.

Bickering over the outcome of these two tournaments may have led to the formation of the United States Golf Association. There was a demand for a national body to establish rules, standardize play, conduct tournaments and serve as a court of appeals. A general meeting of golf clubs was called in December 1894. Delegates from five clubs showed up. They represented St. Andrews of New York, the Country Club of Brookline, Mass., the Newport, R.I., Golf Club, Shinnecock Hills of Southampton, N.Y., and the Chicago Golf Club. Theodore Havemeyer was elected first president of the Amateur Golf Association of the United States, later to become the U.S. Golf Association.

They announced plans for the first U.S. Open and Amateur championships, to be held in 1895 at Newport. And, incidentally, Macdonald won that first amateur title, beating Charles E. Sands 12 and 11.

It was in the third Open championship that mysterious Willie Anderson made his appearance. Little is known of his background or early years because the dour, introverted, silent Scot never talked about it. Registering out of the Watch Hill Club, he shot 163 over the Chicago Golf Club course in that 1897 championship, losing by a single stroke to Joe Lloyd, an English professional. One thing is certain—he had trouble keeping a steady job. He registered out of a different club every year for several seasons until finally settling at Apawamis in Westchester County, N.Y.

He continued to play and play well, but didn't win until 1901 at the Myopia Hunt Club in Hamilton, Mass. Registering this time out of the Pittsfield, Mass., Country Club, Anderson and his close friend Alex Smith tied after 72 holes and Anderson won the 18-hole playoff 85 to 86.

He won his second national title two years later, this time beating David Brown in another 18-hole playoff, 82 to 84. Saying no more than a dozen words a round, he won again the following year at the Glen View Golf Club in Illinois.

History was made the following year, 1905, at the Myopia Hunt Club, scene of his first Open victory. He had rounds of 81-80-76-77—314 for a two-stroke victory and his fourth Open title, matched only by Bobby Jones and Ben Hogan. And even Hogan and Jones couldn't duplicate his feat of three in a row.

Anderson's string was broken the following year by Smith and shortly afterward it was discovered that Anderson had a lung ailment. He died prematurely, one of the great and least known of all American champions.

It remained for a thin, hollow-cheeked gardener's son, a 20-year-old ex-caddie, to excite the general public.

Until 1913, when the annual U.S. Open championship was assigned to the Country Club in Brookline, Mass., golf in America was considered a snobbish, sissy game indulged in only by the elderly and the idle rich. The best players were English and Scottish. When overseas stars consented to play in the American championship, it was not a question of whether a Briton would win but which one.

And that was the attitude in September 1913. The dates of the Open had been changed to permit participation of the two great British professionals, Harry Vardon and Ted Ray. The field included some other notables, Wilfrid Reid of England, Louis Tellier of France and such American stars as Johnny McDermott, Mike Brady and Tommy McNamara. But none figured to match strokes with Vardon and Ray.

Ray was a hulking 200-pounder who cared little for form but threw all his brute strength into every shot, tearing out great divots. He was the longest hitter of the day and the reigning British Open champion.

Vardon was generally acknowledged as the greatest of the time. He was a stylist, a man of fluid grace and power—a picture golfer who had won five British Open titles and went on to take a sixth. He developed the Vardon grip, the left-hand grasp of the club that became the standard.

They were a formidable pair and the least of their opposition was frail Francis Ouimet, the gardener's son who lived across the road from the club and who had learned the game toting clubs at 28 cents a round.

It was no surprise after 36 holes to find Vardon and Reid tied for the top at 147. Ray was two strokes back. No one paid much attention to Ouimet and another 20-year-old from Rochester, N.Y., Walter Hagen, who were tied at 151, well back.

Vardon and Ray led after 54 holes, but they had unexpected company. Ouimet shot a creditable 74 in the third round and moved into a tie for first at 225.

Vardon and Ray each had a final round 79 for a tie for first. Ouimet, playing well behind them, needed two birdies on the final six holes. He got them. He chipped in for a bird on the 13th and rolled in a 20-foot putt on the 17th. He needed a par on the final hole to tie. Ouimet was short in two, chipped five feet short and sank the putt. He had tied Vardon and Ray.

They were all even at the turn in the playoff the next day. The first break came on the 10th, where Vardon and Ray both three-putted and Ouimet got a par three. On the 15th, Ray hit a spectator's derby with his drive, pitched into a trap, failed to get out and took a double bogey six. Vardon hooked into the rough, played back to the fairway, was on in three and took a bogey five. Ouimet seized the opportunity and knocked in an 18-foot putt for a birdie three that gave him a three-stroke lead.

It stayed that way until the 18th, where the great Vardon blew to a double bogey six. Ray was out of it. Ouimet drove up the middle, was on in two and lag-putted to within four feet. He looked a picture of tremendous calm as he lined up the final putt, but recalled later:

"For the first time I thought about the championship. I couldn't breathe. The green began heaving under me. I couldn't even see the hole."

THE BOSTON TRAVELER

AND EVENING HERALD

FINAL EXTRA

BOSTON, SATURDAY, SEPTEMBER 20, 1913. 12 PAGES. ONE CENT.

PUTS DEATH ...TH END

...es and Husband ...ries After ...cued

...OF HEARING BACKYARD

FRANCIS OUIMET, BOSTON AMATEUR, WINS OPEN GOLF TITLE ON PLAY OFF

After the Greatest Battle in the History of American Golf

Woodland Club's Youthful Star Turns in Card of 72; Vardon Second with 77; Ray Third on 78

A RECORD GALLERY OF 10,000 FOLLOWS PLAYERS

HOW THE BETTING RULED ON PLAY-OFF

This was the scene on the final green at the Country Club in Brookline, Mass., when a Boston amateur, Francis Ouimet, won the U.S. Open Golf Championship in a playoff with Ted Ray and Harry Vardon. Ouimet's victory was good for headline news in the Boston papers.

He putted. The ball went in and Francis Ouimet was the new Open golf champion of the United States. He had fired an amazing 72 under the most trying conditions and won a playoff from two of the game's greatest stars. Vardon had a final 77 and Ray 78.

The hilarity at the Country Club over the neighborhood boy's triumph swept over the rest of the country. The story was front page news in the nation's newspapers. It was talked about on street corners, drugstores and drawing rooms. Ouimet became an overnight national hero. Golf emerged as a game for the common man and its popularity boomed.

One English journalist caught the spirit of the event when he wrote:

"There will never be another like it. When we are old men, little golfing children will ask us to tell them again the romantic story of the 20th of September in 1913."

Ouimet won the national amateur title the following year and added another 17 years later.

He remained the true amateur, playing the game for fun and never letting it take a dominant role in his life. As a result, he never was able to add a second Open victory. After finishing fifth in 1914 he didn't make another strong bid until he tied for second in 1925.

The scholarly, soft-spoken Ouimet played on more Walker Cup teams than any other man. He served with the United States international team as a competitor from 1922 through 1934. In 1936 he took over as non-playing captain, retaining the post until he asked to be relieved in 1949.

On May 1, 1951, Ouimet was accorded the highest honor Britain can bestow upon a personality in connection with golf. He was elected captain of the Royal and Ancient Golf Club of St. Andrews, the first non-Briton elected to the post.

The year of his breakthrough, 1913, also marked a milestone for two other giants, the men who were to dominate the professional and amateur games during the '20s, the fabulous Walter Hagen and immortal Bobby Jones, the grand slammer.

Robert Tyre Jones was just 11, and the golf bug was just starting to bite that year when Vardon and Ray played an exhibition at Atlanta's East Lake course. Jones was there and fell under the magic Vardon spell. Jones, who went on to become one of the greatest of all the champions, recalled in later years that the exhibition made a tremendous impact on his young mind. He followed every shot with wide-eyed wonder and Vardon became something of a personal idol.

It was different for the flashy, flamboyant Hagen. He played in that 1913 championship, showing up in striped silk shirt, red bandana, white flannel trousers and white buck shoes. Spotting the defending champion in the locker room, he advanced to Johnny McDermott and stuck out his hand.

"You're Johnny McDermott, aren't you? Well, I'm W. C. Hagen from Rochester and I've come to help you boys take care of Vardon and Ray."

McDermott was speechless. There were giggles from pros within earshot. But it wasn't funny to W. C. Hagen from Rochester. He was dead serious.

He moved to within two strokes of the two English stars after 54 holes, and caught them with five of the final 18 to play. Then Hagen took a triple bogey seven at the 14th and finished at 307, three strokes back. The Boston papers, caught up in the drama of Ouimet's victory, spelled his name "W.C. Hagin."

"I'll be back and show them," he vowed. "They'll spell my name right the next time."

They did. The next time, and the next and the next.

He became the king of the pros while Jones reigned over the amateurs in the Golden Age of Sports. The Haig, as he became universally known, strode the world's fairways with a majestic flourish for a quarter of a century, collecting national championships, entrancing galleries, amassing and spending a $1 million fortune.

He played with caddies and kings, and treated both alike. He kept presidents and princes waiting at the first tee. He was a companion to giants of the financial and business worlds. And he called them all—royalty, rich or commoner—by their first names. He defied and tore down many of golf's stuffiest traditions.

He played on five continents and collected 11 national championships. He set a record of four successive U.S. professional titles. He was the PGA champion five times.

He won the U.S. Open in 1914 and repeated in 1919. He won four British Open crowns and added the national championships of France, Belgium and Canada. He was captain of the U.S. Ryder Cup team seven times.

In matches billed for the unofficial championship of the world, he scored one-sided victories over Cyril Walker in 1924, Bob Jones in 1926, Gene Sarazen in 1927 and Johnny Farrell in 1928. Perhaps no triumph gave the Haig greater satisfaction than the one over Jones in a 72-hole match in Florida.

"Everybody was acclaiming Jones as the greatest golfer in the world and saying I was second best," he recalled. "It rankled me a bit, so I got a friend, Bob Harlow, to arrange the match—36 holes over Bob's course in Sarasota and 36 over my course in St. Petersburg.

"I had an eight-hole lead leaving Sarasota and went on to win 12 holes up with 11 to play. It was my greatest thrill in golf." It also was the worst defeat ever suffered by Jones.

Walter Hagen and Bobby Jones are fabled names in the history of golf. At left, Jones tees off in the Masters at Augusta, Ga., in 1941 and Hagen drives during Ryder Cup match at Southport, England, in 1933.

Hagen brought charm, wit and sartorial elegance to the game. He revolutionized wearing apparel on the golf course. His suits were the wooliest, his shirts the silkiest, his sweaters the fleeciest and his shoes the swankiest.

He lived as lavishly as he dressed in the wild, easy-spending Roaring Twenties. He was a heavy spender who tossed $20 tips around with abandon. Occasionally he gave his entire winning check to his caddie.

It was not unusual for him to attend an all-night party and then, after a shower, take to the course for an important match. Once, the Haig, late for a match, rushed to the first tee still wearing a tuxedo and patent leather shoes. He teed off without removing the satin-trimmed jacket—and shot a 67.

He astounded staid Britons when he arrived for a British tournament in a limousine, complete with chauffeur and footman, and three trunks loaded with clothes.

When he arrived at Deal for the 1920 British Open, he was shocked to learn the clubhouse was off limits to professionals—because they were not regarded as gentlemen. A stiff club secretary directed him to the golf shop, where professionals were compelled to dress. He found it small, dirty and inadequate.

He ordered his big, black limousine parked at the front of the clubhouse. "We'll use my car for a dressing room," he told the club secretary. The club resented it, but had no way of stopping it.

From Deal he went to France. There, he and British Open champ George Duncan went on strike against the clubhouse ban on professionals. They refused to play unless the restrictions were removed. The French, faced with collapse of their tournament, yielded. The British soon followed suit. Hagen was given credit for erasing the ban.

In order to live on the scale he liked, he had to play golf. He was a keen competitor who hated to lose. His theory was that second and third meant nothing. He played to win.

He was sometimes erratic off the tee, but had a marvelous touch around the greens and was a brilliant putter. And he was more than a fine craftsman. He was a psychologist, not averse to using guile to help win an important match.

He often upset opponents by remarking loudly after placing his ball on the tee, "Well, who's going to be second?"

On one occasion, Hagen had the ball 15 feet from the cup and his opponent was about seven feet. Haig started laughing.

"What's so funny?" the opponent asked.

"I was just thinking," Haig replied, "how much harder your putt will look after I make mine."

He rolled it in the cup. The opponent missed.

All the world was a stage to him and he played his role to the hilt.

Once he stroked a long, $3,000 putt and tossed his putter to the caddie while the ball was still rolling. The putt dropped.

He shocked a British gallery by yelling to the Prince of Wales, later King Edward VII of England, "Hey, Eddie, hold that flag, would you, please?"

He had a credo. "You're only here for a short visit. Don't hurry. Don't worry. And be sure to smell the roses along the way."

He retired in 1940 after the PGA championship in Hershey, Pa. Nearing 50 and his skills dulled by high living, he stored the clubs away for good.

"I couldn't stand the thought of probably shooting an 80," he said.

But while Hagen ruled the pros, it was Bobby Jones who dominated the game in the still amateur-oriented '20s. He was young, good-looking, clean-cut. He had a flawless style. Although an amateur, he consistently beat the best professionals of the time.

Between 1923 and 1930 he collected 13 national titles—five U.S. Amateurs, four U.S. Opens, three British Opens and a single British Amateur. In the last nine years of his career he played in 12 Open championships and finished first or second in 11 of them. He considered this a greater feat than the Grand Slam.

But it is for the Grand Slam that he will be remembered. In 1930 he climaxed his career by winning the U.S. Open and Amateur, the British Open and Amateur—an unparalleled sweep of the major championships in a single season. Two months later, in November, he announced his retirement from competitive golf to make a series of instructional films. He was only 28, at the peak of his career.

His father and mother were golfers and he remembers trailing after them as a lad of 5. He won a neighborhood tournament at 6. He won the Georgia state title in 1916 as a 14-year-old and was invited to the National Amateur at Philadelphia's Merion Cricket Club. Spectators there remember him as a boy with a perfect swing and an ungovernable temper. He ranted when he missed a shot. He tossed clubs in disgust. He gradually learned to control his temper, but was doomed to a series of disappointments before he finally was to establish himself.

He became a leading golf figure, widely sought for exhibitions. He won Southern amateur and other regional titles with regularity. But when he got to national events, something always happened.

He adopted a philosophy that he retained even when he had reached the pinnacle. "Every tournament has somebody's name on it," he once remarked. "No matter how well you play, the fellow whom the fates have picked out will win. The ball just falls that way."

He finished second in the 1922 Open and was a loser in the semifinals of the Amateur. But he broke through the next year in the Open at Inwood on Long Island. He had a three-stroke lead over Bobby Cruickshank after 54 holes. But he began pressing in the final round and his game cracked. He played the last three holes five over par and finished with a 76 for 296, and was tied by Cruickshank.

In the playoff they came down to the 18th hole still tied. Cruickshank hooked his tee shot, then played his second short of a lagoon guarding the green. Jones had a good drive and had a decision to make—should he play it safe or gamble for the green?

He walked with quick steps to the ball, jerked an iron from the bag, laced a shot six feet from the flag. The shaken Cruickshank put his third in a trap and eventually took a six. Jones had an easy four and the U.S. Open championship. Jones was dazed as he groped for the clubhouse, oblivious of the turmoil around him. The first conscious thought he had, he said, was, "I've won a championship. At last, I've won a championship." He admitted his morale was getting thin at that point and if this one hadn't come off, he might have given up tournament golf.

But it was the one that set him on his way.

He won the amateur title in 1924 and 1925 and lost in a playoff for the 1925 Open title. He won the Open, his second, in 1926 and came home to a ticker-tape parade down Broadway after taking the British Open the same year. He continued to win at least one national title a year through 1929.

Early spring practices in 1930 convinced Jones that he was headed for an outstanding season. He was hitting the ball better than ever. His confidence was high. But he never dreamed, he said later, he was headed for a Grand Slam.

As captain of the Walker Cup team, he had his chance at the British crowns. He squeaked through some early matches at St. Andrews but finally conquered Roger Wethered 7 and 6 for the British Amateur title—the only one that had eluded him. "I'd rather have won this tournament than any other in golf," he said.

Jones followed with rounds of 70–72–74–75—291 for a two-stroke victory in the British Open at Holyoke. He came home with the British half of the Slam.

America's golf fever was spurred to a new pitch when the game's greats gathered for the U.S. Open at Interlachen in Minneapolis for the U.S. Open. Jones built a five-stroke lead after 54 holes, shooting a blistering 68 in the third round. He had a slumping 75 final round that was good enough to win by two at 287. And it included the famous lily pad shot. On the ninth hole, a 485-yard, par five with a small lake in front of the green, Jones went for the green with a fairway wood on his second shot. But he half topped it, the ball hit the surface halfway across the lake—but skipped onto the other side of the bank and came up just short of the green. Spectators said the ball hit a lily pad.

"It looked like a drowned ball for sure," Jones said. "It would have meant a six or a seven and cost me the tournament. It's perhaps the luckiest shot I ever played in a championship."

The fourth leg of the Slam, the U.S. Amateur, was played at Merion, in the Philadelphia suburbs. And Jones was simply unbeatable. The climactic round sent Jones against Gene Homans. Some 18,000 fans turned out. Homans was nervous and no match for the shot-making robot from Atlanta. Jones won it 8 and 7. He had his Slam.

"He was absolutely perfect," Ouimet said. "It was discouraging and monotonous the way he hit practically every shot exactly as it should be hit."

His retirement in 1930 ended an era. It closed the door on the amateur as a dominant factor in big time tournament competition. And it opened the door to a succession of professional precisionists who proceeded to make a mockery of par. Par was no longer good enough. It took birdies to survive on the rugged, growing professional tour.

But during the period immediately following Jones' retirement, the pros failed to produce one performer who clearly stood over the others. Gene Sarazen still was there, but was nearing the twilight of his remarkable career.

The dapper little ex-caddie, whose career spanned four eras, is one of four men to capture all four major professional titles—the U.S. and British Opens, the Masters and the PGA. A fast-talking, quick-stepping, enthusiastic man, Sarazen won the U.S. Open in 1922 and 1932, took the British in 1932, won the Masters in 1935 and scored three victories in the PGA.

He helped fill the void of the early '30s when the fans had a succession of day-to-day heroes: amateur Lawson Little, Paul Runyan, Johnny Revolta, Denny Shute, Craig Wood and Ralph Guldahl.

But as the war years approached, the interest of the golfing public was stirred anew by the emergence of a small knot of perfectionists who, in their grim struggle for supremacy, launched an unprecedented assault on scoring records.

The hard core of this new breed was a group of leather-tough Texans—Ben Hogan, Byron Nelson, Lloyd Mangrum, Jimmy Demaret and Jug McSpaden, plus a colorful, sweet-swinging Virginia hillbilly, Sam Snead.

Hogan, Nelson and Snead quickly established themselves as the "Big Three." Hogan and Nelson were keen rivals. They had grown up together as caddies in Fort Worth and had battled each other on the links since they were schoolboys. Most of the nation's golf fans were divided into Hogan or Nelson supporters. And everybody loved Snead. He had a captivating backwoods personality, a picture swing and was immune to polish.

The argument between Nelson and Hogan partisans never was satisfactorily settled. They never came face to face at the peak of their careers. Nelson played his finest golf during the war years when he was exempt from military service because of hemophilia. Hogan reached his greatest heights in the early 1950s after Nelson had gone into semi-retirement.

Nelson was christened the "mechanical man." He clicked off pars and birdies with such monotonous ease that his performances tended to be boring. He never scrambled. He didn't have to.

Nelson moved solidly into the big time in 1937. He overtook Guldahl and won the first of his two Masters titles. He went into a temporary slump the following year, but bounced back big in 1939, winning the North and South and Western Opens and climaxing it with a victory in the National Open. He won the first of his two PGA crowns in 1940, beating Snead in the finals, and won his second Masters in 1942. But he still hadn't reached the top.

That came in the two-year period of 1944–45. Fighting raged in Europe and the Pacific. The U.S. Golf Association suspended its national championships.

Gene Sarazen and gallery followed his shot during final round of the 1932 U.S. Open Golf Championship which he went on to win.

But the tour continued, with government encouragement because it was thought to be good for home morale.

Nelson dominated. In 1944 Lord Byron won seven tournaments, including the All-American and Red Cross Opens, and was the leading money winner. He was named Athlete of the Year by *The Associated Press.*

And in 1945 he set records that may never be matched. He won 19 tournaments, an all-time high, including 11 in a row. The incredible string was snapped at Memphis by an amateur, Freddie Haas.

"Every tournament was getting tougher," he said. "I couldn't keep a thing in my stomach."

No other player has won more than three in succession.

Shortly after the string was snapped, Hogan returned and the old rivalry picked up. Nelson won in Knoxville, Hogan hit back at Richland. Nelson won at Spokane and Hogan retaliated at Portland. So it went. Something had to give.

Shortly afterward, Nelson, always bothered by a stomach ailment, retired to his cattle ranch. The door was open to Ben Hogan.

Bantam Ben shot to the top of the money-winning list in 1946 and two years later won the first of his four U.S. Open titles.

Then disaster struck on Feb. 2, 1949. Hogan and his wife, Valerie, were driving from Phoenix to their home in Fort Worth when a huge bus skidded out of control into the path of their car. Hogan threw himself in front of his wife to shield her and she suffered only minor injuries in the accident. Hogan suffered a double fracture of the pelvis, a broken collarbone, a fractured left ankle and a smashed right rib. His golfing future seemed doomed. There was some doubt that he would ever walk again.

But such a thought was ill-founded. It failed to reckon with the grim fighting qualities and flaming determination of the blacksmith's son. He not only walked again, he played golf again. And won. And won again and again and again. He became the dominant figure of the '50s, the one man able to awe and overpower the tough breed who plied their trade on the professional circuit. He became a symbol, not only as a man of fortitude who fashioned an almost incredible comeback—but as one of the great all-time champions of the game.

To the National Open title he won in 1948 before the accident, Hogan added others in 1950, 1951 and 1953. Half a dozen times he came within a shot or two of a fifth title, which would have put him in a class alone. He won two Masters and captured the British Open title in 1953 in his only try at the aged championship. Many rank his feat of winning the Masters, U.S. and British Opens in 1953 equal to Jones' Slam.

He was a dour little man who rarely spoke. He always wore a white cap pulled low over his deeply-tanned face, a cigarette jutting from his mouth. He didn't have the boyish appeal of Jones or the flamboyance of Hagen or the fluid style of Snead, but he was a gallery favorite. They came to watch him bend a course to his will.

He started his comeback from the accident in Los Angeles in 1950 while the sports world watched in fascination. He had a 69 on each of the last three rounds and tied Snead for first place. Snead eventually won the playoff, but one thing was clear—Hogan was back.

A few months later, at Merion, outside Philadelphia, he tied Lloyd Mangrum

Among his many accomplishments on the golf course, Texan Byron Nelson, left, boasts 11 consecutive victories on the pro golf tour.

Right, spectators and the great Ben Hogan follow the flight of his ball from tee in Winnipeg, Canada, in 1946 tournament.

and George Fazio for first in the National Open. A sparkling 69 in the playoff round smothered any lingering doubts that he would be able to regain his old form.

He won the Masters in 1951 and took his third National Open crown two months later. He won the fourth in 1953 and set the Masters record at 274. Then he set his sights on the British Open at Carnoustie, Scotland. He had all the American titles, some of them several times, and needed the British crown to cap it.

It was his first try, under conditions he wasn't used to and using the small British ball. Few conceded him a chance. But he moved into a tie for first with Argentina's Roberto de Vicenzo after 54 holes. Golf-loving Scots came out by the thousands to see the final round. The Wee Ice Mon responded with a winning 68.

But he still wanted that fifth U.S. Open. He appeared to have it in 1955 at San Francisco when he was in the clubhouse with a 287, only to be caught by a little known pro, Jack Fleck. Fleck won the playoff, 69 to 72.

"I will never work this hard to win a tournament again," Hogan announced in a declaration of semi-retirement. He still played the Open and the Masters, and often came close. But he found himself not equal to the birdie pressure of the '60s.

"I just don't have the feel any more," he said sadly.

While the golf world watched in awe and admiration as Hogan piled up his Open crowns, it watched in equal fascination at the trials of Snead.

Samuel Jackson Snead came out of Virginia with a honey-thick drawl, backwoods humor, a brightly-banded straw hat and "the sweetest swing in the land." Blessed with enormous natural talent, he won over 100 tournaments and more money than any other man of his era. He won three PGA titles, three Masters and the British Open.

But he never won the U.S. Open.

He was second in 1937. He needed only a par five on the final hole two years later—and took an eight. He lost in a playoff in 1947. And he was second in 1949 and 1953.

He never quit trying, but turned fatalistic.

"It gives you the eeriest feeling sometimes, like you don't have anything to do with the way a tournament comes out," he said once. "I've won many a tournament I had no business winning. Everything just went right. On the other hand, I've seen tournaments snatched right out of my hands when by all rights they should have been mine. It's destiny."

A new era opened up in the mid-'50s, an era of affluence. The pros were playing for $50,000 to $100,000 a week. With the sport gaining in popularity, there were fringe benefits. Television found the game and its stars. Manufacturers poured millions of dollars into promotion of clothes and equipment.

And a new breed of golfer emerged—smart, tough, educated. He was the businessman golfer, deadly serious and extremely conscientious.

"They are young, strong, confident," Sarazen analyzed. "They are the greatest strikers of the ball the game has ever known, playing with the most perfect equipment man can devise and on courses laid out to accent their tremendous power. They are college-trained, men of trigger judgment who can think under pressure. Many of them are ex-servicemen, afraid of nobody."

Among them were Gene Littler, with a picture swing; burly Mike Souchak; boyish Jackie Burke; slim Art Wall; Doug Ford; Ken Venturi and Tony Lema.

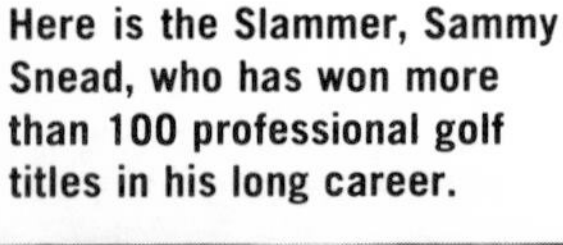
Here is the Slammer, Sammy Snead, who has won more than 100 professional golf titles in his long career.

And there was Billy Casper, the one-time fat man who won two U.S. Opens, a Masters, more than $1 million and put his name on more than 40 titles.

Waiting in the wings were two men ready to scale the heights—Arnold Palmer and Jack Nicklaus.

Golf moved into the jet and electronic age in the late 1950s and early 1960s. Television was the thing. A flick of the switch could bring the most glamorous courses and exciting players into the living room. Saturday and Sunday afternoon channels became choked with live and taped golf competition.

To meet this new development, it was necessary for the game to produce a new hero. It did. His name was Palmer. He was a rugged son of a Latrobe, Pa., greenskeeper. He was a solid 185 pounds with the sloping shoulders of a natural athlete. His hands were large and strong and his arms like pistons. He had a strong, mobile face that registered every emotion.

But personal magnetism was only a fraction of Palmer's amazing appeal. It was his faculty for miracle finishes—dramatic dashes down the stretch to pull out another victory—which really captivated the public. It got to the point that fans flocked to the big tournaments by the thousands, and millions more hugged their television sets, to see another Palmer miracle. No matter how far back, these devoted fans were sure Arnie could pull it out. He often did, usually in major championships where money and prestige were high. He became a legend in his own time, the most popular player the game has known.

His fans weren't restricted to golfers. Housewives, teen-agers, matrons, all counted themselves members of Arnie's Army, that vast, whooping, shouting, stampeding throng that followed his every move on a golf course.

He won the National Amateur in 1954 and his first Masters in 1958, but it wasn't until the Masters of 1960 that he really fired the public imagination.

Ken Venturi was in with a 283 and Palmer needed a birdie on one of the two final holes to tie. They are two of the toughest in golf and his chances appeared to be very, very slim. He knocked in a 25-foot putt on the 17th and decided to play the 18th boldly. It was a long, uphill par four and he put his drive to the left, where he wanted it. He punched a 6-iron into the wind, the ball coming to rest some five feet from the pin. Under tremendous pressure and with millions watching, he assumed that knock-kneed putting stance and stroked it in. He had his second Masters.

"I won't be content," he said, "until I score a professional grand slam. My ambition is to win the Masters, the U.S. and British Opens and the PGA, all in a year."

He seemed to have little chance in the U.S. Open at Denver that year. Going into the final round, he was seven strokes back.

But he drove the green on the first hole, 346 yards, and got a two-putt birdie. He chipped in on the next, wedged to a foot on the next and rolled in a 20-footer on the next.

It was one of the most amazing starts under pressure the game had known. He turned in 30 and came home one under for a 65. That won it. The miracle maker was established.

He missed by a single stroke in the British Open, but the image was there.

He went on to win four Masters and a pair of British Opens. The PGA always eluded him, however. But he was the sports personality of his decade. He was the first to pocket $1 million in prize money. And he parlayed it into a huge fortune through shrewd investments. He hired a personal staff of five to run his interests. He leased his own jet plane. He set up his own golf company.

But golf was the game.

"Golf is my life," he said. "I like to win. I am determined to win. No amount of money can change that."

But he began running into slumps. There was one in 1963. There was another in 1965. As he aged, Palmer found himself fighting a war with his nerves.

The worst slump of all occurred in 1969. He was nearing a year without a victory when he went to the PGA national championship. Troubled with bursitis in his hip, he shot a first round 82 and withdrew, saying he wouldn't play again until he was healthy.

Weeks of treatment and exercises had him back on the fall tour and he spiked the rumor he was through by winning the final two tournaments of the year.

He was named Athlete of the Decade by *The Associated Press.*

Opposing him over the last half of the decade was the bulky form of Nicklaus, an Ohio State product who hit the game with an enormous impact.

Among the trio of present-day pro golfers who have won more than $1 million each in prize money alone are Jack Nicklaus, left, and Arnold Palmer. The other of the trio is Billy Casper.

Pro golfer Ken Venturi tosses his hands in the air and his putter to the ground after dropping putt to win the U.S. Open Golf Championship in the extreme heat at Congressional in Washington on June 20, 1964.

Big, blond and fantastically powerful, he drove the ball higher, straighter and farther than any man who ever lived.

He came to national attention when, as an amateur in 1960, he had a 72-hole total of 269 at Merion, 18 strokes better than Hogan had done 10 years earlier to win the National Open.

Nicklaus, dubbed "the Golden Bear," won the National Amateur and was hailed as another Jones when he decided to turn pro.

And his pro debut was equally dramatic. He won the National Open on his first try as a professional, beating Palmer in an 18-hole playoff at Oakmont, Pa. A few months later he beat Palmer again for the $50,000 first prize in the World Series of Golf.

He won the Masters in 1963, missed by a stroke in the British Open, and captured the PGA at Dallas. He won another Open, and two British crowns before the decade was finished, never failed to win $100,000 a season and, with Palmer and South African Gary Player, made up the Big Three who dominated the game.

Nicklaus really established himself in the 1965 Masters, when he scored a record 271 for 72 holes that clipped three strokes off Hogan's record and left Player five strokes back and Palmer eight.

In four rounds he used a fairway wood only once. He played the par fives on the proud Augusta National as if they were fours. He never used a club longer than a 5-iron for his approaches on the fours. He went 28 holes without a bogey.

The golf world was aghast. Some called it the beginning of a new era. Some talked about scores in the 50s.

Bobby Jones, the Grand Slammer and the founder of the Masters, phrased it differently.

"Palmer and Player played superbly," he said. "But Nicklaus played a game with which I'm not familiar."

Dr. James Naismith in 1891, looking for a new indoor sport for his physical education class, tied a peach basket to a balcony and invented basketball. He is shown, second row right, with his first basketball team.

chapter 4

BASKETBALL

From Peach Baskets to String Beans

by Mike Recht

Mike Recht, 32, is the pro basketball specialist on the New York staff. Born in St. Louis, he served on the sports staff of the *St. Louis Globe-Democrat* for one year before joining *The AP* in 1962. He was a newsman in the St. Louis AP bureau, concentrating on sports, before being transferred to New York in 1966.

James Naismith, a physical education teacher at Springfield College in Massachusetts, sat wrapped in thought one early winter night in 1891. If he was to come up with a new game his classes could play indoors during the cold weather months, it would have to be now. He was running out of ideas.

The instructors had been given complete freedom to experiment with something new, but all they had come up with were modifications of old sports such as lacrosse, soccer and football. All were found too rough or confining indoors.

Body exercise was tried, but it only bored the students. Naismith knew he had to create a game that was competitive, simple, non-contact and could be played indoors. He had one final idea.

The next day, he tied a peach basket to the balcony at each end of the gym. Then he divided the 18 members of his class into two teams. They had no sticks, no pads or any other special equipment. Only a soccer ball.

There were 13 easy-to-learn rules, built around one main objective: shoot the ball into the basket. Naismith tossed up the ball between the two teams, they scrambled for it, and basketball was born.

In those early years, it was a helter-skelter affair, played by little guys who could run, although there was little skill, little scoring, few fans and no money.

By the time Naismith died in 1939, however, his game had grown in popularity into the most popular spectator sport in the country. And even then it was only touching the surface.

From those little gyms with their improper lighting, from those first clumsy players who could manage only scores such as 4–3 and 2–0, basketball rocketed into a multimillion-dollar game that attracted about 150 million spectators a year to thousands of fancy gyms and arenas throughout the country and through much of the world.

By 1970, it was played by such giants as 7-foot-2¾ Lew Alcindor, 7-1 Wilt Chamberlain and little men no smaller than 6-feet. And these were no lumbering, uncoordinated goons. They had the gracefulness of a ballet dancer and were thoroughly skilled magicians on the court, handling the ball, passing it, shooting it into the basket.

The scores and the salaries soared with the popularity.

Professionals, adept individually and as teams, averaged more than 100 points a game, and even college squads scored at a clip of more than two points per minute. Three players—professional Wilt Chamberlain and collegians Frank Selvy of Furman and Bevo Francis of little Rio Grande, Ohio—pumped in more than 100 points in one game by themselves.

With this kind of scoring, this kind of action and excitement, a college game between UCLA and Houston attracted almost 40,000 spectators in the Astrodome. The New York Knicks of the National Basketball Association became the first pro team to draw more than one million fans during a season in 1970, and people paid as much as $12 a seat to see them win the championship.

That kind of money, added to the $6 million television was forking over to televise professional games for three years starting in 1970, multiplied salaries into six figures.

Professional basketball produced perhaps the highest salaries of any sport, with as many as 15 players paid more than $100,000 a year in 1970, and Chamberlain hauling in something like $250,000 each season.

The average salary in the NBA reached about $30,000.

With the emergence of the rival American Basketball Association in the late 1960s, there was fierce competition for outstanding collegians. Graduating seniors such as Pete Maravich and Bob Lanier demanded, and got, contracts that stretched to $2 million.

In the sports-minded United States, Maravich, Lanier and the professionals became heroes to the nation's youth, rivaling the stars of baseball and football for their allegiance. Names like Chamberlain, Alcindor, Bob Cousy, Bill Russell and Oscar Robertson became household words.

Because of the action and excitement these players created, and because of the money they received, and because it was so easy for a young boy to grab a basketball, put up his own basket and learn the game, the sport accomplished just what Naismith had intended, and far more.

It not only was played during the winter months in every school gym in the country, but also by professionals in almost every large city in the nation, providing enjoyment for millions of viewers.

It took kids off the streets, provided those without money the means to a college education and later well-paying jobs, and gave well-regarded status to young giants who might otherwise be looked on only as freaks.

In its simplest form, here's how basketball started—players trying to shoot a ball into a peach basket affixed atop a pole.

The history of the sport and its growth is duly recorded in many books, and the important dates are easily distinguished—the creation of the original Celtics, the introduction of college basketball to Madison Square Garden, the emergence of the NBA, the first television contract.

It is also one of the few—perhaps the only—sports whose origin can be pinpointed to almost the very day in 1891 when Naismith put up those peach baskets. It also is one of the few games of strictly American origin.

Naismith put the baskets 10 feet above the floor, and they still remain at that height, although in recent years there have been suggestions that the baskets be raised because of the many 7-footers now playing the game.

The game became an immediate success, although about the only resemblance to today's game was the ultimate goal—to put the ball in the basket.

In those early years, as many as 50 players competed in one gym class game, bumping into each other on the small court that later was to reach a standard 94 feet long, 50 feet wide.

In other games, instead of a soccer ball, a ponderous, $2\frac{1}{2}$-pound medicine ball was used, a ball so heavy it had to be rolled across the floor instead of passed. By the time players neared the basket, they were too tired to shoot.

There was no dribbling, only passing. There was little team play, no backboards and the players wore long trousers with long-sleeved jerseys.

At first, the game was ridiculed by many who were more accustomed to rough sports like football and lacrosse, and basketball players were called sissies. But it was no sissy game. In fact, during that early period, it more resembled football than today's basketball. It wasn't the non-contact sport that Naismith had intended.

Aside from the elbows, hips, shoulders and body blocks that were prominent on the court, under the rules when a ball went out of bounds it was a free-for-all for possession with players overturning chairs and battling spectators and each other for control.

So rugged did it become that in the first decade of the 1900s, a number of Eastern college teams, who played a rougher brand of ball than those west of Pennsylvania, abandoned the game because it was too violent.

However, once the game came under the jurisdiction of the National Collegiate Athletic Association, rules were passed to make it cleaner, faster and with less contact, and any opposition to the sport faded.

During the incubation period, the basket had a bottom. Fortunately, the scores were low because every time a basket was made, someone had to climb a stepladder to retrieve the ball. It didn't take long for a wire basket and then cord to replace the peach baskets, and they had a small hole at the bottom through which a stick could be used to poke the ball back out after a score.

Naismith, who first intended to be a minister in his native Ontario before getting caught up with football at McGill University in Montreal and then devoting his life to athletics, organized the first team in 1892. It consisted of nine members of the International YMCA Training School, and they toured New York and New England, playing games with scores like 2–2 and 2–0.

The game began to spread like wildfire. It was played in any place there was a soccer ball and a court. The Sioux Indians are said to have played it on a reservation in South Dakota only 16 years after the Custer massacre.

Two girls' schools, Vassar and Smith, also looking for some type of athletics to keep their students busy during the winter, took up the game in 1892, and the popularity of girls' basketball grew in such areas as Iowa where it rivals the boys' game.

The YMCA took the lead in the early years of the sport, organizing teams throughout the country, creating the first ruling group and putting on the first tournament.

Naismith credited little Geneva College at Beaver Falls, Pa., with the first college team, although Vanderbilt University is given the honor in other quarters for its team that beat the Nashville YMCA in March of 1893.

The University of Toronto is recognized as the first foreign college team, scoring a 2–1 victory over the Toronto YMCA in early 1893. Hamline in Minnesota lost to the Minneapolis State School of Agriculture 9–3 in February 1895, in what is reported to be the first all-college game.

Yale walloped Pennsylvania 32–10 two years later in the generally recognized first modern intercollegiate game with five players on each side.

Amos Alonzo Stagg, the famous football coach, introduced the game at the University of Chicago, and the first super team, the Buffalo Germans, began play in 1895.

In that first YMCA tournament held in Brooklyn in 1894, the Brooklyn Central branch won on L. Beattie's basket with 15 seconds remaining, and for the first time a player was carried off the floor by jubilant fans.

Laying the groundwork for bigger scores and better games, a basketball similar to the one used today was introduced in 1894, and Dutch Wohlfarth of the Philadelphia Jaspers later astounded everyone when he dribbled across the floor without looking at the ball.

Before then, the dribble had been put into the rules, but was used mostly as a defensive measure to control the ball. And before a uniform set of rules, players dribbled overhead, tapping the ball over their heads while running.

It wasn't until 1906 that baskets were opened completely at the bottom, and backboards were created about the same time through necessity when rabid fans in the balcony helped their team by giving an errant shot a tap toward the basket.

Wood was tried at first, but it warped and the fans complained that they could not see. Then screening was tried, and finally, in 1909, plate glass backboards. Tennis shoes were introduced six years earlier.

Columbia, Cornell, Harvard, Princeton and Yale formed the first formal college league, the Eastern League, in 1901, and Dartmouth, Holy Cross, Williams, Amherst and Trinity came along with the New England League the same year. By 1905, colleges had accepted the sport as part of their curriculum as it was recognized by the NCAA and the Amateur Athletic Union.

The first pro game? There are claims that it was played in Herkimer, N.Y., in 1893 when the Utica, N.Y., team had its way paid to play there, but more likely the site was Trenton, N.J., in 1895.

The first professional league is generally agreed to be the National Basketball League, which opened with six teams in 1898. The teams were Trenton, Millville and Camden in New Jersey and three Philadelphia teams.

As such, the league lasted only one year when fights, fixes, cancellations and players switching teams from night to night turned off the fans. However, some form of the league is reported to have lasted until 1903.

Around the turn of the century the Buffalo Germans became one of the first super basketball teams.

Other pro leagues came and went in those early years, the best of which were the Hudson River League and the New York State League. Games were played on converted dance floors and in halls with the "court" enclosed in many places with chicken wire, fencing or rope to keep the ball in play and the partisan fans out of play. It was like a cage, and thus the name cage game became synonymous with basketball.

There wasn't much money involved in those early pro games, and the crowds were minimal. It wasn't until 1946 that the pros began to strike it rich with a league that evolved into the highly successful present day operation.

The Chicago West Side team introduced the first "big" man, a skyscraping 6-4, and by 1908, the Wabash team claimed some kind of world title by rolling up a 66–3 record in four years. But the first real winner was the Buffalo club.

The Germans got together as amateurs while they still were in grade school in 1895. Some of the players changed, but by 1929, when it finally disbanded, the team boasted a 761–85 record, including 111 straight victories. They won a tournament at the 1904 World's Fair in St. Louis for what was termed the "world championship" and beat Hobart College in another game 134–0.

But perhaps most impressive was a crowd of 5,000 they were reported to have attracted to one of their games.

In 1903, a promoter named Frank Basloe introduced the Oswego Indians, later known as the Globe Trotters for their travels throughout the country.

In compiling a 1,324–127 mark in 20 years, Basloe told of roughing it on courts in out-of-the-way places where hot steam pipes along the walls and close to the floor burned players as they dashed by. He told of courts with pot-bellied stoves in the way and baskets hidden by boilers forcing the players to shoot over them.

The Troy Trojans, led by Ed and Lew Wachter, was another top team of the era, starting a pattern of play that resembled a fast break. After winning the Hudson River League and then the New York State League titles, they toured the West in 1916 as far as Montana, running up unheard of scores like 64–40 and 115–33.

The colleges were not without their wonder teams of the era. Minnesota was probably the best team at the turn of the century.

The University of Chicago, coached by Dr. Joseph E. Raycroft, was considered the best of the college teams from 1906–10 with 6-3 center John Schommer.

The Western Conference, forerunner of the Big Ten, had been formed in 1905 with Chicago, Illinois, Wisconsin, Minnesota and Purdue, and Chicago tied Wisconsin for the title in 1906 and then won it the following two years. The Chicago squad also won the national championship in 1907–08 by beating Pennsylvania in two straight games.

Until Raycroft came along, the players hogged the spotlight and coaching was not considered of great importance. Phog Allen came along about then, too, and gave the profession an added boost.

After Allen played at the University of Kansas and then coached Baker College to a 12–0 record while still a student at Kansas, in 1906, Baker inquired if he would be available as a regular paid coach.

Naismith, who spent the last 40 years of his career as a physical education professor at Kansas, replied, "You can't coach basketball; you can only play it."

Allen, who went on to a great coaching career at Kansas and won 771 games in almost 50 years of coaching, later wrote Naismith:

"By this token, you can see how many basketball coaches are today obtaining money under false pretenses."

Despite the early success of basketball, the spread of the fever throughout the country, the game didn't really move into the spotlight until the original Celtics came on the scene in 1918. They revolutionized the game with their ability and inventiveness, and with their flashy play and color that made them famous enough to draw 23,000 for a single game in Cleveland in 1922.

Jim Furey, a promoter, put the team together, and it resulted in one of the most successful teams ever, both artistically and financially.

The Celtics were one of the only four teams first elected to the Basketball Hall of Fame at its inception in 1959. The others were the first team of Naismith, the Germans and the New York Rens, a Negro team of the 1930s.

Until the Celtics came along, basketball was mostly a game of individuals, pitting their skills against an opposing player. The Celts were the first to truly make it a team game, developing plays and patterns, great teamwork and pride. They gave the game class and prestige.

Although each was a star, they blended their talents perfectly together.

The Celtics averaged something like 150 games a year, playing anywhere there was money, although they would play for nothing if a title was at stake. In a normal year, they would not lose more than one game in every 10.

The leader of the team was Nat Holman, a forward. He was the brains, the innovator. The center was Joe Lapchick, a thin 6-foot-5, with "Horse" Haggerty, 6-4, 225 pounds, or Johnny Beckman at the other forward. At the guards were Dutch Dehnert and Chris Leonard. On the bench were Davey Banks, Benny Borgeman, Pete Barry and Ernie Reich at various times.

The Celtics had a great spirit of cooperation, a kind of one for all, all for one idea that is best exemplified by Haggerty's protective feeling toward Holman, much smaller and considered the best passer before Bob Cousy came along in the 1950s.

"Anytime I got hit on the court, and that was often," Holman related, "Horse would retaliate by giving the guy a robust nudge in the ribs."

One time, Haggerty floored a fan who was screaming at Holman, and in another game, he is reported to have decked an official who he didn't think was being quite fair about his calls. Of course, in those days, even Haggerty had his troubles when a gang of toughs jumped him after a game before the Celts could get out of town.

The Celtics also started the pivot play, although the reason could be argued. Some say Dehnert got tired during the end of one game and simply stationed himself near the basket, taking passes and then handing off to teammates running by for easy baskets.

More likely, the play began to overcome the standing guard, an opposing player who stood in front of the basket, never moving, and keeping the offensive team from penetrating close to the hoop.

Dehnert circumvented this by standing in front of the guard and his teammates passed him the ball.

"All I had to do was pivot, take one step and lay the ball in the basket, or else

They made their mark on the game of basketball. They're the original Celtics. From left: Joe Lapchick, Chris Leonard, Dutch Dehnert, Pete Barry, Nat Holman, Johnny Whitty, manager, Johnny Beckman and Eddie Burke.

pass off to a cutting teammate," he explained. "This was the pivot play, although we didn't know it at the time."

Holman and Leonard didn't join the Celtics until 1921, when they were stolen away from the rival New York Whirlwinds. Furey made the move after watching his Celts get beat by the Whirlwinds 40–27 in 1921 before 11,000 at the 71st St. Armory in New York. The next night, the Celtics won 26–24 in this meeting between the two best teams of the time, but a scheduled third game never came off because the fans became so unruly.

Furey also revolutionized the stability of the game about this time by signing players to exclusive contracts for an entire year.

The Celtics' own greatness, however, proved to be their demise. They were persuaded in 1926 to join the first real pro basketball league, the American Basketball League, created by George Preston Marshall.

However, they won everything in sight and so demoralized the opposition and made games so one-sided that attendance dropped. Finally, in 1928, to save the league, they had to be disbanded, with Lapchick, Holman and Barry going to the Cleveland Rosenblums, who went on to win the title in 1929 before the league folded.

The ABL started again in 1933 and lasted for 13 years in the big Eastern cities before the Basketball Association of America ran it out of business in 1946. The National Basketball League, meanwhile, operated in small Midwest cities from 1937. Until the 1950s, basketball belonged to individual touring teams, and the colleges.

While the Passaic, N.J., high school team was setting the all-time recognized winning streak of 160 games during the 1920s, St. John's, N.Y., was the top college team of the day. The Wonder Five, as the Redmen were called, posted an 86–8 record from 1927–31 with Matty Begovich, at 6-5 one of the tallest players in the game.

The Redmen began the practice of scouting an opponent, but their main success was due to their defense, which in those days was the result in part of holding the ball as much as 10 minutes at a time. No team scored more than 30 points against them during their final college year.

The St. John's team stayed together as an independent team for two years after college and then entered the ABL as the Brooklyn Jewels before breaking up in 1938.

As in every other sport, there were no Negroes allowed on white teams during this period, so Negroes formed their own teams, such as the New York Rens, 1932–36. Battling against tough competition of both black and white teams, belligerent fans and one-sided officials, the Rens still managed to win 88 games in a row.

Although Bob Douglas first started the team in Harlem in 1922, it wasn't until 1932 that they obtained greatness, rolling up a 473–49 record during the next four years. Players such as Pappy Ricks, Fat Jenkins, Bill Yancy, Tarzan Cooper, Wee Willie Smith and Bruiser Saitch were among the best players of the day, and most of them excelled at other sports from which they were banned.

The Rens lasted until 1948 when Douglas broke them up.

But the greatest Negro team of all time and certainly the most successful team financially of all time, regardless of color, was put together in 1927 by the son of a Jewish tailor on Chicago's South Side. Abe Saperstein, with his rumpled trousers and suspenders, put them on the court in Hinckley, Ill., and they were known as the Savoy Five. The name later was changed to the Globetrotters.

By the time Saperstein died in 1966, the Globetrotters had captured the fancy of the entire world, traveling millions of miles and playing before kings and popes, behind the Iron Curtain, in Africa, the Far East, Australia. In Berlin, outdoors, they played before the biggest basketball crowd in history, 75,000.

Spreading basketball and comedy throughout the world, they were known as the United States' Ambassadors of Good Will. They displayed their trick shots and funny antics in 87 countries for more than 60 million fans before Abe died.

They started as a serious team, but that didn't attract many fans, so Saperstein added the comedy to please the people. The crowds grew.

In their red-white-blue striped outfits, they featured behind-the-back passes,

The Renaissance—or the Rens as they were known—were one of the greatest basketball teams of all time. The team, started in 1922, obtained greatness in 1932, rolling up a 473-49 record during the next four years. They were broken up as a team in 1948.

bouncing the ball into the basket, the dribbling of Marques Haynes, the clowning of centers Meadowlark Lemon and Goose Tatum.

But despite the comedy, Saperstein lived by one rule: "No matter how funny we are, we've got to show how well we play, too. Nobody wants to come out and watch losers, even funny ones."

But it was difficult to convince the pros how great the Trotters were, despite a record of 8,845–322 with a run of 1,476 straight victories under Saperstein.

The Trotters proved themselves once and for all in 1948 and 1949 when they twice beat the world champion Minneapolis Lakers of the top pro league.

When Saperstein died, the Globetrotters were sold in 1967 to Metromedia, Inc., for about $3 million. While the personnel changed, the show, the victories and the crowds remained.

It was in the 1930s that the college game came into its own. In fact, the exact date can be pinpointed at Saturday night, Dec. 29, 1934, when more than 16,000 fans crowded into Madison Square Garden in New York to see New York University beat Notre Dame 25–18 and Westminster defeat St. John's 37–33.

This first college double-header, played for the first time in a big arena between four of the top teams in the country, brought the colleges into the big time. The spotlight remained on them for the next 20 years.

The classy Harlem Globetrotters have displayed their basketball talents and entertainment all over the world for years. Back in 1950 they battled the Minneapolis Lakers, but lost 76–60. With the Lakers then was George Mikan, shown battling Nat Clifton, left, and Babe Pressley for ball.

Ned Irish, a young sports writer who spotted the possibilities for the game when he recognized that it was growing too big to be held in gyms, armories and halls with limited seating, arranged that first double-header. It wasn't long before the Garden became the mecca of basketball teams and players.

Only two years later, a young player with Stanford, little known in the East, came into the Garden and lit another lasting spark by becoming the first bona-fide national basketball hero.

The University of Washington had the first team on the West Coast as early as 1895, but Western teams had little success traveling east until Stanford, and Hank Luisetti, invaded the Garden before 18,000 fans who expected to see Clair Bee and his Long Island University team easily add to their 43-game winning streak.

While the packed house looked in disbelief, Luisetti unveiled his revolutionary one-handed jump shot. Until then, all shooting was done with two hands, and the feet never left the floor except on a layup.

Luisetti scored 15 points and Stanford crushed LIU 45–31. Together they became the darlings of the East. They came back in Luisetti's senior year and scored victories over CCNY and LIU on consecutive nights in the Garden.

For three years, Luisetti was an All-American, astounding the basketball world by scoring 50 points in one game and 1,300 during his three years on the court at Stanford. He led the Indians to three conference titles and records of 22–7, 25–2 and 21–3.

Luisetti also was the first real individual hero on the court. Until he came along, teams and coaches were better known than the players in college.

Coming into the game were coaches such as Bee, the master strategist who helped originate the zone defense and later the 24-second clock and compiled 327 victories in 18 years, including winning streaks of 43, 28, 38 and 26 games.

Phog Allen was in the middle of his career at Kansas, teaching defense and ball control and helping to get basketball introduced into the Olympic Games in 1936.

Ed Diddle at Western Kentucky was on his way to winning 759 games, at race horse speed, and Tony Hinkle was piling up victories at Butler.

George Keogan, credited with creating the switching man-to-man defense, was in the middle of his 20-year coaching career at Notre Dame, and Hank Iba was teaching the patient, deliberate offense at Oklahoma A&M (now Oklahoma State) that won him almost 800 games.

The game itself also was changing. Frank Keaney, who had only one losing season in 27 at Rhode Island, introduced the running game and was scoring 100 points a game before the pros. He also had his teams pressing full court.

Not since he began the fast break style in the early 1920s was the game shifted into a higher gear when the 10-second rule in the backcourt was introduced in 1932 and the center jump eliminated after every basket in 1937.

The tallest man in the 1930s was 6-10, and there were only about 66 collegians more than 6-feet. Tall players were considered goons in those days, and they were uncoordinated and unskilled. But their closeness to the basket and improvement as the 1930s came to a close forced the widening of the foul lanes and the three-second rule for players in the foul lanes, and finally, in 1944–45, the banning of goal-tending.

The game was speeding up, and the fans loved it.

During that first year of double-headers in Madison Square Garden, 99,528 fans paid to see eight twinbills, and Irish was able to bring in top teams from around the country.

By 1937–38, the result was the first National Invitation Tournament, with six of the best squads in the nation. Temple beat Colorado 60–36 in the final.

One year later, the NCAA put on its first national championship, and Oregon edged Ohio State 46–43 at Evanston, Ill., for the crown. That same year, Rhode Island averaged a whopping 70 points a game.

Another landmark occurred the following year in 1940. On Feb. 28, an experimental station, W2XBS, the forerunner to WNBC in New York, televised the first basketball game, a double-header at the Garden matching Pittsburgh against Fordham and New York University against Georgetown.

The National Association of Intercollegiate Athletics also was organized in 1940 for the smaller schools, and the NCAA furthered that end in 1957 by creating its small college division, giving the small colleges a crack at some of the spotlight and glory.

Now college basketball was ready to blossom into its greatest decade with the tournaments providing the focal point. This also was the time the big man, too tall for military service, came into his own, and such greats as 6-10 George Mikan and 7-foot Bob Kurland stepped into the spotlight.

Kurland, who along with 6-9 Harry Boykoff of St. John's helped force the goal-tending rule, led Oklahoma A&M to two consecutive NCAA titles in the mid-1940s, controlling the rebounds and standing out as the hub in Iba's deliberate offense and sticky defense. He also led the nation in scoring with a 19.5 point average one year.

Kurland shunned pro basketball after he was graduated, and instead joined the amateur Phillips 76ers, working for the company while playing basketball. He led them to six straight AAU titles and also played on two winning United States Olympic basketball teams.

Mikan's star rose even higher, and he later was selected by *The Associated Press* as the outstanding player of the half-century.

Mikan proved beyond a doubt that a big man can be agile, graceful, and skillful, erasing the image of the goon. Playing at DePaul, the near-sighted, bespectacled giant averaged more than 19 points a game during his four years in college, and he was still greater as a pro. In fact, his presence played a great part in the survival of the pro leagues. He was pro basketball's first big drawing card.

Joe Lapchick, with his patient, intelligent defense, made St. John's a college power during the 1940s, and the Redmen were to win four NIT titles in 17 years under him.

Holy Cross, coached by Doggie Julian and led on the court by Cousy, rose from nothing to an NCAA title in 1947.

The '40s also saw the beginning of Adolph Rupp's dynasty at the University of Kentucky, where the controversial and outspoken "Baron of the Bluegrass" won more than 800 games and four NCAA titles as the winningest coach in history.

It began during the 1945–46 season when Rupp came up with three outstanding freshmen—Alex Groza, Ralph Beard and Wah Wah Jones.

That year, Kentucky broke into the spotlight by winning the NIT, although

Rhode Island, beaten by one point in the final, captured the fancy of the fans. Ernie Calvarley hit a desperation 50-footer at the gun to send Rhode Island's first round game against heavily-favored Bowling Green into overtime.

By the 1953–54 season, with Frank Ramsey, Cliff Hagen and Lou Tsioropoulos leading the way to an undefeated season, Kentucky rolled up a record of eight Southeast Conference crowns, three NCAA titles and one NIT crown, plus No. 1 ranking in the first *Associated Press* basketball poll in the 1948–49 season.

Beard also made the first *AP* All-American team in 1947–48, along with Murray Weir of Iowa, Jim McIntyre of Minnesota, Ed Macauley of St. Louis and Kevin O'Shea of Notre Dame.

Kentucky also played in what was considered then "the greatest game of all time," losing to the Phillips 76ers and Kurland 53–49 in the 1948 Olympic trial finals at Madison Square Garden. Beard scored 23 points, Kurland 20, including the final six points.

CCNY, coached by the brainy Nat Holman, closed the decade by becoming the only team ever to win both the NCAA and NIT titles in one year. That team, led by 6-2 Ed Warner and 6-6 Ed Roman, had the brains, the muscle and the height.

But Kentucky, CCNY and the 1940s also laid the groundwork for basketball's most disgraceful era, her most trying time. The scandals, matched only perhaps by baseball's World Series fix of 1919, deflated the balloon, and it took years for the game to recover.

Because basketball is a high-scoring game, and because with only five players, one outstanding player can have greater control of the outcome than in most other sports, basketball was hard hit. It was particularly vulnerable because betting was done not just on winning and losing, but on point spreads—the number of points by which a team wins, or loses.

"What's the difference if you win by eight or 10 points?" a gambler could use as a talking point in persuading young college kids to maybe miss a basket on purpose, or allow an opposing player to score.

The first signs began in 1945 when rumors of fixes infiltrated and damaged the reputation of the game after five Brooklyn College players admitted accepting bribes to throw a game against Akron for $1,000 each. The game never was played, the players were expelled and two gamblers were arrested. But it was just the beginning.

In 1948, Joe Fulks, a star with the pro Philadelphia Warriors, swore out a warrant against a Philadelphia pool hall operator, charging him with attempting to fix a game. The operator later was cleared.

But the next year, a George Washington player, Dave Shapiro, reported being approached by gamblers to throw a game in the Garden against Manhattan, and four men were arrested and sent to prison.

The stage now was set for the great collapse, and it came in 1951 when young Junius Kellogg, a 6-8 star for Manhattan, reported a bribe offer of $1,000 to control the point spread in a game. Two of his teammates were arrested, along with three gamblers.

An investigation between 1947–50 resulted in the disclosure that 86 games in 23 cities and 17 states had been tampered with during that period.

Thirty-three players were named to be involved, including such stars as Beard, Groza and Bill Spivey of Kentucky and members of that 1950 CCNY team. Eight schools were affected, one official and 25 gamblers.

All this after Rupp claimed gamblers couldn't touch any of his boys "with a 10-foot pole."

The Southeast Conference suspended Kentucky for the 1952–53 season for recruiting practices, and the Wildcats didn't even play basketball that season.

But more lasting was the affect on big time basketball and its alliance with Madison Square Garden. Because New York was the betting center of the country, schools began declining invitations to play there. And the best New York teams, CCNY and LIU, de-emphasized the sport, and LIU refused to play a game in the Garden for almost 20 years.

The result of the scandal almost proved fatal to big time college basketball. Yet the sport still had more problems ahead.

In 1954, the former Columbia All-American, Jack Molinas, was suspended from the Fort Wayne professional team after being accused of betting on games, and seven years later, he was at the center of another scandal that rocked the basketball world. Some $70,000 was allegedly paid to tamper with 43 games throughout the country between 1957–61.

Some 47 players were believed approached and 33 admitted taking bribes from 22 schools. Molinas and several others were sent to prison and six former players received suspended sentences.

In 1965, a Chicago night club owner was found guilty of trying to fix a basketball game between Seattle and Idaho. He testified that he gave one Seattle player $130 as "a token of friendship." Three Seattle players later were expelled.

The problems didn't always stem from outside gamblers or fixes. In May 1967, Illinois was put on two-year probation by the NCAA for discovery of a $21,000 slush fund used to recruit athletes. Coaches Pete Elliott, football, and Harry Combes and Howard Braun, basketball, were forced to resign and 14 players were declared ineligible, five of them permanently, for being recruited illegally.

Although its reputation had been badly tarnished, college basketball managed to survive, with the help of colorful teams such as San Francisco, Cincinnati, Ohio State and UCLA, and players such as Bill Russell, Clyde Lovellette, Bob Pettit, Frank Selvy, Wilt Chamberlain, Oscar Robertson, Jerry Lucas, Bill Bradley, Lew Alcindor and Pete Maravich.

During the 1953–54 season, a guard named Frank Selvy, playing for little Furman, shocked even the most offensive-minded basketball experts by scoring the incredible total of 100 points in one game against Newberry. Selvy led the nation in scoring that year with a 41.7 point a game average.

And then in 1954, a giant named Bevo Francis of Rio Grande College in Ohio did even better, pumping in 113 points against Hillsdale, Mich., for an NAIA and NCAA small college record.

By 1966, Syracuse, not a great basketball team, averaged 99 points a game, and that same year, Stillman, Ala., scored 169 points in a victory over Miles, Ala.

In 1968, Elvin Hayes of Houston set a record of 1,214 points in one season, and in 1969–70, Pete Maravich of Louisiana State, a shooting and passing wizard, broke the one season scoring mark and the career standard with more than 3,000 points.

But one man proved, both in college and then in the pros, that scoring still had to take a back seat to defense. He was 6-10 Bill Russell, the winningest basketball player of all time.

He wasn't much of a shooter, but he had the jumping ability, the timing and the coordination that enabled him to play defense as no one before or after ever matched. Rebounding, blocking shots and intimidating opposing players just by his presence in the center, he led San Francisco University to 60 consecutive victories and two straight NCAA titles.

That team, coached by defensive genius Phil Woolpert, also featured K. C. Jones, perhaps the finest defensive guard in history, and led Lapchick to call them "the best college team I've ever seen. They played a defense I never saw before," he added.

As great as he was in college, it was just the start for Russell, who went on to lead the U.S. Olympic team to victory in 1956, then turn professional and transform the Boston Celtics into a 13-year dynasty. Finally, he became the first Negro coach in the National Basketball Association or in any major professional league.

For all of this, he was named by *The Associated Press* the Basketball Player of the Decade, covering 1960–70.

Bill Russell (6) of the Boston Celtics dominated the professional game of basketball in the '60s as no other player did. He reintroduced the art of defense to the game and intimidated opponents by his mere proximity to the basket.

Following Russell as the dominant force in college basketball was a 6-foot-5 Negro who, first in college and then in the pros, could lay claim to being the greatest backcourt man ever to play the game. He was the Big O, Oscar Robertson.

"There's never been one like him," Lapchick said. Phog Allen called him the "greatest of all time for a fellow his size."

He was big for a guard but, despite his height, he was as quick and could handle the ball as well as any smaller player. He could score almost at will and completely control a game. In three years at the University of Cincinnati, he scored a record 2,973 points for a 33.8 point a game average. For three years he led the nation in scoring and became an All-American all three seasons while leading the Bearcats to records of 25–3, 26–4 and 28–2.

However, oddly, Cincinnati never won an NCAA crown until after he left, although he took them to the final one year and the semifinal another, losing to California each time.

He did start a brief dynasty at Cincinnati, which won five straight Missouri Valley Conference titles and five consecutive NCAA regional championships. After Robertson was graduated, with a better balanced team the Bearcats beat Ohio State and Jerry Lucas twice in the final for two NCAA titles and missed a third when they blew a 15-point lead against Loyola of Chicago with 12 minutes left in 1963.

That Ohio State team with the 6-8 Lucas, 6-5 John Havlicek and guards Mel Nowell, 6-2, and Larry Siegfried, 6-3, battled cross-state rival Cincinnati tooth

Oscar Robertson of Cincinnati drives past Iowa defender in a 1960 college game. Robertson was to go on and become a professional basketball star.

and nail during this period, winning 32 games in a row and three Big Ten titles, compiling a 78–6 mark between 1959–62.

After those two defeats by Cincinnati in the NCAA final, the Buckeyes finally won it all.

But the greatest college reign came in the mid-1960s with the appearance of 7-2¾ Lew Alcindor on the UCLA campus.

Clyde Lovellette, 6-9, started the college trend of high-scoring centers back in the early 1950s with Kansas. Previously, centers had been used mostly for rebounding. But Alcindor presented the best of both, and also could pass and run for his size, and he was a team player.

Under scholarly John Wooden, a shrewd basketball mind, Alcindor and UCLA dominated the game as never before. UCLA won 45 straight games during one stretch and lost only two games in three seasons, easily winning three consecutive NCAA titles.

One of the two defeats was to Houston and Elvin Hayes in the Astrodome before more than 37,000 spectators, by far the largest college basketball gathering ever. However, Alcindor played that game with an injured eye, and when the Bruins faced Houston in the NCAA final later, they demolished the Texas team.

UCLA had won two NCAA titles in the three years preceding Alcindor's reign, but when he left, there was speculation whether the Bruins could win without him. They answered that question in 1970 by sweeping past Jacksonville 80–69 for their fourth championship in a row.

Only Adolph Rupp and Kentucky had won as many as four NCAA titles, and only Oklahoma A&M under Iba, San Francisco, Cincinnati and Kentucky had won two in a row—before UCLA.

Wooden led UCLA to six titles in seven years, and with his deliberate but fast, quick teams, he won more than 500 games in 34 years of coaching for a winning percentage of better than .800.

Another big name in college basketball before Alcindor to capture the fancy of the fans was 6-foot-5 forward-guard Bill Bradley, who did it all for the Ivy League Princeton University. A three-time All-American, he averaged 30.1 points a game during his three years in college. But what really brought him to the attention of the nation was the fact that he played for an Ivy school. Although the Ivy is not considered a match for the more recruiting-minded football and basketball schools, Bradley made Princeton competitive.

His incredible performance against Michigan in Madison Square Garden during the Holiday Festival will always be remembered as he outdueled fellow All-American Cazzie Russell until the final moments when Bradley fouled out. He left to a standing ovation and his team led by 12 points, only to have Russell lead Michigan in a stirring finish that pulled out the victory.

Bradley, a scholar, went on to two years of study at Oxford, but returned to sign a $500,000 contract with the New York Knicks, one of the first of the high-monied signings.

Just starting at Louisiana State while Alcindor was finishing at UCLA was a gangling, wavy-haired 6-5 guard with floppy socks who became the pride of the South and the greatest scorer in college history. Pete Maravich, who also could pass like Cousy and Robertson, scored more than 40 points a game in each of

Pete Maravich (44) of the Atlanta Hawks, hair flying, is in action here against the Knickerbockers in New York early in 1971. Maravich was an outstanding college player with LSU and holds an abundance of scoring records.

his three varsity seasons with LSU, breaking the single season scoring record and the career mark with a total of 3,667 points, a 44.2 average. Although LSU was only a .500 team, they were writing songs about Pete Maravich, the most colorful performer of his day.

With the emergence of the modern basketball era when that first double-header was played in Madison Square Garden in 1934, the college game hogged all the glory from the pros until the scandals.

Aside from scattered touring teams like the Globetrotters, the only real pro league in existence during the first part of that period was the National Basketball League, formed in 1937. But how big league could it be with teams like Anderson and Hammond in Indiana, Oshkosh and Sheboygan in Wisconsin and Davenport and Waterloo in Iowa?

Then, a group of men who owned the country's largest arenas gathered in a New York hotel on the night of June 6, 1946, and formed the Basketball Association of America.

Max Kase, the sports editor of the *New York Journal-American,* and Walter Brown, president of Boston Garden, originated the idea, and joining them that night were arena owners from Cleveland, Washington, D.C., Philadelphia, Pittsburgh, St. Louis, Toronto, Providence, Chicago, Detroit and New York, the last represented by Ned Irish and the Madison Square Garden.

Irish wasn't the most enthusiastic member of the group, but in the end, he got the New York franchise instead of Kase. So the league started with those 11 members.

Most of them also owned hockey teams in the National Hockey League or the American Hockey League. For their first president, they picked Maurice Podoloff, a 5-foot bundle of energy from New Haven, Conn., who was president of the American Hockey League. He was a lawyer who knew little about sports, but who could handle the legal matters and, what turned out just as important, keep the owners away from each other's throats in working toward the best interests of the league. He is credited with holding the league together in those early years.

On Nov. 1, 1946, the New York Knickerbockers defeated the Toronto Huskies 68–66 in Toronto, and the league was under way.

Fulks, a jump-shooting forward with Philadelphia, was the first big star, leading the league in scoring that first season with an incredible 23.2 points a game average.

The Washington Capitols, coached by then unknown Red Auerbach, a 29-year-old local boy who had never coached before but got the job because he knew a number of stars coming out of the military, was the first great team. The Caps set a record of 17 straight victories that first season, a mark that stood for 14 years. They also won three Eastern Division titles, only to lose each year in the playoffs, although they were without doubt the best.

"They weren't quite the greatest, but they were awfully close," Auerbach says, looking back. He had players such as Fred Scolari, Bob Feerick and Bones McKinney.

In the spring of 1946, Mikan, the best-known basketball player in the country, was graduated from college, and the BAA and the NBL battled to get him. The NBL Chicago franchise signed him, but just his presence in the pros—Kurland, the other great giant, decided to play AAU—created new excitement and interest and stature for all pros.

The BAA lost four teams, Pittsburgh, Toronto, Cleveland and Detroit, after that first year because of financial difficulties.

The teams traveled by train in those days and few players made more than $6,000. The crowds were meager.

In 1947, Baltimore made it an eight-team league with a 48-game season for each team. That year, the BAA also inaugurated the college draft under which teams in the league drafted the rights to college stars, with the last place team of the previous season getting the No. 1 choice. It not only strengthened the weaker teams, it cut out the bidding by teams in the same league against each other for players.

That same year, the Chicago team in the NBL folded and Mikan moved to the Minneapolis franchise.

However, the shorter season and the bidding that remained between leagues still presented financial problems, and Podoloff knew the only answer to survival was a merger of the BAA and the NBL.

The NBL still had a majority of the better players, while the BAA had the big arenas in the big cities. A union seemed natural.

Podoloff convinced general manager Paul Walk of the NBL Indianapolis team and Carl Bennett, who ran the Fort Wayne club for Fred Zollner, that their future lay in joining the bigger cities. The two teams decided to jump to the BAA.

Perhaps seeing the handwriting on the wall, Minneapolis and Rochester also decided to jump leagues, taking the two best teams out of the NBL. Suddenly, the BAA had Mikan and teammate Jim Pollard plus Arnie Risen and Bob Davies of Rochester. It was a tremendous victory for the BAA and all but spelled an end to the NBL, although it continued with eight teams but branded then as a minor league.

Mikan filled arenas in the BAA wherever he went, and few collegians would choose to go to the NBL, ending much of the competition for new players.

Thus, the BAA started the 1948–49 season with 12 teams, and Mikan led the Lakers to the first merged championship in the playoffs. Mikan, who had signed a five-year contract with the Chicago team for the unheard of sum of $60,000, led the Lakers to four titles in five years, along with Pollard, Vern Mikkelsen, Whitey Scoog and Slater Martin. The giant center led the league in scoring with a 28.3 average.

This new merged league was named the National Basketball Association.

The following season, the size and structure of the league changed again, with Providence and Indianapolis giving up and Syracuse, Anderson, Tri-Cities and Sheboygan brought in from the NBL, along with Denver and Waterloo, which had not finished the NBL season.

The 17th team was the Indianapolis Olympians, composed of the ill-fated Kentucky team of Groza, Beard and Jones. The scandal later put them out of business.

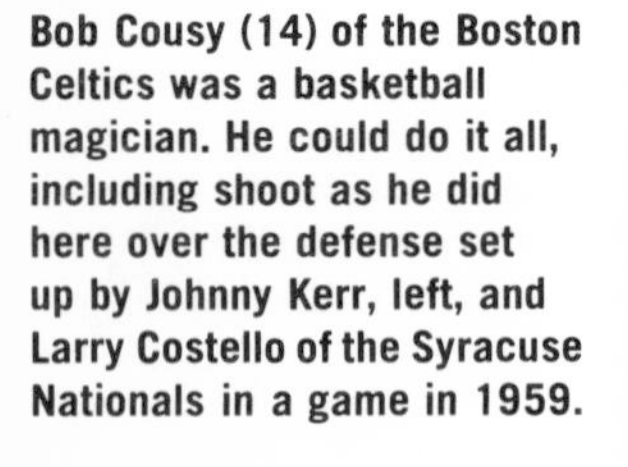

Bob Cousy (14) of the Boston Celtics was a basketball magician. He could do it all, including shoot as he did here over the defense set up by Johnny Kerr, left, and Larry Costello of the Syracuse Nationals in a game in 1959.

Teams came and went, but with the colleges supplying the players, there always were new stars to replace the old—players such as Dolph Schayes, who was to score 20,000 points before he retired; Ed Macauley, Carl Braun, Paul Arizin, Red Rocha, Bill Sharman and Cousy, the player most responsible for bringing the league to the forefront during the 1950s.

Although he was a star at Holy Cross in college, Cousy was not highly thought of in the college draft, and after being bounced around that first year, he wound up with Boston for $8,500.

With his sensational passing that excited fans, his brains, his shooting and dribbling, Cousy attracted enough people to Boston games to keep the Celtics in existence. Together with coach Red Auerbach, who had taken over the last place Celtics at the end of 1950, Cousy helped start the Celtics on the road to one of the greatest dynasties in all sports history.

The Celtics finished second four times in the next five years, and then Russell returned from giving the United States another Olympic victory to join the Celtics in December of 1956.

With Russell providing the big man to rebound, the Celtics won the NBA title in 1957, lost to the St. Louis Hawks in 1958 when Russell missed the last game because of injury, and then reeled off seven consecutive NBA crowns.

With people such as Frank Ramsey, Tom Heinsohn, Sam Jones and John Havlicek to replace retiring stars, the Celtics won 11 titles in 13 years before Russell finally retired after the 1968–69 season.

Their major rivals during this period were first the Hawks, with Bob Pettit, Macauley, Lovellette, Cliff Hagen and Martin, who won five straight division titles; then Philadelphia, which cut the streak with Wilt Chamberlain, Hal Greer and Billy Cunningham, and finally the Los Angeles Lakers, with Jerry West, Elgin Baylor and, later, Chamberlain.

Pettit replaced Schayes as the all-time high scorer. Then the 7-1 Chamberlain came along in 1959 and won the season scoring title for seven straight years, shattering all records. In Hershey, Pa., in 1962, against the New York Knicks, he pumped in that incredible total of 100 points, the only pro ever to do it.

Chamberlain, the scorer, and Russell, the defensive wizard, staged many brilliant duels during this period, and while Wilt managed most of the time to get his points, Boston usually was the winner. Only once, in the 1966–67 season, did Chamberlain and Philadelphia beat Russell and the Celtics for the NBA title.

One of the most significant players ever to sign an NBA contract was Chuck Cooper of Duquesne, drafted after the 1950 college season. Cooper played only briefly with the Boston Celtics, and never really made it big, but his name will always be in any basketball history book. He was the first Negro to sign a contract.

Sweetwater Clifton came to the Knicks that same year from the Globetrotters, and both he and Cooper started the 1950–51 season in the NBA. The trickle of Negro talent quickly turned into a tidal wave, and by 1970, many of the greatest players in the NBA were Negro.

John McLendon, who coached at a number of Negro colleges, became the first Negro coach in a pro league in 1960 when he took over a team in the short-lived American Basketball League.

Finally, it was Russell who truly became the first black coach in a major league sport when he took over the Celtics as a player-coach in 1967 from Auerbach, who moved up to general manager after more than 1,000 victories in 20 years of coaching in the NBA and BAA.

Russell was earning well over $100,000 a year by then, and Chamberlain was pulling in something like $250,000 per season.

The one most important factor in the actual playing of the game occurred in 1954. Until then, it was a rough and tumble game of pushing, blocking, shoving. A slow big man such as Mikan could control play, and teams such as Minneapolis, with big centers, would slow play to adapt to their centers. And the team leading in the final minutes would stall, holding or dribbling the ball to run out the remaining minutes.

A number of things were tried to speed up the game and keep it exciting, but it was Dan Biasone, the owner of the Syracuse team, who came up with the master stroke—the 24-second rule. A team had to shoot the ball within 24 seconds, and it was adopted after the 1955 season.

From then on, everything took off. The shooting improved, the scoring increased, the excitement never lessened in a close game.

In 1954, the great Lakers team shot only 37.6 per cent from the field. By 1970, teams were shooting in the high 40 per cent, and every team in the NBA averaged more than 100 points a game.

In 1960, the NBA became a true national league when the Lakers moved to Los Angeles. There were eight clubs then, and a ninth was added in 1961.

Walter Kennedy replaced the retiring Podoloff as commissioner in 1963. Kennedy had been the league's first public relations man when it still was the BAA. When he took the commissioner's position, he was the mayor of Stamford, Conn.

Kennedy's two major achievements during his first seven years was expansion of the league to 17 teams by the 1970–71 season, with five of those teams on the West Coast, and the alliance with television.

Some games had been televised during the 1950s, but the real breakthrough came in 1964 when the NBA signed a five-year contract with the American Broadcasting Company to televise the NBA Game of the Week.

Like pro football and baseball, the money from television raised players' salaries, created more fans, interest and attendance, and increased the value of teams to an extent that the Los Angeles team was sold in 1965 for a reported $5,175,000, the highest ever paid for an NBA franchise.

In 1965, total attendance for the league was just more than two million spectators; in 1969–70, the Knicks alone drew more than one million, and the entire league attracted 5,146,858 fans.

In 1970, the NBA signed a new three-year contract with ABC for a reported $17 million, more than four times the previous pact.

In 1967, a new force entered the pro basketball scene—the American Basketball Association, started by a number of wealthy men who realized the growing popularity of pro basketball and the profit from it.

It started with a 10-team league and Mikan was named the first commissioner. He immediately declared war on the NBA for players.

At first the ABA lured away only those fringe players in the NBA, or those who couldn't make NBA teams. But in the spring of 1967, the new league coaxed away Rick Barry, the NBA's scoring leader. Barry's NBA team, San

Francisco, sued, but the case still was in the courts in 1970, and meanwhile, Barry played in the ABA.

Several other name players jumped to the ABA, and the new league also fiercely entered into a bidding war with the NBA for the graduating college talent.

The ABA managed to sign at least 10 college stars in 1970, including the outstanding Spencer Haywood. The ABA slowly was catching the NBA in talent, and costing the established league a lot of money.

By 1970, a merger was discussed. It was inevitable. However, NBA players, who realized that a merger would sharply cut their negotiating power for more money because they no longer could threaten to jump leagues, filed an antitrust suit against the merger.

When a merger seemed imminent, Kennedy of the NBA abruptly closed the door on such negotiations. The war continued.

Basketball had indeed come a long way from peach baskets and dance floors. It is still great exercise, but now it also is national heroes, millions of dollars, television, court cases, mergers, world championships, Olympics, college drafts, and perhaps most of all, the frenzied enthusiasm of a fan for his favorite team. By the 1960s, it had become the favorite sport—over baseball and football—of many fans.

It no longer was played in gym classes just for the exercise, but rather had become a status sport where season tickets were high-priced and at a premium in many cities, college and pro. A basketball game had become a big evening out, an occasion that attracted the kids and lower classes along with the wealthier people.

Basketball players were recognized, highly thought of, national celebrities.

As the sport entered the 1970s, the popularity seemed to be just beginning. More teams, jet travel, more money, more exposure all pointed to even higher pinnacles.

Basketball giants Wilt Chamberlain, left, of the L.A. Lakers, and Lew Alcindor of the Milwaukee Bucks are shown in action in 1970. The strong, agile big man has become the base upon which all pro teams find they must build.

Kelso, with Eddie Arcaro in the saddle, was an imposing figure in finishing first in the Suburban Handicap at New York's Aqueduct race track in 1961. Kelso was Horse of the Year in 1960.

chapter 5

HORSE RACING

Pari-Mutuels Hum for Sport of Kings

THE THOROUGHBREDS by Charles Morey

Charles Morey, 55, is radio-television sports editor of *The Associated Press* with a deep and abiding interest in horse racing. He doubles by making the picks for *The AP* race wire. New York-born and bred, he formerly was a staff member of the *Daily Racing Form*. He has never ridden a horse.

Thoroughbred racing, once the "Sport of Kings," long since has gone public and even more so, political. It is the oldest American spectator sport. It is the richest in money handled and the greatest revenue producer for state treasuries. It often is controversial. It is exciting, dangerous, expensive and habit-forming.

It began in 1665, more than a century before the Declaration of Independence, on Salisbury Plain, Long Island, just east of New York City. The first sponsor was Richard Nicolls, the colonial governor of New York. Nicolls was a colonel in the British army and an amateur phrasemaker. His contribution to racing was to lay out a course and donate a silver trophy to be raced for in the spring and fall. But he also established a creed still honored.

"Racing is for the improvement of the breed," he said. "It is not for the divertissement of youth." The first part of that quote still echoes throughout the turf world. The second part, well, the divertissement is for all ages.

More than 100 tracks hold meets in the 30 American states where it is legal. Something like 42,893,379 people have paid their way into thoroughbred tracks in one year for the privilege of betting $3,813,204,069 on the races. Those are official figures for 1969. They are greatly increased, of course, by the figures for harness, quarter-horse and country-fair racing.

The money wagered in the pari-mutuel machines is taxed heavily. The state takes its share, the tracks get theirs. It varies from state to state on the percentage and even whether the government or the racing promoters get the larger share of the financial pie. The tracks, of course, lay out the purses for the horsemen, who in turn pay the jockeys.

Almost a half-billion dollars was taken by the states in 1969, most of it from thoroughbred racing. The thoroughbreds produced $309,218,745 in state revenues. Harness racing accounted for $147,518,108. Country fair and quarter-horse racing added $4,762,033.

These astronomical sums clearly show the turn racing has taken, from the old sport-against-sport, horse-against-horse for a side bet custom to the colossus of today. Most legislatures now consider themselves partners in racing operations in their states.

Racing is a year-around sport, running from Jan. 1, the automatic birthday of all North American race horses, to Dec. 31. Until the 1950s, it was usually shut down in the winter in the northern part of the country but that has changed. New England and Maryland have racing virtually year-around. The long New York season begins in March and runs into December, roughly nine months.

Pari-mutuel wagering long has been the established method of betting, bookmakers having gone underground with the exception of Las Vegas, Nev., where they are legal. The last state where they operated openly was New York, which did not adopt the mutuel system of betting until 1940. However, in 1970, New York State passed legislation to permit off-track betting parlors.

It is the horse, however, that makes thoroughbred racing the glamor sport that it is. Without him, it would be open-air roulette. The thoroughbred is such a beautiful animal that to the average eye a cheap claiming horse often looks as handsome as a Kentucky Derby winner.

Although the Romans had chariot racing, which was a form of horse racing, the first race course which bore any resemblance to the tracks of today was the Smithfield track in London. It was staked out in 1174 and was the beginning of organized racing as we know it.

For more than three centuries after that, England had racing of a sort at its country fairs. Until 1512 it was just for the fun of it, with perhaps a shilling or two changing hands on the result. But in 1512 at the Chester Fair in England a prize was awarded—the first. It was a wooden ball, festooned with flowers. By 1540 that had been built up to a silver ball, worth four shillings or about $1.

In 1607 that evolved into a golden ball for the winner, value $10. But the real breakthrough came in 1609. A silversmith in Chester made a silver ball which was to go to the winner of a race. It was deemed not good enough. He made another, also rejected. After he made a third, which was accepted, the steward in charge realized he had three prizes.

That's when the win, place and show awards were born. It wasn't until 1714, under the sponsorship of Queen Anne of England, that cash prizes were paid and entry fees demanded for sweepstakes. It was in that era that the three horses appeared on the scene who are regarded as the forerunners of all accepted thoroughbred lines of today. Their names, and in racing they are legends, were Byerly Turk, Darley's Arabian and Godolphin's Arabian.

Racing grew in popularity in England in the 18th century. Late in the century races were founded which have lived on as headline events. The St. Leger Stakes was first run in England in 1776. It is the oldest race in the world.

The Epsom Oaks was first held in 1779. It still is run over a mile-and-one-half course but confined to 3-year-old fillies. The Epsom Derby—or "English Darby"—began in 1780. It also is a run of a mile-and-one-half but is for both colts and fillies.

England's celebrated Grand National Steeplechase was run for the first time in 1839. Many racing people consider it the toughest race in the world to win. It is held over a course of four miles and 856 yards at Aintree in Liverpool.

Racing is very popular in Ireland, France and other European countries and is rated the national sport of Australia, where the Melbourne Cup is rated among the world's greatest races. So, too, is the celebrated Arc de Triomphe at Longchamps in Paris. In 1969, the winner of the Arc, Levmoss, won $213,188 of a total purse of $358,700. That was topped only by the Arlington-Washington Futurity in Chicago where Sonny Werblin's Silent Screen was the winner. The gross purse was $366,075. Silent Screen earned $206,075, a bit less than the Arc winner.

Most of the racing outside the United States is on grass and some of it—but not all—is clockwise. All the racing in the United States is counterclockwise, meaning the horses always make left turns whereas some foreign runners turn right.

If the Kentucky Derby winner were to race a cheap plater, the difference would be obvious and startling. Class would show instantly. The claiming horse would appear to be pulling an invisible plow.

There have been many horses who became household names in the United States. In the 20th century, the still incomparable Man O'War; Kelso, who earned almost $2 million and is the all-time money-winnings champion; Native Dancer, the great Gray Ghost; Citation, the one the professional horsemen rave about; Dr. Fager, possibly the fastest of them all; and Whirlaway, not really a great horse but a legendary crowd-pleaser with his prairie twister style of finishing.

Spectators lined a wooden rail in 1953 to watch the running of the ABC Cup race, most important race at Burnette Downs on the Barkly Tableland in Northern Territory in Australia. Note clockwise direction of track.

Ten horses, headed by Kelso with his record earnings of $1,977,896, have joined the millionaire's club. The others include Round Table, the grass specialist with $1,749,869; the brilliant Buckpasser with $1,462,014; Nashua with $1,288,565; courageous Carry Back, $1,241,165; flashy Damascus, $1,176,781; Citation, $1,085,760; turf-loving Fort Marcy, $1,043,280 (through 1970); the crack Californian, Native Diver, $1,026,500; and Dr. Fager, who squeezed in at $1,002,642.

There were great horses who did not make it to the million mark but would be rated over many of those who did. The reason usually was that they raced at a time when purses were much smaller. Man O'War, for instance, earned only $249,465. Swaps went to stud after earning $848,900. The golden gelding, Armed, retired with earnings of $814,475. Native Dancer's earnings were $785,240. Assault gathered in $675,470 in purses. Tom Fool picked up $570,165 and Equipoise won just $338,610.

The most spectacular phase of racing is the Triple Crown, the name given to three races held in the spring of the year which are exclusively for 3-year-olds. That's the time a race horse grows up, although he is not considered fully mature until 4. The Triple Crown races are the Kentucky Derby at Churchill Downs in Louisville, the Preakness Stakes at Pimlico in Baltimore and the Belmont Stakes in New York.

There have been eight Triple Crown winners, the last in 1948. Sir Barton was the first to do it in 1919, Gallant Fox in 1930, his son, Omaha, in 1935, War Admiral in 1937, Whirlaway in 1941, Count Fleet in 1943, Assault in 1946 and Citation in 1948.

Racing has been more thoroughly reported and spotlighted in the current century but there were giants in the dim past. They include Kingston, the horse who still holds the record for most races won; Domino, the Black Whirlwind; the swift Salvator, Hindoo and Henry of Navarre and a little red horse named Aristides, who won the first Kentucky Derby in 1875.

If the horse is king on the race course, the jockey is crown prince. There have been many great riders but none better than Eddie Arcaro, the swarthy Kentuckian who was "Banana Nose" to the railbirds. When he rode a winner the name was affectionate. On a loser Heady Eddie heard it derisively.

Eddie, who quit the saddle on Nov. 18, 1961, rode for 31 years. He was on 4,779 winners and his mounts earned $30,039,543. In number of winning mounts he is surpassed by the all-time champion, Willie Shoemaker, who took over as No. 1 in 1970 when he handled his 6,033rd victorious mount and then kept right on going. Arcaro also is topped by the retired Johnny Longden, who stopped after 6,032 winners.

Arcaro was hot-tempered and even ruthless in his younger days. In 1942 he drew a one-year suspension for trying to put another jockey, Vincent Nodarse, over the rail at Aqueduct. Arcaro was riding Occupation and Nodarse was on Breezing Home in the Cowdin Stakes. Nodarse had angered Eddie and he was still blazing when the stewards called him up. He allegedly said, "I wanted to kill him."

The stewards gave Eddie a year to think that over and when he returned in September of 1943 he had matured. He became The Master, acknowledged as such by the other jockeys.

Eddie Arcaro, who was to pilot five Kentucky Derby winners in his career as a jockey, was aboard Nashua (5) in winning the Preakness over Saratoga (4), Nick Shuk aboard, in 1955.

Arcaro could do it all: rate a speed horse in front and save something for the lung-lancing final quarter of a mile; drop back with a one-run horse and gun the leaders down in the stretch; come through an opening so narrow an alley cat might flinch and turn away.

Eddie won the Kentucky Derby five times, sharing the record for that race with Bill Hartack. He captured six renewals of the Belmont, holding the mark for that stake jointly with Jimmy McLaughlin, a star of the 19th century. He scored in the Preakness six times, an all-time record. He is the only jockey to win the Triple Crown twice, with Whirlaway in 1941 and Citation in 1948.

Shoemaker became an outstanding rider. He possessed all the finesse that Arcaro had. But Wee Willie, at 4-11 and 100 pounds, lacked something of Arcaro's wiry strength. In 1966 he rode Dr. Fager, a heavy-headed horse, to a second-place finish in the Champagne Stakes at Aqueduct and trainer Johnny Nerud replaced The Shoe after that with another boy. That sort of thing never happened to Arcaro, who rode at between 112 and 115 pounds in his prime.

In any rating of jockeys, Longden, despite his great number of victories, would not be ranked with Arcaro or Shoemaker in all-around horsemanship. Whatever he could do, they could do just a little better. The moody Bill Hartack, he of the five Derby victories and frequent controversies, went past the 4,000 mark in winners in 1970 and appeared headed for a bid at Shoemaker's record.

Other great riders of modern times included Gentleman Johnny Rotz, restless Bobby Ussery, Eddie Belmonte, Angel Cordero Jr., and the matchless band of boys from Panama who have dominated the riding ranks in the decade of the

Jockey Johnny Longden, left, chatted with Sunny Jim Fitzsimmons at Aqueduct race track in New York in 1961. Longden amassed a total of 6,032 winners in his racing career. Fitzsimmons was one of the most famous of all trainers in the sport.

1960s. Included in their number were Braulio Baeza, Manuel Ycaza, Jorge Velasquez, Jacinto Vasquez, Laffit Pincay Jr., and Heliodoro Gustines.

In previous generations there were Earl Sande, who was immortalized by Damon Runyon as a "Handy Guy Named Sande"; George Woolf, the money-riding "Iceman"; Sonny Workman, strong and smart and fast with his fists; Cowboy Wayne D. Wright, Pony McAtee and Charlie Kurtsinger.

Going back to the turn of the century and beyond, there were Tod Sloan, the toast of Broadway and the man who invented the "monkey on a stick" style of riding; Jimmy McLaughlin, "Snapper" Garrison, Walter Miller and a quiet, patient Negro named Isaac Murphy, the first to ride three Kentucky Derby winners.

The two-dollar bettor undeniably supports racing today but it has always attracted wealthy people of a sporting turn of mind. At one time they not only dominated it but kept it going—the Belmonts, Vanderbilts, Whitneys, Woodwards, Wideners, among others. It also attracted people such as Diamond Jim Brady and Harry Sinclair, the oil magnate, who did a stretch in jail.

Among the great trainers were Sunny Jim Fitzsimmons, Max Hirsch and Hirsch Jacobs, Ben Jones and Jimmy Jones, James Rowe, Sam Hildreth, Preston Burch, R. H. McDaniel and Eddie Neloy.

Fitzsimmons, the beloved "Sunny Jim," trained for the Phipps and Woodwards and handled such champions as Gallant Fox, Omaha, Granville, Johnstown, Nashua and Bold Ruler. He had been a jockey in his youth.

Ben Jones, the hard-fisted perfectionist from Missouri, was the king of Kentucky Derby conditioners. He saddled six Derby winners, a record. Rowe sent out eight Belmont champions with Hildreth on his heels at seven and Fitzsimmons next with six. The all-time Preakness leader among trainers was Robert W. Walden, who won the race seven times in the 19th century.

There is no record of the trainers in Gov. Nicolls' time. Racing was pretty much catch-as-catch-can. It was done in heats with two needed to win. The heats were either three-mile or four-mile events. The horses got little rest in between. There was a 30-minute rest between four milers and a 20-minute respite between three-mile heats. The pace of those races was much slower than the pell-mell action of the later period.

Certain other factors slowed the growth of racing in colonial America. In the 17th century in Jamestown, Va., a famine forced the colonists to put thoroughbred steak on the menu for a time. Nobody ever grew to like it. But it did keep people alive.

Late in the 17th century things began to pick up. In 1699 when Williamsburg became the capital of Virginia, it was noticeable that the population of that busy town increased from 2,000 to 6,000 during racing week.

In the 18th century racing centers sprang up in Maryland, still one of the great turf states. In mid-18th century, Gov. Samuel Ogle of Maryland founded the Belair Stud, the forerunner of the great stable that two centuries later was to produce outstanding horses such as the father-and-son Triple Crown combination of Gallant Fox and Omaha and the brilliant Nashua for the Woodwards, William Sr. and William Jr.

There were other turf centers dotting the colonial map. Charleston, S.C., founded the first Jockey Club in 1734. The Quakers in Pennsylvania showed a surprising relish for racing. William Penn imported an English stallion, Tamerlane, in 1699. In 1766 the Philadelphia Jockey Club was formed.

In the 18th century there was racing at various times in New Jersey, New Hampshire, Rhode Island and Connecticut. Connecticut later abandoned the sport but in 1970 a big push was started to bring back racing in that state.

George Washington was partial to horse racing. He was a familiar figure at race meetings in Philadelphia and Annapolis. He even took time out from fighting the Revolutionary War to buy a stallion named Ranger, who was standing in Windham, Conn. Gen. Washington purchased Ranger for 125 hogsheads of tobacco, worth about $3,000.

Ranger became a successful sire. He sired a horse named Magnolia who raced for Washington until 1788 when the first president sold the horse to "Light Horse Harry" Lee, the father of Gen. Robert E. Lee, of Civil War greatness. The purchase price was 5,000 acres of Kentucky land. Kentucky then was part of Virginia.

Another president of the United States, Andrew Jackson, was an active horse racing enthusiast. U. S. Grant was rated a superb handler of horses. More recently, President Nixon saw Majestic Prince win the Kentucky Derby in 1969 and Dwight D. Eisenhower, shortly after leaving the White House in 1961, attended the Belmont, won by Sherluck.

After the Revolutionary War, with the United States on a going basis and anti-English feeling running high, there was some anti-racing legislation in the 13 original states. Racing began to drift westward, to Kentucky, Ohio, Illinois, Tennessee and finally to California.

But in 1821 the celebrated Union Course opened on Long Island, not too far from Salisbury Plain or the sites of the Belmont and Aqueduct tracks. It had a skinned racing surface which became the model for tracks of the future.

Match races provided most of the color in racing at that time. They usually began with strong drinks which turned to strong talk. There were no racing associations to put up fat purses. The matches featured side bets with a sizable forfeit in case of a scratch.

In May 1823, a match race at the Union Course featured the North versus the South. The Northern champion, Eclipse, raced the Dixie representative, Henry, for a side bet of $20,000. Both horses were backed by syndicates.

The population of New York at that time was 150,000. It was claimed that 60,000 fans saw the match race, which seems unlikely. However, a large contingent of Southern fans, estimated at 20,000, made the trip. One of them was Andrew Jackson, then governor of Florida. Daniel Tompkins, vice president of the United States, was present.

There were three heats of four miles. Henry won the first, Eclipse the next two. It was estimated that $200,000 changed hands in bets between the Northern and Southern sports. That was a fantastic figure for those days.

Just before the opening guns of the Civil War in 1861, the face of racing was beginning to change. The distance of the average event was shrinking from four miles to one. Formal racing was being held as far from Long Island as San Francisco and Sacramento, Calif.

Southern breeding centers, at least the old line ones, were devastated by the war. Kentucky emerged as the leading breeding center after Appomattox. Something new, handicaps in which weights were assigned arbitrarily, came into being. Organized bookmaking began to take hold.

The battle of Gettysburg was fought in July 1863, and one month later Saratoga Springs, destined to become one of the most popular tracks in the country, held its first meeting. The famed Spa in upstate New York is the oldest continuing race course in the country.

In the last third of the 19th century racing began to bloom in earnest. The first running of the Belmont in 1867 saw a filly, Ruthless, finish in front. The Preakness was next to get going as Survivor won the initial running in 1873. Aristides took the first Kentucky Derby in 1875.

Bookmakers dominated the betting at this time. The pari-mutuel system of betting which allows the public to make its own odds, originated in France. In the latter part of the 19th century it was tried without success in New York, New Jersey, Kentucky, Maryland, Chicago and Washington, D.C. It was a failure each time. The legislatures either did not realize the full potential of the taxes that could be placed on it or more likely could not have passed that kind of law in the political climate of the times.

The tremendous change in pari-mutuel betting is dramatically illustrated by these facts. In the 1890s just about the largest betting setup in the country was at the Brighton Beach track in Brooklyn. There were 60 licensed bookmakers, each of whom paid the track $100 a day to operate. The state received nothing. No figures on betting were ever announced but it was estimated the total bookmaker handle was close to $1 million a day.

Going into the 1970s at New York's massive "Big A," Aqueduct, and Belmont, the betting ran better than $3 million a day. The state took out $300,000 or more each day as its share. The tracks got close to $200,000 for purses and operating expenses. The world record handle for one day was set at Belmont on June 7, 1969, when $6,371,829 was bet.

Brooklyn was the racing capital of New York in the late 19th century although there are no tracks there now. Among the colorful owners of that time were the Dwyer brothers, sons of a Brooklyn butcher. They were high-dollar plungers and owned some famous horses, including Hindoo, Miss Woodford, Hanover, Tremont and Kingston. Kingston won 89 races, tops in turf history.

Other prominent owners of that period were the Keenes, J. R. and his son, Foxhall; the Belmonts; Marcus Daly, the Montana copper king, and a man with the unusual name of James Ben Ali Haggin. The middle part of that name was a tribute to his grandfather, a Turkish army officer. Haggin was a Kentuckian and around the turn of the century controlled, in partnership with Lloyd Tevis, a sprawling breeding operation.

The partners owned 400,000 acres of grazing land in Southern California, 100,000 additional acres in New Mexico and Arizona and the Rancho del Paso near Sacramento, Calif., a little layout of 44,800 acres. They had 30 stallions standing at their farms, servicing hundreds of broodmares. For the 1900 Futurity Stakes, Haggin made 196 nominations.

He won the 1886 Kentucky Derby with Ben Ali, named for his grandfather. Haggin finally centered his holdings in Kentucky where he had the Elmendorf Stud. Many of the great breeding farms of the Blue Grass region later were located on land he formerly owned.

In the latter part of the 19th century new race tracks sprang up. The Fair Grounds in New Orleans was opened in 1872. In 1894 the old Aqueduct course was built and was so rickety that the Gay Ninety wisecrackers called it, "A shanty on stilts."

Racing in those days was not supervised as it was later when there were film patrols to record rough-riding and patrol judges stationed at strategic spots around the course. The jockeys believed in the free enterprise system. They got away with anything they could.

The 1893 American Derby at Washington Park was a perfect example. There were 25 false starts and the field was at the post for more than an hour. Some of the smarter riders helped effect the false starts. One of the greats of that period, "Snapper" Garrison, had wisely dismounted from his horse, Boundless, each time there was a false start. When the break came he had a fresh mount. He won the race.

This was a time when Tod Sloan was rocketing to the top. He was the first "monkey on a stick" rider. He rode hunched over and leaning forward, instead of straight up in the saddle as a cavalryman in full charging order.

Tod was a Broadway personality and inspired at least one George M. Cohan musical. He married two actresses, demonstrating in the most sincere manner his love of the theater. At one time he was the personal jockey for the Prince of

From the Keenland Library comes this historic finish of Man O'War's hardest race, against John P. Grier in the Dwyer at New York's Aqueduct race track in 1920.

Wales. Two of his closest friends were Diamond Jim Brady and Lillian Russell. In spite of his playboy proclivities, Tod was a great jockey.

It was around the turn of the century that political reformers wheeled up some big guns in an attempt to blast racing out of the picture. Many tracks closed in the early 1900s, both in the United States and Canada, which had entered the picture with the first Queens Plate at Woodbine in 1860.

The governor of New York, Charles Evans Hughes, backed legislation which closed racing down in that state for two years, 1911 and 1912. It was resumed in 1913.

For three decades in New York, racing was conducted with oral betting, a unique system in which the bettor more or less whispered his wager to a bookmaker. First, however, he established his credit with a sizable cash deposit. There was no revenue to the state. In 1934 New York State gave its legal assent to open bookmaking which lasted until the mutuels arrived in 1940.

Pari-mutuel betting in other areas took root just before World War I. Matt Winn, Mr. Kentucky Derby, got into a hassle with the city fathers of Louisville on Derby Day, 1908. To block their drive against bookmaking he used the mutuels. The $2 mutuel ticket was born in 1911. In 1912 Maryland passed pari-mutuel legislation.

History was made at Churchill Downs in 1915. A filly named Regret belied her name by winning the Kentucky Derby. She is the only member of her sex to do it, although fillies have won both the Belmont and Preakness.

Greater history was made at the Nursery Stud in Kentucky, owned by August Belmont II, on March 29, 1917. A red chestnut colt by Fair Play from a mare named Mahubah was foaled. The mare's name, in Arabic, meant, "May good things be with you." The colt was named Man O'War. Fair Play's principal claim to fame before that had been in 1908 when he came within a head of beating the classy Colin in the Belmont. Colin never lost a race.

Man O'War was consigned to the Saratoga Yearling Sales. He had already been named, which is unusual. Samuel Riddle purchased him for $5,000, a fair price in 1918 but hardly headline news. In fact, that same day J. E. Widener went to $14,000 to buy a colt named Fair Gain. F. M. Taylor paid $13,600 for Rouleau, never heard of again.

If Man O'War wasn't the greatest horse ever to race in America—and there are plenty of facts to support the theory that he was—he was the most spectacular. He was a roaring red comet. He was an odds-on favorite every time he raced. He won 20 races in 21 tries, each victory by a sizable margin.

His only defeat came in his 2-year-old year, in the 1919 Sanford Stakes at Saratoga, to the incredibly named Upset. Big Red was ridden by Johnny Loftus, who had him in trouble for most of the race and did not get him clear until the final stages. Man O'War was a flying second at the wire.

Long after his retirement to stud in Kentucky, Man O'War's groom, in showing the aging stallion to visitors, referred to him as "The Mostest Hoss." It's a phrase hard to dispute.

Man O'War set three world records, two American marks and three track records. He obviously would have set more. But he was put to a drive only once, in the 1920 Dwyer Stakes at Aqueduct, where a game colt named John P. Grier hooked him at the furlong pole and may have headed him for one stride. Big Red just bounded away to win by a length-and-one-half.

A contemporary of Man O'War, although they never met, was the extraordinary campaigner, Exterminator. He raced for Willis Sharpe Kilmer and won the Kentucky Derby of 1918. Like Kelso a gelding, Exterminator was known as "Old Bones" because of his country-like appearance. He was no show horse. But he was a horse of high heart and great stamina.

Exterminator appeared in 100 races and won 50 of them. He was second 17 times and third 17 times. He won at distances from 5½ furlongs to 2¼ miles. He won on 16 different race tracks. His earnings for eight years of campaigning came to $252,996. In 1942, at the ancient age of 27 for a horse, he was paraded at Belmont as part of a War Bond rally. The old swaybacked charger pranced before the crowd as though he were in a parade to the post.

One of the most colorful owners in the 1920s and 1930s was the courtly Col. E. R. Bradley, who became "One-Two Ed" in Kentucky Derby history. Bradley won the Derby four times and twice saw his horses run one-two. In 1921 it was Behave Yourself and Black Servant in that order. Bubbling Over and Bagenbaggage did it in 1926. In 1932, the colonel won with Burgoo King and in 1933 with Brokers Tip. That last was the race in which Don Meade, riding the winner, and Herb Fisher, on the second horse Head Play, belted each other with hand and whip in the stretch run.

Colonel Bradley, testifying before a congressional committee, was asked his occupation. He replied simply, "I am a gambler." He then asked to be excused in order to watch one of his horses run at a nearby Maryland track. Half the committee went with him.

A number of new and famous tracks opened in the 1920s, Hialeah Park in Miami in 1925, the new Washington Park in Chicago in 1926, Lincoln Fields in that city that same year and the Arlington Park in Chicago in 1927.

It was in 1927 that another turf milestone was passed. A race was announced on the public address system for the first time. It was at Bowie in Maryland. The caller was the inimitable Clem McCarthy, of the gravel voice and machine-gun delivery.

After Sir Barton's first Triple Crown victory in 1919, it was 11 years before any horse did it again. The second was Gallant Fox, the Bear from Belair, who carried those famous silks home in front in the 1930 Kentucky Derby, Preakness and Belmont. His son, the long-striding Omaha, did the same thing in 1935.

The year 1930 was one of the greatest vintage seasons of all time. Among the 2-year-olds that year were Equipoise, Twenty Grand, Mate and Jamestown, the last a great sprinter. The others were redoubtable stayers.

In the 1930 Pimlico Futurity, Equipoise was left at the post with Sonny Workman in the saddle. He was sent after the field and with a sensational stretch charge got up to win from no less a pair than Twenty Grand and Mate. Twenty Grand won the 1931 Kentucky Derby and Belmont while Mate took the Preakness.

Equipoise was sidelined with a hoof injury early in the 1931 season but came back in 1932 to rule as handicap king for three years. He figured in the climactic scene of the classic Broadway comedy, "Three Men on a Horse." It revolved around the 1934 Metropolitan Handicap at Belmont which he won on the track but lost on a disqualification in the stewards' stand to Mr. Khayyam. That same Metropolitan carried added drama. A horse named Chase Me, who had been used as a saddle mount by Mrs. John Bosley and then became a racing star, broke his leg on the stretch turn and was destroyed.

Probably the most incredible and mysterious horse death of all time occurred in 1932 when the Australian ace, Phar Lap, was brought to this country. He raced once, scoring a galloping victory in the Agua Caliente Handicap. A short time later he died while grazing in a California meadow. There were loud cries that he had been poisoned.

Eventually, however, a theory was accepted that he had eaten grass which had been sprayed with an insecticide. His carcass was mounted by a taxidermist and was on display in the Belmont paddock for a short time before it was shipped back to Australia. An autopsy on this great runner showed that his heart weighed 14 pounds, about five more than the average.

In 1933 no fewer than 10 states legalized pari-mutuel betting. At the end of 1934 the Santa Anita track near Los Angeles opened. The feature of its first meeting was the $100,000 Santa Anita Handicap, the forerunner of the dozens of hundred-grand races which became almost routine.

In the mid-1930s the photo finish camera came into being. Until then all races had been called by the placing judges on the finish line. The great majority were unquestionably honest, competent men. But a few years after the camera was introduced many people wondered how many races of the past had been miscalled at the finish.

In 1933, with no photo finish cameras, there was one dead heat recorded. In 1934 there were six. In 1935, an experimental year with the camera, the number went to 20. In 1936, the first full season, there were 115 dead heats on American tracks. Every year since they have been numbered in the hundreds.

There was no photo finish camera needed for the most ballyhooed match race of the 1930s, the one between Seabiscuit, the California champion, and War Admiral, the pride of the East. It was held at Pimlico on Nov. 1, 1938, and Biscuit, with Iceman Georgie Woolf up, whipped under the wire a winner by four lengths. Woolf swiveled in the saddle at the wire to make a derisive gesture at the losing jockey, Charlie Kurtsinger, whom he didn't like.

It was in 1938 that Arcaro won his first Derby, which also happened to be the first for trainer Ben Jones, who saddled five more in later years for the Calumet Farm. In 1938, however, Jones was training for the Woolford Farm of Herbert M. Woolf of Kansas City. He boosted Eddie into the saddle on Lawrin, who saved ground all the way under the canny Arcaro to beat the late-running Dauber by a length.

Arcaro and Jones also teamed up for Derby victories on Whirlaway in 1941, Citation in 1948 and Hill Gail in 1952. Jones was a resolute type and when he was saddling Hill Gail for the Derby the horse began to act up. Big Ben hauled off and clouted the colt across the nose.

Hill Gail quieted down and won the race by two lengths. Citation was Jones' favorite. In 1948 Calumet started an entry of Citation and Coaltown, a racy runner of intense speed. Arcaro wasn't sure which horse he wanted to ride. Jones told him to take Citation.

Halfway down the backstretch at Churchill Downs, it was Coaltown by six lengths. Arcaro was wondering what he was doing on Citation. He found out at the head of the stretch. Citation went by Coaltown in an eighth of a mile to win by three-and-one-half lengths.

The Derby, the first of the Triple Crown races each year, is $1^1/_4$ miles in length. The Preakness is 110 yards shorter, measuring $1^3/_{16}$ miles. The Belmont is the longest, stretching a mile-and-one-half.

By the time Arcaro reached the Belmont he knew Citation was a super horse. He told some people in the hearing of Ben and Jimmy Jones, his son, that the only way he could lose was to fall off. He nearly did when Citation stumbled leaving the gate. But after that it was an open gallop, Citation by eight.

Arcaro never classed Whirlaway with Citation and few others did, either. But Whacky Whirly, as he was called for his erratic behavior, posted spectacular victories in the Triple Crown of 1941. His Derby triumph was his greatest. Jones had put special run-out equipment on him to keep him on a straight course. Arcaro got through on the inside on the stretch turn and knocked out the contenders in the stretch to win by eight lengths.

Count Fleet, the 1943 Triple Crown champion, was probably the nearest thing to Man O'War in his way of running. The Count ran in front. He was unbeaten as a 3-year-old and virtually unchallenged. He won the Belmont by 25 lengths.

Gallant Fox, Earle Sande in the saddle, romped to finish line to win the 56th running of the Kentucky Derby at Churchill Downs in Louisville in 1930. Gallant Fox won the Triple Crown of racing that year, adding the Preakness and the Belmont to the Derby win.

Other prominent horses of the 1940s included Alsab, probably the greatest bargain buy of all time; Assault, the club-footed comet who won the Triple Crown in 1946 for the King Ranch of Texas, and Stymie, the most incredible claim in racing history.

Chicago attorney Al Sabath purchased Alsab for $700 as a yearling and the colt won $350,015. He won the 1942 Preakness and was second in both the Kentucky Derby and Belmont. In September of that year Alsab defeated Whirlaway in a desperate match race finish, winning by a slim nose at Narragansett Park.

Assault, who injured one hoof by stepping on a pointed object as a yearling, won the Derby by eight lengths, the Preakness by a neck and the Belmont by three lengths.

Stymie was bred by the King Ranch in Texas and his trainer, Max Hirsch, thought so little of him as a juvenile that he put him in a $1,500 claiming race at Belmont on June 2, 1943. Another great trainer, the renowned Hirsch Jacobs, liked the colt. He claimed him and went on to win $918,485 with the stormy stretch runner.

Racing managed to stay open for most of World War II, although the West Coast tracks were closed down and Florida was blacked out in 1943. But on Jan. 2, 1945, the ax fell. All racing was suspended for the duration. It was not resumed until after VE Day on May 8, 1945. The war was still on in the Pacific at that time.

One of the more memorable happenings in racing during the war years was the triple dead heat in the 1944 Carter Handicap at Aqueduct in which Brownie, Bossuet and Wait A Bit finished all even. There have been 10 others of that kind since the photo finish camera was introduced but none in stakes races.

A poignant turf drama was played out in mid-January 1951, although the full extent of it was not realized at the time. A speedball of a colt from California, Your Host, fell during the running of the San Pascual Handicap at Santa Anita. His right foreleg was fractured in four places. Normally this would have meant a quick death.

But not this time. The veterinarians fought to save the colt, who was owned by William E. Goetz, and they did. He went to stud and ultimately sired the superb Kelso.

One of the most handsome and strongest horses ever to run on the American turf was foaled in 1949. His name was Tom Fool. He raced for the Greentree Stud. He was the handicap champion of 1953 and, over-all, won 21 of his 30 races while earning $570,165.

One of Tom Fool's rivals for the racing headlines, although plans to match them never materialized, was Native Dancer, Alfred Gwynne Vanderbilt's gray champion. The Dancer came out the year after Tom Fool and won 21 of his 22 races. His only defeat was in the 1953 Kentucky Derby which cost him the Triple Crown, since he won the Preakness and Belmont.

Willie Shoemaker was the riding sensation of 1953. He rode 485 winners, an all-time record. The Shoe was only 22 years old at the time.

In 1955 there was a fierce coast-to-coast rivalry between Nashua, of the Eastern Belair Stud, and Swaps, the speed-burning California colt owned by Rex Ellsworth. They met only twice and honors were even. Swaps hung it on Nashua

Native Dancer, one of racing's all-time champions, was piloted by Eric Guerin in this driving finish to win the Preakness at Pimlico race track over Jamie K (2), Eddie Arcaro aboard, in 1953.

in the Kentucky Derby and the Belair bay blistered his rival with a six-and-one-half length trouncing in a match race at Washington Park.

A stretch runner named Needles, racing for the D & H stable, made a splash in 1956 by winning the Kentucky Derby and Belmont, although losing in the Preakness to Calumet's Fabius. Needles was the first Florida-bred horse to win a classic race. Since that time, however, there have been many and Florida sought to challenge Kentucky as the horse capital of the country.

There was a rich crop of 3-year-olds in 1957. Bold Ruler, who later became a fantastic sire, won the Preakness after Iron Liege nosed out Gallant Man in the Derby. That was the Derby in which Shoemaker, on Gallant Man, misjudged the finish line, stopped riding for one second, and lost the race to Iron Liege, with Hartack up.

Gallant Man won the Belmont as Shoemaker made amends. That was the race that established the classic quote. As The Shoe went by Bold Ruler and Arcaro at the head of the stretch, a grinning Shoemaker shouted at Eddie, "Hey, look at the hold I have on this horse." Gallant Man won the race by eight lengths.

The most successful member of the class of 1957, however, was Round Table, who couldn't handle either Gallant Man or Bold Ruler on a dirt track but who turned out to be a champion in grass racing, which was just beginning to zoom in popularity. It now plays a major part in American racing.

Round Table, who raced for Travis Kerr, was a durable colt. He started 66 times and won 43 races while finishing second eight times and third on five occasions. His earnings of $1,749,869 put him in second place among all-time winners. He raced 16 times on the grass and won 14 of those races.

Round Table did a lot of his racing in California where in 1958 one of the most unusual horses of the century had a brief fling. Nobody would ever put in a claim of greatness for Silky Sullivan but he may have packed more thrills to the furlong than most great horses. At least, he did when he won.

Silky would drop so far out of it as to seem not only in the next race but on the next day. He would explode in the final quarter of a mile and sometimes he would pass everybody. He once came from 41 lengths behind the leader to win a 6½-furlong race. He won the 1958 Santa Anita Derby with a roaring rally but never got out of a gallop at Churchill Downs in the Kentucky Derby, which went to Tim Tam. Silky was a laboring 12th. In the Preakness he moved up to eighth. He skipped the Belmont.

In 1960 a horse named Kelso came along and for the next five years everything in racing was measured against him. He was owned by Mrs. Richard C. duPont. He started only three times as a 2-year-old in 1959 and won just one of those. He had been gelded. It was explained later that it was because of stifle trouble. There are many reasons why horses are gelded and that's just one of them.

Kelso was "Horse of the Year" for five consecutive seasons, from 1960 through 1964. No other horse has come close to that. He ran 63 times, won 39, was second 12 times, third twice and out of the money in 10 races.

He won the Jockey Club Gold Cup, run at both Aqueduct and Belmont, five straight times, starting in 1960. This two-mile event is probably America's premier race for stayers, at least on a dirt track. Kelso, while not really a grass runner, took four shots at the Washington International at Laurel. He was second in 1961 to TV Lark, second in 1962 to Match II, second in 1963 to Mongo and a winner finally in 1964 in the record time of 2:23⅘ for a mile-and-one-half on grass. That mark was reduced by Czar Alexander to 2:23⅖ five years later at Santa Anita, where the turf course is partly downhill.

Kelso, being a gelding, raced until he was 9 years old, starting once at that age and finishing fourth in his final race at Hialeah in March of 1966. That brought in $500 to boost his total earnings to $1,977,896. Mrs. DuPont then made him the most expensive saddle horse in the history of the bridle path.

Jack Price's Carry Back, another of the exclusive turf millionaire's club, provided a Cinderella chapter in the early 1960s. He won the Derby and Preakness, racing in the silks of Mrs. K. Price, Jack's wife, but failed to stay in the Belmont. He defied his own bloodlines, being by an obscure sire, Saggy, from a mare called Joppy, who was purchased for $150 after being barred from racing because she was unruly.

The next great horse—and he was truly that—was Ogden Phipps' Buckpasser, a son of Tom Fool and a foal of 1963. He was the first horse ever to make a million by the time he was 3. In two seasons of campaigning, as a juvenile in 1965 and a 3-year-old in 1966, he won $1,218,874. An injury kept him out of the Derby, Preakness and Belmont.

He won 13 straight races in 1966 after finishing second in his first start of the year at Hialeah. He was a lazy workhorse in the morning but a tiger in the afternoon in the heat of a race. He made one of the most amazing finishes ever seen on an American race track to win the so-called "chicken" Flamingo Stakes in 1966 at Hialeah.

There were nine horses in the mile-and-one-furlong race but the track had decreed no betting because of the presence of Buckpasser. A minus pool and subsequent loss of money by the track was feared. Buckpasser took the lead at the head of the stretch and seemed on his way to an easy victory when he decided to loaf in mid-stretch.

Abe's Hope, with a furious rush, went by him and opened up a daylight lead with less than a furlong to go. It was then that Buckpasser got mad. He thrust his head out and began to take two strides for one by Abe's Hope. He nailed the leader one jump from home and was a nose in front at the wire. Some people who saw the race refused to believe it.

In winning the Arlington Classic, Buckpasser lowered the mile record to 1:32$^3/_5$, a mark since topped by Dr. Fager's clocking of 1:32$^1/_5$ in 1968 at the same track.

Mrs. Edith Bancroft's Damascus and Tartan Stable's Dr. Fager were both 3-year-olds in 1967 and both wound up millionaires. They were entirely different types, however.

Damascus was a well-mannered colt who could be rated well off the pace and sent after the money as the field wheeled past the three-eighths pole. That's the way he won the 1967 Preakness and Belmont. Dr. Fager, who ducked the Triple Crown races in 1967 on advice of trainer John Nerud, was a fuming front-runner. He did not want to be passed. It cost him dearly in some big races when pacemakers took him too fast in the early going and he tired in the stretch.

The two stars met four times over a two-season span, 1967 and 1968, and broke even. Dr. Fager defeated Damascus in the 1967 Gotham at Aqueduct and lost to the stretch-runner in the Woodward Stakes that fall at the same track. In 1968, Damascus captured the Brooklyn, beating Dr. Fager, after losing to the good Doctor in the Suburban.

In 1968, the most controversial Kentucky Derby since the 1933 shoot-out between Meade on Brokers Tip and Fisher on Head Play took place. It seemed routine enough at first. Peter Fuller's Dancer's Image defeated Calumet's Forward Pass by a length-and-one-half under a brilliant ride by Bobby Ussery.

The real race started afterward and was still being run more than two years later in the courts. The stewards announced they had found evidence of a pain-killer called butazolidin in a urinalysis taken of the winner after the race. The Kentucky Racing Commission ordered that first money be given to the owners of Forward Pass.

Fuller decided to fight and a long legal hassle began. More than two years later, in December 1970, a circuit court judge in Kentucky, Henry Meigs, ruled that Fuller was entitled to the purse money and not the Calumet Farm. Meigs found fault with the actions of the Kentucky Racing Commission and the chemist who ran the test.

But the Kentucky Commission voted to appeal Judge Meigs' verdict and as the field headed into 1971 another long legal race appeared inevitable.

There was no controversy surrounding the 1969 Derby, which went to Frank McMahon's Majestic Prince, with Hartack up and with President Nixon looking on. Or in 1970 when a longshot, Dust Commander, was an upset winner.

Majestic Prince also won the Preakness but failed in the Belmont, taken by the racy Arts and Letters. It was the fifth time since 1948 that a horse which had won the Derby and Preakness failed to stay the testing mile-and-one-half of the Belmont.

Others who had tried and failed were Tim Tam in 1958, Carry Back in 1961,

Northern Dancer in 1964, and Kauai King in 1966. Majestic Prince did not race again after the Belmont. Trainer Johnny Longden had not wanted to run him, suspecting some latent hurt, but was overruled by owner McMahon. Longden was right. The Prince came out of the race with a leg ailment.

In the 1970 Keeneland yearling sales, McMahon purchased a full brother to Majestic Prince for the record sum of $510,000. The colt was named Crowned Prince and sent to England for racing there.

At about the same time, the 1970 champion in England, Charles Engelhard's

Below, Diane Crump, second from right, became the first woman to ride in a regular race at a major track when she rode Bridle 'N Bit in the seventh race at Hialeah in Florida in 1969. At right, she's a bit mud splattered after a win in the first race of the 1970 Kentucky Derby program.

Nijinsky was flown to the United States to take up stud duty. Nijinsky was just one of a long line of European champions to make that journey, although he was American-owned. He was syndicated for stud for the record sum of $5,440,000, which broke down to 32 shares at $170,000 each. He is standing at Claiborne Farm, Kentucky.

A bright new page was written in racing in 1969 and it was only coincidental that it came along at a time when the women's liberation movement was accelerating.

On Feb. 7, 1969, Diane Crump became the first woman to ride in a regular race at a major track. She handled Bridle 'N Bit in a race at Hialeah and finished 10th. Slightly more than a year later she became the first girl to ride in a Kentucky Derby, winding up 15th in a 17-horse field aboard a horse named Fathom.

It remained for slim Barbara Jo Rubin to become the first girl to make it to the winner's circle at a race track. On Feb. 22, 1969, she rode Cohesian to a neck triumph in a race run under the lights at Charles Town, W.Va.

Television has not played the part in horse racing that it has in the post-World War II boom in other sports, baseball, football and basketball, for instance. Most television of racing is regional. Only the Triple Crown events get national coverage. There are many reasons for this. The networks don't want to use prime time for racing on TV. Some track owners are fearful that television might hurt the gate in some way.

One luxury available to the American racing fan—at a price, of course—not accessible to devotees anywhere else in the world is printed past performances of horses and daily charts of the races. These are compiled by the Triangle Publications, which publish papers in seven cities—New York, Chicago, Los Angeles, Miami, Toronto, Seattle and Vancouver.

The New York paper is the *Morning Telegraph,* the others are all Daily Racing Forms, sacrilegiously but affectionately known as "The Bible" to turf followers.

The Jockey Club, a posh organization with offices on Park Avenue in New York, was for a long time the dominant rules-making body in American racing. But gradually the various state organizations began to take over in that area. There are rules which vary from state to state but they all respect each other's power in areas such as jockey and trainer suspensions.

The Jockey Club maintained control of the naming of all American horses, however, and each year received reports of about 24,000 foals. About half of those reached the race track. The others fell by the wayside for one reason or another.

As racing began its run through the 1970s, it appeared to be still on the upbeat from a point of view of attendance and betting. But the leaders of the sport had grown a new worry—they were disturbed over the lack of young people at the courses.

Most fans seemed to be in the over-30 group and the majority had reached middle age. It all seemed to flash back to Gov. Nicolls and his solemn observation that racing was not for the divertissement of youth.

But the turf fathers comforted themselves with one timeless thought. No matter how many young people there were they would have to reach 30 eventually and then progress to middle age. The inescapable conclusion was that they—some of them, anyway—would develop new interests, such as horse racing.

THE STANDARDBREDS by Ted Meier

Ted Meier, 64, is a former all-around athlete at the University of Pittsburgh, playing football under coach Jock Sutherland. A 36-year veteran with *The AP*, starting in the Philadelphia bureau, he has covered all phases of sports but has specialized in harness racing, boxing and college basketball. He broke into journalism by covering scholastic sports for the *Erie (Pa.) Dispatch-Herald*.

The thoroughbred always has been the aristocrat of horse racing and, until the middle of the 19th century, the standardbred was the country cousin.

The trotter and the pacer never reached the glamorous public image of the flat racer. They were bred to compete under harness and at different gaits. And they had to pull a two-wheeled sulky.

But, as any country boy can look at the gleaming city lights and dream, so did the standardbred sport. It left the county fairs and moved to the big town. There it found a home in glistening multimillion-dollar plants.

It never overtook thoroughbred racing in popularity and financial investment, but it grew to tremendous stature.

Figures in 1970 showed an annual attendance of 24,000,000 at harness tracks in the United States with wagering that reached close to $2 billion.

The sport, which started booming after World War II, also extended to Canada and gained in popularity in France, Italy, New Zealand, Germany, Sweden, Australia, The Netherlands, Austria and the Soviet Union.

The sport was hardly recognizable as that at the turn of the 20th century when the legendary Dan Patch toured America in a private white railroad car.

In 1969, according to figures from the United States Trotting Association, the attendance in the United States was 24,695,063 and the betting $1,819,965,781. Canada reported its 1969 wagering as $344,977,382.

This was big business.

It provided tax revenue to the 17 states which legalized betting on the trotters and pacers as well as fortunes and an amount of fame to owners, drivers, trainers and breeders.

The growth of harness racing made millionaires of drivers; among them Billy Haughton, left, and Stanley Dancer, right.

The 1969 USTA figures showed that the various states received $138,093,800 as their share of the betting, topped by New York's $80,193,699.

Total purse money in 1969 was $80,683,497, with many races worth more than $100,000, and the number of horses registered was 11,851.

A comparison with 21 years before revealed the tremendous expansion of the sport.

In 1948, attendance in the United States was 5,494,636 and the betting $198,781,327. Purses totalled $9,805,079 and the number of horses registered 3,427.

In 1940, when pari-mutuel betting on the trots was authorized by the New York State Legislature, the attendance was 126,238 and the betting a mere $1,703,538. The 1969 figures for New York showed attendance of 9,278,071 and $810,517,364 in wagers.

Breeders, such as the Hanover Shoe Farm in Pennsylvania, and the Castleton Farm in Kentucky, prospered with the increase in prices at the various yearling sales.

The growth of the sport made millionaires of drivers such as Billy Haughton and Stanley Dancer, who started from scratch in the late 1940s, and led to the building of new tracks such as the $30-million trot palace at Roosevelt Raceway in Westbury, N.Y.

Other tracks modernized their plants. Yonkers Raceway at Yonkers, N.Y., became a competitor of Roosevelt for metropolitan New York's gambling dollars.

Yonkers and Roosevelt became the recognized giants of trotting, but it was at the Freehold, N.J., Raceway, the only major track that continued to operate solely in the daytime, that Cardigan Bay emerged as the first standardbred to win more than $1 million. That was in 1968 and the Cardigan Bay Room at Freehold was named in honor of that achievement.

These luxurious, air-conditioned dining spots, a feature which many other tracks in the United States and Canada adopted, were a major reason for the popularity of the sulky sport.

Another point in its success was an attraction to women who seemed to love the atmosphere and the attendant excitement.

During the Depression of the 1930s, the sport was at a low ebb. The automobile changed the lives of most citizens. They wanted to be on the open road. Few had an interest in a horse and sulky.

The tedious method of starting a race from a walkup start, resulting in numerous recalls, also tended to turn persons who desired more action away from harness racing.

The introduction of legalized pari-mutuel betting and the development of a mobile starting gate, an auto with a fast getaway which virtually eliminated recalls, helped boost the sport.

The formation of the USTA in 1939 also played a major role in reviving the trots as did the later formation of the Harness Tracks of America (HTA). The Grand Circuit, organized in the 1880s and often called the major league of the sport, helped in the revival.

George Morton Levy of Westbury, N.Y., generally was credited as being the father of modern harness racing.

When pari-mutuel betting and night-time racing for the trots was legalized in New York State in 1940, Levy organized a group which took over the old auto racing track, near which Charles Lindbergh took off on his historic solo flight across the Atlantic Ocean in 1927, and called it Roosevelt Raceway.

For the entire meeting that first year, the attendance was less than 75,000. In fact, Levy was hard pressed to keep Roosevelt going for the next six years.

Levy, who was still president of the track after reaching his seventies, liked to recall that those employes who took stock in lieu of wages at the time, made hundreds of thousands of dollars when the public took up the sport in a big way in 1947.

That was the year the mobile starting gate, developed by Stephen G. Phillips, came into general use.

Levy inaugurated the world famous $125,000 Roosevelt International Trot for the World Trotting Championship, a glamorous spectacle that in 1960 drew a crowd of 54,861 for an all-time attendance record at a pari-mutuel harness track.

The International became one of the big money races that reflect the vastly increased purses. The other races worth $100,000 or more included the Hambletonian, sometimes termed the Kentucky Derby of the trots; the Dexter Cup Trot; the Colonial; the Yonkers Futurity Trot; the Messenger; the Cane Pace; the Little Brown Jug, and the American Pacing and Trotting classics in California.

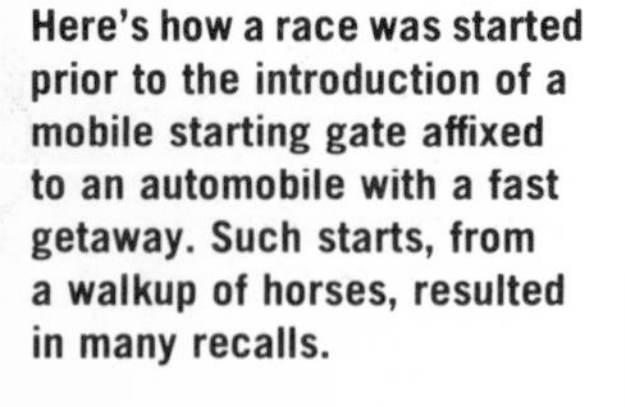

Here's how a race was started prior to the introduction of a mobile starting gate affixed to an automobile with a fast getaway. Such starts, from a walkup of horses, resulted in many recalls.

The trotter moves its left front and right rear legs forward at the same time. This is Nevele Pride.

The pacer moves both legs on one side of its body forward in unison as shown here by Miss Conna Adios.

E. H. Harriman, E. Roland Harriman and Lawrence B. Sheppard were names prominently identified with harness racing along with William H. Cane, Octave Blake, Henry Knight and Robert Bonner.

Before the turn of the century, Leland Stanford of California, R. A. Alexander of Kentucky, C. J. Hamlin of New York, J. Malcolm of Massachusetts and L. U. Harkness of Ohio and Kentucky lent their names and efforts to the development of harness racing.

Trotting history goes back to ancient times, but the sport of light harness racing as we know it in North America today dated from Colonial days and the importation of the great sire, Messenger, from England in the 1780s.

Messenger was recognized as the founding father of the standard breed. Hambletonian, Peter the Great and the latter day Adios and Star's Pride ranked among other famous stallions.

From the first record performance by an American trotter named Yankee, who did the mile in 2:59 in June 1806, down to the latter day world record holders, Nevele Pride and Bret Hanover, there has been a long list of famous standardbreds.

Nevele Pride set the world mile trotting record of 1:54⁴⁄₅. Bret Hanover, who won his first 35 races in a row, held the world mile pacing mark of 1:53³⁄₅.

Their times compared to the world mile record of 1:32⁴⁄₅ for a thoroughbred.

In contrast to the thoroughbreds who run, a trotter moves at a diagonal gait. His front right leg and rear left move at the same time, then his left front and rear right. The pacer moves at a lateral gait. His right front leg and right rear move in unison, then his left front and left rear.

These characteristics generally are inherited, but have to be developed by trainers.

The trotter was considered the elite of the standardbreds long before the advent of the pacer. The pacer was developed by breeding in Colonial days to meet the needs of the population for a saddle horse with an easy gait to ride the forest trails.

Among the first pacers were the so-called Narragansetts of Rhode Island. This breed became extinct around 1850 as roads were built and a bigger horse was needed to serve not only as a saddle horse, but to pull a wagon or carriage as well.

Pacers once were looked down on, but they gradually were accepted for formal races at organized tracks. This contrasted to 1970 when most of the races at betting tracks were for pacers.

Dan Patch, foaled at Shebanse, Ind., in 1896, earned close to $3,000,000 in exhibitions and races during a legendary career. Driving him here is Myron McHenry.

Bret Hanover was the Harness Horse of the Year in the United States in 1964, 1965 and 1966, before being retired to stud. Nevele Pride was Harness Horse of the Year in 1967, 1968 and 1969 before being retired for breeding purposes.

Other leading trotters and pacers over the years included Henry Clay, George Wilkes, Lou Dillon, Star Pointer, Su Mac Lad, Dame Winnie, Axworthy, Bingen, Hamburg Belle, McKinney, Lady Suffolk, Flora Temple, Maud S., Dexter, Billy Direct, Peter Volo, Volomite, Dean Hanover, Single G., Titan Hanover, Greyhound, Overcall, Peter Manning, Uhlan, Adios Butler, Bye Bye Byrd, Speedy Scot, Cardigan Bay, Lindy's Pride, Romeo Hanover, Fresh Yankee, Roquepine, Dan Patch and Goldsmith Maid.

Goldsmith Maid was an extraordinary mare who raced 100 years ago, starting in 1865 at the close of the war between the states.

Foaled in New Jersey in May 1857, she was sired by an unknown colt named Edsall's Hambletonian out of an undistinguished road mare known as Old Ab.

She ran wild until she was 8 years old when Alden Goldsmith bought her for $650 and a second-hand buggy and managed to break her to wearing harness.

Goldsmith Maid won her first race in September 1865, at Goshen, N.Y., for a purse of $100. Thereafter she toured the country while winning 95 of 119 recorded starts, finishing second in 17, third in five, fourth in one and being unplaced just once.

She broke the world trotting record seven times during her career at such places at Milwaukee, Boston, East Saginaw, Mich., Buffalo and Rochester, N.Y., lowering the mark to 2:14 in 1876.

Crowds gathered everywhere when word got around that Goldsmith Maid was passing through town. On her 20th birthday in 1877, she closed out her racing career by winning a special match race against Rarus at Chico, Calif. She then was retired for breeding purposes and died at the age of 30.

Goldsmith Maid earned $364,200 during her career. Had she raced for purses in the 1960s and 1970s, she probably would have been the first standardbred to win $1 million, an honor which went to the New Zealand-bred Cardigan Bay virtually a century later in 1968.

A decade after the death of Goldsmith Maid, Dan Patch was foaled at Shebanse, Ind., in 1896. The pacer toured the country in a private white railroad car attended by four grooms and raced hitched to a white sulky.

The private car was hooked onto first class trains and stories of the era proclaimed Dan Patch Day wherever the white car stopped. The picture of the magnificent animal was on the side of the car along with his name in capital letters.

Dan Patch loved the excitement as much as the people loved him. He enjoyed the music of the bands which played whenever he appeared and was gentle with everyone.

He had been raised more or less as a pet by his breeder, Dan Messner Jr. of Oxford, Ind., and hence treated humans in an affectionate manner.

Dan Patch, sired by Joe Patchen out of an obscure mare, Zelica, didn't start racing until he was a 4-year-old in 1900.

He easily won his first race in 2:35 at Boswell, Ind. From there he went on the Grand Circuit and won 52 of 56 heats, never losing a race, before Messner sold him to M. E. Sturgis of Buffalo, N.Y., for $20,000.

In December of 1902, Marion Willis Savage of Minneapolis, Minn., paid

$60,000 for Dan Patch. That started a memorable lifetime association between man and beast.

Savage was proprietor of the International Stock Food Co. His business expanded tenfold after he acquired Dan Patch.

"Three feeds for one cent," said an advertisement of the time. And of Dan Patch's stud service for $300: "A colt by Dan Patch is just like a government bond."

Dan Patch was commercialized, a trick picked up years later by leading athletes and teams. There were Dan Patch cigars, Dan Patch chewing tobacco, Dan Patch silk scarfs, Dan Patch pillows and even a Dan Patch two-step tune for dancing.

Savage was reported to have turned down offers as high as $180,000 for his pride and joy whom he occasionally hitched to a buggy or a sleigh to enjoy a private ride.

It is estimated that Dan Patch earned close to $3 million for Savage from his numerous exhibitions and races against the clock.

In October 1905, Dan went a 1:55¼ mile at Lexington, Ky., leading Savage to believe his horse was capable of a 1:52 mile by pacing four 28-second quarters.

In 1906, Dan Patch, driven by Harry Hersey, did 1:55 in a time trial at Hamline, Minn. The mark was never officially recognized because a running horse had been used as a pace-setter. His best time without cover was 1:58 at Memphis, Tenn., in 1905.

Dan Patch made his last public appearance in New Orleans in an exhibition on Thanksgiving Day in 1913. He died on July 11, 1916, at the International Stock Farm in Minnesota, aged 20.

Multiple exposure? No, it's a head-on view of entries in a harness race bunched up in a turn.

"The King Is Dead" read a newspaper headline at the time. Savage died the day after Dan Patch.

Where big money is involved, some evils usually are found. Harness racing proved no exception. The twin double was abolished at most tracks after irregularities developed in connection with fantastic payoffs as high as $172,000 for $2.

The Harness Track Security Office, headed by John Brennan, came into being and worked in conjunction with the USTA.

As a rule, the leading drivers, such as Joe O'Brien, Del Insko, George Sholty, John Chapman and Herve Filion, in addition to Haughton and Dancer, seldom, if ever, bet.

Other top reinsmen included Clint Hodgins, Del Miller, Vernon Dancer, Bob Farrington, Eddie Cobb, John Simpson Sr., William Myer, Jimmy Cruise, Frank Ervin, Lucien Fontaine, Ralph Baldwin, Carmine Abbatiello, George Phalen, Earle Avery and Sanders Russell.

All were high on the all-time money winning list which was topped by Haughton's $15 million and Stanley Dancer's $13 million.

Before their time, noted drivers included Sep Palin, Pop Geers, Tom Murphy and Henry Thomas. Hirman Woodruff, who died in 1867, was a noted driver-trainer of the 19th century.

In 1968, the 30-year-old Herve Filion won the driving championship with an unprecedented 407 victories. And on Aug. 1, 1970, he made harness racing history by driving five winners, each under two minutes for the mile, at Brandywine Raceway in Delaware.

Filion made 1970 even more memorable for himself by breaking his own world record for the most wins in one year. On Nov. 1, he scored his 408th victory, breaking the record 407 mark he had set in 1968. He added several more victories before the year was out.

The harness sport could not escape the women's liberation movement of the 1960s. But only a few women were licensed to drive.

One of the leading female drivers was Bobbe Huntress. In July 1970, she won at Vernon Downs in New York State with the trotter, Seymour J. in 1:59$^{1}/_{5}$, the fastest race mile ever by a woman driver.

Previously, the swiftest female drivers in a betting race had been June Dillman in 1:59$^{4}/_{5}$ with the pacer Red Dominion and Marian Brewer in 2:01$^{2}/_{5}$ with the trotter Rodare.

Mary McCune of Coraopolis, Pa., became the first woman to be elected to the Hall of Fame of the Trotter at Goshen, N.Y.

Miss McCune was a leading amateur driver. She set a then world record for a lady driver of 2:04$^{1}/_{2}$ with the trotter, Mignola, on Sept. 15, 1917.

The trotters and pacers continued to perform at many state fairs, but harness racing could no longer be considered a hayseed sport. It found wealth and success in the big city.

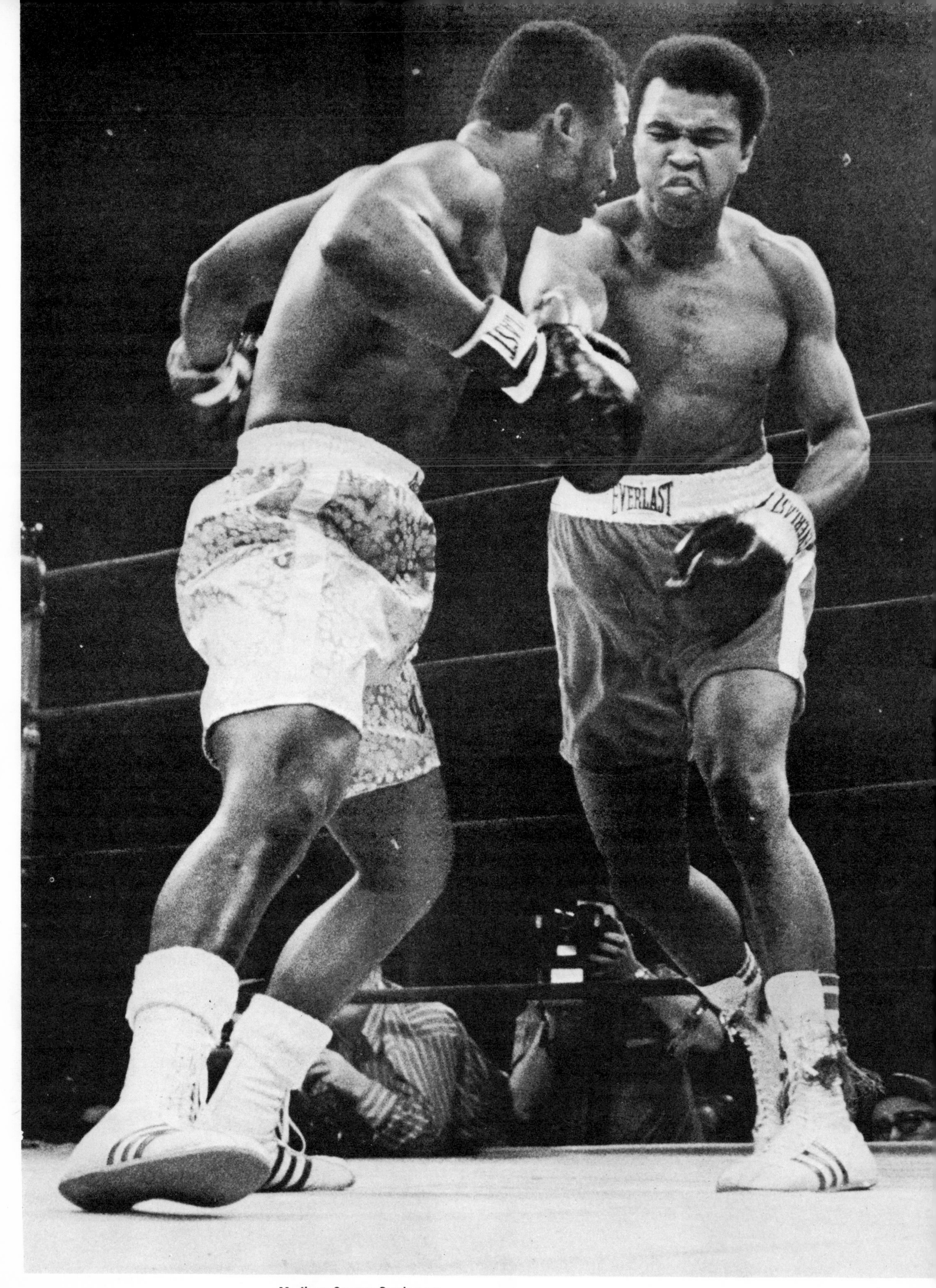

Madison Square Garden on March 8, 1971: Joe Frazier, left, won on a unanimous 15-round decision over Muhammad Ali in "The Fight."

chapter 6

BOXING

Throwback to the Gladiators

by Ed Schuyler Jr.

They called it "The Fight."

For one brief period in history the world shunted aside its burden of problems —the Vietnam War, tensions in the Middle East, youth rebellion, drugs, runaway inflation and poverty—and centered its attention on a spotlight on a 20-foot-square ring with blood red ropes in New York's Madison Square Garden.

The principals were a 27-year-old ex-butcher from a Philadelphia slaughterhouse, Joe Frazier, recognized heavyweight champion of the world, and Muhammad Ali, 29, descendant of a runaway Kentucky slave, loud, bombastic, egotistical, whose boasts and braggadocio had made him as despised as he was loved.

The 15-round bout, between two unbeaten and unmarked giants of the ring, was more than a mere boxing match. There were deep social factors, brought about when Ali, formerly known as Cassius Clay, adopted the Muslim faith and refused to enter the military service. Passions ran deep. All over the world, there were people pulling either for Ali to win or to get his brassy tongue knocked down his throat. It was difficult to be neutral.

The date was March 8, 1971. It was boxing's most resplendent hour.

The largest indoor fight crowd in history—20,455—paid a record $1,352,961 to see the action live in the Garden, the glistening new reproduction of one of sport's most famous arenas. More than 300 million reportedly watched via

Ed Schuyler Jr., a native of Bloomsburg, Pa., joined *The Associated Press* in Pittsburgh in June 1960, after serving two years in the Army and graduating from Washington & Lee University. He handled a variety of *AP* jobs and assignments in Pittsburgh, including sports. In October 1965, Schuyler transferred to New York Sports and since has concentrated mainly on horse racing and boxing.

satellite on closed circuit and home television all over the world. The show was beamed to 35 countries outside the United States.

It is easy to understand the universal interest. Boxing, unlike many sports, has no boundaries. It appeals to man's baser instincts. It is man against man. Whereas cricket interest may be confined to British Commonwealth nations, baseball and basketball to the United States, boxing is practiced and followed as a spectator sport on every continent.

Boxing fortunes have declined and escalated with the popularity of its individuals. Once outlawed, it grew to manhood through the fistic exploits of such men as John L. Sullivan, James J. Corbett, Jack Dempsey, Gene Tunney, Joe Louis and Rocky Marciano.

It is ironic that the game, which went into the doldrums in the 1950s because of overexposure to television, should rebound and, because of television, produce the most watched single sports event of all time.

The new boxing boom of the 1960s and 1970s could be attributed largely to Ali, a tall, handsome figure with an engaging yet often abrasive personality. He spouted poems of his prowess and rhymes that predicted the rounds his victims would fall. He ranted and raved at times and other times became a subdued personality with the puckishness of a small boy.

Ali, who turned pro Oct. 29, 1960, after winning the Olympic gold medal in Rome as a light heavyweight, reeled off a series of successes, often knocking out his foe in the round he previously had specified in rhyme.

In April 1967, contending he was a Muslim minister, the former Cassius Marcellus Clay refused to take the step for military induction at Houston. He was sentenced to five years in prison—a sentence he never served after taking his case to the courts. He was stripped of his title and denied license to fight. Then followed 3½ years of ring idleness.

While the controversial case—which divided Americans and brought criticism from the rest of the world—bounced around the courts, Ali ballooned to 240 pounds, took to the stage and bolstered his finances by speaking on college campuses.

In 1970, a federal court ruled that the New York State Athletic Commission was in error in not granting Ali a license. The door was opened for him to return to the ring.

His first comeback fight was against Jerry Quarry, a bullish slugger, in Atlanta Oct. 26, 1970. The world was intrigued by the Great Man's return. Had Ali lost any of his old speed and skills? Could he regain his championship?

Ali opened an ugly four-inch gash over Quarry's eye in the third round and the fight was stopped. Five weeks later—on Dec. 7—he scored a 15-round technical knockout over Oscar Bonavena, the rugged Argentine who had twice gone the limit with Frazier and once floored Frazier twice in one round.

Now Ali and his handlers felt he was ready for Frazier.

In the wild bidding for the so-called Fight of the Century, Jerry Perenchio, an enterprising Hollywood theatrical agent, outbid all rivals by promising the two combatants an unprecedented purse of $2.5 million each. He borrowed a grub stake of $4.5 million from Jack Kent Cooke, a Los Angeles sportsman, and the other one-half million from the Garden. Then he set about setting up a vast closed circuit television project that he predicted would bring in $15 million.

Over-all, he set his sights on a $30 million gross, including a post-fight screening at theaters and other ancillary rights. His aim fell short and he grossed close to $20 million instead.

The fight at the Garden was a sports spectacular. Diplomats, business tycoons, astronauts and celebrities of screen and Broadway rubbed elbows with the "soul people," most of them attired in flamboyant mink, feathers and silk.

The fight proved half-theater and half-sport. In a bruising brawl in which Ali, the clever boxer, matched his rare skills against Frazier's brutal, buzz-saw style, Frazier was declared the unanimous winner by decision.

The fight provoked controversy—as did most of Ali's bouts. Some observers at ringside thought Ali won. *The Associated Press* card matched that of the two judges and referee.

But the stage was set for a multimillion-dollar rerun. The game had a new lease on life.

The fight game is many things to many people. To some it is the most exciting of sports. To others it is a disgrace. But perhaps it is the most natural sport. It is man against man, with their fists as weapons and their wits and courage as armor.

Human traits are more magnified in boxing than in team sports. Cowardice as well as courage, viciousness as well as compassion, humor as well as pathos are naked in the prize ring.

And there always has been another human quality connected with boxing—greed. And greed has brought a lust for power which has only been satisfied through devious means.

But it has been the men who personify the good and the bad who have made the sport of boxing a controversial one, a colorful one, an honest one, a crooked one and, mainly, a lasting one.

Boxing has been Jack Dempsey, Joe Louis, Rocky Marciano, John L. Sullivan, James J. Corbett, Bob Fitzsimmons, Jim Jeffries, Jim Braddock, Floyd Patterson, Gene Tunney, Jack Johnson—the gladiators.

Boxing has been Tex Rickard, Mike Jacobs, James D. Norris—the wheelers and dealers.

Boxing has been Frankie Carbo, Blinky Palermo—the undercover operators, men of a shadowy nature.

Boxing is a world sport and one of several weight divisions from which have come such colorful figures as Sugar Ray Robinson, Marcel Cerdan, Rocky Graziano, Luis Firpo, Benny Leonard, Willie Pep, Joe Gans, Stanley Ketchell.

But ever since John L. Sullivan, the Boston Strong Boy, the United States has been the sport's hub and the heavyweight division always has been its main cog. So the chief lines to follow in tracing a history of boxing are the development and practice of it in the United States, particularly in connection with the heavyweights.

Although men have been beating on one another with their fists since time immemorial, fist fighting really didn't develop as an athletic event until the Greeks and Romans. However, excavations on the island of Crete have revealed that a form of boxing was practiced there as early as 1500 B.C.

The writings of Homer describe a boxing match held as part of the festivities celebrating the fall of Troy. There are other references by Homer that Greek athletes boxed in Athens and other city states. Leather coverings protected the fists.

Boxing as practiced in the Roman Empire underwent the transition from an athletic contest between two men to a spectacle staged to satisfy the blood lust of Coliseum crowds. The fighters wore elbow-length gloves studded with pointed metal knobs and slugged it out until one or both were dead.

When the Roman Empire fell, boxing apparently also vanished. There seem to be no records of boxing being practiced during the Middle Ages.

Then, in the 18th century, boxing appeared as a sport in England and 100 years later it got started in the United States.

It was in England that boxing, in the general form practiced in the 20th century, began. The rules that have governed the game since the 1700s originated in England. They were Broughton's Rules in 1743, the London Prize Ring Rules in 1838 and revised in 1853, and the Marquis of Queensberry Rules in 1867.

James Figg was the first recognized heavyweight champion of England, gaining the honor in 1719. He was one of the most famous of the early bare knuckles champions as was John Broughton, author of the first set of rules.

Broughton won his title in 1740 and held it until 10 years later when he was defeated by Jack Slack. The Broughton-Slack fight brought forth a charge that has become an inglorious part of boxing—the charge of "fix."

Other famous English champions of the 18th century were Daniel Mendoza, a major early contributor to the science of boxing; Tom Cribb, and Deaf Burke.

Those great fighters of the first century of modern boxing fought under Broughton's rules. Under both the Broughton and London Prize Ring rules, a round ended when a fighter was knocked or wrestled to the ground. The man who had been knocked or thrown down had to toe a mark in the middle of the ring in a prescribed time or be declared the loser.

Under the later Marquis of Queensberry Rules, drawn up by John Sholto Douglas, eighth Marquis of Queensberry, no wrestling or hugging was allowed and each round lasted three minutes with a minute's rest between rounds. A man knocked down had to get up before the count of 10. These rules also called for the use of boxing gloves.

Jim Corbett, right, and Bob Fitzsimmons are shown in action in the 14th and last round of their heavyweight title fight at Carson City, Nev., in 1897. Fitzsimmons knocked out Corbett later in the round.

The first fight in America under English bare-knuckle rules took place in New York City in 1816 between Tom Beasley and Jacob Hyer. However, there were earlier bouts in America. Two early American fighters were Bill Richmond and Tom Molineaux, both of whom went to England to fight. More significantly, both were Negroes, the sons of slaves.

Boxing is the one sport is this country in which blacks played a prominent role right from the start. Many of the early fights matched slaves from various Southern plantations. Many of these men, after becoming free, fought for a living. Throughout the history of the American prize ring there have been many black champions, among them Jack Johnson, the first of his race to win the world heavyweight title and the victim of one of American boxing's saddest chapters.

The first recognized heavyweight champion of the United States was Tom Hyer, the son of Jacob Hyer. The younger Hyer gained this honor in 1841 when he beat Country McClusky. The fight went 101 rounds and lasted two hours, 55 minutes.

The next American champion was one of the most colorful men in the annals of the American ring. He was Irish-born John Morrissey, who, after retiring from the ring, made money on the stock market, opened a gambling house in Saratoga, helped organize a horse race meeting in that New York town, helped found the Jockey Club, served two terms in Congress and served in the New York State Legislature.

Morrissey succeeded the retired Tom Hyer as champion by beating Yankee Sullivan in 1853. He then brought a family feud to a culmination by beating John C. Heenan, like Morrissey from Troy, N.Y., Oct. 28, 1858, in Canada. Then he retired.

After Morrissey's retirement, Heenan claimed the championship and it was he who took part in the first big international fight. Heenan met British champion Tom Sayers in England April 17, 1860, for what was billed as the heavyweight championship of the world.

Heenan, who at 6-foot-2 and 195 pounds, towered over the 5-8, 149-pound Sayers, was having the better of the going in the 37th round when someone cut the ropes and the crowd invaded the ring. A draw was declared and each man was given a silver championship belt. After Sayers retired, Heenan was universally recognized as world champion, an honor he held until he was beaten in England in his last fight by Tom King in 1863.

Five days before Morrissey beat Heenan in 1858, there took place an event that was little noticed but one that would greatly affect boxing in America. The event was the birth in the Boston suburb of Roxbury of John Lawrence Sullivan, who would go on to punch himself into boxing lore as John the Great and the Boston Strong Boy.

Sullivan was the first American fighter to gain national recognition. He was a true folk hero, a hard hitting, hard drinking man whose exploits were praised in verse and whose downfall shocked the nation.

John L. got his shot at the title when he signed Oct. 5, 1881, for a fight to the finish with champion Paddy Ryan. The fight was with bare knuckles. At this time, gloves of a fashion were used in some fights.

Sullivan met Ryan Feb. 7, 1882, at Mississippi City and beat him senseless in the ninth round. At age 23, John L. Sullivan was champion of the world, a position he held for the next 10 years during which he fought throughout the country and also appeared on the stage.

While he was still champion, Sullivan took part in a historic fight with Jake Kilrain. It was the last championship bout fought with bare knuckles.

Prior to the fight, Sullivan was confined to bed from August to November of 1888, a victim of his wenching and hard drinking. But on July 8, 1889, in a clearing near the center of Richburg, Miss., under a blazing noontime sun, Sullivan beat Kilrain into submission after 75 rounds which took two hours, 16 minutes.

The sporting public was in a state of shock Sept. 8, 1892. On the night before, John L. Sullivan, who had boasted he could lick any man in the world and who had made that boast stand up for a decade, was knocked out in the 21st round by James J. Corbett in New Orleans. The fight also was significant in that it was the first in which big gloves were used. Gloves had been used before but they had little or no padding.

Gentleman Jim Corbett was a classic boxer and has been recognized by some observers as the greatest boxer ever to hold the heavyweight championship. But at the time he won the title Corbett's skill was not acknowledged. In fact he was very unpopular for some time for having committed the "crime" of shattering an idol.

Corbett knocked out Charley Mitchell in 1894 and then lost his crown to one of the most remarkable fighters in history, Bob Fitzsimmons, who was called Ruby Robert.

The English-born Fitzsimmons was one of the most improbable looking champions ever to get into the ring, yet he won three world titles—the middleweight, then the heavyweight and later the newly formed light heavyweight. Only one other fighter has ever won three titles. Henry Armstrong simultaneously held the featherweight, lightweight and welterweight crowns in the 1940s.

Fitzsimmons was a freckle-faced, spindly-legged man with sparse red hair who weighed only 167 pounds when he beat Corbett. He never weighed much more than that but he had a powerful torso and a mighty punch. He also was a good defensive fighter, had great recuperative powers and tremendous stamina. He fought more than 300 times and his last bout was a six-round no-decision affair in 1917 when he was 53.

A left to the pit of the stomach in the 14th round at Carson City, Nev., March 17, 1897, knocked out Corbett and made Fitzsimmons the champion. The punch was nothing new, but a sports writer overheard two doctors saying that the blow had landed on the solar plexus, the nerve center in the diaphragm, and the knockout punch went into boxing lore as the "solar plexus" punch.

Two years later on June 9, Fitzsimmons lost the title to powerful Jim Jeffries on an 11th round knockout. Jeffries, the boilermaker from San Francisco, weighed over 200 pounds and was a ponderous, numbing puncher who fought out of a position known as the Jeffries Crouch.

Jeffries defended his title six times, including two knockouts of Corbett and another knockout of Fitzsimmons, before retiring in March 1905.

Marvin Hart laid claim to the title after beating Jack Root, but Hart then lost to Tommy Burns of Canada. Burns didn't gain general acknowledgment as champion until he beat Philadelphia Jack O'Brien over 20 rounds in Los Angeles on May 8, 1907.

Burns, who usually weighed about 180 and stood only 5–7, was a busy champion, defending his title eight times in a little more than a year. But Burns' main contribution to fighters who followed him was that he pointed the way toward big money. He earned a record $30,000 in defending his title Dec. 26, 1908, in Sydney, Australia.

The outcome of that bout also had a profound effect on the fight game. For the man who fought and beat Burns, by a knockout in 14 rounds, was Jack Johnson.

Johnson was the first black heavyweight champion of the world and as such he was the target of the White Hope campaign, which was a search for a white man who could dethrone Johnson, a search that at times bordered on frenzy.

Helping bring the cries for his defeat to fever pitch were Johnson's arrogance and his amorous adventures with white women.

But there was no doubt about Johnson's skill in the ring. He was the complete fighter and some people, such as boxing authority Nat Fleischer, called him the greatest heavyweight that ever lived.

On April 5, 1915, in the heat of Havana, Jess Willard had just floored Jack Johnson in the 26th round. The referee was taking up the count. Johnson was on his back with his gloves above his face. There were cries of "fix" on the contention that this picture showed Johnson shielding his eyes from the sun and that he was not unconscious. It has been the general belief the fight was legitimate.

Some of Johnson's toughest fights came before he won the title, when he beat men like Hank Griffin, Denver Ed Martin, Sam McVey, Joe Jeanette and the legendary Sam Langford, the Boston Tar Baby. These men belonged to a group that has always been a part of boxing—the Negro fighters who are praised for their skills but because of them are avoided by champions.

After beating Burns, Johnson fought a few no-decision bouts before he knocked out Stanley Ketchel in 12 rounds in 1909; Jim Jeffries in 15 rounds in 1910, and won from Jim Flynn in nine rounds in 1912 when police stopped the bout.

The Ketchel fight was one of boxing's classics. Ketchel, known as the Michigan Assassin, was the world middleweight champion and one of the most colorful fighters in a division that produced such great champions as Harry Greb, Mickey Walker, Tony Zale, Marcel Cerdan, Rocky Graziano and Sugar Ray Robinson.

Johnson, who outweighed Ketchel by 45 pounds, had agreed with the middleweight king to go the distance, but Ketchel tried to cross his opponent. In the 12th round he stunned the crowd at Colma, Calif., by dropping Johnson with a right below the ear. It was a mistake by Ketchel. Johnson bounced on his feet and met Ketchel's rush with a thunderous right uppercut which floored him. Ketchel did not regain consciousness for several minutes from the blow that broke his front teeth off at the gums.

Less than a year after the fight, Ketchel was dead, fatally shot in a dispute over a girl, and Johnson was headed for trouble.

Johnson had no difficulty in beating the great Jeffries at Reno, Nev., in a fight in which Tex Rickard, destined to become one of the great boxing promoters, was referee. Jeffries was persuaded to come out of almost six years retirement by the White Hope craze.

In the latter part of 1912, Johnson fled to Europe after being convicted of violating the Mann Act and being sentenced to a year in prison. At the time he had been married twice to white women and it was an affair with another white woman which got him into trouble with the federal government.

With Johnson in exile, a tourney for white heavyweights was held and Luther McCarty was proclaimed white champion of America. Then, McCarty collapsed in the first round of a bout with Arthur Pelkey, May 24, 1913, and died. Pelkey lost to Gunboat Smith, Jan. 1, 1914, and then Georges Carpentier gained the white heavyweight title by winning from Smith on a foul in six rounds, July 16, 1914.

Meanwhile, Johnson knocked out Andre Spul, drew with Jim Johnson and decisioned Frank Moran, all in Paris.

Then on April 5, 1915, in the heat of Havana, the White Hope crusade finally was culminated when giant Jess Willard knocked out Johnson in 26 rounds.

A controversy resulted from a picture of the knockout that showed Johnson on his back with his gloves above his face. There were cries of "fix" on the contention that the picture showed Johnson shielding his eyes from the blazing sun and that he was not unconscious. Years later Johnson made a statement that he had thrown the fight, but he was paid for the statement. It has been the general belief that the fight was legitimate.

Johnson was killed in an auto accident in 1946. A play based on his life and called "The Great White Hope" was a Broadway hit and a success as a motion picture.

The Twenties was the decade of Dempsey, the Manassa Mauler, and Gene Tunney, the fighting Marine. It also was the decade of Tex Rickard who brought the million-dollar gate to boxing, and of great fights such as Dempsey-Carpentier, Dempsey-Firpo and the famed Battle of the Long Count between Dempsey and Tunney.

The 1920s also was a period for great fighters in other divisions.

Fighting during those wild years were three of the great light heavyweights—Tommy Loughran, Jack Delaney and Paul Berlenbach. Also in action were Mickey Walker, who won both the welterweight and middleweight titles, and middleweight king Harry Greb, the Pittsburgh Windmill, who was the only man ever to beat Tunney.

Among those in the lighter weights displaying their skills in the '20s were Benny Leonard, ranked with Joe Gans as the greatest of the lightweight champions; featherweight champion Johnny Dundee; Panama Al Brown, king of the bantamweights, the class that produced the great George Dixon, and three men who ranked with Jimmy Wilde as the greatest of the flyweight champions—Pancho Villa, Franky Genaro and Fidel Le Barba.

But the boxing idol of the '20s, possibly the greatest hero of any sport in an era that had such greats as Babe Ruth, Ty Cobb, Bobby Jones and Big Bill Tilden, was Dempsey, who became one of the most popular sports figures of all time.

Dempsey won the heavyweight title in one of the legendary fights promoted by Rickard. Although Willard towered over Dempsey, he didn't have a chance. Before the unbelieving eyes of the crowd in the open-air arena, Dempsey knocked the giant Willard down seven times in the first round.

Because of the crowd noise, the referee counted Willard out after the last knockdown, not realizing the bell had saved Willard. Dempsey, thinking he had won, had left the ring and had to be summoned back. Dempsey continued to cut up Willard in the second round but he could not floor him. In the third round, Willard took another fearful beating but amazingly jarred Dempsey. However, at the end of the round, Willard could not continue and Dempsey was champion.

After winning the title, Dempsey knocked out Billy Miske in five rounds and Bill Brennan in 12 rounds in 1920, then knocked out Georges Carpentier in four rounds July 2, 1921, at Boyles Thirty Acres in Jersey City, N.J., in the first million-dollar gate—$1,789,238.

He then was idle until July 4, 1923, when he outpointed Tom Gibbons in 15 rounds at Shelby in a fight that was supposed to put the Montana town on the map.

It almost wiped Shelby off the map. Dempsey got his guarantee of $300,000. Gibbons and the investors in the fight got nothing. Three banks failed and many townsmen went broke.

Next for Dempsey, on Sept. 14, 1923, came the unforgettable fight with Luis Firpo, the Wild Bull of the Pampas.

For drama, no fight ever surpassed the three minutes, 57 seconds of fighting put on by Dempsey and Firpo in New York's old Polo Grounds before a crowd of 82,000 that paid $1,188,603.

Seven times in the first round Dempsey hammered the Argentine to the floor, but Firpo came back with a crashing right that sent the champion through the ropes and into the press section. Sports writers, in a reflex action of self protec-

Luis Angel Firpo, Argentina's Wild Bull of the Pampas, stands behind referee Jack Gallagher after knocking Jack Dempsey out of the ring in the first round in a title bout at the Polo Grounds in New York. Dempsey climbed back and floored Firpo nine times before finishing him off in the second round.

In their 1927 championship bout, Jack Dempsey has just floored Gene Tunney with a left hook. Dempsey's failure to retreat to a neutral corner resulted in what has become famous as "the Long Count."

tion, helped shove Dempsey back into the ring. Dempsey was badly hurt but Firpo was unable to follow up his advantage. In the second round, Dempsey floored Firpo twice, the second time for the count.

The Firpo fight was Dempsey's last for three years and his last successful defense of his title.

Dempsey's reign came to an end Sept. 23, 1926, when he was outpointed by Gene Tunney in 10 rounds before a crowd of 120,757, paying $1,898,733, in Philadelphia's Sesquicentennial Stadium. At the end, the exhausted Dempsey was on the verge of being knocked out.

So one-sided had Tunney's victory been, that Dempsey was forced to earn a rematch. He did this by knocking out Jack Sharkey in seven rounds July 21, 1927, at New York's Yankee Stadium, thus setting the stage for another fight with Tunney, a fight that turned out to be the famed Battle of the Long Count.

The fight was another highlight of Rickard's promotional career. It was the first $2-million gate and the richest fight in pre-closed circuit television history. A crowd of 104,943 in Soldier Field in Chicago paid $2,658,660. It also was the fifth $1-million-plus fight in Dempsey's career, his tune-up bout with Sharkey also having topped $1 million.

Tunney began to take control of the fight in the third round and he maintained it through the sixth.

Then, in the seventh round, the crowd was brought to its feet when Dempsey caught Tunney near the ropes and knocked him down with a long left hook to the jaw. The timekeeper began to count, but referee Dave Barry did not because Dempsey was hovering near the stricken Tunney.

What had happened was Dempsey had failed to obey an Illinois State Athletic Commission rule—a rule that has become universal—that a fallen boxer is not considered down until his opponent goes to the corner farthest from the man he has knocked down. By the time Dempsey did this and Barry began his count, several seconds had passed and Tunney had recovered. At the count of nine, Tunney got up and held off Dempsey for the rest of the round.

Tunney recovered so completely that he came back in the eighth round to floor Dempsey, who got up without taking a count. Tunney boxed his way through the final two rounds and retained the championship.

Dempsey protested in vain to the Illinois State Athletic Commission, and so his colorful career ended on a controversial note.

During the years after he left the ring, Dempsey's popularity seemed to increase. In fact, the low spot in Dempsey's popularity came while he still was fighting. During World War I, Dempsey chose to work in a shipyard rather than serve in the military, and this provoked heavy criticism. Dempsey saw action as a Coast Guard officer in the second world war.

Tunney was the exact opposite of Dempsey. The former Marine was, as they say in the newspaper business, "poor copy." In the ring he was a precision fighter but not brutally destructive like Dempsey and out of the ring he preferred to keep to himself and choose his company.

Tunney fought just once more after the Battle of the Long Count. On July 23, 1928, he knocked out Tom Heeney in 11 rounds in New York.

After Tunney's retirement, the heavyweight throne was vacant for almost two years. It finally was filled when German Max Schmeling won from Jack

Sharkey in the fourth round in the only heavyweight championship decided on a foul. The fight was in New York, July 12, 1930.

Schmeling defended his title in 1931 by knocking out Young Stribling in 15 rounds and then lost the championship on a 15-round decision to Sharkey in Long Island Bowl, June 21, 1932.

Sharkey, born Joseph Paul Cukoschay of Lithuanian parentage and called the Boston Tar because of his Navy service, lost the title in his first defense. On June 29, 1933, he was knocked out in the sixth round in the Long Island Bowl by Primo Carnera of Italy, the first non-American to hold the title since Tommy Burns.

Carnera stood 6-foot-5¾ inches and weighed around 260 pounds, but his main weakness as a fighter was his inability to take a hard punch.

Carnera arrived in this country Dec. 31, 1929, accompanied by his manager, Leon See, a Parisian promoter. Once in the United States, Carnera underwent one of the great ballyhoo campaigns in boxing history.

Carnera embarked on a fighting tour of the United States, a tour arranged mainly by Bill Duffey, a New York night club owner and racketeer who handled fighters as a sideline. Carnera posted a 23–0 record against such setups as Big Boy Peterson, Farmer Lodge and K. O. Christopher before he was upset on a 10-round decision by Jim Maloney, who was supposed to be another setup.

Carnera returned to Europe to post two victories and then came back to the United States to go on another successful barnstorming tour before losing a 15-round decision to Jack Sharkey. But by going the distance with Sharkey, Carnera convinced his handlers he was ready to take on good fighters. He ran off an impressive number of victories and then was matched with Ernie Schaaf in New York Feb. 10, 1933.

It was a dull fight and then in the 13th round Schaaf collapsed from an apparent light punch and was counted out to the cry of "fix." Three days later Schaaf died. Many believed that fatality stemmed from a brutal beating Schaaf had received from Max Baer a year earlier.

After Carnera won the title, he defended it by winning a 15-round decision from Paolino Uzcudun, the Basque, in Rome in 1933 and over Tommy Loughran in Miami in 1934 before being floored repeatedly and knocked out in the 11th round by Max Baer in New York, June 14, 1934.

Baer had a magnificent physique, strength, stamina and tremendous punching power. Some students of boxing have contended that he could have been the greatest heavyweight champion of them all.

But Baer was the madcap of boxing, a man who looked on training with disfavor and viewed women and good times with relish.

Baer almost quit boxing in 1930 when Frankie Campbell died after being knocked out by the Californian in five rounds. But promoter Ancil Hoffman convinced Baer to continue, and he went on to win the title.

After his smashing victory over Carnera, Baer fought a series of exhibitions before defending his title in the Long Island Bowl, June 13, 1935, against Jim Braddock.

If Carnera was a perfect example of a manufactured fighter—one who has been carefully built up—Braddock was a top example of the underdog. Hardly given a chance, Braddock outpointed Baer in 15 rounds in one of the great upsets in the annals of sport.

Braddock had quit the ring in the fall of 1933, after eight busy years of boxing, to work on the Hoboken, N.J., docks to support his family. But, with a chance to pick up some money, he returned to serve as a trial horse for Corn Griffin, a promising young heavyweight. Braddock upset Griffin by knocking him out in three rounds in the semifinal match on the Carnera-Baer card.

Braddock then upset top light heavyweight John Henry Lewis in 10 rounds in 1934 and outpointed Art Lasky in 1935 to gain his match with Baer.

After the Baer fight, which put Braddock into boxing legend as the Cinderella Man, he fought only one exhibition in 1935 and did not pull on a glove in 1936.

But there occurred in 1936 another of boxing's big upsets. In New York on June 18 Max Schmeling scored a 12-round knockout over a rapidly rising young heavyweight from Detroit named Joe Louis who already had to his credit knockouts over Primo Carnera, Max Baer and Paolino Uzcudun.

But Schmeling, who missed a chance to fight Baer for the title because he refused to fight Braddock in an elimination bout, also missed out on a title fight with Braddock.

Schmeling was signed by the Garden to fight Braddock, who was under contract to the Garden, but Braddock would not fight the German. He remembered Schmeling's refusal to face him in an elimination match to see who would fight Baer. Braddock also apparently feared that if Schmeling won he would take the title back to Nazi Germany where it would remain.

Another reason Schmeling was bypassed was a dispute between the Garden and Uncle Mike Jacobs, the exclusive handler of Louis' affairs as head of the Twentieth Century Sporting Club.

Jacobs induced Braddock to defend against Louis, and the fight was held June 22, 1937, in Comiskey Park in Chicago.

Joe Louis dances away from Max Schmeling whom he KOed in two minutes and four seconds of the first round of their bout in New York on June 22, 1938. Schmeling had upset Louis three years before.

Billy Conn goes down and out at the hands of heavyweight champion Joe Louis in title bout at Yankee Stadium in New York in June 1946. Eddie Joseph is the referee.

Since being upset by Schmeling, Louis had bounced back to win seven in a row and he was too much for Braddock. Louis became the champion with an eighth-round knockout.

So began the reign of Joe Louis, the Brown Bomber, a reign that would last until he retired as undefeated champion in March 1949.

During Louis' rule he defended his title 25 times against fighters such as Schmeling, big Buddy Baer, Abe Simon, Arturo Godoy, Billy Conn, Jersey Joe Walcott, Tony Musto, Johnny Paycheck, Gus Dorazio and Red Burman. Louis fought often and well and was a popular champion.

With the era of Louis came the era of Mike Jacobs, who succeeded Tex Rickard as boss of boxing in Madison Square Garden. Jacobs promoted 61 world championship bouts, more than 1,500 boxing cards and sold tickets worth $30 million at face value from 1937 through 1947. His promotions involving Louis had gross receipts of more than $10 million.

Jacobs also was accused of creating a monopoly and of associating with men such as Paul John Carbo, also known variously as Paul Carbo, Paul John, Frank Russo, John Paul Carbo and Frankie Carbo.

Carbo, an arrogant man of some charm who had five arrests for murder, had a stable of fighters and became known as the boxing commissioner of the underworld.

In 1947, Carbo made a bet killing when Jake LaMotta was stopped in four rounds by Blackjack Billy Fox, which LaMotta later admitted was a fixed fight. Two years later LaMotta got a middleweight title fight, which he won, with Marcel Cerdan. The fight was the first promotion of James D. Norris and the International Boxing Club. Norris inherited the association with Carbo.

Another associate whom Norris inherited from Jacobs was Frank Palermo, known by his friends as Blinky, the manager of lightweight champion Ike Williams, the guide of the fortunes of Billy Fox and owner of a police record that included two arrests for assault.

In 1938, Louis defended three times, knocking out Nathan Mann and Harry Thomas and then turning in perhaps the highlight performance of his brilliant career, a one-round knockout of Max Schmeling, the man who had upset him three years before.

A crowd of 70,000, paying $1,015,012, turned out in Yankee Stadium. What they saw was a short but memorable fight.

After several seconds, Louis forced Schmeling to the ropes with a right to the jaw and then battered the German's body and head. Louis took a right, then landed a left hook, a right, another hook and a right to the jaw that dropped Schmeling for a three count. He then dropped Schmeling with two lefts and a right and finished off the machine-like destruction with a left hook and right cross to the jaw that dropped Schmeling on his face. It was over in two minutes, four seconds.

In December 1940, he launched his so-called "Bum of the Month" campaign which ran through June of 1941. He knocked out Al McCoy, Red Burman, Gus Dorazio, Abe Simon and Tony Musto and won on disqualification from Buddy Baer in a total of 42 rounds, 13 of them involving Baer.

Louis concluded his "Bum of the Month" campaign against a fighter who turned out to be anything but a pushover—light heavyweight champion Billy Conn.

Conn put on a tremendous exhibition. At the end of 12 rounds before 60,071 in the Polo Grounds, June 18, 1941, the Pittsburgh Irishman was ahead and had the title in his grasp. But the cocky Conn went out in the 13th to try for a knockout and ended up being knocked out with just two seconds left in the round.

Except for a four-round exhibition, Louis did not fight in July and August and his last fight of 1941 was a six-round knockout of Lou Nova Sept. 29. He had two fights in 1942. He knocked out Buddy Baer in Madison Square Garden Jan. 9 and donated his purse to the Naval Relief Fund, then kayoed Abe Simon in six rounds in the Garden March 27 and donated his purse to the Army Relief Fund.

Louis, who was inducted into the Army a month before the Simon fight, then donned khaki for the rest of the war and the title was frozen. While in the service, Louis entertained troops by boxing and refereeing exhibitions.

Louis returned to the ring in 1946 and the first thing on the agenda was a rematch with Conn, a fight that had been built up while the two men were in the service.

A crowd of 45,266 at Yankee Stadium paid $1,925,564, the second biggest pre-television gate, June 19, 1946, for the privilege of seeing a fight that was far different from the first Louis-Conn battle and far below expectations.

Although 32, Louis was in top shape as a result of all the exhibitions he fought in the Army and of a strict training program. But Conn was well below his old form. He put up a poor fight.

Louis knocked out Conn in eight rounds.

There were some exciting fighters in action during that postwar year of 1946.

Middleweight champion Tony Zale and Rocky Graziano staged a donnybrook in Yankee Stadium that Zale won on a sixth-round knockout. A year later these two put on another brawl, this one in Chicago with Graziano winning on a sixth-round knockout.

On Dec. 6, 1946, the French middleweight champion made his American debut by outpointing Georgie Abrams in New York. He was Marcel Cerdan. Cerdan, who became a legend in France and one of her greatest heroes, went on to win the middleweight title from Zale and lose it to Jake LaMotta before losing his life in a plane crash in the Azores in 1949 as he was returning to the United States for a rematch with LaMotta.

Fourteen days after Cerdan fought Abrams, there was a welterweight title bout in New York between Tommy Bell and one of the most colorful and talented fighters who ever lived—Sugar Ray Robinson.

Robinson, a picture boxer and a deadly puncher, beat Bell, went on to win the middleweight championship five times and barely missed joining Bob Fitzsimmons and Henry Armstrong as the only triple champions. Robinson was beating light heavyweight champion Joey Maxim but he collapsed from the

heat after 13 rounds and had to settle for being a double champion such as Barney Ross, Tony Canzoneri, Emile Griffith and Dick Tiger.

Canzoneri, featherweight and lightweight champ, and Ross, lightweight and welterweight king, were on top in the 1930s and were contemporaries of such men as Armstrong, Jimmy McLarnin, Lou Ambers and Fritzie Zivic. Griffith, welterweight and middleweight champ, and Tiger, holder of the middleweight and light heavyweight titles, were at their peaks in the 1960s.

Another great fighter at the height of his powers in 1946 was featherweight champion Willie Pep. He had a historic four-bout series with Sandy Saddler.

On Oct. 22, 1946, Beau Jack, the former lightweight champion, lost a 10-round decision to someone called Buster Tyler. The story of Beau Jack is boxing legend. He was a Georgia shoeshine boy who became a world champion and ended up as a shoeshine boy.

Louis spent most of 1947 fighting exhibitions, then on Dec. 5 in Madison Square Garden he defended his title against Arnold Raymond Cream who borrowed the name of Joe Walcott, the welterweight champion around the turn of the century, and called himself Jersey Joe Walcott.

At the end of 15 rounds, during which he twice was on the floor, Louis found himself the winner of an unpopular 15-round split decision.

Walcott's showing earned him another shot at Louis, June 25, 1948, in Yankee Stadium. This time Louis won by a knockout in the 11th round. It was his last fight as champion.

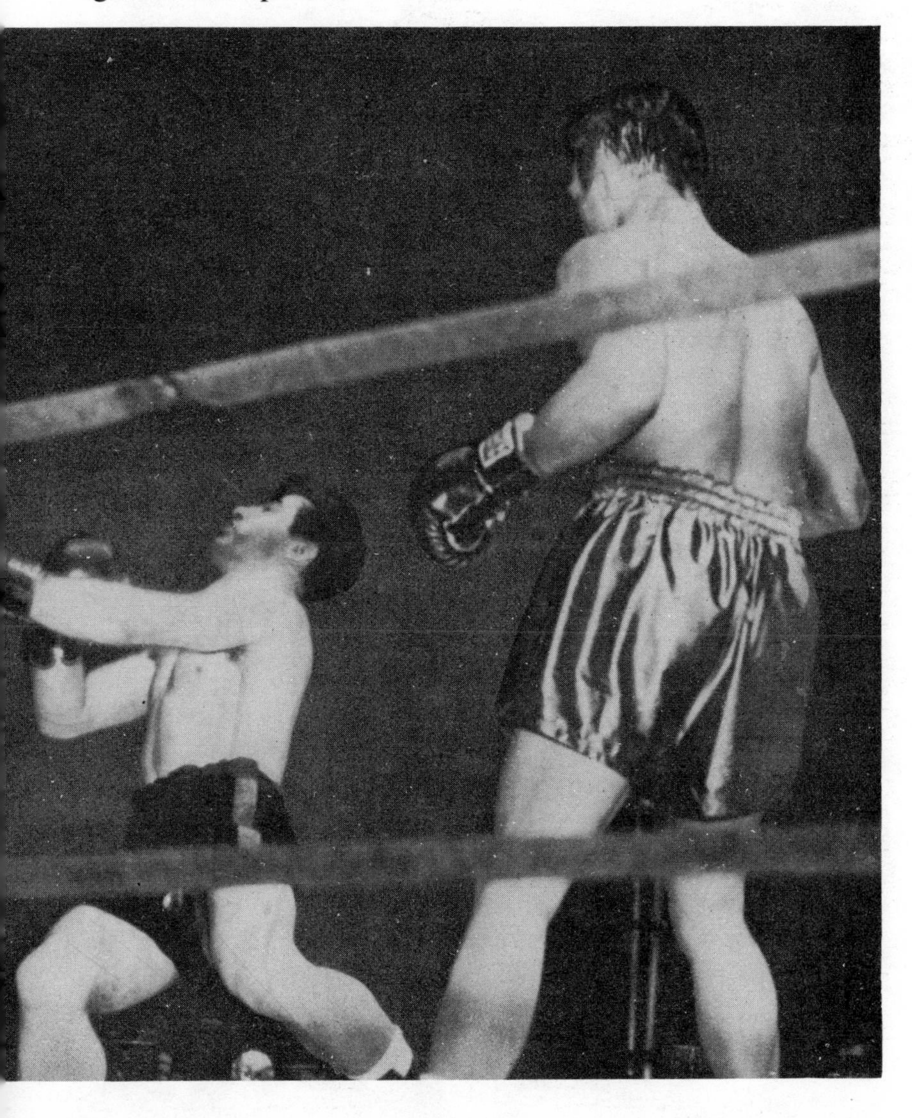

Middleweights Rocky Graziano and Tony Zale swapped knockouts in these bouts in the late '40s. Left frame, Graziano in this sixth round TKO strips Zale of the crown on July 16, 1947. Right frame, Graziano goes down for the count in the third round of bout in Newark, N.J., June 10, 1948, as Zale regained the title.

Above, Willie Pep tosses jaw-distorting right at Sandy Saddler on Feb. 11, 1949, in 13th round of title bout in which Pep regained his featherweight crown.

Sugar Ray Robinson was a picture boxer and a deadly puncher . . . one of the most colorful and talented fighters who ever lived. At right, he has just bounced a right off the head of Jake LaMotta in a middleweight title bout in Chicago on Feb. 14, 1951. Sugar Ray won on a TKO in the 13th.

With the retirement of Louis, boxing entered another era. It was the era of James D. Norris and the International Boxing Club. It was the era of weekly televised fights, a practice which strangled boxing by drying up the small clubs.

It was an era that brought on the Kefauver committee hearings into the monopoly aspects of boxing and ended the International Boxing Club, busted as a monopoly.

By 1951 the International Boxing Club offered televised fights three nights a week. There was a minor network show from New York's St. Nicholas Arena, a Wednesday night fight over CBS under the promotion of the International Boxing Club of Illinois and a Friday night fight on NBC under the promotion of the IBC of New York.

To meet his television contracts, Norris needed fighters. Carbo had what Norris needed, controlling many good fighters and also managers.

Besides losing many of the small clubs that provided fresh talent, boxing gained with Carbo's involvement something it didn't need—a diet that included fixed fights.

On March 8, 1957, Federal Judge Sylvester J. Ryan ruled that Norris, his associate Arthur Wirtz, Madison Square Garden and the International Boxing Clubs had engaged in a conspiracy to restrain trade and had monopolized the promotion of world championship fights in the United States in violation of the Sherman Act.

Carbo and Blinky Palermo, convicted on conspiracy and extortion charges, were sentenced Dec. 2, 1961. Carbo was given 25 years in prison and a $10,000 fine while Palermo got 15 years in prison and a $10,000 fine. Their appeals were rejected.

The last weekly televised fight was in 1964.

With Joe Louis in retirement, Ezzard Charles became heavyweight champion by outpointing Joe Walcott June 22, 1949. He followed this by knocking out Gus Lesnivich in 10 rounds and Pat Valentino in eight and stopping Freddie Beshore in 14.

Then he gained universal recognition as champion on Sept. 27, 1950, in Yankee Stadium by winning a 15-round decision over Louis, who, plagued by financial problems, came out of retirement.

Never a popular champion, Charles outpointed Joey Maxim in 15 rounds in the spring of 1951 and then decided once again to fight old Jersey Joe Walcott. So on July 18, 1951, in Pittsburgh's Forbes Field, the two met again and in the seventh round a smashing left hook to the jaw made Walcott champion. He was 37.

Walcott defended against Charles and outpointed him in 15 rounds and then accepted the challenge of an unbeaten fighter known as the Brockton Blockbuster—Rocky Marciano.

Marciano was a brawling-type fighter who could absorb tremendous punishment. Usually weighing only about 185 pounds for a fight, Marciano was one of the most superbly conditioned fighters of any era.

On his way to the title shot, Marciano outpointed Roland LaStarza, knocked out Rex Layne and scored an eighth-round knockout of Joe Louis, a 37-year-old shell of his former self.

Marciano and Walcott met on the night of Sept. 23, 1952, in Philadelphia in what was a slugfest from beginning to end.

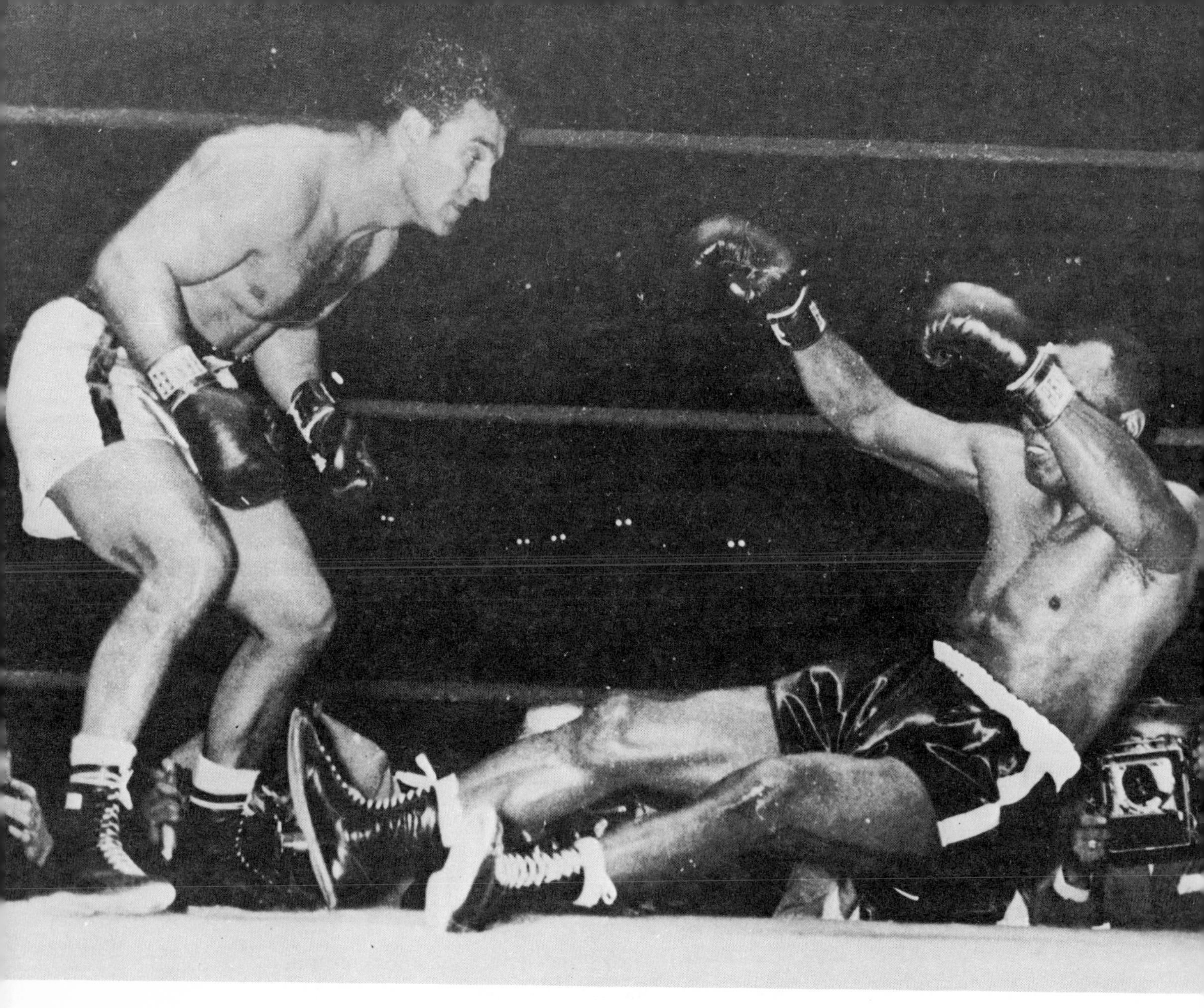

Rocky Marciano, the Brockton Blockbuster, watches challenger Jersey Joe Walcott suffer a first round knockout in bout on May 15, 1953, in Chicago. Marciano was killed in a light plane crash on Aug. 29, 1969, on the eve of his 46th birthday.

Walcott floored his younger opponent in the first round and was ahead after 12 rounds. Then in the 13th, Marciano connected with a thunderous right hand to the jaw and he was the champion. He would remain champion until he retired in 1955, saying he wanted to spend more time with his family.

Like Dempsey and Louis, Marciano remained extremely popular with sports enthusiasts after his retirement. He was killed in a light plane crash Aug. 29, 1969, on the eve of his 46th birthday.

The Marciano-Archie Moore fight in 1955 was the last heavyweight title bout promoted by Jim Norris. Cus D'Amato, manager of the next heavyweight champion, Floyd Patterson, said even before Patterson won the crown that he would never let the boxer fight for the International Boxing Club.

Patterson knocked out 43-year-old Archie Moore in the fifth round in Chicago Nov. 30, 1956, to become at 21 the youngest man ever to win the title. He also was to become the first to regain the title.

Patterson's reign as heavyweight champion was a series of highs and lows. A gentle man, who shunned publicity, Patterson was a complex personality in the realm of prize fighting.

Patterson had speed, a good punch and dedication to his craft but did not possess a heavyweight's chin. He often was on the canvas.

In June 1959, Patterson stopped Brian London of England in 11 rounds at Indianapolis and then accepted a fight with a big, undefeated Swede named Ingemar Johansson. Johansson had gained prominence by knocking out top contender Eddie Machen in one round.

Johansson and Patterson met in Yankee Stadium June 26, 1959, and Johansson stunned the sports world by knocking Patterson down seven times and finishing him off in the third round.

The Swede lost the title on his first defense when Patterson regained the crown with a five-round knockout June 20, 1960, in a Polo Grounds fight that was the highlight of his career. The knockout punch, a right hand, left Johansson unconscious for several minutes.

Patterson fought Johansson for a third time, knocking him out in six rounds at Miami Beach, Fla., March 13, 1961, but lost the title to Charles "Sonny" Liston on a one-round knockout in Chicago's Comiskey Park Sept. 25, 1962. Patterson tried to regain the crown again July 22, 1963, in Las Vegas, Nev., but Liston again knocked him out in the first round.

Liston, a brute of a man, was once managed by John Vitale, a St. Louis racketeer, and Blinky Palermo. He learned to box in the Missouri State Penitentiary at Jefferson where he was sentenced to two concurrent five-year terms in 1950 on two counts of armed robbery and two counts of larceny.

Liston's tremendous punching power, his ferocious appearance and his two quick knockouts of Patterson built around him an aura of invincibility. This bubble burst the night of Feb. 25, 1964, in Miami.

On that night Liston lost the title to a fast-talking, poetry-spouting young man called Cassius Clay. Liston quit in his corner after the sixth round, saying he had injured his shoulder.

Cassius Clay won the Olympic light heavyweight championship for the United States in Rome in 1960. He turned pro in October of that year and fought his way up the heavyweight ladder, clowning, couching his predictions of victories in poetry and emitting bombastic boasts. He annoyed some people but many found him entertaining.

The day after he beat Liston, Clay announced he was a member of the Black Muslims and his name was Muhammad Ali, not Cassius Clay. He turned his contract over to the Black Muslims, breaking with the Louisville, Ky., syndicate that backed him from his start as a pro.

The word for Ali changed from colorful to controversial.

Controversy certainly followed his first defense of the title May 25, 1965, at Lewiston, Maine, an implausible New England village selected because suspicion surrounding the first Ali-Liston bout had discouraged the major centers.

At Lewiston, Ali knocked out Liston in the first round with a phantom right-handed punch many people who were there or watching in theaters said they never saw.

The cry of "fix" was heard and as usual there were calls for the outlawing of boxing. As usual, boxing survived.

Ali's next defense came Nov. 22, 1965, when he toyed with Floyd Patterson before stopping him in 12 rounds in Las Vegas. He was busy in 1966 with five defenses. He outpointed George Chuvalo and knocked out Henry Cooper of

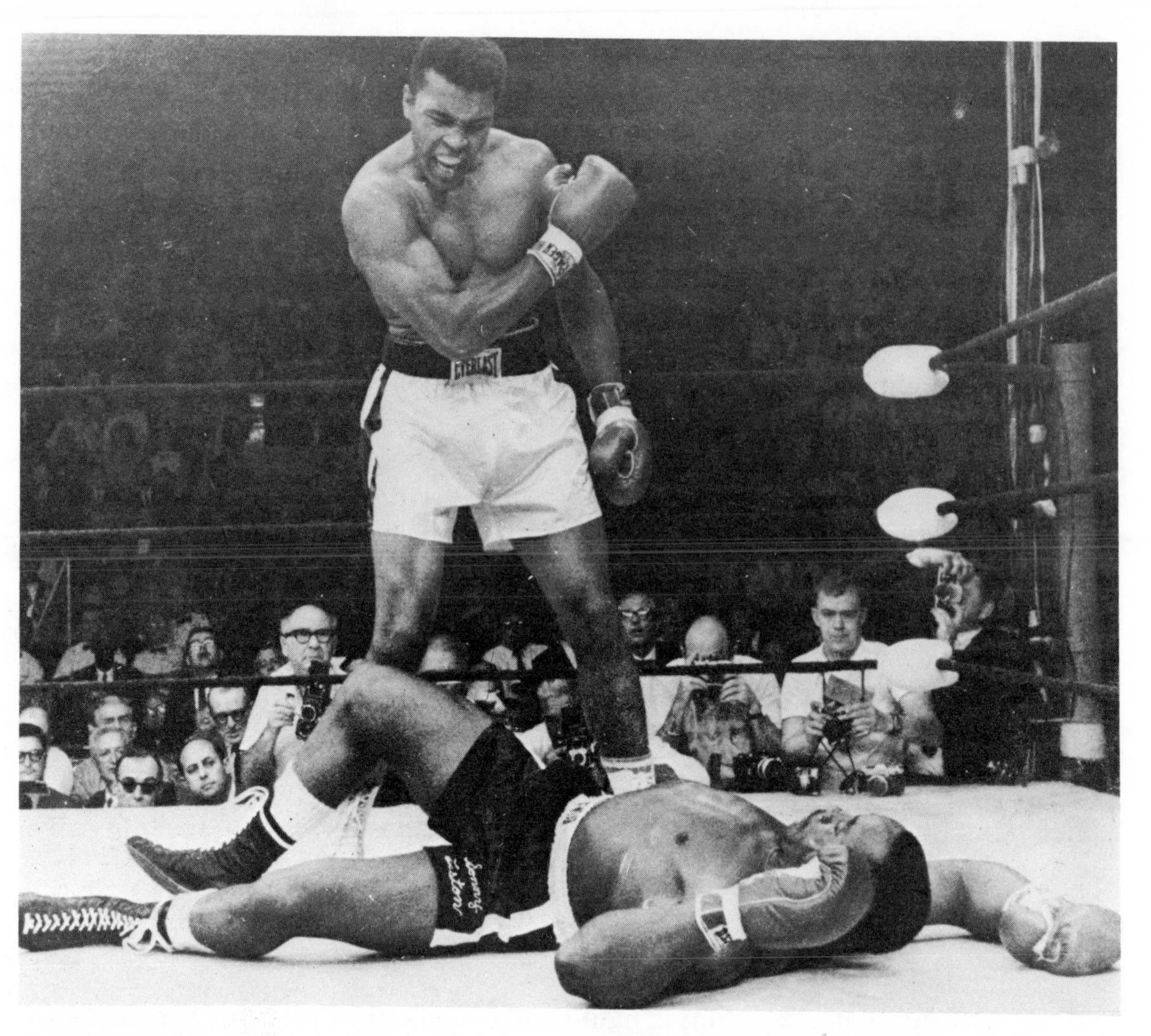
Muhammad Ali shouts at Sonny Liston whom he floored in first round of return title bout in Maine on May 25, 1965.

England in six rounds, Brian London in three, Karl Mildenberger in 12 and Cleveland Williams in three.

He opened 1967 by outpointing Ernie Terrell Feb. 6 and then knocked out Zora Folley in seven rounds March 22 in Madison Square Garden.

Shortly afterward, Muhammad Ali refused to take the step for military service—contending he was a Muslim minister—setting off a series of events that rocked the foundation of boxing. He was fined $10,000 and sentenced to five years in prison, but he never served. He entered into a series of appeals, but he was stripped of his title.

The Folley fight was Ali's last until, with an appeal of his conviction still pending, he was given a license to fight Jerry Quarry in Atlanta, in October 1970, a fight he won when it was stopped after three rounds because Quarry had a split left eyebrow.

With Ali stripped of his title by the governing bodies of boxing, there was no universally recognized heavyweight champion until Feb. 16, 1970.

In the meantime Jimmy Ellis, a former sparring partner of Ali's, won the World Boxing Association elimination tournament. But Joe Frazier, thought by many to be the best heavyweight with Ali on the sidelines, refused to enter the WBA tournament and became recognized as champion by six states, including New York.

The question of the recognized heavyweight champion of the world was settled—insofar as the official authorities were concerned—Feb. 16, 1970, in Madison Square Garden when Frazier floored Ellis twice in the fourth round and Ellis was unable to answer the bell for the fifth round.

But Ali was still in the wings, screaming loud enough for the whole world to hear: "Frazier is a phony. He is still an amateur. He is not the champion. I am the champion."

Frazier, a quiet family man, father of five who disdained any militant role in the civil rights movement, listened and smiled. He said little.

Then on Nov. 18, 1971, in Detroit, he sharpened his punches by knocking out light heavyweight champion Bob Foster in the second round.

Ali was next—much to Ali's regret, but boxing was healthy and thriving again.

Promoters began laying the groundwork for a bigger and better rematch.

A happy Joe Frazier is embraced by manager Yank Durham after retaining his heavyweight title by whipping Muhammad Ali over the 15-round distance in New York March 8, 1971.

Pros Pancho Gonzales, forecourt, and Rod Laver battle for high stakes at Madison Square Garden in June 1970.

chapter 7

TENNIS

It Started with a Wall and a Ball

by Will Grimsley

Instead of grass, the white lines of the court were inscribed on a huge green rug made of some synthetic material. There was no sun overhead but thousands of kilowatts of light beamed down from the ceiling, as on a theatrical stage. The place was New York's Madison Square Garden, a scene of prize fights, hockey matches and rodeos.

On one side of the net stood Pancho Gonzales, holding an aluminum instrument that flashed as would a surgeon's tools. On the other side was Rod Laver. The weapon in his hand was sleek and looked as if it were made of shining gold.

"The score is 6–6," barked the umpire, from his adult high chair. "We now go into sudden death."

The crowd of more than 16,000—it looked like a fight crowd or fans in a bull-ring—leaned forward expectantly. The big arena became deathly quiet.

There were a few swift swishes of the rackets. The balls sped back and forth over the net almost too quickly for the human eye to follow.

"Set to Gonzales," announced the umpire.

If Maj. Walter Clopton Wingfield suddenly had come to life and been transported to this indoor scene in one of the world's most populous cities, would he have recognized the game he introduced to a few intimate friends at a lawn party outside London in December 1873?

Probably not.

Will Grimsley is a Special Correspondent, whose assignments are not confined to sports. However, since joining *The AP* in 1943 at Memphis and moving to New York in 1947, his concentration has been on sports. He has covered five Summer Olympics, starting with Helsinki in 1952 and the 1968 Winter Games at Grenoble, France. Assignments also have taken him to Moscow, Tokyo, Stockholm, Budapest, Dublin and other overseas sites. Ten trips to Australia in the 1950s and 1960s to cover the Davis Cup helped background him in tennis. He formerly worked on the *Nashville Tennessean*.

Lawn tennis, a snobbish sport appealing to the affluent and fashionable and restricted in its formative years to the country club set, was slow to change. No other game adhered so strictly to tradition. If most of the authorities had been given their way, the sport would have continued to be played on manicured lawns by a favored few, all wearing the traditional white garb and mouthing such obscure phrases as "fifteen-forty," "deuce," "advantage" and "love."

Tennis, like golf, however, spilled over to the masses. Change was inevitable. Progress could not be deterred.

On July 8, 1968, the *Wall Street Journal,* America's business barometer, found it necessary to turn its attention from the ticker tape machines and industrial charts and take a long, hard look at what it called the tennis explosion.

"What happened to golf a generation ago and to skiing a few winters ago now is happening to tennis," the financial journal reported. "Suddenly, the courts are full."

A survey showed the number of active players in the United States alone had soared to nine million, increasing at the rate of almost one million a year. There were 100,000 tennis courts in the country with new ones arising at the rate of 7,000 every 12 months. Tennis balls sold in 1968 numbered 15.8 million, almost double that of 1962. Sporting goods companies were producing rackets of wood, steel and aluminum—costing between $40 and $65, depending on the quality of the strings—as fast as their factories could turn them out, yet not fast enough to meet the demand. One could still buy a racket at department stores for $8.

The big time promoters moved in. Madison Avenue joined the parade. War developed in the scramble for talent and the spectator dollar.

A young Dallas, Tex., sportsman named Lamar Hunt, already with financial involvements in pro football, baseball, basketball and soccer, bought the contracts of the leading professional players, wiped out one rival promoter and in one bold stroke siphoned off three-fourths of the United States' successful 1970 Davis Cup squad.

He announced a tournament schedule for 1971 with total prize money of $1 million. The various national associations, which had dominated the game for half a century, became jittery and took countermeasures in an effort to prevent the wholesale stampede of leading tournament players into the Hunt corral. The International Lawn Tennis Federation, cooperating with a soft drink company in the sponsorship of a Grand Prix program in tennis similar to that in auto racing, set in motion a rival circuit with $1.5 million in purses.

Tennis, once the pastime of bored monks in European monasteries and later recreation for the idle rich, finally had come of age.

The origin of the game—even the origin of its name—is a mystery. Historians contend that the early forms of tennis came down to us through France, dating back to the 13th century, although there are roots reaching out to ancient Greece and the Orient.

Homer, in the *Odyssey,* related how the white-armed Princess Nausicaa, playing at the game with her hand maidens, hit the ball into the river. Horace, in describing his journey from Rose to Brundusium in the Vth Satire, tells that during one of the stops Maecenas "goes to play at Tennis while he and Virgil to sleep."

An English writer who signed himself Antiquarius said the game found its way into France through the Saracen invasion and the Greeks picked it up from

Persia or Egypt, probably as far back as the 5th century before Christ. Another reported that in the 4th century A.D., Persians were found playing a game called "tchigan" in a closed space with rackets four feet long.

Most historians pick up the game in France in the 13th century. It was called "jeu de paume," or a game played with the palm of the hand. It was played at first by striking a ball made of cloth fabric with the palm of the hand—not to be confused with handball, which originated in Ireland in the 10th century. The balls were made of a soft cloth fabric sewn into a hard, round shape. A pile of dirt formed the first nets.

The game first was played by bishops and priests in court yards and monasteries. Later it became the game of kings. In 1245, the Archbishop of Rouen prohibited priests from indulging in the sport. King Louis IX outlawed tennis in France but his edict was ignored. Nearly a century later, the game invaded the British Isles and Edward III (1327–77) had a court constructed on the palace grounds.

The common belief is that the name is derived from the French word, "ten-ez," meaning "to play." Some say it can be traced to the lost city of Tennis, renowned for its fabrics from which the balls were made. The Egyptian city supposedly sank into the sea in 1226.

The players first hit the ball with bare hands. Later the hands were taped. Then crude bats developed and finally precision rackets strung with sensitive sheep gut—not cat gut as generally supposed. The cloth balls were replaced by balls made of leather, stuffed sometimes with human hair, and later in the early 1900s by balls made of rubber with a flannel coating. The net, dating back to early fishermen, preceded tennis. Dirt and wooden barriers were originally used, replaced first by a single cord and later by the net, varying in height over the years.

Major Walter Clopton Wingfield, a member of one of England's most distinguished families, a handsome man with beard, sideburns and flowing mustache, was a student of court tennis, an indoor game played by batting balls against a wall and into crevices, and a man adept at racket games. He often confided with friends that he thought an outdoor game could be devised, using rackets and balls, which would be a delight to players and spectators alike.

In December 1873, he invited some friends to a lawn party at Nantclwyd and sprang a surprise. He had marked out a court on the lawn—a court with an

This painting depicts lawn tennis, a favorite game, on Staten Island, N.Y., where the game enjoyed popularity early in its development.

hour-glass figure, narrower at the net than at the baselines. He had spoon-shaped rackets with long handles and uncovered hollow rubber balls. A net, four feet in the center and five feet at each end, was strung between two fragile poles. Scoring was similar to that used in racquets, with each point counting one—1-2-3, etc.—and 15 points constituting a game.

The major called his brainchild "Sphairistiké," a name he said had been given the game centuries before, from the Greek, meaning "to play." He said he borrowed features of the game from other racket games, principally court tennis and badminton.

The lawn party was a howling success. The guests became so excited that they bantered the major on how they might acquire rackets and balls of their own so they might play on their own lawns. Wingfield applied for a patent in 1874 and began marketing the game of "Sphairistiké, or Lawn Tennis." The commercial venture failed but the major earned his place in history as the father of lawn tennis.

A year after the major's lawn party, a group of British army officers, one or more of them perhaps a guest on the eventful occasion, were found batting a ball back and forth over a newly-laid court in Bermuda. An interested spectator was Mary Ewing Outerbridge, member of a socially-prominent family living on Staten Island, N.Y., in Bermuda on a holiday.

When Miss Outerbridge returned home—in March 1874—she brought a package containing tennis rackets, balls and net. The parcel was confiscated by suspicious Customs officers but released when Miss Outerbridge's brother, A. Emilius Outerbridge, prominent in shipping circles, brought pressure on higher authorities.

The Outerbridges were a sports-minded family. Emilius was a very good cricket player and with his brother, Eugenius, served on the board of directors of the Staten Island Cricket and Baseball Club, to which the family belonged.

Through the influence of her brothers, Miss Outerbridge received permission to lay out a tennis court on the edge of the cricket field. It was immaterial that the court only roughly met specifications. It was 24 feet wide at the net and 30 feet wide at the base line. There was a large service area.

On a bright spring day in 1874, Miss Outerbridge donned high button shoes, a tightly-drawn corset, half a dozen frilly slips and a dress that dropped to her shoe tops. Her long hair was held in place by a floral hat. Then she, her brothers and a few curious friends proceeded to christen the court.

Thus, so far as can be ascertained, the first game of lawn tennis was played in the United States.

Miss Outerbridge's claim of being the "mother" of the game in the United States was disputed later by a group of New England men, who insisted they were the first to strike a ball with a racket in a formal contest in this country.

Dr. James Dwight, who was prominent in later forming the U. S. Lawn Tennis Association and who served for a long period as its president, wrote years later:

"The first set of lawn tennis in New England—indeed, I fancy, in this country—was played at Mr. William Appleton's place at Nahant. In the summer of 1875, a set of Sphairistiké, or lawn tennis, was brought out from England, where the game was just coming into fashion.

"Mr. F. R. Sears, the elder brother of the champion, and I put up the net and tried the game . . . That is the first tennis that I know of that was played in New England, and for two years we played incessantly. At the end of our second summer, in August 1876, we held our first tournament."

It is true that the game took more quickly in New England. At the Staten Island Baseball and Cricket Club, Miss Outerbridge found difficulty getting up a match. Most of her lady friends demurred, arguing it was not feminine to go leaping across the grass in pursuit of a rubber ball. They preferred croquet. The men considered it a sissy game.

While Miss Outerbridge was languishing for want of partners, courts began bobbing up on the Atlantic Seaboard. Within a few years there were several private courts in Newport, R.I. William H. Young, returning from England, in 1879 established a crude court in Santa Monica, Calif., on the site where the municipal pier now stands. A tournament was organized at Nahant in 1875.

Newport, however, emerged as the early tennis capital. It was only natural. The city was the shrine of the white flannel set. It was there that industrial tycoons built multimillion-dollar mansions, presidents and princes rubbed elbows with the rich and ultra-rich.

The first National Championships were played at Newport in 1881 and they remained there until 1915 when the tournament was shifted to Forest Hills, N.Y.

The first American champion was Richard D. (Dick) Sears, who won the title at the age of 19 and held it for seven years. He wore steel-rimmed spectacles and a mustache. He played in long white flannels, a striped blazer and a cap. A tie was knotted at his neck.

Dick Sears had become interested in the game when he watched his older brother, Fred, and Dr. Dwight play their historic match on the Appleton Estate at Nahant in 1875. He was 11 at the time. Often Dr. Dwight allowed the youngster to come onto the court and practice swinging the racket at the heavy balls. The doctor also took his protege with him on a trip to England where young Sears became acquainted with the great English players, William Renshaw and Herbert Lawford.

Renshaw presented Sears with a racket which the young man took home as a prized possession, polishing and restringing it and using it in winning his string of championships. From Lawford, Sears got the "Lawford stroke" which became the envy of all players in those early days. It was a wide, sweeping shot on which the racket was brought over the ball, producing a looping trajectory and confusing top-spin.

In those early years before the turn of the century, tennis in America was dominated by a handful of men, largely Easterners and largely players from the Ivy League colleges. Henry W. Slocum Jr., a wiry athlete with a handlebar mustache and brilliantined hair, succeeded Sears. Oliver S. Campbell was a Columbia student who was an aggressive net rusher. Robert D. Wrenn, a Harvard student who won four titles, was an all-around athlete who lettered in football, hockey and baseball. He was a powerful left-hander who scampered all over the court in making returns and who seemed indefatigable.

Meanwhile, tennis was not standing still in England where the modern version of the game originated. At the time Maj. Wingfield thought of the idea of bringing the game out of its monastery shell into the daylight, croquet, a pleasant pastime in which wooden balls were nudged through wickets with wooden mallets, was enjoying wide popularity among the British social set.

One day, so the story goes, three eminent English sportsmen—Julian Marshall, Henry Jones and C. G. Heathcote—were strolling past the All-England Croquet Club when they happened to notice the magnificent turf on which the games were being played. An idea struck them almost simultaneously.

"What an ideal court for lawn tennis," Marshall remarked.

"Indeed," said Jones.

"An excellent place for a tournament," added Heathcote.

The three gentlemen took their notions to J. H. Walsh, editor of *The Field Magazine*. A meeting was held in the magazine's office at 346, The Strand, in London. An influential man, Walsh persuaded the All-England Club to introduce tennis into its program and change its name to the All-England Croquet and Lawn Tennis Club.

On June 9, 1877, the notice was posted:

"The All-England Croquet and Lawn Tennis Club, Wimbledon, propose to hold a lawn tennis meeting open to all amateurs on Monday July 9 and following days. Entrance fee, one shilling. Two prizes will be given–one gold champion prize to the winner, one silver to the second player.

A set of rules was agreed upon. Scoring would be in the "fifteens," the original system of scoring, rather than the 1–2–3–4 racquets formula. The court should be rectangular, 26 yards long and nine yards wide, and not shaped like an hourglass. The net would extend from poles three feet outside the court. One service fault would be permitted without penalty no matter where the ball was hit. These regulations became the foundation of the game, almost inviolate for close to 100 years.

The first Wimbledon tournament was held in 1877. It was won by a Harrovian named S. W. Gore, a big, strong, athletically-inclined man with tremendous reflexes. Opponents marvelled at his wrist shots.

Nevertheless, a modern-day player would have snickered at the inaugural Wimbledon. Both players served sidearm. The service offered little or no advantage. Twenty-two players competed in the event. There were only 200 spectators, who paid a shilling each. There were no deuce sets. When the score reached 5–5, the next player to take a game won the set. Players changed court at the end of each set instead of on odd games. The tournament was postponed one day so that everybody could attend the Eton-Harrow cricket match.

The early Wimbledons were Challenge Round matches. The champion sat out the tournament until eliminations produced a challenger. The titleholder thus had to play only one match. This practice continued until 1922 when the rules were changed making it necessary for the defending champion to take his chances in the regular field.

The first of Wimbledon's many legends was a man named Willie Renshaw, whose all-court ability and remarkable stamina made him the terror of the pre-1900 era. In 1881 Willie won his first championship by crushing the Rev. J. T. Hartley in 37 minutes, a record never threatened. To this title, he added six more between the years of 1881 and 1889, establishing a mark untouched by such subsequent heroes as Big Bill Tilden, Fred Perry, Don Budge and Rod

Laver. It took a woman, America's Helen Wills Moody, to overshadow that imposing string of Wimbledon triumphs. Helen won eight.

Wimbledon was rich in history from the beginning. The Doherty brothers, R. F. and Lawrie, won nine championships between them between 1897 and 1906. A 15-year-old schoolgirl named Charlotte (Lottie) Dod beat the defending champion, Blanche Bingley, with the loss of only two games in 1887, becoming the youngest winner. Bill Baddeley won in 1891 at the age of 19, the youngest men's champion.

The event soon became a social as well as a sporting spectacle. Kings and queens sat in the royal box. Players from other parts of the world poured in to make a challenge in what was acclaimed the tennis championship of the world. Two of the first American invaders were Dwight Davis and Holcombe Ward.

Dwight Filley Davis was a member of a prominent St. Louis family. While attending Harvard, Davis, a member of the varsity tennis team, conceived the idea of an international match between top players of the United States and Britain, which was considered more advanced in the game than the Americans.

"I think we could beat them," Davis said. "We play a more aggressive game."

The plan was laid before the U. S. Lawn Tennis Association, which contacted the British Lawn Tennis Association. A match was scheduled for the Longwood Club in Brookline, Mass., outside Boston, in 1900.

Davis contacted a Boston jeweler and together they agreed on specifications for a suitable trophy. It was a silver bowl lightly washed in gold, 13 inches high, 18 inches in diameter and weighing 217 ounces, troy weight. The cost: $700. Davis paid the bill.

The British were a confident team when they arrived in their blue jackets and gold buttons, but they were in for a shock. Having agreed upon a format of two opening singles, a doubles match and two closing singles for a best-of-five match series, the Americans proceeded to clinch the match on the first two days. Malcolm Whitman beat Britain's Arthur Gore 6–1, 6–3, 6–2. Davis won over E. D. Black 4–6, 6–2, 6–4, 6–4. Davis and Ward teamed to win the doubles.

This is the Davis Cup, the trophy put on the line each year in international competition between top players of more than 50 nations.

So the Davis Cup was born, but it was not to be strictly a two-nation affair. Davis' concept was for an international competition which would spread good will through tennis. Belgium, Austria and France entered the lists in 1904 as did Australasia, a combined team from Australia and New Zealand. Then came South Africa in 1911, Germany and Canada in 1913, Holland in 1920. By 1970, more than 50 nations, including the Soviet Union and her Communist satellites, were vying for the big silver bowl, to which it was necessary to add a tray and polished walnut base—or plinths—for the inscription of names.

The two decades preceding World War I in American tennis were dominated by three personalities—Bill Larned in the men's division, Hazel Hotchkiss and Molla Mallory among the women.

Larned was a graduate of Cornell University who rode with Teddy Roosevelt's "Rough Riders." A stocky, muscled man with a daring go-for-broke philosophy and a searing backhand, he returned from the Spanish-American War to win the first of his seven championships in 1901. He ranked No. 1 for eight years and was in the Top Ten 19 times.

"There is little doubt that William A. Larned was the most consistently brilliant player this country had turned out before Tilden's skill ripened," wrote one contemporary.

Hazel Hotchkiss was the daughter of a pioneer who drove a covered wagon from Kentucky to California where he became a farmer and a wine maker. The sturdy farm girl won three straight women's titles, starting in 1909, and captured a fourth 10 years later. In the interim, she was married to George Wightman, a prominent New Englander.

In a fabulous career, Mrs. Wightman achieved a total of 45 national crowns, the last a seniors' championship when she was 68 years old. She originated the Wightman Cup competition between top women players of Britain and the United States in 1923. She became the dowager queen of American tennis.

During its teething years, ladies' tennis was looked upon with scorn in some quarters. The girls wore long, frilly dresses that dropped down to the ankles. Underneath were layers of petticoats. They wore floppy, wide-brimmed hats, some of them decorated with flowers. Some of them played a slow, pat-ball game, giggling and chatting as they skipped across the court. A few served underhand.

The image of the feminine tennis player was changed drastically with the appearance on the courts of a supple, shapely French mademoiselle named Suzanne Lenglen, who seemed to delight in defying tradition.

Suzanne was 20 years old when she crossed the English Channel to play in her first Wimbledon in 1919 and challenge the aging British star, Mrs. Lambert Chambers, who had been virtually unbeatable for 10 years. Tennis fans in England were anxious for a view of the French girl, who had been the rage of the Riviera circuit, but they hardly were prepared for the shock they got.

Mlle. Lenglen appeared on the courts in a low-cut, one-piece dress that dropped only midway to her calves. Instead of a cumbersome hat, she wore a scarf around her dark tresses. Women spectators were shocked. They gathered in small clusters and whispered about the scandal of it. The males were goggle-eyed with delight.

Suzanne was no dazzling beauty. She had a long, Gallic nose and large mouth. She was stocky and swarthy, with heavy shoulders. Yet she was light as a kitten on the court, charged with an electric personality and full of fire and temperament.

Driven by doting parents, she practiced by the hours, becoming so proficient that she was able to hit a coin on a court five times in a row. She was a fierce competitor, begrudging every point scored against her. She also was tense and high strung but many old-timers who lived through succeeding eras rated her the greatest striker of the ball who ever lived.

Suzanne once crushed Molla Mallory, the American champion, 6–0, 6–0, dropping only 18 points in the entire match. She beat the great Helen Wills in their only meeting. She won her first Wimbledon in 1919 and went on to take five others. She captured six French championships over a period of seven years.

The French girl was a relentless but frail tennis machine. She suffered from pernicious anemia. She became a court prima donna. She demanded private limousines, special treatment. She had her clothes made by hand by the best French designers, who did it free. She sulked and stormed and threw tantrums. She died at the age of 39, in the prime of her life.

Nevertheless, she left an indelible mark on the game. She became the darling of the masses, who poured out by the thousands to watch her play. It was largely through Mlle. Lenglen that tennis dropped its cloak of country club conservatism and began to dwell among the people. A worldwide heroine, Suzanne pricked the interest of the masses.

It remained for two Americans, Big Bill Tilden and Helen Wills, to pick up the torch from Mlle. Lenglen and turn tennis into a big time spectator sport.

They were the court sovereigns in the mad age known as the Golden Twenties, an era of free-spending and sports hero worship that spawned such idols as Jack Dempsey in boxing, Babe Ruth in baseball, Bob Jones in golf and Babe Didrikson in Olympic track and field and other sports.

William Tatum Tilden II was a frustrated Shakespearean actor from Philadelphia's Main Line who took his thespian proclivities to the tennis court and became the greatest player in the world. Polls conducted in 1951 and in 1969 to pick the No. 1 player of all-time placed Tilden on top by a comfortable margin.

Big Bill was a gangling, lantern-jawed man with broad, sloping shoulders and a mincing step. There was an electric quality about him that captivated audiences. He had a thundering cannonball service but rarely followed it to the net, as is the custom of the modern day serve-and-volley, quick-kill artisans. Yet he had no equal off the ground. His forehand and backhand drives were both flawless and deadly. He cut opponents to pieces with mixtures of pace, spins, slices, lobs and drop shots. He was the master craftsman.

Shot-making excellence, however, was only a fraction of Tilden's appeal. He carried on an unending feud with administrators, umpires and linesmen. He was always exciting. He was never predictable.

Tilden, who grew up in the tennis tradition around the turf courts of Germantown and Merion outside Philadelphia, matured late. Once he took off from the game for nearly a year to perfect a backhand. He was 27 when he won his first American championship.

The year was 1920. Tilden went on to win six straight U. S. titles and return to Forest Hills in 1929 at the age of 36 to capture a seventh. He was the first American to win the Wimbledon men's singles title—in 1920. He won three in all, his last in 1930 when he was 37 years old.

Here's Big Bill Tilden as he appeared in 1950.

Big Bill's chief rival was a frail, intense player, Little Bill Johnston, destined to die at an early age of tuberculosis. Little Bill concentrated on Tilden's then vulnerable backhand to beat the tall Philadelphian in the 1919 Forest Hills final 6–4, 6–4, 6–3. A proud man, Big Bill brooded over the defeat, went into seclusion at the home of a New England friend and spent months reconstructing his backhand stoke.

The secret practice worked. Returning the next year, he won at Wimbledon and then defeated Johnston in a historic match for the championship at Forest Hills.

He emerged as the undisputed king of the courts, reigning until he turned professional in 1931, taking his talents on the road. His life remained a tempestuous one. He ran afoul of the law and late in life served two jail sentences on morals charges. He was preparing another tennis trip when he died of a heart attack at the age of 60.

Tilden's career paralleled that of Helen Wills, later to become Mrs. Helen Wills Moody. They called her "Little Miss Poker Face." Her trademark was a green-lined white eyeshade, pulled low over a sphinx-like chiseled Grecian countenance.

Bill Tilden's chief rival was Little Bill Johnston shown here in 1945 and in action in the 1920s.

Her trademark was a green-lined white eyeshade and she was known as "Little Miss Poker Face." She's Helen Wills Moody and in her career she won seven American championships, eight Wimbledon and four French titles.

She was an enigma. To the general public, her rivals and the news media, she was a cold and unemotional automaton. She seldom spoke on the court. She never made a gesture. She went about her work dourly, frequently freezing a linesman with an icy stare. Yet, in off moments, she could be a giggling, effervescent schoolgirl in pigtails.

One writer of the period, discussing her lack of expression, said: "This did not mean she was grim, or tense; it meant that she was calm. She was placid. She showed only equanimity."

Helen, a doctor's daughter born in Berkeley, Calif., won her first U. S. women's title at the age of 17. She captured seven American championships, eight Wimbledon and four French, winning her last Wimbledon in 1938 at the age of 32.

As Helen's conquests multiplied, demands grew for a match between Miss Wills and Mlle. Lenglen. The Frenchwoman, ill and moody, was accused of avoiding a confrontation. Miss Wills, confident she could win, was eager for a chance to prove it.

The opportunity came in January 1926. Miss Wills learned that Suzanne was campaigning in the south of France. She took leave of her studies and headed for the Continent. A carnival atmosphere prevailed when the match of the century finally took place in an obscure tournament at the Carleston Club in Cannes. Mlle. Lenglen, playing in a low cut blouse and a calf-length skirt, played brilliantly, winning 6–3, 8–6. Helen was stricken later that year with appendicitis. Suzanne turned professional.

Miss Wills' greatest rival was Helen Hull Jacobs, who grew up in the San Francisco Bay area and, younger than Miss Wills, became heir apparent to the latter's tennis throne. Both Californians, they met frequently with the older Helen usually the victor.

But in 1932, when Queen Helen passed up the National Championships, Miss Jacobs won and the following year had to defend her title against the former champion, who now was Mrs. Moody. The concrete horseshoe at Forest Hills was jammed for the battle of the Helens. Miss Jacobs won the first set 8–6, the third set Queen Helen had yielded in six years. Mrs. Moody took the second

6–3. Miss Jacobs spurted to a 3–0 lead in the third and decisive set when suddenly there was commotion on the center court.

Mrs. Moody strode to the umpire's chair, said, "I can't continue," and then without a word to Miss Jacobs strode to the clubhouse. Spectators and Miss Jacobs were stunned. The fans became outraged and called Mrs. Moody a quitter. Mrs. Moody never apologized publicly but she confided to friends that she had injured her back lifting some rocks in her garden and was unable to play further.

She divorced Frederick S. Moody, a California broker, in 1937 and in 1939 married a long-time friend, Aidan Roark, a well-known polo player. She retired to Southern California, where she kept busy writing and painting. She disappeared completely from the tennis scene.

Departure of Tilden and Mrs. Moody left a great void in the game. They were followed by a succession of champions—some great, some good and some indifferent—but tennis itself moved into a period of controversy and unrest.

Players became what were known as "tennis bums." Although regarded as amateurs, they fed on the game. They traveled the world circuit at someone else's expense. They accepted bonuses and appearance monies under the table. The ruling associations were fully aware of the violations but discreetly—or indiscreetly—looked the other way.

Professional promoters moved in. As soon as a player reached a championship pinnacle—with only a Wimbledon or Forest Hills title or two to his credit—he was offered a tempting contract and put on an exhibition tour. This was theater on a canvas court. As the pro ranks grew, so did demands for open competition, tournaments pitting the pros against the so-called amateurs.

An ugly impasse occurred. The pros wound up with the best talent. The national associations possessed all of the attractive big time tennis venues—Wimbledon, Forest Hills, Roland Garros in Paris, Kooyong in Melbourne. They refused to get together. Tennis was the victim.

Through the first 26 years of Davis Cup competition, Dwight Davis' silver bowl had been dominated by English-speaking nations. The United States won it 10 times, Australasia six and Britain five, with no matches between 1915 and 1918 because of World War I.

In 1927 France broke the stranglehold with a quartet of dashing clay court wizards who were labeled "The Four Musketeers." They were Rene Lacoste, son of a millionaire automobile magnate in Paris; city-bred Henri Cochet, from the silk capital of Lyons; Jean Borotra, the scrambling and unorthodox Bounding Basque, and Jacques Brugnon, the classic stylist who never reached his potential.

The Frenchmen wrested the Davis Cup from Bill Tilden and Little Bill Johnston at Germantown Cricket Club in Philadelphia in 1927 and took the trophy back to the red clay of Paris where they held it for six years. For a period in the 1920s they ruled the world of tennis. Lacoste won two U. S. titles and Cochet one. For half a dozen years, starting in 1924, they had Wimbledon to themselves, Lacoste, Borotra and Cochet each winning twice. They also dominated the doubles.

Then came Fred Perry. He was a tall, good-looking Englishman with a head of raven-black hair, never a strand out of place, and a tennis game just as immaculate. Perry came out of the London suburbs and with a companion, Henry W. (Bunny) Austin beat the French in the Davis Cup Challenge Round 3–2.

It marked the first time since 1912 that Britain had held the cup and, with Perry

Fred Perry, the tall Englishman out of the London suburbs, won three consecutive Wimbledon titles in the early '30s, later adding three U.S. crowns plus the championships of France and Australia.

as chief of the defenders, the British reign lasted four years. He won the first of three consecutive Wimbledon titles in 1933—the first Briton in 24 years to take his country's title—and to that he added three U. S. crowns plus the championships of France and Australia.

Perry had no sooner reached his peak and whetted his country's appetite for tennis success than he—as in the case of Bill Tilden, Ellsworth Vines and others before him—succumbed to the lure of quick riches on the professional tour.

First of the big time pro tennis promoters was a colorful character named Charles C. (Cash and Carry) Pyle, who operated on P. T. Barnum theory: "A sucker is born every minute." He promoted six-day bicycle races, dance marathons, flag-pole sitters and tennis exhibitions. He paid Suzanne Lenglen $75,000 for a 1926 appearance in New York's Madison Square Garden against Mary K. Browne, winner of three U. S. women's titles. Four other players divided around $100,000 and Pyle himself pocketed $80,000.

Cash and Carry had proved to himself and to the world that good professional tennis players were a commodity the public would buy. Pro tennis was born.

Cash and Carry moved on to other lucrative adventures and turned the pro tour over to Vincent Richards, a former doubles partner of Tilden. Tilden turned pro in 1931 and assumed charge of the tour with an entrepreneur named William O'Brien. A match between Tilden and Czechoslovakia's Karol Kozeluh packed Madison Square Garden in the midst of the Depression.

Although banks closed and businesses went bankrupt and hungry people queued for apples on the streets, Tilden's magic name kept crowds pouring through the turnstiles in the early 1930s. Players flocked to pro ranks—Cochet of France, Bruce Barnes, Berkeley Bell and George Lott Jr.

When the tour needed an injection of new blood it dipped into the amateur ranks and plucked the player currently in the spotlight.

In 1933 it was Ellsworth Vines, a dynamic Californian who won the U. S. Nationals in 1931 and 1932 and captured Wimbledon in 1932. He was a powerful hitter but unpredictable, given to patches of wildness. On his best day, many observers said, he was the greatest player who ever lived.

Tilden and O'Brien signed Vines after the 1933 season and launched a Tilden vs. Vines tour in Madison Square Garden in the winter of 1934, the extravaganza drawing a crowd of 14,637 and a gate of $30,125. On the cross-country series, Vines overwhelmed the 41-year-old Tilden, 47 matches to 26.

Fred Perry was the next to be drawn into the pro venture, which passed from the hands of Tilden and O'Brien to Francis T. Hunter, and the steady Briton proceeded to beat Vines in their Garden debut although he lost to him in the overall series. The tour grossed $412,181.

A 1938 repeat of the same act, in which Vines beat Perry 48–35, drew only $175,000, and the promoters agreed they should look around for a new face.

They didn't have to look long or hard. It was right in front of them—florid, freckled, gaunt. It belonged to Donald Budge.

Like Vines, Budge also came out of California, a red-haired comet who ended a 10-year Davis Cup drought for the United States, scored tennis' first Grand Slam and set the phenomenal record of not losing a tournament match over the 1937–38 two-year span.

Sidney Wood, former Wimbledon champion and a contemporary, said Budge was a player without a weakness. "Playing against Don was like hitting against a concrete wall," Wood said. "There is nothing to attack."

Budge had a cannonball service. His forehand was powerful. He moved around the court with long, graceful strides. He volleyed and smashed with deadliness. But the weapon for which he was most remembered—and feared—was his backhand. It was a ferocious weapon.

Budge, as a tyke, played with a racket too big for him. He started hitting his backhand as a youngster with a baseball grip. The left hand was used to stabilize and guide the swing and it released itself once the stroke got under way. The result was a whip-like action, similar to that of an uncoiling spring, which unleashed a mighty shot from any position.

In 1937 Budge won both the Wimbledon and U. S. championships. He repeated in 1938 and that year also added the French and Australian crowns for a Grand Slam of major championships that escaped such predecessors as Johnston, Tilden,

Lacoste and Perry and such later stars as Jack Kramer and Pancho Gonzales. It was not until 24 years later, in 1962, that a player was able to duplicate the feat and it was done by another redhead, Australian Rod Laver. Laver repeated as a pro in 1969.

Budge was involved in a historic match with Germany's Gottfried Von Cramm in the 1937 Davis Cup Inter-Zone final, played at Wimbledon. Hitler was at the height of his power in Nazi Germany. War fever was high. Before the vital match,

Don Budge scored the first Grand Slam in tennis history and set a record of not having lost a tournament over the 1937–38 two year span.

Von Cramm was summoned to the telephone. It was Hitler, exhorting him to win for the Fatherland. Von Cramm was pale and serious when he came onto the court. He played as if his life depended on every point.

The German won the first two sets. Budge won the next two. Then Budge fell behind 1–4 in the fifth. Resorting to desperate, attacking measures, the American pulled level at 4–4, 5–5 and 6–6. Budge broke Von Cramm in the 13th game and had five match points on his service in the 14th before he finally scored a forehand placement. Those who saw it said it was perhaps the greatest tennis match ever played.

Budge made his pro debut at Madison Square Garden Jan. 3, 1939, beating Vines. He beat Vines in their series 21–18 and later took on Perry in another tour, winning 18–11. Returning from service in World War II, he lost a series to Bobby Riggs. That was the signal for him to retire.

Another player in the service was a young Coast Guard cadet named Jack Kramer. Another Californian with an imposing shot repertoire, Kramer won the U. S. Championship in 1946 and 1947, captured Wimbledon in 1947 and then turned professional where he not only established himself as the undisputed king of the touring pros but also became chief bankroller of tennis' traveling circus. He left a tremendous impact on the game.

Kramer signed Australia's Frank Sedgman and Ken McGregor in 1952 after they'd taken the Davis Cup to Australia and successfully defended it; grabbed Pancho Gonzales, colorful winner of the U. S. Nationals in 1948 and 1949, and paid a record $125,000 to Lew Hoad after the blond Australian had won at Wimbledon in 1957.

Big Jack carried on a running feud with Gonzales, both on and off the court and sometimes in the courts, not dropping a decision, but in the late 1950s bowed out of the picture and let the pros set up their own organization, with Tony Trabert the first director.

Kramer had other plans. Feared as a promoter, he was nevertheless trusted and respected by most of the officials in the national associations. Believing that the game might destroy itself through its blatant hypocrisy, Jack set about on an intensive and largely personal campaign to bring about open tennis. Authorities stubbornly had resisted it down through the years.

Twice in the early 1930s, the Germantown Cricket Club outside Philadelphia made an application to stage an open tournament but both times the efforts failed. In 1937, the fashionable Greenbrier Golf and Tennis Club staged what it called "The First U. S. Open Tennis Championships." Six amateurs joined the field of professionals. The U. S. Lawn Tennis Association withdrew the club's membership and suspended the players.

The open issue lay dormant for close to two decades, only to be revived in 1957 by the then USLTA president, Renville McMann. He set up a committee, headed by the influential Perry Jones of Los Angeles. The committee recommended that open tournaments be held on an experimental basis. The proposal was rejected by the Executive Committee of the USLTA, 20 to 8.

Meanwhile, there were rumblings of discontent among the Big Four tennis nations—Britain, France, Australia and the United States. The pros had all of the leading players but no organization. The amateur game, riddled with dissension and badgered on all sides by charges of hypocrisy, appeared to be dying.

In the United States, where opinions were sharply split among top officials on the open issue, resistance against change began to weaken noticeably as American tennis continued to drop into the doldrums. Men with progressive ideas, such as Robert Kelleher of Los Angeles, a Davis Cup captain and president of the USLTA, moved into places of power.

They realized something had to be done.

After Kramer and Gonzales went into the pro ranks, American tennis talent and tournament success dropped proportionately. Vic Seixas, an ageless athlete from Philadelphia's Main Line, won the U. S. Championship in 1954 and his Davis Cup teammate, Tony Trabert, an ex-basketball player from Cincinnati, won in 1955. There wasn't another American victor until Arthur Ashe Jr. captured the inaugural U. S. Open in 1968.

During that period of 13 years, Australians dominated with Rafael Osuna of Mexico breaking the string in 1963 and gifted Manuel Santana of Spain in 1965. During that period eight different Australians won the championship. As quickly as one might take the crown and turn pro, another was ready to step into his place.

Little Ken Rosewall started the streak in 1956, crushing the Grand Slam bid of his teammate, Lew Hoad. Then followed Malcolm Anderson, Ashley Cooper, Neale Fraser (twice), Roy Emerson, Rod Laver, Emerson again, Fred Stolle and John Newcombe.

Australia is a country the size of the United States with only as many people as New York City. It has always prided itself on its beaches, its beer and its tennis players, who since 1900 have ranked among the world's best.

As soon as a child is old enough to walk, he is given a tennis racket which he lugs to school with his books. Entire families play on lighted courts in every neighborhood. Scouts go into the bushes and country towns, pick the best talent and bring it into one of the big cities—Melbourne, Sydney or Brisbane—for special instruction.

Australia always has had an unending assembly line. Another factor in the

Alice Marble, shown in 1937 and in 1964, ruled women's tennis in the mid and late '30s.

The '50s belonged to such women as Maureen "Little Mo" Connolly, right, who, in 1953, was the first woman to win the Grand Slam of tennis and Althea Gibson, below, who learned to play tennis using wooden paddles on the sidewalks of Harlem.

country's tennis progress was a scrubby little man with sandy hair, a Cockney accent and a hidden whip. His name was Harry Hopman. A stern disciplinarian, he became Australian Davis Cup captain in 1950 and during the ensuing 18 years led Australia to 15 Davis Cup victories.

With virtually all of Australia's best talent siphoned off by the pros and Hopman tired and on the verge of retirement, the United States recaptured the Davis Cup in 1968 and defended it successfully against inferior teams from Romania and West Germany the next two years while arguments raged over opening up the international competition to the pros.

The United States suffered a similar letdown among the women. After Helen Wills Moody retired, Helen Jacobs ruled for four years and pretty, talented Alice Marble for four of the next five, starting in 1936. Statuesque Pauline Betz won four titles, dark-haired Sarah Palfrey Cooke two, Margaret Osborne duPont three and then came Maureen Connolly.

Maureen, nicknamed "Little Mo," a back court precisionist out of San Diego, Calif., was only 16 when she won the first of her three straight U. S. championships at Forest Hills in 1951. In 1953, she won the Australian, French, Wimbledon and American crowns to become the first woman ever to achieve the Grand Slam. She suffered an accident while riding a horse in 1954 and never played the game seriously again. She died of cancer in 1969.

Althea Gibson, a big, strong Negro girl who learned the game with wooden paddles on the sidewalks of Harlem, was queen of the game in 1957 and 1958

During the '60s, Billie Jean King won three straight Wimbledon titles and consistently ranked among the top women players.

Wimbledon veteran Arthur Ashe won the U.S. Open at Forest Hills as an amateur in 1968.

before trading her rackets for a set of golf clubs, and she was followed by Darlene Hard, a Californian who quit after winning successive titles in 1960 and 1961.

Then the foreigners took over. Maria Bueno, a slender Brazilian with rapier-like shots, won three championships and Margaret Smith Court, a 5-foot-9 country girl from Australia, moved in to battle Billie Jean King of Long Beach, Calif., for world honors. Billie Jean won three straight Wimbledons, starting in 1966, but a brief pro career and knee problems took her out of the fight temporarily, leaving the field clear for Margaret Court.

Its tennis prestige diminishing, the United States delegates were in a more conciliatory mood when they went to the International Federation meeting in Paris in July 1960. They were committed to vote in favor of experimental opens but oppose a British proposal for a special class of registered players, who could accept purses without being designated as professionals.

The open proposal almost carried. A delegate with 12 proxy votes in favor of open tennis was in the men's room when the vote was taken. The move lost by a margin of five votes.

On Dec. 14, 1967, the stubborn British, weary of back room politics, announced that the 1968 Wimbledon tournament would be open. It was a declaration of war on the ILTF. From the ILTF came threats of suspensions and boycotts. On March 30, 1968, at the Place de la Concorde in Paris the 82 nations of the ILTF voted in favor of sanctioning a limited number of open tournaments.

The first open was scheduled for April 22, 1968, the British Hard Court Championships at Bournemouth, England. If there was any fear this move signalled a complete takeover by the pros it was erased when a British Davis Cup player, Mark Cox, beat Pancho Gonzales and Roy Emerson in consecutive rounds. The event was won by Ken Rosewall, the Australian pro. At Wimbledon, two American amateurs, Arthur Ashe Jr. and Clark Graebner, swept into the semifinals before Laver finally won to take another leg on his second Grand Slam. At the 1968 U. S. Open at Forest Hills, the pros, apparently unaccustomed to five-set marathons, were toppled early and Ashe, the amateur, beat Tom Okker, the registered player from Holland, for the title.

Tennis peace, however, did not come with open tennis. A money war erupted between the pro promoters and the national associations. The pro promoters, who contended they owned all of the main gate attractions, demanded special fees to appear at tournaments. The national associations balked. The 1970 Australian and French Championships were among those boycotted by the big names.

For a few years there were two major pro groups—the National Tennis League, with such established pros as Rod Laver, Ken Rosewall and Pancho Gonzales, directed by ex-Davis Cup captain George MacCall of Los Angeles, and World Championship Tennis, made up of the younger pros such as John Newcombe, Tony Roche and Dennis Ralston. Early in 1970, Lamar Hunt, Texas millionaire sportsman who bankrolled the latter group, bought out MacCall's interests and turned the pro tour into a monopoly.

The tennis structure remained in confusing disarray. During the 1970 U. S. Open Championships at Forest Hills, Hunt announced a series of 20 tournaments with a total prize list of $1 million. The International Federation, in an

One of the many tennis greats from Australia is Grand Slam winner Rod Laver shown in action in New York in 1970.

Margaret Court of Australia, in action in 1969 at Forest Hills, completed the first women's Grand Slam of tennis since the late Maureen Connolly.

open declaration of war, countered with a plan for 30 tournaments in 1971 with $1.5 million in prize money.

Lamar Hunt had another card to play. A few days after the tournament, he announced the signing of Arthur Ashe, Bob Lutz and Charles Pasarell, three members of the U. S. Davis Cup team, to contracts which would join them with 24 other pros already on his payroll.

"I think the idea of differentiating between the contract pro (a Hunt man) and a registered pro (who owes allegiance to the ILTF) is hypocritical," said Ashe. "I like Hunt's style of professionalism."

Tennis found itself faced with other problems—a strong move to simplify and make over the game's traditional scoring system and a threatened revolt by women players.

James Van Alen, a Newport, R.I., socialite and millionaire, led a one-man campaign to change the involved scoring system of "fifteens, deuce, advantage and love" to 1–2–3, as in table tennis, and to obtain a terminal point with a sudden-death tie break.

He succeeded in the latter effort. Several tournaments tried the tie-break on an experimental basis and the plan was used successfully in the 1970 U. S. Open Championships. Instead of deuced sets and interminable matches, a best-of-nine point sudden death, with services alternating, was played when the score reached 6–6.

The players had some reservations. The fans loved the tension. The plan appeared ready for universal adoption.

Margaret Court, the Australian who completed the first women's Grand Slam since the late Maureen Connolly, was among more than a score of leading women players who threatened to boycott tournaments in which there was a disparity in the size of the men's and women's purses. An example was the 1970 Pacific Southwest Tournament in Los Angeles in which the men's first prize was $12,500 and the women's first prize $1,500.

"Twelve to one—that is ridiculous," said Billie Jean King. "I am better known than Stan Smith and a lot of the men players."

"We practice as hard and we play as hard as the men," said Rosemary Casals. "We deserve as much money."

"Money is going to be the fall of us," moaned a top USLTA official. "I would like to go back to the amateur days."

Britain's Roger Bannister gasped for breath as he hit tape at Oxford, England, on May 6, 1954, to become the first man ever to run the mile in under four minutes. His time was 3:59.4 and the floodgates were open.

chapter 8

TRACK AND FIELD

They'll Never Forget Jesse Owens

by Jerry Liska

Jerry Liska, a former Marquette University athlete, has been Midwest Sports Editor for *The Associated Press* since 1956. He played for Marquette's football team in the early 1930s as a 168-pound end (he's swelled to 230 since) and has been an *AP* sports staffer since 1944. In 1960, Liska was honored with Marquette University's By-Line Award, presented annually to graduates who have achieved success in the journalistic field. He has covered the Olympic Games in Rome, Tokyo and Mexico City, specializing in track and field.

Born in the dim dawn of civilization, the sport of track and field plodded through the ages in evolutionary leisure until it exploded in the 20th century with an era of fantastic and incredible feats of swiftness, strength and endurance.

Historians depict the very earliest man as the hunted instead of the hunter, a fearful creature whose fleetness and agility measured his survival against the wild beasts.

Primitive man gradually refined his skills of running, jumping and throwing—until, in ancient Greece about 1500 B.C., the first known competitive prize was awarded.

Coroebus, citizen of Elis, was crowned with a wreath of wild olive as the first Olympic victor at the stadium of Mt. Olympus, overshadowing the shimmering, blue sacred rivers of Alpheus and Kladeos on the Greek-Macedonian border.

Centuries blotted out the Olympic glories of ancient Greece, but not the stentorian cry attributed to their athletes of: "Citius, Altius, Fortius."

That echoed and re-echoed down the corridors of time until a resolute Baron Pierre de Coubertin of France revived the Olympic Games in 1896 at Athens, Greece.

Fewer than four decades after the modern Olympics made their Victorian era debut, track and field athletes indeed had complied with the ancient exhortation to run faster, jump higher and throw further.

A host of super athletes, ranging from Jim Thorpe and Jesse Owens to Bob

Beamon in a span between the 1912 and 1968 Olympic Games, strained brilliantly to performances often beyond belief or long-cited human limitations.

Beamon, a lanky 22-year-old with iron-springed long legs, authored the most memorable moment in the history of track and field with his "leap of the ages" on Oct. 18 in the XIX Olympiad of 1968.

Beamon's long jump of 29 feet, 2½ inches in one pulsating, electrifying catapult through the thin air of Mexico City rates as the greatest single track record of all time.

Track and field's Sensational Sixties, incomparable as a decade in track history, left no world record of pre-1960 vintage still standing!

But no world record ever was obliterated so devastatingly as Beamon surpassed the target long jump of 27 feet, 4¾ inches, shared by Ralph Boston and Russia's Igor Ter-Ovanesyan.

Beamon, a 6-foot-3 black from Texas-El Paso University via Jamaica, N.Y., rocketed entirely over the 28-foot stage to better the former record by almost two incredible feet. The achievement is calculated the equivalent of a 7-foot, 10½-inch high jump, or a 5,000-meter clocking of 12 minutes, 56.4 seconds, both regarded as humanly unattainable.

Beamon's prodigious feat came on his opening jump in the final round of competition in which Boston, 1960 Olympic champion and 1964 runner-up, and Ter-Ovanesyan were co-favorites.

Beamon, whose previous career best was 27-4, fairly flew through the air when he exploded from the takeoff board along the east side of the colorful Estadio Olympico.

At first, a huge roar burst from the crowded stands when Beamon finally landed almost beyond the sanded pit. This faded to a nervous hum of expectancy as long jump officials had to call for a tape measure. So great was the jump, it eluded the range of the specially installed semi-automatic Cantabrian recording device.

Told of his incredible distance, Beamon dropped to the ground as if felled by lightning. Recovering quickly, he bounced into a prayerful pose and then cavorted in wild joy around the jumping pit, embracing his older friend, Boston.

Beamon may have been the most easy-does-it of all athletes who have crumpled barriers once regarded impregnable, the 4-minute mile . . . the 7-foot high jump . . . the 17-foot pole vault . . . the 70-foot shot put . . . and the 28-foot long jump.

At Mexico City, he watched nonchalantly as co-world record holders Boston and Ter-Ovanesyan and other world class stars painstakingly measured their run-ups and marked them off with little flags.

"I was just lucky and everything fell together," commented the uninhibited, run-hit-and-jump leaper, who took off the board perfectly on his epochal flight. Beamon's luck included a following wind of 2.0 meters per second, exact maximum allowable velocity for a record. And he performed on the same lightning-fast runway used the previous day when five finalists in the triple jump broke the world record a staggering nine times.

Track and field may long be contested before there is a repetition of such a world record massacre as transpired in the 1968 Olympics on the pink all-weather running strip and jumping approaches and in the reduced air resistance of 7,300-foot-high Mexico City.

In 1968, Bob Beamon took off on a practice leap during the Olympic trials at Lake Tahoe, Calif. and landed in the Olympics long jump event at Mexico City with a record-shattering jump of 29 feet 2-1/2 inches.

Eyes straight ahead and legs churning, Jesse Owens takes baton from teammate on last leg of 400-yard relay event in dual U.S.–Great Britain meet in London in 1936.

Among 38 men's and women's events in the XIX Olympiad, 15 new world records were fashioned and two equalled. Beamon's leap was one of nine world marks erupting in the 24 men's events.

Jesse Owens, the aging, still trim "Greatest Track Athlete" selected in an *Associated Press* poll for the first half-century, watched the Mexico City Olympics in his quadrennial role as technical consultant.

That was 32 years after Owens, then a silk-smooth sprinter-hurdler-jumper from Ohio State, had won everything except a handshake from Nazi Germany's Adolf Hitler in the 1936 Games at Berlin.

"The tartan track and Mexico City's high altitude were two reasons for the greatest assault on records the Olympic Games has ever known," commented Owens. "However, I don't want to take anything away from the athletes themselves. These men and women were better conditioned, stronger and better trained than ever before.

"But I think the departure in the 1968 Olympics from the standard cinder or clay track may have been a turning point in the history of international track and field."

Owens' own selection as the "Greatest Track Athlete" of the 1900–1950 period reflected the most stunning demonstration of versatility in the sport's history. This was a stupendous one-day performance in the 1935 Big Ten outdoor track and field meet in which Owens shattered three world records and tied a fourth within a two-hour span.

One year later, Owens was to dominate the Berlin Olympics, running away from the world's best in the 100- and 200-meter dashes, capturing the long jump, and anchoring the victorious United States 400-meter relay team for a total of four gold medals. Only Finland's Paavo Nurmi, first of the classic world distance runners, previously won three individual Olympic gold medals. The Flying Finn scored a grueling sweep of the 1,500, 5,000 and 10,000-meter runs in the 1924 Paris Games.

But a day to remember in all the annals of track and field was May 25, 1935, when a slender black athlete clad in the scarlet and gray of Ohio State University tore the record book apart on a sunny afternoon at the University of Michigan's Ferry Field.

Here was Jesse Owens' timetable in track's greatest one-day exhibition:

At 3:15 P.M., Owens streaked to victory in the 100-yard dash, equalling Frank Wykoff's world record of 9.4 seconds.

At 3:25 P.M., Owens took his first and only long jump, clearing 26 feet, 8¼ inches to surpass by nearly a half-foot the world record of 26-2⅛ by Japan's Chuhei Nambu.

At 3:34 P.M., Owens flashed home an easy victor in the 220 dash with a 20.3 clocking, slashing three-tenths of a second from Roland Locke's world mark.

And at 4 P.M., Owens scissored over the 220 low hurdles in 22.6, shaving four-tenths of a second from Charles R. Brookins' 11-year-old world record.

Owens' 220 dash and 220 low hurdles efforts also encompassed officially recognized world marks at the 200 meter distance for both events.

"I was just a sophomore, you know, and what I remember best about that afternoon was leaning against a flag pole, watching the people come into the field and wondering if I could run at all," Owens recalled on the 35th anniversary of his great day.

"When it came to the pre-meet warm-up, I couldn't even jog because of a stiff back from a stairfall at a fraternity house two weeks before. When the call came for the 100, Larry Snyder, our Ohio State coach, suggested I scratch because of the sudden strain in the jolting start of the 100.

"But I told Larry: 'Let me try it, maybe I'll snap out of it,' even though my buddy, Charlie Beetham (ace half-miler), had to help me remove my sweatsuit at the 100 start. Charlie slapped me on the back and said: 'You'll be okay, kid.'

"My back hurt when I went into the starting crouch, but when the starter said 'Get set,' I felt no pain at all. I jumped in front with the gun and stayed there. I could hear Bobby Grieve (Illinois) pounding behind me, but I took him by five yards."

By that time, the long jump was under way. After a 10-minute rest, Jesse went to the jumping pit with Snyder's instruction to take only one leap and rest for the 220 dash and low hurdles.

"I skipped a practice jump, but put a handkerchief aside the pit at the world distance mark of the Japanese Nambu," recounted Owens. "I tried a couple of runs for stride and then barreled down the runway for keeps. I took off perfectly and thought I'd never come down. When I leveled off in the pit, I saw that handkerchief behind me and knew I had a world record when Larry grinned at me."

Two more times, after the 220 dash and 220 low hurdles, the megaphone of field announcer Ted Canty again intoned to an awe-stricken crowd: "I wish to introduce a new champion and new world record holder."

As track and field surged into the final half of the century, the era of shattering "impossible" barriers was triggered by a gangling, 25-year-old British medical student.

Dr. Roger Bannister made the first moonshot of the track world on May 6, 1954, in the comparative obscurity of an Oxford-British Amateur Association team dual meet at Oxford, England.

He ran the first sub-four minute mile in history with a clocking of 3:59.4 before a crowd of 1,200 which abandoned British aplomb and roared approval at the achievement of the most coveted goal in the sport.

Six runners started that epic race over a track soaked by heavy rains earlier in the day and fanned by a 15-mile-per-hour wind. Bannister, billed a super runner who failed England in the 1952 Olympics, decided to go full blast just 15 minutes before the race started.

The 6-foot-1, 150-pound Bannister first let Chris Brasher, Olympic steeplechaser, set the pace—urging "faster" at 220 yards. Brasher wilted after 2½ laps and Bannister called out "Chris," urging his old Oxford teammate, Chris Chataway, 5,000-meter star, to push the pace.

Chataway accelerated the dangerously slowing pace and was leading Bannister with 300 yards to go. But here Bannister exploded his fine stretch kick and burst first over the finish line, his usual pleasant face contorted from complete exhaustion.

There was hushed silence as the field announcer, fighting to retain Oxford poise, solemnly and distractingly began:

"Ladies and gentlemen. Here is the result of event No. 9, the one-mile run: First, No. 41, R. G. Bannister, Amateur Athletic Association and formerly of Exeter and Merton Colleges, Oxford, with a time which is a new meeting and track record, and, which, subject to ratification, will be a new English Native, British National, British All Comers', European, British Empire, and world record.

"The time was three . . . " The roar of the hilarious crowd cut him off. History had been made. All three official timers caught Bannister in 3:59.4. One alternate watch had him in 3:59.4 and another in 3:59.2.

History also will record, however, that Bannister simply opened the flood gates and was a sort of Lindbergh of track and field. Less than 15 years after the British doctor ran his unbelievable race, any recital of sub-four minute milers found Bannister nearly dropped out of sight and mind.

Moving into the 1970s, the world mile record still was held at 3:51.1 by America's Jim Ryun, accomplished in the same year of 1967 he also blazed to a world 1,500-meter record of 3:33.1.

Wilma Rudolph, above, was one of the world's best woman runners in the late '50s and early '60s. Here she wins the 200-meter race in the 1960 Olympic Games. In 1966, 19-year-old Jim Ryun set a world mile record of 3:51.3 here at Berkeley, Calif. The next year, he cut it down to 3:51.1.

Cornelius Warmerdam, right, used a steel pole to soar to a height of 15 feet 8-11/16 inches in Chicago in 1943. Technology, in the form of a fiberglass pole, helped Christos Papanicolaou of Greece become the first man to break the 18-foot barrier in Athens in 1970.

But the bright promise of Ryun as the world's premiere runner from 800 to 1,500 meters faded in the thin air of Mexico City. The leggy Kansan ran out of gas and was defeated by Kenya's Kipchoge Keino in their 1968 Olympic 1,500-meter showdown.

Bannister, who carved two full seconds off the previous world mile mark of 4:01.4 by Gunder Haegg in 1945, and Ryun, may have written the beginning and end of the whirlwind era of record-breaking in track's glamor race.

Underscoring the impact of Bannister's 1954 breakthrough, it took more than 30 years to reduce the mile record from the great Nurmi's 4:10.4 clocking in 1923 to the Briton's cracking of the four-minute barrier.

It had been attacked by such other past standouts as Bill Bonthron, Glenn Cunningham, Gil Dodds, Archie Romani, John Lovelock, Syd Wooderson, Louis Zamperini, and Arne Anderson. They were among some 20 milers who ran under 4:10 during the first half of the century.

But at the end of 1970, the International Amateur Athletic Federation, world track governing body, noted a slowdown in the mid-century assault on records from 800 meters up, and especially the 1,500 meter, or metric mile.

Olga Fikotova of Czechoslovakia prepares to toss discus in meet at White City Stadium in London in 1956. She later was to marry U.S. Olympic athlete Harold Connolly.

Between 1952 and 1960, 13 records for the 1,500 meter run were fashioned. But Australian Herb Elliott's 3:35.6 victory in the 1960 Rome Olympics then held up until Ryun's 3:31.1 in 1967.

One of the ironies of track's Swinging Sixties was that another Australian great, Ron Clarke, retired from major racing after setting 17 world records from 3,000 to 20,000 meters. The tireless Aussie never won an Olympic title, trying in the 1964 Tokyo Games and at Mexico City in 1968.

Even in his quest to set a world record for setting world records, Clarke became a cropper. He trails the total of 19 by Paavo Nurmi in the 1920s and 18 by Emil Zatopek, Czechoslovakia's post-World War II winner of four Olympic gold medals from 5,000 meters through the marathon.

The Olympic marathon, won by Zatopek in 1952 at Helsinki, reached colorful heights when a barefooted policeman from Ethiopia, Abebe Bikila, swept the 26-mile, 385-yard grind in both the 1960 Rome Games and at Tokyo in 1964.

The wiry Bikila, Olympic record-setter in 1964, faltered on a bid for a third straight Olympic crown in 1968 at Mexico City. He had to quit after 15 kilometers because of stomach cramps and a heavy cold. Bikila's countryman, Mamo Wolde, captured the classic race with enough remaining steam to jog a victory lap in the Olympic Stadium.

Beyond Beamon's fantastic long jump, the adage that records are made to be broken seems destined to prevail the rest of the 20th century.

The bamboo valuting pole which gave Cornelius Warmerdam the first 15-foot vault in the 1940s, and cinder track which sizzled under Jesse Owens' flying feet have surrendered to a steady succession of mechanical improvements. They include composition tracks, fiberglass poles, foam rubber landing pits, brush spikes and all-metal javelins.

The "Fosbury Flop," spectacular backward dive over the crossbar invented by 1968 Olympic champion Dick Fosbury, could be encouraged by the foam rubber pit to menace the 8-foot barrier in the high jump. The first 18-foot pole vault already has been claimed by Greece's Christos Papanicolaou, a San Jose State College exchange student, using an American-made fiberglass pole and landing on rubber cushions.

Other young athletes may be lurking in every corner of the world readying to surpass such rarefied performances as the 71-foot, 5½-inch shot put of Randy Matson . . . the 7-foot, 5¾-inch high jump of Russia's Valery Brumel . . . or the blazing dashes of Tommie Smith, Bob Hayes, John Carlos, Jimmy Hines, Charlie Greene, Cuba's Enrique Figuerola and Italy's Livio Berruti in the jet-propelled '60s.

It will take some doing, however, to match the discus skill and endurance of golden-armed Al Oerter, who at the age of 32 won his third successive Olympic title in 1968 at Mexico City. In the amazing process of winning three Olympic crowns in an eight-year span, Oerter wore a brace for many competitions because of a damaged neck which bothered him from 1964 through 1969.

With the same mid-century splurge as men's track, women athletes around the world proved their masculine counterparts had no monopoly on talent and record-breaking prowess.

Mildred (Babe) Didrikson, Stella Walsh and Betty Robinson just about blanketed the female field at the start of women's competition with the 1928 Olympics at Amsterdam. By the 1960s, world class feminine competitors were smashing world records by the dozens.

The parade of talented women included Wilma Rudolph, Wyomia Tyus, Madeline Manning, Edith McGuire, Barbara Ferrell, Russia's Tamara and Irma Press, England's Ann Packer and Mary Rand, West Germany's Ingrid Becker, and the remarkable Chi Cheng, Taiwan's super gal.

Track's honor list of countless superb performers since the first track and field meet in modern history between Oxford and Cambridge in 1864, offers in Jim Thorpe a true pioneer in the lineage of the world's greatest athletes.

Thorpe, a full-blooded Sac Indian from Carlisle, Pa., won both the pentathlon and decathlon in the 1912 Olympics at Stockholm. The tremendously versatile Thorpe was stripped of his Olympic medals for previously sullying his amateur status. Big Jim had played minor league baseball for a pittance and, naively, under his own name.

Valery Brumel, top, and John Thomas thrilled the world with their head-on duels in the high jump pit in the '60s.

In the mid '60s, Dick Fosbury came upon the national scene with his "Fosbury Flop." It was his unique way of competing in the high jump. Here he is in various stages of an effort during the 1968 Olympic Games in Mexico City. It earned him a gold medal in the event.

Thorpe, performing when track and field techniques barely were emerging from the comparative privacy of blue-blooded athletic clubs, won four of five pentathlon and four of the 10 decathlon tests at Stockholm.

In the Olympic list of decathlon winners, the 1912 champion is given as Sweden's Hugo Wieslander, runner-up to the disqualified Thorpe. But the United States since has been vindicated many times in that greatest of all challenges of track talent and endurance.

The United States won eight of the subsequent 11 Olympic decathlon championships with Bob Mathias a historic back-to-back winner in 1948 and 1952. World record holder entering the 1970s, Bill Toomey set an Olympic record of 8,193 points in winning at Mexico City in 1968.

In this event, which is the closest throwback to the one-man athletic displays of the ancient Olympics, Toomey labored to a world record total of 8,417 points at Los Angeles, Dec. 11, 1969, fittingly closing out track's most magnificent decade in history.

Entering the 1970s, U.S. track still had to resolve the now historic impasse between the governing Amateur Athletic Union and the National Collegiate Athletic Association.

It has been a jurisdictional squabble which even bounced into the halls of Congress, mystifying federal folk as much as the general public and, to a certain extent, the track athletes themselves.

The AAU, steeped in tradition, zealously guarded its international mandate from the IAAF for sanction of meets leading to world competition. The NCAA challenged the AAU's right to call most track and field shots, contending that the

collegiate realm provides most of the talent for the Olympics and international meets.

The athletes themselves became restless under the ancient code of ironclad amateurism which they claim is unrealistic in competition with the career athletes of many foreign countries. They also sought equitable treatment of black performers, who formed the backbone of the nation's sprint, middle distance and jumping talent.

Lee Evans, left, surged ahead of Vince Matthew to successfully defend his title in the 400-meter race at the National AAU meet in Sacramento, Calif., in June 1968.

Yoshinori Sakai, the last torch runner at the 1964 Olympic Games in Tokyo, climbs steps with the Olympic flame to the caldron at the National Stadium during opening day ceremonies.

chapter 9

THE OLYMPICS

Dedicated to Good Will, the Games Have Seethed with Controversy

by John Farrow

John Farrow, 48, has been a sports writer in the London office for 19 years and European sports editor since 1959. One of the most traveled of the world's sports writers, he covered the Olympic Games in Rome in 1960, Tokyo in 1964 and Mexico in 1968 plus Winter Olympics in 1964 at Innsbruck, Austria, and Grenoble, France, in 1968. He also has covered World Cup soccer tournaments in Sweden, Chile, England and Mexico.

"Citius, Altius, Fortius"—"Faster, Higher, Braver"—is the clarion call of the Olympic Games and supposedly they are dedicated to the principles of fair play and sportsmanship and the creation of international amity and good will.

"The essential thing is not to have conquered but to have fought well," said Baron Pierre de Coubertin, the French founder of the modern version of the great international spectacle.

There is no question that the clarion call—the Games' motto—has been heeded well. As the years passed, decades turning into new decades and centuries into new centuries, men and women athletes have shown they could run faster, throw farther and jump higher than their predecessors. Every four years of the Games, records tumble at an unbelievable rate. A mark is no sooner etched into the book than it is shattered. Barriers once thought unattainable—the four-minute mile, the 17-foot pole vault, the seven-foot high jump—are breached and sights set upon new horizons.

But the other phase of the Olympics' lofty goal—that of a greater understanding through sport—has failed miserably. Almost from the beginning, the Games have seethed with controversy.

Jealousies and national pride have usurped the pedestals where friendliness and good will should have stood. Politics have moved in. Racism has become a divisive issue. The powerful nations turned the Games into a sounding board for political philosophy and propaganda. Commercialism and professionalism became a festering sore.

As the Games moved into the 1970s, creeping professionalism posed the greatest threat to the giant athletic festival. The amateur codes were being flagrantly abused. Virtually every athlete who went to the line was guilty of a violation in some form or another. These infractions were countenanced by the nations themselves, each anxious to enhance its athletic power and prestige. Hypocrisy became rampant.

One man, almost alone, stood as a break against these sinister influences—a sort of modern-day Horatius at the bridge. He was Avery Brundage, a straight-backed, grim-jawed millionaire from Chicago who served as president of the International Olympic Committee.

Brundage, a former Olympian himself, was roundly criticized in many quarters as being unrealistic and a man of another century. A strong man, he was hated as he was admired. He was respected and feared.

It was Brundage, then president of the U.S. Olympic Committee, who created a worldwide furore by kicking Eleanor Holm, beautiful American swimmer, off the 1936 team because of the high jinks during the team's transatlantic ocean voyage.

It was Brundage who resisted efforts to have medals restored to Jim Thorpe, the big Indian who won both the decathlon and pentathlon in the 1912 Games at Stockholm only to have the honors stripped from him later when it was learned he had signed a semiprofessional contract.

The King of Sweden had hailed Thorpe as "the greatest athlete of the century." Other royalty honored him and America gave him a hero's reception on his return home. Yet Thorpe died a broken man, the whereabouts of his Olympic medals unknown.

Brundage, who became head of the IOC in 1952, seemed always in the center of a controversy. He never dodged it. Some critics insisted he sought it.

The tall, rugged Olympic official defended South Africa when that country's Olympic eligibility was on trial and it was largely through his influence that the IOC voted to allow South Africa back in the Games in 1968 after being barred for its apartheid policies.

"Politics have no place in the Olympic movement," Brundage insisted, never wavering from his firm belief in the basic integrity of the Games.

However, Brundage was beaten down. When a group of African nations with the support of the powerful Soviet Union and the Communist bloc threatened to boycott the Summer Games at Mexico City, the IOC had to surrender. After a bitter battle which left lasting wounds, South Africa was barred.

Once asked for comment on the Soviet Union's policy of subsidizing athletes —all are trained and paid by the state—Brundage replied:

"Under the Soviet system, everyone is subservient to the state. The Russians are no more professional than the Americans, who give their athletes free college scholarships."

The 1968 Winter Games at Grenoble, France, were almost wrecked when Brundage threatened to cancel the Alpine skiing events—the most spectacular event of the competition—because many of the skiers insisted on flaunting the brand names of the ski manufacturers, from whom they received a nice subsidy.

The Alpine races were saved through a compromise. The skiers could keep the manufacturer's name on the skis but must cover them up when exposed to photographers and television.

The issue was raised again prior to the 1972 Games when a manufacturer underwrote a clinic in California for which leading foreign skiers were given free transportation and paid fees to attend.

Professionalism, use of drugs and stimulants and mandatory tests on all women athletes to confirm they were of the proper sex brought turmoil to the 1968 Olympic Games at Mexico City. The turmoil was turned into an eruption by a black power display on the part of two American sprinters.

After receiving their medals on the victory stand following the 200-meter dash, Tommie Smith, who won the gold, and John Carlos, who won the bronze, raised their black-gloved fists in a black power salute.

The purpose was one of shock—a gesture intended to jar the watching world into realization of black injustices. It succeeded. The crowd was stunned into silence. This silence later turned to chagrin and anger on the part of many.

The International Olympic Committee ordered the U.S. Committee to take punitive action or face the prospect of having its entire Olympic force removed from the Games. Smith and Carlos were ejected from the Olympic Village. At first, many companion Negro athletes threatened to bolt the team. Some sympathetic whites joined in, but the situation was alleviated and the 1968 Olympic Games—for the medal-caching American team—ended on a victorious though sour note.

With all of its inner strife, politics and emphasis on nationalism, there is a grandeur about the Olympic Games that no other sports spectacle can begin to match. In some ways, it is like a pagan festival. In others, it embodies all of the spirit of competition. The gathering of thousands of athletes of varying skills, races, colors and political persuasions from throughout the world—dressed in native costumes, a Babel of languages, tossed into one giant arena—presents a setting that Cecil B. DeMille would find difficult to duplicate on a Hollywood screen.

No observer can escape a spinal chill when an athlete from the host nation pronounces the Olympic oath—"In the name of all competitors, I promise that we will take part in these Olympic Games, respecting and abiding by the rules which govern them, in the true spirit of sportsmanship for the glory of sport and the honor of our teams"—and a runner races to the top of the stadium to put a torch to the Olympic flame.

Ceremony has been the integral part of the Games since their pre-Christian birth in a sacred valley at Olympia in Elis near the western coast of Greece. The earliest recorded competition was in 776 B.C.

Religious festivals in honor of Olympian Zeus were observed for several centuries prior to that date. The Greek Games were celebrated in the belief that the spirits of the dead were gratified by such spectacles.

Every four years trading was suspended, the fighting tribes laid down their arms and all the people went forth in peace to pay tribute to the manhood of the nation. For the first 13 Olympiads, the competition consisted of a single race of around 200 yards. The race was called the "stade" because it was about the length of the stadium. The first recorded winner was Coroebus of Elis in 776 B.C.

Later the race was lengthened to twice the length of the stadium and in the 15th Olympiad an endurance race was added with athletes running around the stadium 12 times, or approximately three miles. The spectators watched from grassy slopes.

In 708 B.C. the pentathlon and wrestling were added to the program. Boxing became an event in 688 B.C. and the four-horse chariot race in 680. In 648 a fierce combination of boxing and wrestling was introduced under the name of "pancration." The victors at first received crowns of wild olive. Later, if an athlete won an event three times, a statue was erected in his honor.

The Games appeared to reach their climax in the fifth century before Christ. Then decay set in. Records and specialization became paramount. After the invasion of the Macedonians, the Greeks quit training their youth but hired athletes and nationalized them. The Games continued but they lost their savor. Ideals were discarded and profit became the main motivation. In 393 A.D., the Emperor Theodosius ordered an end of the spectacle that had survived 1,200 years.

Credit for revival of the Olympics goes to a French nobleman, Baron Pierre de Coubertin, who after the Franco-Prussian War became concerned about the moral fiber of his people and decided that there was need for development of the individual to revive hope and self-respect.

Wealthy and widely traveled, he was not an athlete but he made a study of sports and saw in the Olympics a chance to bring countries together in friendly competition. He proposed revival of the Olympic Games at a meeting of amateur sports officials in Paris in 1892 but he received a bland response. He repeated the proposal at an international athletic congress in 1894 and the idea bore fruit. The first of the modern Games was assigned to Greece. De Coubertin lived to see his brainchild gain universal recognition before he died in Geneva, Switzerland, Sept. 2, 1937 at the age of 74.

Only 13 countries and 285 athletes took part in the first of the modern Games at Athens in 1896. By 1968, through steady growth, the list had grown to more than 100 competing nations and 7,000 athletes. IOC officials were concerned the Games might choke on their own affluence.

The inaugural of the modern Games in Athens was dominated by the United States, which grabbed off 10 gold medals in track and field alone. The team's star was Tom Burke, who won the 100-meter dash in 12 seconds flat, and the 400 meters in 54.2. John W. Tewksbury was also a double gold medalist, winning the 200 meters in 22.2 and the 400-meter hurdles in 57.6.

Burke and Tewksbury set a pattern that was to prevail throughout the Games —dominance of the dashes and hurdles by the United States. While the Finns, Poles and Argentines and later the Russians showed superiority in the longer distances, the Yanks' blinding speed rarely was challenged.

Burke and Tewksbury were forerunners of a brilliant array of sprinters that included Archie Hahn, Charlie Paddock, Eddie Tolan, Jesse Owens, Bobby Morrow, Bob Hayes, Tommie Smith and John Carlos.

The Olympics, with all of their machinations, myths and mysteries, have nevertheless produced a long line of athletes of heroic stature whose feats have become living legend.

One of these never won a gold medal.

Paavo Nurmi, foreground, left center, who was to carve a name for himself in Olympic competition, is shown in the steeplechase event at the 1928 Olympic Games.

Pietri Dorando was a pastry cook from Capri who went to the 1908 Games in London and competed in the marathon, the most grueling of tests. No one gave him passing notice.

Yet at the end of the muscle-stabbing 42-kilometer race, he loped into the stadium with his arms flailing and his head sagging from fatigue. The crowd let out a deafening roar, because no other runner was in sight. Then the cheers turned to gasps of dismay. Pietri stopped suddenly, staggered momentarily and collapsed on the track.

Officials and doctors, without stopping to think, rushed onto the track, hoisted Pietri to his feet and helped him the remaining few yards to the finish line.

The crowd again roared with delight. But their enthusiasm was soon doused. John Hayes of the United States burst through the gate and ran to the finish line. He was declared the Olympic victor. Pietri, the cook, was disqualified.

No assistance was needed 16 years later for Paavo Nurmi, the fabulous Finn whose distance running exploits occupy some of the most exciting pages in Olympic history.

Nurmi made his Olympic mark at Paris in 1924, an obscure entry in the 1,500-meter race—the metric mile, always regarded as the "blue riband" event of the Games. He had proved himself a distance runner by winning the 10,000 meters in 1920, but no one figured him for the 1,500.

Outstanding milers were plentiful. There were Britain's Douglas Lowe and Henry Stallard and the Swiss champion, Willi Scherer. They were favored to grab off the three medals, it was just a question of what the order might be.

Above, three great distance runners are shown in Olympic action. From left to right, Emil Zatopek of Czechoslovakia winning at Helsinki in the 1952 marathon event; the Soviet Union's Vladimir Kuts winning the 10,000-meter race at Melbourne in 1956; and barefooted Abele Bikila of Ethiopia on his way to victory in the 1960 marathon in Rome. At the right, Kipchoge Keino of Kenya outdistances Jim Ryun and the rest of the field to win the 1,500-meter event at the 1968 Games in Mexico City.

While the spectators watched the three favorites jockey for advantage, Nurmi surged to the front on the final lap, passed the early leaders with a burst of power and finished the dramatic winner in 3 minutes, 53.6 seconds. Scherer beat out his British rivals for the silver medal in 3:54.8.

An hour later, when the 5,000-meter race was announced, fans could hardly believe their eyes when they saw Nurmi at the starting line. Willie Ritola, a fellow Finn, and Edwin Wide of Sweden, the world record smashers, were expected to battle it out for the gold.

Nurmi asserted his challenge quickly. The three set a crackling pace. Neck and neck, they raced around the track—the lead changing constantly—while the crowd became delirious from excitement. Then the race became a duel of the two Finns. Nurmi moved in front. Ritola time and again made a move but each was countered. It was Nurmi across the line first in 14:31.2, Ritola only two-tenths of a second behind.

Nurmi competed in three Olympics, failing only in the fourth in 1932 because of allegations of professionalism. During his career, he won four gold medals and three silver and set more than 20 world records while racing in distances from 1,500 meters to 10,000.

The Finns erected a statue of their hero in front of the stadium which housed the 1952 Games in Helsinki.

Ironically, it was at Helsinki that the Olympics witnessed the greatest feat of long-distance running in all history, a one-man performance overshadowing any in the life of the fabulous Nurmi and setting a mark that most observers contend probably will never be duplicated.

The 1952 Games in the Land of the Midnight Sun were distinguished in themselves because they brought together the United States and the Soviet Union

for the first time and launched an international rivalry that was to supersede anything that the Games had ever witnessed.

It was the emergence of the big Russian bear from behind its Iron Curtain after the destructive World War II. The Soviet Union, having already made its bid to become a world power, now was prepared to challenge America on the playing fields as the No. 1 sports power. Its strength and attitude a deep mystery, the Soviet Union and her satellites declined to mingle with other nations in the Olympic Village but set up a village of their own some 30 miles from the heart of Helsinki.

It was from one of these Communist satellite nations—Czechoslovakia—that came the most miraculous distance runner of the age.

His name was Emil Zatopek. He was a small, lean man with thinning blond hair. He could be seen running for hours around the hillsides outside Helsinki, keeping largely to himself, avoiding interviews. His wife, Dana Zatopekova, was a javelin thrower on the women's team.

The thousands who had gathered in Helsinki for the Games were impressed when Zatopek, an officer in the Czech army, won both the 5,000 and 10,000-meter races, two of the most demanding in the track and field program. He won many admirers with his unique style. He ran with his arms flying loosely and his head bobbing from side to side. He always appeared on the verge of collapse.

Everyone was stunned when Zatopek, after capturing the two distance races, entered the 26-mile-plus marathon. Could he do it? Could he pull off the distance triple that had seemed out of the reach of mortal man?

Zatopek answered with a thrilling victory. He was lionized by the Eastern and Western world alike and the Communist bloc dropped the pervading curtain to allow the amazing Czech to receive the attention which he was due.

The story had a tragic ending. In the next Olympics, Zatopek was succeeded in both the 5,000 and 10,000-meter races by an indefatigable Russian, Vladimir Kuts. Sixteen years later, Zatopek was invited by the International Olympic Committee to be a special guest at the Summer Games in Mexico City.

Zatopek and Kuts, once the closest of friends and friendliest of rivals, met on the village promenade at Mexico City. Zatopek looked at Kuts and coldly passed on by, as if he didn't see him.

All of the Czechs scorned their onetime Russian allies similarly. Only a short time before Russian tanks had moved across the border and into the heart of Prague to put down a freedom-craving Czechoslovakian government.

"How foolish they are," lamented Zatopek, referring to the powerful Soviet nation. "Don't they realize that communism cannot live if it isn't given a chance to breathe?"

Zatopek, who had risen to high army rank and then to virtual Cabinet status, was stripped of all of his government positions and reduced to the position of a lowly gym teacher. But his spirit was never broken.

The Helsinki Olympics also produced the first great power struggle between nations in the Olympics. Avery Brundage's oft-repeated admonition that the Olympic Games are a contest of individuals and not of nations went unheeded as America and the Soviet Union struggled madly for medals and unofficial points.

At the end of each day, the medals were counted—the gold, silver and bronze.

Eddie Tolan of the U.S. hits the tape to win the 200-meter final at the Olympic Games in Los Angeles in 1932. George Simpson was second and Ralph Metcalf was third to make it an all-United States finish. Tolan also won a gold medal in the 100-meter event.

Who had the most—Uncle Sam or the Soviet Bear? The Russians captured a cache in gymnastics, an event in which they excelled. The United States countered by counting one medal for each member of the basketball team. An American basketball team never lost in the Olympics.

There is no official point formula in the Games. The United States devised one of its own. The Soviets had their own, but different, point system. A Helsinki department store each day flashed the point standings—America's and Russia's. America led by the American system. Russia led by the Russian system. When the Americans pushed ahead by the Soviet formula, the Russians resorted to a new system. So it went.

Nationalism—of a different sort—was a major factor in the 1936 Games at Berlin, called by one reviewer as "the most ominous pagan spectacle of modern times."

These Games proved to be the mark of America's greatest triumph and at the same time its most humiliating affront.

The echoes of Adolf Hitler's goose-stepping legions were shaking Middle Europe. War clouds darkened the skies. Yet the IOC, over the protests of many nations, went through with its plans for holding the Games in war-indoctrinated Berlin.

Star of the American team was a lithe Negro named Jesse Owens, born in Danville, Ala., and educated at Ohio State. A year earlier Owens had ripped the record book apart in a dual meet at the University of Michigan, running the 100-yard dash in 9.4 seconds, winning the high jump with a fantastic leap of 26 feet, 8¼ inches, taking the 220-yard dash in 20.3 and climaxing his record burst with a 22.6 performance in the 220-yard low hurdles, all world marks.

Meanwhile, Hitler was espousing the superiority of the Aryan race. It was only natural to wonder how the Fuehrer would take this athletic marvel whose ancestors came from darkest Africa and who was flying the red, white and blue colors of the enemy United States.

Those who wondered did not have long to wait.

Hitler was in his loge the first day of the Olympics, Aug. 2, 1936. When Hans Wollke, a German, broke the Olympic shot put record he was led to the Hitler box for personal congratulations. The same occurred for three Finns, who finished 1-2-3 in the 10,000-meter run.

Then Owens began his surge. He won the 100 meters in 10.3 and the 200 in 20.7. He captured the long jump with a leap of 26 feet, 5³/₈ inches. Then he anchored the 400-meter relay team to victory, capturing his fourth gold medal.

No man before in the history of the Olympics had won four gold medals in a single year.

Even the Germans were yelling "Yes-sa Ov-enss!" "Yes-sa Ov-enss!"

Hitler watched coldly from his loge. When time came for Jesse to receive his medals and hear the strains of the *Star-Spangled Banner,* Hitler looked the other way. Once he strode out of the box after watching Jesse, the Negro, capture his fourth gold medal.

A four-medal sweep in the Olympics proved to be a rare achievement but, although his feat was the most dramatic, Owens was not destined to hold this honor alone.

Fanny Blankers-Koen, a Dutch housewife and mother of two who at the age of 30 was considered well past her prime, duplicated Owens' medal slam in the 1948 Games at London, the first to be held after World War II.

The Flying Hollander won the 100-meter dash in 11.5 seconds, the 200 in 24.4, the 80-meter hurdles in 11.2 and anchored the women's 400-meter relay to a victory for The Netherlands. In the 1964 Games at Tokyo, a blond, teen-age water sprite from America, Don Schollander, dominated the freestyle swimming races and came away with four gold medals.

Schollander's remarkable sweep marked the fruition of the United States' youth program in swimming. In the early 1960s, after a decade of domination by the Australians, United States swimming officials launched a training program that was destined to make America king of the Olympic pool. Tykes were tossed into the water as soon as they were big enough to walk. Then they were disciplined through long hours of training until at the age of 12 and 13 they became seasoned competitors and at 15 world champions. Some of them found they were "over the hill" at 20.

The U.S. whiz kids brought water mastery back to America.

Americans had been in the forefront in the early years of Olympic swimming, particularly in the freestyle sprinting races. Champions had included Charles Daniels, 1906–08; Duke Kahanamoku, of Japanese descent, 1912–20, and Johnny Weissmuller, later the movie Tarzan, 1924–28; backstroker Warren Kealoha, 1920–24, and such women stars as Helene Madison, Martha Norelius and Ann Curtis.

But in the mid-1950s Australians, employing new training techniques, pushed the Yanks out of the limelight. Jon Henricks, John Devit, Murray Rose and Jon Konrads were best of the freestylers and David Thiele led the backstrokers, grabbing most of the medals in the 1956 and 1960 Games. Meanwhile, Dawn Fraser, the first to crack the one-minute barrier in the 100-meter freestyle, and Lorraine Crapp were showing the same supremacy over the girls.

The tide turned dramatically at Tokyo in 1964 and it continued to flow in the direction of the United States in succeeding races at Mexico City. In the 1968

Without question, Jesse Owens was the standout performer in the 1936 Olympics in Berlin. Here he wins a heat in the 200-meter dash, one of the four events in which he won gold medals. Repeatedly snubbed by Hitler, Owens offered this salute from the winners' stand. Note other salutes.

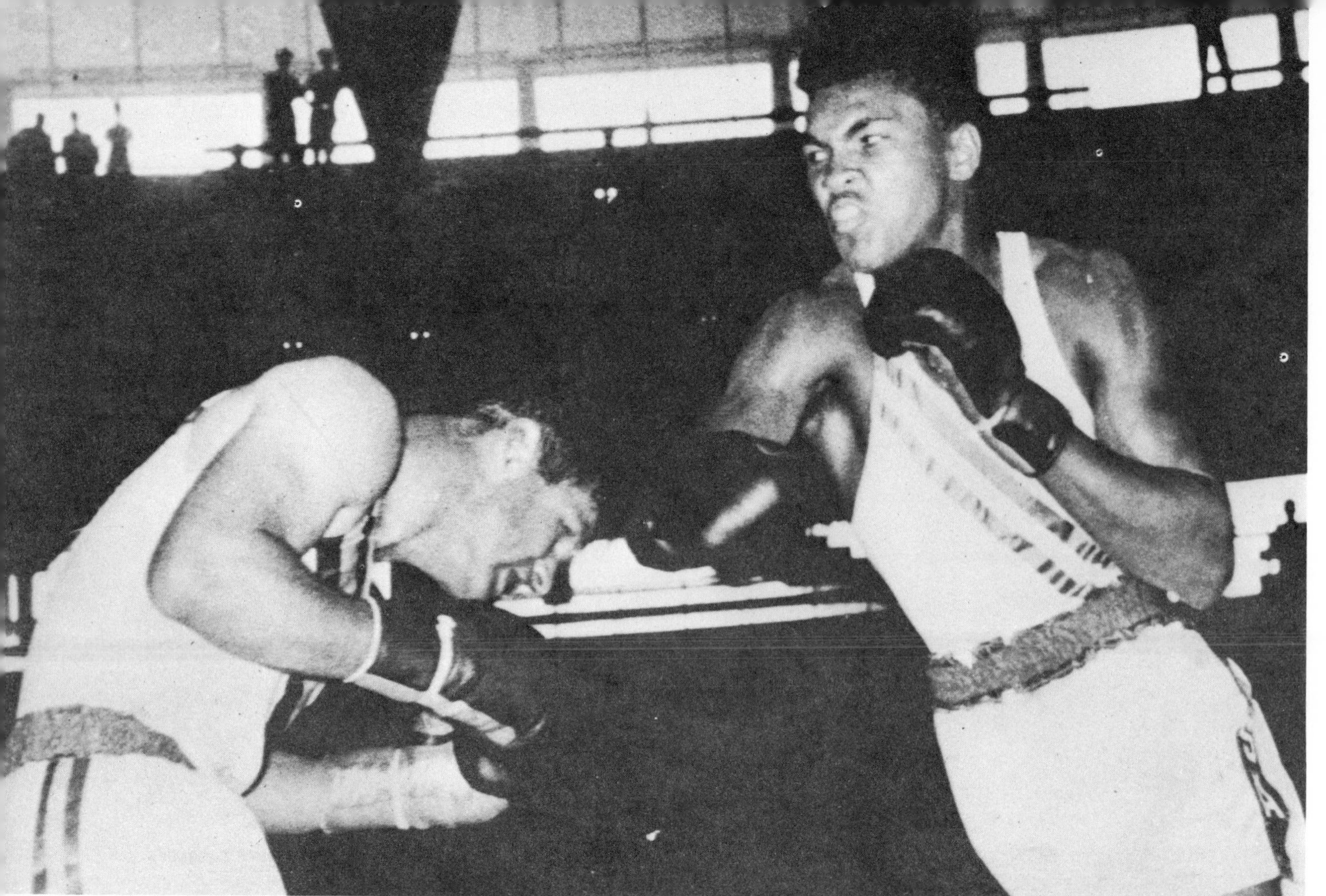

One day these two men would meet each other in one of the richest boxing matches in history, but here, they were concerned with winning gold medals. Above, Cassius Clay defeats Australia's Tony Madigan in 1960 in Rome and four years later, in Tokyo, Joe Frazier beat Germany's Hans Huber.

Games, American swimmers and divers, most of them in their teens, made a harvest of 73 of the available 104 medals, capturing 23 gold, 15 silver and 20 bronze. Schollander won only one of the golds, in the relay. Charles Hickox was the team star, winning three. Michael Burton, Don McKenzie and Mark Spitz won two each.

Debbie Meyer, still in her teens, collected three gold medals, winning the 200 meters, 400 meters and 800 meters freestyle, all in Olympic record time. Just by way of showing the great strides the sport had taken in four decades, Johnny Weissmuller won the men's 100-meter freestyle in 1928 in 58.6 seconds. Mike Wenden of Australia won it in 1968 in 52.2. Weissmuller's time in the 400 meters was 5:04.2. Debbie Meyer, just a wisp of a girl, cut that time down in winning the women's 400 meters in 1968 in 4:31.8.

The modern Summer Games had been in progress 28 years before cold weather athletes—the skiers, skaters, bobsledders and figure skaters—forced the International Olympic Committee to start the Winter Games. There had been strong opposition from the Scandinavian nations, which held their own series of prestigious winter events.

However, the popularity of ice and snow sports was gaining such momentum throughout the world that the IOC finally had to give its official blessing. It was determined that the Winter Games should be held every four years—in the same year as the Summer Games—but always at a different date and on a different site.

The inaugural Winter Games were staged at Chamonix, a famed French resort, in 1924. Sixteen nations competed. There were 293 athletes, only 13 of them women. This ratio increased in succeeding years, with the list at Grenoble, France, in 1968 including more than 1,000 athletes from more than 30 nations, some 200 of them women.

One event was transferred from the Summer to the Winter Games. That was figure skating, which had been added to the Summer Games in 1908.

Figure skating became one of the most glamorous events of the Winter Olympics program, rivaled later only by Alpine skiing, and the person most responsible probably was a dimpled Norwegian beauty named Sonja Henie.

Sonja, a graceful ballerina on razor-sharp blades, won the women's figure skating gold medal in three consecutive Olympics—1928, 1932 and 1936—capturing the fancy of Hitler at Garmisch-Partenkirchen, Germany, in 1936. Then she turned professional and came to America to star in the movies.

Most of her movies were fresh, young love productions staged in a winter wonderland setting. Americans were enchanted with the dimpled Scandinavian skating queen. After witnessing the movies, many of them rushed home and immediately bought ice skates for their daughters and sons. Figure skating reached high popularity in the United States. Years later—when the kids had grown up—America found itself with a brood of world and Olympic class figure skaters.

Observers have given the credit to Miss Henie.

Dick Button, a Harvard student who introduced a repertoire of daring spins and jumps to his routine, won Olympic men's titles in 1948 and 1952, succeeded by a pair of brothers—Hayes Alan Jenkins in 1956 and David Jenkins in 1960. Tenley Albright, a statuesque medical student from Boston, gave the United States its first ladies' crown in 1956. Carol Heiss, a baker's daughter from the borough of Queens in New York, won in 1960 and dazzling Peggy Fleming, a green-eyed whirling dervish, took the gold medal in 1968 after the United States had built back from a plane accident that wiped out most of the country's leading skaters after the 1960 Games. Miss Heiss already had turned professional and became the wife of Hayes Alan Jenkins.

The United States has been unable to exercise in the Winter Games the overwhelming dominance that track and swimming permitted it to do in the Summer Games. The Scandinavian countries, for whom snow and ice are a way of life, have cached most of the medals in the Nordic skiing events—cross-country racing and jumping. Austria and France have seemed to produce most of the best Alpine stars—the downhill and slalom racers.

In recent years, the Russians have moved in to challenge in the cross-country races and have developed brilliant figure skaters, particularly the pairs. Also, the tough, professional-like Soviet hockey team wrested superiority in that sport from Canada, which won six of the first seven championships. The United States scored its first and only ice hockey conquest in the 1960 Games at Squaw Valley, Calif., upsetting the heavily favored Soviets.

The Winter Games have produced their own set of heroes and heroines. Sonja Henie was only 16 when she won the first of her figure skating crowns. Thorleif Haug, a hardy Norwegian, won three gold medals in Nordic events in the in-

Gold medal winner Peggy Fleming's performance in a round of the compulsory figures is carefully studied by officials during the 1968 Winter Olympics at Grenoble, France.

Frenchman Jean Claude Killy sweeps to victory in the 1968 Olympic giant slalom event at Chamrousse, France. He went on to become the star at the Games.

augural Games in 1924. Hjalmar Andersen, also of Norway, captured three golds in speed skating in the 1952 Games at Oslo. A Soviet girl, Lydia Skoblikowa, made history by winning four gold medals in speed skating in 1960.

The most glamorous of the winter stars have come from Alpine skiing, an event in which the contestants speed down a mountainside at break-neck speed, taking treacherous curves in the downhill and spinning around fragile flag poles—or gates—in the slalom.

A tall, handsome Austrian named Anton "Toni" Sailer became the fascination of all skiers when he won three gold medals in the 1956 Olympics at Cortina D'Ampezzo, Italy. He won the downhill, the slalom and giant slalom in a sweep that had never been achieved before. The undisputed world champion, he turned to a movie career and then became an instructor in his native Austria.

Sailer was a spectator at Grenoble in 1968 when he saw Jean Claude Killy, a handsome Frenchman who brought new daring to the sport, match his sweep on a cloud-shrouded and controversy-marred mountainside.

With the entire French nation, including Charles de Gaulle, at his feet, Killy gave a brilliant show in winning the three Alpine specialties, the final under bitter protest from Karl Schranz of Austria.

Schranz demanded and received a repeat run when he contended that an interloper crossed his path on the descent. On the repeat performance, the Austrian

Italy's Eugenio Monti is at the helm of his team's bobsled as it zoomed down the 1,500-meter course at Alpe D'Huez, France, in the 1968 Olympic Games.

recorded a better time than Killy. Later, however, an international jury threw out the repeat run on the grounds that there was no evidence of an obstruction.

Schranz objected violently. The jury held its ground.

IOC President Avery Brundage, still contending that Alpine skiers violated the amateur code, gave the Alpine performers the brushoff. He refused to present medals.

Although the United States has a talented and dedicated group of Alpine skiers—trained on the slopes of California, New Hampshire and Vermont—Americans have had only moderate success in world and Olympic skiing.

Gretchen Fraser, a pig-tailed housewife from Vancouver, Wash., brought the United States its first gold medal in Alpine skiing in 1948 at St. Moritz, Switzerland, winning the women's slalom and finishing second to Trude Reiser of Austria in the combined (downhill and slalom). Four years later, Andrea Mead Lawrence, 19, of Rutland, Vt., scored a double triumph at Oslo by winning both the slalom and giant slalom events.

Billy Kidd and Jim Huega gave the United States its first men's medals in Alpine skiing at Innsbruck, Austria, in 1964, Kidd winning a silver and Huega a bronze in the slalom.

Meanwhile, the giant struggle continued between the United States and the Soviet Union in the Summer Games.

At Helsinki in 1952, the Americans won 14 gold medals in track and field while the Russians won none. Yet the huge Soviet delegation piled up points in such events as gymnastics, boxing and wrestling.

The United States continued to hold an edge over the improving Russians at Melbourne, Australia, in 1956 but at Rome in 1960 Soviet track and field stars began making their presence felt. They won five gold medals and showed particular strength in the women's competition.

Stars of the Rome Olympics, however, were Abebe Bikila, a bodyguard of Ethiopia's Emperor Haile Selassie, who won the marathon running barefoot over the cobblestones of the Appian Way; leggy Wilma Rudolph, a Negro speedster from Nashville, Tenn., who captured three gold medals in the women's sprints; and Ralph Boston, also from Nashville, who shattered Jesse Owens' 24-year record in the broad jump.

The United States won half of the 24 track and field gold medals in Tokyo in 1964, setting eight Olympic records in the process. Billy Mills, an ex-Marine, scored the major surprise in winning the 10,000-meter race, which always had been a European specialty. Bikila repeated his marathon victory.

The Games went to Mexico City in 1968, the first time ever in a Latin American country, and immediately a raging controversy arose over the mile-high altitude. Exhaustive tests were made before the Games. There were forecasts that the thin air might result in serious injuries and perhaps even death. Some athletes collapsed because of the heat but the fears of fatalities and permanent damage proved groundless.

Shortly before the scheduled opening, students rioted on the streets of Mexico City and scores died under the guns of police. The IOC held an emergency meeting to decide whether to go on with the Games. The vote was affirmative.

The Games were highlighted by Bob Beamon's incredible long jump of 29 feet, 2½ inches and Dick Fosbury's triumph in the high jump, using an unorthodox technique in which he soared over the bar backwards and landed on the nape of his neck. He popularized the "Fosbury Flop."

The Mexico City Games saw the United States overpower the Soviet Union in track and field, monopolize the swimming pool, win again in basketball and pick up enough medals in other events to make it a red, white and blue Olympics.

Out of these games came America's greatest Olympic giant of them all—Al Oerter, a 32-year-old Long Islander who won the discus throw for the fourth time with a heave of 212 feet, 6½ inches. No other athlete in the long history of the Games had ever before won four consecutive gold medals in the same event.

Sir Frederick Wells, lord mayor of London, holds the Olympic flag as state trumpeters blare the official end of the 1948 Olympic Games at Wembley Stadium in London at the first resumption of Olympic competition after World War II.

"Sports" is defined as a form of recreation or diversion, but more than that, it is . . .

determination . . .

frustration . . .

speed . . .

power . . .

15

21

13
19
6
21
15
NEW YORK
16

timing . . .

style . . .

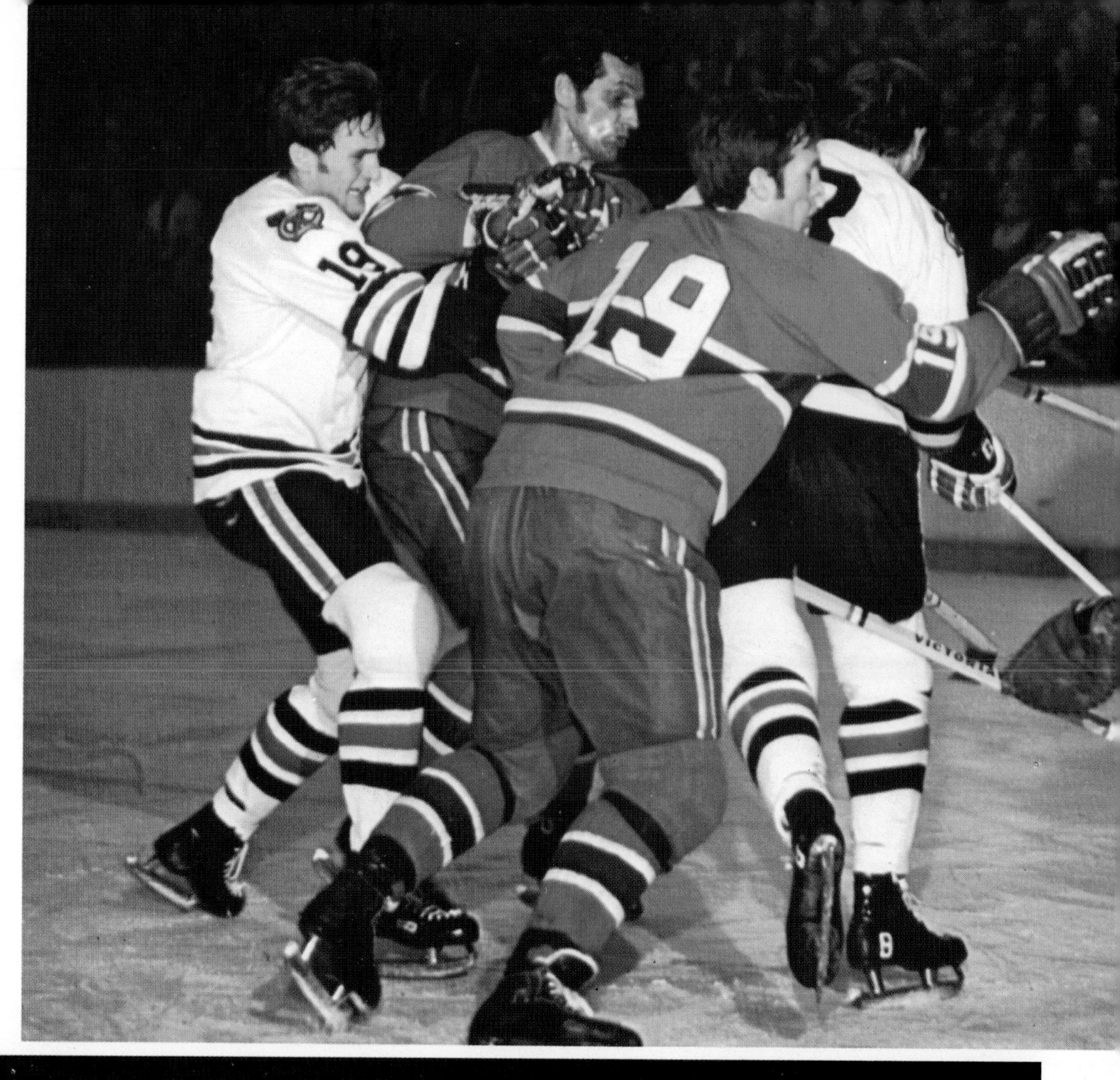

endurance . . .

concentration . . .

exhilaration . . .

hustle . . .

AND
THANK YOU FOR COMING
PLEASE ARRIVE HOME
SAFELY
METS
BALT. ORIOLES
N.Y. METS
NO THROWING
OF OBJECTS
LONGINES
Meet The Corner
371

and victory!

These photos, taken by Henry Ford, show some of the action of the first Indianapolis 500 in 1911. Top, the drivers line up in front of their cars before the start (photographic car is at right). Ray Harroun, the eventual winner of the race, center, slows for a pit stop and the second place finisher, Ralph Mulford, right, approaches the infield area during the race.

chapter 10

AUTO RACING

Fastest Growing of Spectator Sports

by Bloys Britt

Bloys Britt, a graduate of the University of North Carolina, began his *Associated Press* career in 1942 in Raleigh, N.C., and did general editorial work until he was assigned to Carolina auto races in the late 1950s. Then he became an expert. In 1969, he was made Auto Racing Editor of *The Associated Press*. Since then, he has followed the belching machines around the tracks throughout the United States.

There are those who say the first motor race occurred shortly after the second car was built. It is certain that the first owner started looking for the second one within due time. Exactly when they found each other isn't known.

Americans have been thrilled with the speed of moving things and with the spirit of competition down through the ages, and it was logical that the transition of this urge to match machinery, skill, horsepower and bravery should move from the age of horses and carriages to the age of motors.

In the early days of the auto, this fascination first worked its magic on the affluent, the blooded scions of the nation's great families. But it also cast its spell on the neighborhood kid who stood under the elms and watched in awe as the carriages putt-putted among the dusty city streets.

This love affair with motors has continued down through the years, at first because of the novelty and excitement generated by machines that responded, however reluctantly and capriciously, to human direction, then to one of acceptance as Detroit produced autos in the millions.

It is accepted that the seeds of competition spring from ownership. And it is this tiny spark of identification with motors, however limited and however sprung, that causes more Americans to pay their way into racing tracks and courses each year than to any other non-pari-mutuel sport.

It is also this identification of the individual with cars—his ownership, his being a part of his machine—that has caused U.S. auto makers to dump untold millions of dollars into motor sports. The thesis is simple and uncomplicated: Every competitive event involving machinery brings with it technical improvements to the vehicles that participated; and, it follows, victory on Sunday makes for more sales in the showrooms on Monday. After all, as Henry Ford once put it, nobody sells horses anymore.

Racing actually got the automobile started. The leading families of the country took to the motor-driven carriages and with their approval the auto became the socially accepted fifth rung in the ladder of success, the others being wealth, castle, bloodline and politics. As one historian put it at the turn of the century, it was a question of keeping up with the Vanderbilts and the Whitneys rather than the Joneses.

History records many planned excursions in the sport of motor racing well before 1900. The sport already was flourishing by the time Ford built his first prototype in 1896. Europe was a hotbed of racing, with village bucks filling the main roads with the bark of two-cylinder engines. The French coined the words "Grand Prix" to designate the "grand prize" in thoroughbred horse racing. With the coming of the motor racing age the term was used to isolate the premiere motor races from the lesser ones.

The first race of major proportions apparently was the one from Paris to Rouen in 1894, won by a man named De Dion in a fragile little steam car. It is said that crowds that swarmed up and down the route slowed his progress to an average speed of just over 11 miles per hour.

A year later, in June 1895, Emile Levassor drove a Panhard-Daimler round trip from Paris to Bordeaux, a distance of 732 miles, in 48 hours, 47 minutes for an average speed of 15.01 m.p.h. A durable camel could have done better.

On Dec. 18, 1898, Count Gaston de Chasseloup-Laubat set the first recognized land speed record for motor cars—a sparkling 39.24 m.p.h. for the measured kilometer—at Acheres, France. Gaston's electric Jeantaud ran out of power and stalled just as it crossed the finish line.

The motor racing urge already was beginning to spring forth in America even as the first organized events were pulling huge crowds in Europe. It is said that several of this country's blooded and landed gentry were touring Europe at the time of the Paris-Bordeaux race. They stopped off to witness it and came home imbued with prospects of a financial harvest in a new sport for kings.

In the next five years there were a number of "exhibition" races in the Northeast, mostly on back roads, without supervision or rules, and out of eye and earshot of the police.

Then on July 25, 1900, there was a series of exhibitions for various types of motor carriages in New Haven, Conn. The program, staged on a half-mile dirt horse track at Bransford Park, drew an astonishing 15,000 people. Now recognized as America's first closed course race for more than one type of machinery, the New Haven race included heats for gasoline engine tricycles, four-wheeled gasoline motor cars and for electric and steam vehicles.

Later, on Sept. 6, 1900, William K. Vanderbilt swept a series of races for all types of horseless carriages in a gala program staged at Aquidnick Trotting Park in Connecticut. Sponsors included such socially-elite families as the Belmonts, the Oelrichs, the Davises and the Astors.

Vanderbilt was declared the sweepstakes winner, his chauffeur acting as mechanic and riding shotgun. It is said that the brother of a shipping magnate came in fourth, riding in the back seat of his monstrous sedan with his chauffeur and a mechanic riding up front. Newspapers of the day carried pictures or drawings of the vehicles, generally with ladies in high fashion togs swarming around them.

Henry Ford, then 38 and a proven mechanic and tired of the life of being a house painter, built his first car in 1896. A light weight runabout, the engine produced only 29 horsepower from its massive two-cylinder, 540 cubic inches, but it was the forerunner of engines that during the next 60 years were to win more competitive races than any other U.S. powerplant.

Ford, looking for money to begin building his own line of motor cars, entered a 10-mile race at Grosse Point, just outside Detroit, on Oct. 10, 1901. He had got his prototype up to 72 m.p.h. during tests a few months earlier—the world land speed record then was 65.79 m.p.h. held by the Belgian Camille Jenatzy—and was ready to take on all comers.

The winner's purse was $1,000. There were three entries, but one dropped out with mechanical troubles, leaving Ford and Alexander Winton, who was then building his own cars in Cleveland, as the only contestants. Winton was a proven racer and was acclaimed the favorite.

Ford, with mechanic Spider Huff riding along as ballast, took the lead on the eighth of 10 laps over the one-mile Detroit Driving Club oval as Winton's engine began to sour. Winton managed to finish but Ford's victory was an impressive one. He covered the 10 miles in 13 minutes, 23.8 seconds for an average speed of 44.8 m.p.h.

Ford, jubilant but grease and dust covered, announced on the spot that he was quitting as a race driver, having accomplished what he set out to prove—that he could build a fast and durable car. He also got his name in the public press and, with the prize money, formed the first company bearing his name. There were changes later, of course, and Ford raced again, many times, but his name was established.

The early races in Europe and the United States were road races—that is, they were run on public roads, from one town to another. For various reasons, including the obvious dangers involved, plus the impracticality of policing miles and miles of country lanes, closed circuits came into being. These at first involved no more than choosing a route that started and finished in the same place. Roads also were selected that provided fencing or barriers, giving drivers some assurance that when they came around a bend they could be reasonably sure that the route wouldn't be filled with stray spectators, flocks of geese or chickens, or a local yokel pedaling the wrong way on his bicycle. Time-keeping was made easier and the same crew of officials could be used for starting and stopping it. Also, it was easier to tell who won.

The massed start, as it is used today, was still a long way off. Competitors in the early days were sent off at intervals, their eyes covered by goggles, their faces swathed in kerchiefs against the dust, their long outer coats flapping in the breeze. But there was none of the wheel-to-wheel action that enlivens the modern race. The daredevil drivers of yesterday technically were neck-and-neck in the scoring but could be miles apart on the long, pock-marked courses.

It was not until about 1905 that any semblance of rules to govern racing began to appear and with these came the modern pattern of starting several cars abreast. The first set of rules covering an entire series or season was applied to one of the early Vanderbilt Cup circuits, and mostly had to do with machinery. Drivers could be anyone who either had his own machine or the courage to drive someone else's. It is said that many a young villager who started early manhood as a chauffeur ended up by gaining a country club membership because of his ability to drive his employer's car to victory.

As cars became more plentiful and more evenly matched, results depended more and more on the skill of the driver. By the time auto racing began to blossom as an organized sport, and with prize money becoming a major factor, many of the European drivers either hustled to America on their own or were imported by wealthy owners and manufacturers.

There was a growing number of events for which their services could be used. Vanderbilt, who became perhaps the leading early pioneer of speed in this country, holding the land speed record at least five times in the early 1900s, inaugurated the first big series of road races in the Northeast in 1904, calling it the Vanderbilt Cup. The courses were laid out mostly over dusty public roads, with laps ranging from 14 to 24 miles. The racers were mostly production models but the entry lists were heavily laden with some of the more powerful, more advanced European makes. Accidents were frequent and spectacular, often taking the lives of drivers, mechanics and spectators. The European makes dominated this series, and it was not until 1908 that an American entry finally won—a chain-driven Locomobile with a massive 16-liter engine.

By then, however, the domestic auto makers were turning out production models by the thousands, of every shape and size, by every method of propulsion known. The need to gain recognition of a particular make became so great that the makers themselves staged at least 200 speed runs or "exhibitions" during 1908 alone.

In addition to public roads and streets, beaches and private courses came into use for racing events. Promoters everywhere appropriated any enclosure that had a protective fence or barrier, and the horse tracks at fairgrounds were among the more prized locations. In the colder climates, frozen lakes also were fair game.

The Florida beaches, particularly the white-washed sand at Daytona-Ormond, became a mecca for speed as early as 1902 when Winton's "Bullet" of the Ford-Winton race at Grosse Point and the "Pirate" of R. E. Olds ran at 75 m.p.h. in a match race.

Vanderbilt, who on April 9, 1902, had set a land speed record of 65.79 m.p.h. in a Mercedes-Simplex at Acheres, France, went to Daytona in January 1904, and flashed to a new mark of 92.30 m.p.h. in a Mercedes. Ford had posted the existing record only two weeks before, driving his own creation to 91.37 m.p.h. on the ice at Lake St. Clair, Mich.

Vanderbilt's achievement was the forerunner of many speed records set at Daytona during the next 25 years. The warm winter climate was especially attractive to the Northern sportsmen, their wives and socially-prominent friends. The last record of note set there was Sir Malcolm Campbell's 276.82 m.p.h. in his famed "Bluebird" in March 1935. The Bonneville Salt Flats in Utah then became the chosen site for speed runs and Daytona settled down to become one of the key sites for stock car racing.

Other beaches ran races in the period from 1902 through 1908, including Cape May and Atlantic City, N.J. It was at Cape May in the late summer of 1905 that a Swiss mechanic named Louis Chevrolet made his debut in auto racing. He and brothers Gaston and Arthur were to become famous as race car builders.

Many of the early races were strictly exhibition runs for one make of car and sponsored by the manufacturer for publicity purposes. These exhibitions frequently were endurance runs. In this connection, it may be said that Le Mans, in France, was not the birthplace of 24-hour racing. There were a number of events in the United States prior to World War I that stretched around the clock. Indeed, Packard Motors ran one of its cars 1,000 miles in 29 hours, 53 minutes at Grosse Point in 1904. And a Pope-Toledo covered 825.5 miles during a 24-hour run at Columbus, Ohio, in July 1905.

Other endurance events were held at such widely separated points as Brooklyn, Birmingham, Ala., and St. Paul, Minn. There were eight 24-hour runs at Brighton Beach, now a residential section of Brooklyn, before the first world war.

There also were many cross-country runs as manufacturers sought to gain attention in the press, even to advertising well ahead the exact moment their entourage would reach a given point. Some of these endurance runs were limited to distances between Eastern and Midwestern cities, others spanned the continent. A corps of drivers took a Packard from New York to San Francisco in 15 days, 2 hours, 15 minutes early in 1906 to claim the first transcontinental record. Another such effort in 1907 ended in tragedy. The crew of one auto ran out of water, got stranded in the desert and died before they could be rescued. The crew of another car was similarly stranded for two days during which one member was bitten by a rattlesnake and died.

After 10 years of the new century, auto racing was about to come of age. Auto makers in the Midwest cities were matching the Europeans in technology and styling, and horse-drawn carriages were going out of style. Newspapers almost daily carried news of the exploits of the daredevils who were risking their lives on the tracks.

But U.S. auto makers had no large track on which they could prove or test their theories on such things as four-wheel brakes, hydraulic shock absorbers, carburetion, suspensions and tires. Nor was there an enclosure that could accommodate large crowds—one that could be policed to the extent that everyone who got in to watch paid to do so.

Thus it was that in 1908, Carl G. Fisher, James A. Allison, Arthur C. Newby and Frank H. Wheeler pooled their ideas and resources to build the Indianapolis Motor Speedway. They selected a flat 400-acre field on the northwest fringe of Indianapolis as the site for their "proving ground" for automobiles. They capitalized at $250,000.

The field assembles in front of the main grandstand just before the May 30, 1912, Indianapolis 500.

Ralph DePalma's dramatic breakdown two laps from the finish cost him the 1912 Indianapolis 500. He attempted to push his car across the finish line.

Work started on the mammoth 2.5-mile course in the fall of 1908 and when the thaws lifted the next spring, hundreds of mules and a work brigade of 100 men, most hired at $2 per day, gradually "plowed out" the outlines of the oval that was to bring maturity to racing in America.

But it wasn't long before Fisher realized that something would have to be done about the dirt surface. There had been many wrecks and injuries in the first series of sprints and dust clouds floated over that section of the city for days.

Too, there had been pandemonium in the parking lots and streets outside. Horses, singly and hitched to carriages and wagons, roamed loose in the fields, dragging hitching blocks with them. They knocked down fences and shrubbery and sometimes wound up in barns of irate property owners who ransomed them back to their owners for princely sums of cash.

During the winter and much of the following year, workmen laid 3,200,000 paving bricks, each weighing 10 pounds, on the dirt surface of the oval. New fencing was put up to replace that knocked down in the turmoil of the previous August. Garages were built for cars and crews and drinking fountains made their appearance.

Fisher and his cronies felt by then that auto racing was ready for its first "spectacular." European makers and drivers were ready to challenge the growing influence of the Americans in the motor car market and, indeed, had more than held their own against domestic machinery for years. The only place of any significance available for such a confrontation was Indianapolis. The Fisher group scheduled a 500-mile race for Memorial Day, 1911. Prize money was $35,000.

Few rules were set for the race. One limited engine sizes to 600-cubic-inch displacement. Another specified that only drivers who had exceeded 75 m.p.h.

in practice would be allowed in the field. A third rule limited the starting list to 44 cars. Spots in the lineup were determined by entry dates; thus, many of the faster machines, arriving at the track late, were relegated to rear starting positions.

America had some experienced drivers to throw against the Europeans. There had been a championship circuit in operation since 1902. Harry Harkness had won the national driving title in 1902 and the great Barney Oldfield had taken the crown in 1903. Such personages as George Heath, Vic Hemery, Joe Tracy, Eddie (Cannon) Bald, Louis Strang, George Robertson and Bert Dingley also had won national championships. Two other greats, Ralph Mulford and Ralph DePalma, and comparative newcomers Joe Dawson and Howdy Wilcox were just beginning to exploit their talents.

Race day was bright and sunny. The management, taking a lesson from the year before, had installed 3,000 hitching posts in the adjoining lots.

More than 75,000 people crowded through the gates. They witnessed drama, tragedy and frustration.

Arthur Greiner, who had started his Amplex in 38th position, lost control in the southwest corner on the 12th lap and hit the wall. His riding mechanic, Sam Dickson, became the first man to lose his life at the Speedway. Greiner was hospitalized with a broken shoulder. Later, the Pope-Hartford of Louis Disbrow and the Lozier of Teddy Tetzlaff collided on the front straight but neither driver was hurt.

The real drama came on lap 87 when mechanic C. L. Anderson fell from Joe Jagersberger's racer as the two roared down the front straight. Harry Knight, who was trailing Jagersberger closely, swerved to avoid the sprawling Anderson as the crowd screamed in horror. Though he managed to avoid hitting Anderson, Knight careened into the car of Herbert Lytle in the pits, then flipped over on Caleb Bragg's machine. Knight came out with a mildly fractured skull and his riding mechanic, John Glover, a strained back.

Roy Harroum was among the late arrivals. He had started his Marmon "Wasp" in 28th position. A slightly-built, dark-haired man of 35, Harroum had retired from racing the previous year and hadn't planned to race in the "500" until urged to do so by friends.

Driving with "dexterity and determination," as the press reports put it, Harroum began picking off car after car as he brought his black and yellow, bullet-like car steadily to the front and romped home the winner by a good margin over the second place Mulford. His average speed for the 500 miles was 74.59 m.p.h.

Harroum's six-cylinder, 447-cubic-inch machine was the only single-seater in the starting order and thus he had no room to carry a riding mechanic. The extra man in the cockpit not only served as an observer to keep an eye on the other cars and the pits, but to listen for sounds of trouble from the engine. Harroum had to make up for the loss of his observer. To compensate, he mounted an eight-by-three-inch mirror on a tripod attached to the hood cowling—and thus put into use the first rear-view mirror on any kind of motor vehicle.

The Indianapolis Motor Speedway was a success from the start. During its long history it has provided a mixture of thrills and poignancy, success and bitter failure for drivers and car owners, tragedy and turmoil for others and their families.

Ralph DePalma, who observers say was one of the best drivers ever to race on American tracks, led the 1912 race for 196 of the 200 laps, only to have a connecting rod break and stall the car within sight of victory. DePalma and his mechanic, Rupert Jenkins, gallantly tried to push their heavy Mercedes the rest of the way, a crowd of 80,000 yelling support. They failed.

Joe Dawson, who had finished fifth the year before, unexpectedly found himself with the lead that year and coasted home with a check for $35,000. Member of a poor family, Dawson was so overwhelmed that he slipped away from well-wishers in victory lane and drove to his nearby home to tell his mother. Mrs. Dawson, who had refused to go to the track, asked, "Joe, did you get any bumps and bruises?"

The 1913 race brought an influx of European entries, forerunners of powerful machines that were to dominate the event for the next 10 years. Among those who came was a Frenchman named Jules Goux, manning a Peugeot that obviously was one of four or five cars to beat.

But Goux had a problem: He couldn't speak a word of English. Johnny Aitken was assigned as his American coach, his principal duties being to keep the driver abreast of the rules. Aitken had to communicate with Goux through an interpreter.

The story is told that during the race, the interpreter informed Aitken that there had been an oversight, a vital one, in the arrangement of Goux's pit, already cluttered with spare parts, tires, gasoline and helpers. The missing item was the bottle of chilled wine that the Frenchman always demanded when he drove.

Suffice to say that the interpreter was sent to a nearby dispensary and a supply of champagne was waiting when Goux made his first pit stop. Much refreshed, Goux went on to win the race handily.

Oldfield, the best known driver in America at the time, had missed the first two "500s" while sitting out his fourth "lifetime" suspension from the American Automobile Association (AAA), which sanctioned the early Indianapolis races.

Oldfield had received the suspension for racing on outlaw tracks and "against horses, other animals and airplanes." The suspension was lifted in time for the great Oldfield to make the 1914 race, when European cars swept the first four finishing positions. Oldfield came in fifth—a magnificent effort considering that his Stutz was relegated to a last place start as a result of the draw for spots in the lineup the night before.

DePalma won his only victory in 10 tries at Indianapolis in 1915. But among the entries were Eddie Rickenbacker, the World War I flying ace, and Louis Chevrolet. Rickenbacker went on to compete in the "500" several times before buying the Speedway in 1927.

Gaston Chevrolet later became a winner of the race and his brothers, Arthur and Louis, also were competitors. They also were to become famous as car builders and engineers.

Rickenbacker was credited with wearing the first steel crash helmet at the Speedway.

Indianapolis served as a proving ground for the U.S. auto makers. Most of the cars that raced there during the years prior to World War I were production models, though modified somewhat for track use. Makes included Marmon, Buick, Fiat, Mercer, Stutz, Simplex, Mercedes and National.

General view looks down rainy track of the Indianapolis Speedway on Memorial Day in 1931 during the running of the 500. Lou Schneider of Indianapolis won the rain-delayed race.

For two makes, however, one trip and one victory was enough. Marmon never came back after winning the first race, and National quit after Dawson's triumph in 1912. Over the years, however, every domestic car that became popular and remained on the American scene any length of time raced at Indianapolis.

The Roaring Twenties brought the first major changes in machinery. For the first time, the Speedway adopted the international formula for Grand Prix cars, dropping the engine size to 183 inches and making obsolete all of the production and semi-stock cars that had kept things going in former years.

In the early days, it had been a contest between the Stutz and the Peugeot, the Mercedes and the Delage, the Maxwell and the Mercer. Thus, it came that on Memorial Day, 1920, every car entered in the race was built solely for racing, most in small shops around Indianapolis. The auto makers weren't missed as the era of exotic engines, chassis and body designs, together with a new breed of skilled and strictly professional drivers took over in racing.

The '20s became a period when it was the Millers against the Frontenacs, the Duesenbergs and a special collection of other mounts, mostly handmade.

As one historian put it, drivers had changed from the leather-helmeted, mustachioed daredevils handling huge, ungainly machines to young jousters in low-slung bombs. The drama of Jimmy Murphy, Tommy Milton, Leon Duray, Frank Lockhart, DePalma, Howdy Wilcox, Mulford and Oldfield passed and brought on the Pete DePalos, the Ralph Hepburns, Harry Hartzs, L. L. Corums, Wilbur Shaws, Louis Meyers, Billy Arnolds, Ray Keeches, and Cliff Bergeres.

The first double-overhead cam engines produced by Fred Miller made their appearance in the 1920 race. They were designed by two brothers, Harry and Fred Offenhauser, and were forerunners of the famed little "Offys" that long have been among the best in racing.

In another development that was to have its impact on the future of the transportation industry, Charles Kettering brought his new ethyl-formula gasoline to the Speedway in 1923. It powered Tommy Milton's winning car.

In 1925, winner DePalo became the first driver to average more than 100 m.p.h. for 500 miles. Dave Lewis drove the first front wheel drive car to appear at the Speedway to second place in the same race.

The 1927 race was notable for two reasons: 1. It was the last one under the Fisher regime; 2. it marked the debut of Wilbur Shaw, Lou Meyer and George Souders, all of whom were to leave their impact on the Brickyard in future years.

Shaw's Indianapolis career spanned 14 races, but he raced 10 times before he became the first three-time winner. Meyer, who served as Shaw's relief driver in 1927, also went on to win three times—all of them coming before Shaw finally broke his streak of hard luck. Souders won the 1927 running in his first start, becoming only one of three rookies ever to accomplish the feat.

Rickenbacker bought the Speedway from the Fisher group on Aug. 1, 1927, for a sum reported in excess of $750,000. One of the major changes he instituted came in 1930 when he threw out the international Grand Prix engine formula and raised the limits to 336 cubic inches. It was a move to encourage more participation by the major domestic auto makers, and it worked. The entry list that year was full of names such as Buick, Chrysler, Ford, Hudson, Packard, Studebaker and Reo.

It also brought a new influx of foreign cars, and Shaw's 1939 victory in a Maserati was the first for a European-made machine since 1919.

The 1940s at Indianapolis, marked by a wartime shutdown that lasted four years—1942–1945—brought still another new crop of drivers and more specialty machinery, including the supercharged Novis, V–8 powerplants, designed by the Winfield brothers. The engine became famous as the "screaming" Novi because of the ear-splitting howl it emitted when running full bore. The Novi set fast time and it led many races, but it never made the victory circle at Indianapolis.

Fire destroyed the garage area in the early morning of Memorial Day, 1941, though drivers and crews managed to save all but one of the cars that were scheduled to start that day. Victory went to Mauri Rose—first of his three before he retired in 1951—and he was followed across the finish line in order by three men who were to become famous drivers but who died before they could win the big one. They were Rex Mays, Ted Horn and Ralph Hepburn. Hepburn's car was the first use of the supercharged Novi.

Anton (Tony) Hulman, a Terre Haute businessman, bought the Brickyard from Rickenbacker on Oct. 15, 1945, paying $750,000 for the plant that was then a collection of wooden buildings and bleachers.

It was shortly after that that Hulman started refurbishing the place and over the years increased the permanent seating to 215,000 and made the infield available for an additional 100,000, plus parking space for 25,000 cars. It was during this period, also, that the course was paved with asphalt over the old bricks. It was under Hulman that the purse began to skyrocket—from $115,450 his first year to the first $1 million payoff in auto racing history in 1970.

The 1950s were years of development as Detroit carried on the streamlining of passenger cars that started in the late 1940s, and as engines moved out of the six-cylinder to eight-cylinder acceptance.

The joy of victory and the horror of tragedy are familiar to the Indianapolis 500. At top, Bill Vukovich waves to the crowd as he receives the checkered flag giving him his second straight 500 victory, in 1954. Vukovich was to die at Indy the following year attempting to win his third consecutive 500. The bottom photo catches the spectacular crash in the 1964 Indy that claimed the life of veteran driver Eddie Sachs.

It was an era of dominance by the little Offenhauser—and a signal for the later development of the Ford overhead cam powerplants. These exotic little bombs, first mated to superchargers, then to turbochargers, shot speeds out of sight. They became so reliable and so strong that they survived a dramatic challenge from turbine power in the 1960s.

There also was new emphasis on special fuels, new metals, better and bigger tires, and improved methods of spring suspension.

Jimmy Snyder had set the pre-World War II four-lap qualifying record at 130.138 m.p.h. in 1939. In 1946, Hepburn raised the single-lap mark to 134.449 and the four-lap standard to 133.944. Floyd Roberts, a promising young driver, had set the 500-mile race record at 117.200 in 1938. This mark was to stand for 10 years, but beginning with Mauri Rose's 119.814 in 1948, scarcely a year passed without the speed barrier going up. Joe Leonard set the modern-day standard of 171.953 for one lap and 171.559 for four in a turbine in 1968.

The national championship circuit for Indianapolis-type cars had been established in 1902, strengthened in the 1920s with the addition of a dozen dirt and board tracks, then solidified with the building of a number of paved and modern dirt ovals. The Brickyard was the hub of this activity and the combination produced many drivers whose names are hallowed in history.

There was the "Mad Russian," Billy Vukovich, who won the 1953 and 1954 Memorial Day races and died in a crash in 1955 while trying to make it three in a row. There was the "clown prince of racing," Eddie Sachs, who made eight starting lineups, always was a contender, but was still without victory when he died in a flaming crash in the 1964 race. Jimmy Bryan won the 1958 race, collected $111,328, but was killed a month later at Langhorne, Pa. Tony Bettenhausen and Jerry Parsons, whose sons later were to follow in their footsteps as drivers, had tremendous careers at the Speedway.

And there was Jerry Unser, oldest of three driving brothers from Albuquerque. Jerry made his debut at Indy in 1958 by sailing over the wall seconds after the race got under way. He was a prime candidate when he returned the next year, but his car crashed in the northwest turn and he died of his injuries. Brothers Bobby and Al Unser were later to win the most prestigious race of them all.

A rear-engined car had first appeared at the Speedway in 1938 and 1939 with little success. There had been other odd cars, like the screaming Novi and the front-wheel designs. None had ever won at the "500." Thus, when Australian Jack Brabham showed up in 1961 with a flimsy-looking, small and light contraption called a Cooper-Climax, the railbirds brushed it off as another novelty that wouldn't work.

Furthermore, the car was mated to a Ford engine—mounted in the wrong place, in the rear! Nobody could conceive of this Ford-powered, English-built, rear-engined lightweight challenging the brute strength of the standard Indianapolis roadster.

But it did. Brabham drove it to a ninth place finish, and his car owner, Art Lathrop, told all who would listen in the garage area, "Gentlemen, you are looking at more than a million dollars worth of obsolete machinery."

Other rear-engined machines, more powerful and with top European and Grand Prix drivers at the wheel, were to follow.

In 1963, Colin Chapman's Lotus-Fords, sleek, low-slung machines in which

Lloyd Ruby (40) in a turbo-charged Offenhauser, speeds into the first turn the leader with a tight pack following in the Indianapolis Memorial Day race in 1969.

the driver viewed the roadway from a reclining position, arrived to challenge the hefty roadsters.

The little cars brought more chuckles from the Gasoline Alley faithful, but most experts agreed that Chapman had some things going for him. Not the least of these was the fact that Jim Clark, the great Scottish driver, and the international star Dan Gurney were his drivers.

The 1960s had brought a new crop of American drivers to the fore, many destined to become wealthy from the sport. A. J. Foyt had arrived at Indianapolis in 1958 and had won the race in 1961. There was three-time winner Rodger Ward, and a tough, dedicated Californian named Parnelli Jones. There were the Rathmann brothers, Dick and Jim, and Roger McCluskey, Lloyd Ruby, Jim McElreath, Art Malone—the cream of the championship trail regulars. And there was the second of the Unser brothers, Bobby, a lean professional who was to make his debut by crashing on the third lap.

It was a spine-tingler. Clark and Gurney stalked pole-sitter Parnelli from the start and at one time, while Jones was pitting, actually were running one-two at the front. Jones finally won, though there were protests from other drivers that his roadster had dumped so much oil on the track that it was too slippery for anyone to pass him. Clark finished second, Gurney seventh. But the handwriting was on the wall.

Thus, another revolution had begun at the Brickyard. Foyt's unexpected victory in a roadster the following year was the last for the front-engined cars. And in that race, 12 of the 33 starters were lightweight rear-engined machines.

The 1964 race was notable in several respects, one tragic. It heralded the demise of the dinosaur roadsters. It established the European road-racing stars as distinct threats every time they appeared at Indy. Clark was to win in 1965 and Grand Prix star Graham Hill in 1966.

Tragedy occurred when Dave McDonald and the loquacious and much-loved Sachs were killed in a flaming seven-car pileup on the front straight. The accident resulted in a new rule requiring that all fuel tanks be made of metal, with rubber bladder inserts, and that no tanks be positioned ahead of the driver or project beyond the inner edge of the wheels.

Clark's 1965 victory was the first for a foreign driver since World War I. Rear-engined cars swept the first three places, Jones coming in second and a new star, Eastern dirt track champion Mario Andretti, taking third in his first start in the big one.

But the revolution was not complete. The switch had been made from front to rear engine mountings, but the choice of power was reserved for a later decision.

Though the "funny car" was plainly the machine of the day, a few builders were looking toward innovations. Thus it was that old Indy veteran Andy Granatelli appeared at the Speedway in 1967 with a race car so odd that many veteran fans laughed out loud.

The new car was turbine-powered and was immediately dubbed the "whooshmobile." It was different from the still new rear-engined machines in that the cockpit and engine were side by side in the chassis. Power came from a small 260-pound Pratt and Whitney turbine engine designed for small aircraft, but it rated 500 horsepower—enough to propel it down Indy's back chute at 200 m.p.h.

Parnelli Jones, who as the winner in 1963 and second place finisher in 1965 could have had his choice of machines, chose to drive the turbine. In practice, Jones proved that the car would handle. It stuck to the track corners as though it was nailed to the course, it had fantastic acceleration from its four-wheel drive, and it had power to spare.

By race day, the Gasoline Alley veterans agreed that it would be Parnelli against the field. And so it was. Jones had the lead from his sixth place starting position by the time the cars went into the second turn. By the end of the first lap he was in solid command—and a rain delay and restart the following day made no difference.

Except for brief times in his pit, Jones led almost every lap of the race. By the 196th lap, it was obvious that everybody else was running for second place. Then, incredibly, Jones slowed down. The turbine had lost power when a $6 bearing in the transmission failed. Threading his way through a last-lap pileup of crashing, spinning cars, A. J. Foyt fought his way to his third Indy triumph.

The 1967 turbine brought the usual chorus of protests from the Brickyard purists, and during the winter severe new restrictions were placed on future turbine designs by the United States Auto Club.

Granatelli, this time in tandem with Chapman's Lotus builders, was back at the Speedway in 1968 with four wedge-shaped turbines and a battery of the world's best drivers—Jones, Clark, Hill, Jackie Stewart and Joe Leonard. Before qualifications began, the driving staff had dwindled with the death of Clark in Europe, the retirement of Jones and injury to Stewart in a Formula 2 accident.

Three of the cars made the field, with Hill, Leonard and Art Pollard manning them. Pole-sitter Leonard either led or dogged the other front runners from the start. It was obvious that a turbine would win if one could survive. Leonard was in the lead when his red monster quit on the 190th lap. Pollard's machine had failed about the same time farther back in the pack, and Hill had crashed earlier.

Bobby Unser went on to win his first "500," and the turbines were relegated to history when still more restrictions were placed on them for the future.

In retrospect, Indianapolis has, indeed, been a proving ground for automobiles, keeping apace and often ahead of developments in the industry.

It has also proved the stepping stone to wealth for many. Al Unser, third of the Albuquerque breed to drive there, won the 1970 "500" and went on to gain almost half a million dollars in prize money. He won again in 1971 with a record speed of 157.735 m.p.h.

But the Speedway also has had a tragic history. In its first 50 years, 40 drivers and mechanics lost their lives either in practice, qualifying or the race itself. There also had been six spectator deaths.

Stock car racing is the oldest form of motor sports. Most of the autos that ran in the early days were prototypes of what became limited or full production models as the industry grew. It wasn't until the early 1920s that cars especially designed for racing began to make their appearance at the tracks.

But while Indianapolis was drawing more and more attention and its attendance soared, there were thousands whose interest remained with the racing of purely production cars—stock cars that could be purchased from showrooms and, with slight modification, raced.

It wasn't until the early 1930s that stock car racing broke away from the Indianapolis influence. The production cars began to appear more frequently in races all their own at small ovals in the Northeast and South. Most of the stock car ovals were carved out of wheat or cotton fields, or were originally dirt horse racing tracks at county fairgrounds. And most were without adequate safety features.

It isn't generally known, but the famed Roosevelt Raceway on Long Island was originally built for multiple use as a horse and auto racing track. The first auto racing in 1936 drew 75,000 people, but subsequent promotions were less successful and the facility was turned over to the horses in 1938.

Atlanta, among other cities in the South, started a racing tradition in the early 1900s and missed by only 90 days the honor of having the first track in America built especially for automobile racing.

Indianapolis had its first race, a scheduled 300-miler that was halted after 235 miles because of wrecks, in August 1909. The Motordrome opened in Atlanta in October with Louis Chevrolet winning a 250-miler in a Buick.

There is no record of the Motordrome running races after 1910, but Lakewood Speedway, a one-mile dirt oval, came into being in 1911 and became the spawning ground for stock car racing as it is known today. Names such as Lloyd Seay, Roy Hall, Ed Samples, Red Bryon, Jack Etheridge, Gober Sosebee, the fabulous Flock brothers, Fonty, Tim and Bob; Glen (Fireball) Roberts, Joe Weatherly and Curtis Turner, among others, either were first heard from there or were among the Speedway's early stars. Their names became household words in Dixie, much like the famed Indianapolis drivers.

Charlotte also contended with Atlanta and Daytona Beach, Fla., as a center for stock car racing in the early '30s. North and South Carolina were stomping grounds for such stars as Buck Baker, Cotton Owens, Lee Petty, Herb Thomas and Jim Paschal, men tough as nails, fearless and with colorful backgrounds.

Both Charlotte and Atlanta entered the super speedway era in 1960 when huge 1.5-mile racing plants accommodating up to 90,000 people were built. They held two stock car "spectaculars" each year.

The early days of auto racing and the national success of the sport created many small tracks in the South, but stock car racing actually got its momentum from the pioneering efforts of two communities, Darlington, S.C., and Daytona Beach.

Darlington, a town of 7,000 in the rich agricultural area of northeastern South Carolina, was the most unlikely spot in the nation to pioneer anything in the speed age. The area was low in population, the economy was geared to cotton and tobacco, and income was almost entirely dependent on the whims of nature. It was an area of unpaved roads, limited transportation, little tourist housing, and, more importantly, lacking in racing know-how.

Nevertheless, in December 1949, a group of local businessmen, headed by Harold Brasington, decided to build the first high-banked, paved speedway designed especially for stock cars. Using much equipment from nearby farms, they completed the Darlington International Raceway in the summer of 1950.

South Carolina lies in the heart of the so-called "Bible Belt" and it never had allowed stock cars to run on Sunday. The Darlington promoters selected Labor Day, 1950, for their first race, though this holiday isn't recognized formally in the state.

It was one of the big financial gambles in the history of motor sports. The first race was to be 500 miles. The field would be limited to strictly stock cars, without modification of engines or chassis. Automotive experts viewed the project with skepticism and some publicly acclaimed it as foolhardy.

But the race pioneered many facets of the industry and it served to answer many and varied questions of sanctioning, rules, promotion and race engineering.

It also proved to be a financial harvest for the promoters. More than 50,000 people jammed into the place and many others watched from scaffolds erected outside the oval by farmers who owned the land and cashed in on their vantage points.

The race itself presented many problems. No stock car had ever been asked to go 500 miles at top speed on asphalt banking, and even the Detroit engineers, who came in droves, predicted that none of the starting cars would finish.

More than 80 cars showed up—Cadillacs, Lincolns, Fords, Chevrolets, Hudsons, Buicks, Chryslers, even the little Henry J. The entry list is said to have included rental cars, taxis, even stolen vehicles.

Seventy-five cars started the marathon, but by the end of 250 miles only half of them were running. The fender-banging, the break-neck driving of the pilots and the high banks had taken their tolls, either through spins or engine failures. Yet no one was hurt.

The winner was Johnny Mantz, a Midwesterner who spent the night before the race partying at nearby Myrtle Beach and didn't get to the track until just before race time. His car was a boxy little Plymouth sedan. Technical inspection was at a minimum or someone might have detected that it was equipped with taxicab shock absorbers and springs—stiff enough to hold the banking better than most of the others.

Mantz completed the 500 miles in 6 hours, 38 minutes and 42.25 seconds for an average speed of 76.26 m.p.h. Modern day speeds at the same track hover around the 130 m.p.h. level for 500 miles.

Daytona Beach had long been a mecca of speed, its long, sweeping ocean front of white, washed sand having first been used for auto sports as far back as 1900.

Sir Malcolm Campbell, Alexander Winton, Ransom E. Olds, H. L. Bowden, William K. Vanderbilt, Fred Marriott, Barney Oldfield, Ralph DePalma and Tommy Milton were among the early pioneers of speed who used the Daytona-Ormand Beach strip for speed record runs. And Henry Ford had once lived off sardines and crackers while his cars were using the beach.

The speed phase of the Daytona strip ended in 1935 when Campbell made the last of his runs in his famous Bluebird, averaging 276.82 m.p.h. for the measured mile. Campbell then transferred his trials to the Bonneville Salt Flats in Utah, where most of the modern land speed marks were set.

The next era of Daytona racing began on March 8, 1936, when the first event limited to stock autos took place. The 3.2-mile course utilized the beach for one straightaway and a blacktop road for another, with turns cut through sand dunes to connect the two straights.

The first race was a combined city-county venture with a distance of 250 miles and a purse of $5,000. Sanctioned by the AAA, the entry list included Bob Sall, Bill Cummings, Bill France, Sam Collier, Maj. Goldie Gardner, Jack Rutherford, Bill Schindler, Dock McKenzie, Ben Shaw and Milt Marion, all of whom could already claim a measure of fame.

Marion was declared the winner after 200 miles, his Auburn averaging 70.39 m.p.h. Only 10 cars of the original 27 were running, but the race opened a new era that was to see Daytona the home of one of the world's great speedways, the Daytona International Speedway, with two 500-mile classics for stock cars and a 24-hour race for sports endurance cars listed on its annual "Speedweeks" calendar.

At about the same time or immediately afterward, stock car racing ovals popped up in Charlotte, Winston-Salem and Raleigh, N.C., and at Spartanburg and Greenville, S.C., Atlanta and in Virginia, Ohio, Pennsylvania, Connecticut, New Jersey and New York.

Hardly a weekend passed during the summer months that racers with shiny souped-up engines and battered body shells weren't at it somewhere in the nation. Drivers worked in factories or garages during the week, taking every free hour to practice their mechanical skills on their cars, which were usually propped up on blocks under a tree or in a lean-to garage to block out the sun's warm summer rays. Then on Friday night, Saturday or Sunday, the hell-for-leather drivers, mechanics, car owners, friends and thrill-seekers moved to the tracks.

There was fierce battling on the dirt tracks for small purses, even those frequently not paid, but the drivers became heroes to their local followings. Many had grown up on farms or in mill villages, and many had gained their first driving experience following a mule down rows of cotton or tobacco.

And a few during the Depression years had resorted either to making or hauling "moonshine" liquor and gained valuable driving experience by outwitting revenue agents on backroads in the Virginia, Carolinas and Georgia foothills.

All of the early confusion, chaos and color of stock car racing provided spice

Sir Malcolm Campbell is shown in cockpit of his giant speedster "Bluebird" near the Bonneville Salt Flats in Utah in 1935. At the time he held the world land speed record of 276 miles per hour.

for the racing fan and scripts for the Hollywood movie makers. But for auto racing, it pointed up the need to bring organization to the sport—protection for promoters, drivers, owners and spectators alike.

The first move toward organization evolved from the first Daytona race, when there was bickering about rules, prize money distribution and eligibility of drivers and cars.

But it wasn't until 1947 that the National Association for Stock Car Auto Racing (NASCAR) was formed at a meeting in Daytona. Principals were Bill Tuthill, then a promoter in Lonsdale, R.I., and Bill France, a towering 6-foot-4 former service station operator who had moved to Daytona from Washington, D.C., with $35 in his pocket in the late 1930s.

Tuthill, France and 16 other promoters, drivers and friends of the sport came up with the first set of rules and regulations to govern and bring stability to stock car racing. The task of establishing specifications for cars, setting safety rules and lining up tracks, drivers and car owners was completed in time to sanction and supervise the first Southern 500 at Darlington.

The organization's first Grand National race, however, was run at Charlotte on June 19, 1949. Until then, stock car racing had been a loose conglomerate of promoters, mostly operating under their own rules, settling their own disputes and frequently the target of irate fans because of dishonesty.

The first race under NASCAR sanction not only was a financial success for the embryo organization but it brought a semblance of law and order to the sport.

The late Glenn Dunaway took the checkered flag in a Ford as 13,000 watched. But a post-race inspection of his machine, something hitherto unheard of, showed the car was equipped with extra supports for the rear springs—a clear violation of the new NASCAR specifications. Dunaway was disqualified and the victory was given to Jim Roper, who had finished far behind in a Lincoln.

Dunaway's owner brought suit in the courts seeking to have the disqualification overturned. It was the first challenge of the new sanctioning body's authority and, when Dunaway lost the decision, it was established for the first time in racing history that a sanctioning body could enforce its technical rules.

NASCAR became the largest of the groups involved in stock car sanctioning. Its 1970 program included 71 events ranging in length from 100 to 600 miles and carrying prize money in excess of $3 million.

Moreover, many of its star drivers, notably Richard Petty, Cale Yarborough, David Pearson, Pete Hamilton, Bobby Isaac, Lee Roy Yarbrough, Bobby and Donnie Allison and Buddy Baker, frequently earned more than $100,000 a year.

Among its race sites were modern new speedways at Daytona, Talladega, Ala., Atlanta, Charlotte, Riverside, Calif., Jackson, Mich., College Station, Tex., North Wilkesboro, N.C., and Martinsville, Va.

From the early days of motor sports, professionals and amateurs alike gathered on weekends on small tracks and road courses throughout the country to match their skills and machinery against all comers. The entry lists not only included the big pro names of the early part of the century, but amateur enthusiasts—bankers, lawyers, socialites and ordinary citizens.

It was only occasionally that the amateurs could win against the full-time pros, who were equally proficient on the "left turn only" oval tracks and the road courses, where braking, acceleration and cornering determined a driver's ability.

Not only that, the pros usually came with better prepared machinery, frequently factory-backed and supported by technicians furnished by the makers.

Long before World War II it was obvious that there was a need to separate the amateurs from the pros. The traditions of road racing, as opposed to the less demanding skill of oval racing, had been set in the Vanderbilt Cup events on Long Island and New England, together with the two unsuccessful Grand Prix events at Roosevelt Raceway in 1936 and 1937.

All of the organization for amateur racing centered in the Automobile Racing Club of America, but there was little attempt to classify cars or drivers and supervision of the races themselves was lax.

The Sports Car Club of America came into being after the second world war, organized by a small group of enthusiasts, most of whom were members of ARCA. But even the SCCA in its early days directed most of its efforts toward the restoration and collecting of vintage sports cars, rather than toward active racing.

Nevertheless, the SCCA was called on to sanction the first sports car race in the United States after World War II. Held at Watkins Glen, N.Y., on a 6.6-mile course of city streets and country roads, it drew a wide variety of sports cars, most of which were driven by area residents, although there was a sprinkling of "name" drivers from both the United States and Europe.

The old ARCA rules for road racing were rewritten under direction of Alex Ulmann, a Russian by birth whose family had immigrated to America prior to World War I. Ulmann, who became a power in the affairs of international racing, founded the famed 12-Hours of Sebring (Fla.) and brought the first FIA-sanctioned world Grand Prix to this country in 1949. The U.S. Grand Prix was held in 1950 at Riverside, Calif., later transferred to Watkins Glen where it became an October fixture.

The first Glen road race was followed in 1949 by others at Bridgehampton, L.I., Floyd Bennett Field, Allentown, Pa., and at Palm Beach Shores, Fla. Thus began the first stage of the present-day SCCA program for club and amateur racing that has spread into seven geographic divisions throughout the United States.

Club or amateur racing probably involves more drivers and cars than any other segment of motor sports. The SCCA sanctions more than 3,000 events yearly, including rallies, auto-crosses, races for sports and production cars, each carefully graded by class, horsepower and weight; hill climbs and cross-country events.

A professional division was added by the SCCA in the mid-1960s and the body sanctioned a number of races for Formula, sedan and unlimited sports racing cars.

Hot-rodding has been a part of the American scene since the early days of the automobile. Now a major segment of auto racing, with a spectator attendance of more than 10 million in 1970, hot-rodding—or drag racing as it is known today—bases its appeal on the natural desire of the car owner to give his own machine that little extra bit of acceleration that will take him away from the stop light just a bit quicker than the guy sitting in the next lane.

The early drag races were usually impromptu affairs, with the local "top gun" challenging the best driver and machine from the next village. Most of these match races were held on darkened streets or on country roads, away from the eyes and ears of the constabulary.

The first organized hot-rodding was concentrated in California. The draggers used the flat, smooth surface of Muroc Dry Lake, in the desert 100 miles north of Los Angeles. Many of the future stars of American racing got their start at Muroc.

These early races, for modified Model T roadsters, Model As and lightweight Chevvys, were over a quarter-mile distance and usually pitted several cars of a class against each other. The idea was for over-all speed, not acceleration, and there was little regard for safety. Meets frequently ended in battle royals among drivers and spectators.

Some semblance of organization came in 1937 when some of the early hot-rodding clubs formed the Southern California Timing Association, which laid down rules governing safety and car classification and, eventually, set up technical committees to see that the cars met the standards.

The first move to take hot-rodding off the streets and highways—and to rebuild its image—came after World War II. Penalties were imposed on members caught in the act of hot-rodding on the streets. Even so, the reputation of drag racing became so bad that there were threats to outlaw it through legislation.

In 1948, the SCTA clubs, led by President Wally Parks, became associate members of the National Safety Council and organized hot rod meets moved from Muroc to airport runways and to isolated streets and roads that could be more properly supervised by civic officials and police.

The American Hot Rod Conference was formed in 1950 in an effort to coordinate the mushrooming sport. It failed, but Parks organized the National Hot Rod Association (NHRA) two years later. The NHRA's purpose then, as now, was to help clubs obtain sites for meets, run them with safety, unify records and serve as a clearing house for safety rules and regulations. More importantly, the NHRA set out to gain more favorable acceptance of hot-rodding from the press and public.

The Detroit auto makers inevitably got into the business in the 1950s and early 1960s, coming up with new engines, pieces and bits that lent themselves to sheer horsepower. Drag racing, more than any other form of racing, was responsible for the so-called "muscle cars" produced in quantity by the auto makers in the 1960s.

Drag racing today is the simple task of matching two evenly equipped cars, from exotic fuel and gas dragsters to the lowliest standard production sedan, and seeing which of them can move from a standing start down a 1,320-foot strip in the fastest elapsed time. Full-time professionals raced against weekenders, but the advantage of the pro over the amateur proved less than in perhaps any other form of racing competition.

Hot-rodding gained a measure of respectability through the NHRA and with the formation of the American Hot Road Association in 1956. Today, the NHRA holds full international status through membership in the Fédération d'Automobile Internationale.

The four major sanctioning groups in the United States—the SCCA, NASCAR, USAC and NHRA—paid an estimated $10 million in prize money in 1970 and, without the added attraction of pari-mutuel betting, played to about 45 million spectators. In addition, more than 100 small tracks across the country operating without sanction from either of the major groups played to steady crowds by featuring local drivers.

So, from the early road courses, auto racing progressed to Indianapolis, Daytona, Charlotte, Darlington, and more recently to a new $25.5 million racing complex at Ontario, Calif., then to a bright new jewel in the Pocono Mountains of Pennsylvania.

It has established itself as one of the world's most exciting, most popular and most rewarding of major sports.

Spectators line the way along a twisting turn in the 190-mile Road Atlanta Can-Am road race at Gainesville, Ga., in September 1970.

The Stanley Cup signifies supremacy in professional hockey. The Montreal Hockey Club of 1893 won the first Stanley Cup and in 1970 the Cup returned to Boston for the first time in 29 years. It's held aloft by Harvard hockey coach Cooney Weiland.

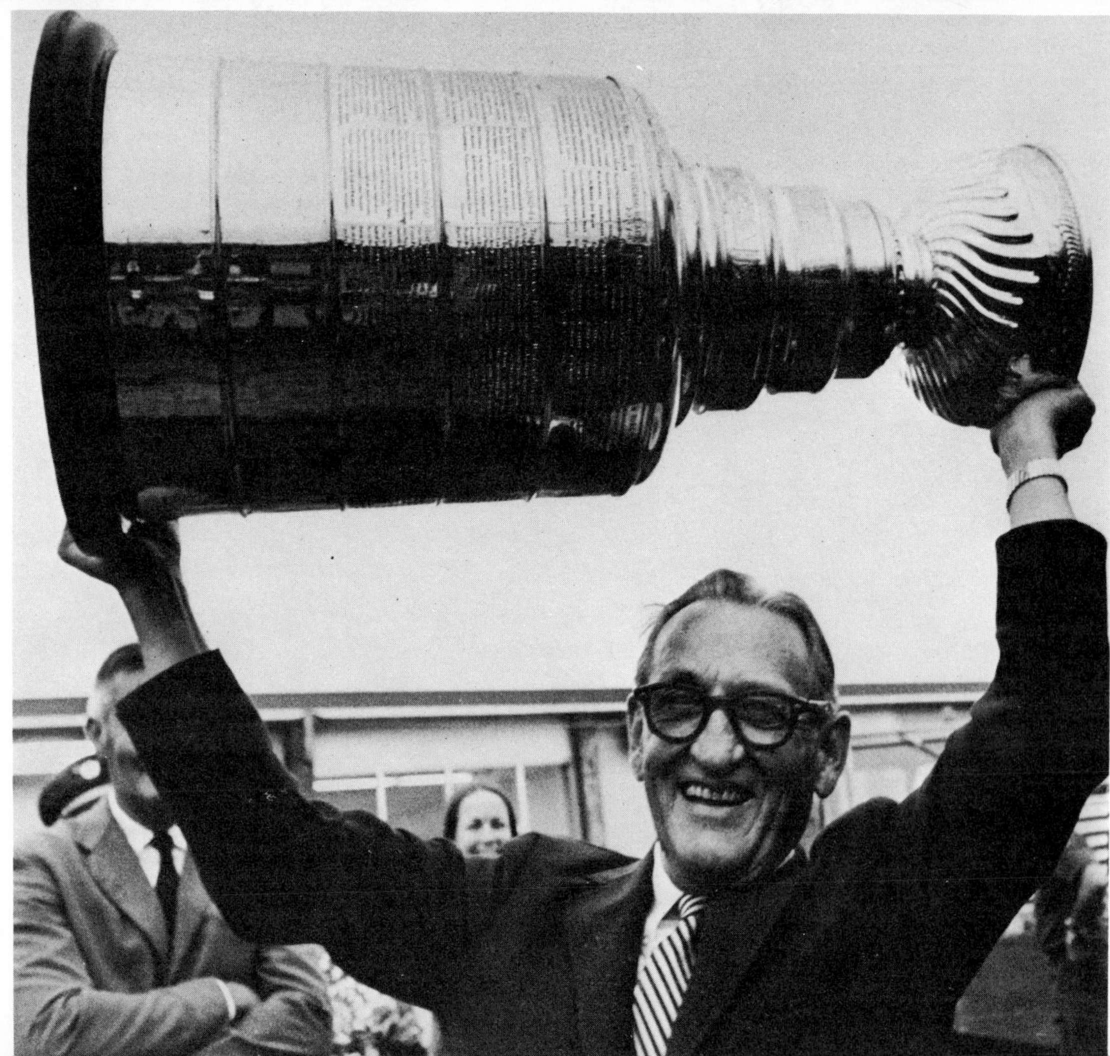

chapter 11

ICE HOCKEY

Speed and Fierce Action Thrill Fans

by Hal Bock

Hal Bock was born and grew up in New York City. He graduated from New York University in 1961 with a degree in journalism and an abiding interest in sports. In 1963, he joined *The Associated Press* and has been in NY Sports since. His specialties are baseball and hockey and over the years he has covered the World Series, the Super Bowl, Stanley Cup playoffs and All Star games.

Ice hockey, a game born and nurtured in the frozen northern hemisphere, was ordained for growth and popularity. Played on flashing skates with a stick and a puck, it is the fastest of all contact sports. It pulsates with action. It is tough and rough and has a masculine appeal that stirs red-blooded men and fascinates the ladies.

As far as anyone can ascertain, hockey breathed its first frosty breath in Canada, with its cold climate and its stretches of snow and ice. Youngsters were unable to play baseball and football as did their neighbors below the border. So they took crude-shaped sticks, donned skates and learned to compete against each other on frozen lakes and ponds.

Sometimes the ice was thin and dangerous. Sometimes it was filled with ruts. But always there was ice. And wherever there was ice—in obscure villages, in the neighborhoods of the big cities—the game was played. As popularity grew, the game moved indoors to the rinks. Then it reached out to captivate first a nation, then a continent, finally the world—becoming in the 1960s one of the proud conquests of the Soviet Union in the Olympic Games.

Originally confined largely to Canada, the fad for the fast, exciting game afflicted the United States—if for no other reason than close-hand exposure. It

moved first into the big cities near the border—Detroit, Chicago, New York—and then flowed west to the Pacific Coast and then into the sultry South, where minor league teams operated with remarkable success.

The National Hockey League was formed in 1917, the outgrowth of a series of other leagues and the result of internal strife and problems. By 1970, the National Hockey League had expanded to 14 teams—11 in the United States and three in Canada. It had taken its place as a big time spectator sport, regularly filling big city arenas and holding its own with basketball, an American invention, in the battle for the spectator dollar.

The league grew so large that it was necessary to split it into two divisions, East and West, following no geographical lines. Philadelphia competed in the West while Vancouver played in the East. Other West Division teams were Los Angeles, Oakland, St. Louis, Minnesota, Pittsburgh and Chicago. In the East with Vancouver were New York, Buffalo, Boston, Montreal, Oakland and St. Louis.

The league produced superstars whose names were splashed across newspaper headlines in just as big and just as black type as that accorded the heroes of baseball, football, golf and tennis.

Some of them became legendary. Gordie Howe of Detroit scored more goals, more assists and more total points than any man in the history of the game. Bobby Hull of Chicago set a record for the most goals in a single season—58. He boosted his career total to more than 500. Boston's Bobby Orr became the first and only

Maurice "Rocket" Richard of the Montreal Canadiens shoots the puck past Chicago goalie Al Rollins to score one of his 545 career goals.

defenseman to win a scoring title. Phil Esposito set an all-time mark with 126 points in one season.

These were the latter day giants of a game that had a primitive beginning. The early stars were those who played on obscure frozen ponds in the provinces of Quebec and Ontario, across the vast prairie land of Saskatchewan, Alberta and Manitoba and on to British Columbia in the West.

There were no crowds to cheer. Barren trees were the spectators. But the checking was just as sharp, the stick work just as furious and the competition as keen as that shown by latter day pros.

Hockey in the 1880s was a seven-man game played with upright posts embedded in the ice to serve as goals. There were no nets, no blue lines, no red lines and no face-off circles. All there was was the ice, the sticks, the pucks and the players.

The sport became a widespread diversion for citizens from all walks of life and even the aristocratic governing class became involved. Finally, in 1893, came the first significant development in the evolution of hockey as an organized sport. Frederick Arthur, Lord Stanley of Preston and son of the Earl of Derby, became so fascinated by the sport that he invested £10 (about $48.67) in a trophy to be presented to the amateur hockey champions of Canada. In time, this punch bowl-shaped trophy became known as the Stanley Cup and the 14 NHL teams now compete for it each spring.

The Stanley Cup trophy itself has been battered and booted by one team of winners who over-celebrated their victory, stolen by an ambitious admirer, completely forgotten by another winning team and used as a flower pot when discovered by an unsuspecting citizen who didn't know what it was. It remains the oldest trophy competed for by professional athletes in North America.

Ironically, Lord Stanley never saw a Stanley Cup game. Shortly after he introduced the Cup, he returned to his native England and that's where he was on March 22, 1894, when Chauncey Kirby scored the first Stanley Cup goal and the Montreal Athletic Association defeated the Ottawa Generals 2–1 in the first Stanley Cup game.

Each year amateur teams challenged for the Cup but none was as sincere as the 1905 challenge by a team from the Yukon. Colonel Joe Boyle, a wealthy Dawson City prospector, bankrolled the team for its 23-day journey from one end of the continent to the other to challenge the Ottawa Silver Seven for the Cup. The team traveled by dog sled, boat and train to cover the 4,400 miles, most of it through temperatures well below the freezing mark.

When the team finally arrived in Ottawa, it was all in vain. They lost the first game to the Silver Seven 9–2 and the second 23–3. Frank McGee scored 14 goals in the second game, eight of them in eight minutes, 20 seconds, even though he was blind in one eye.

Another Cup defense by Ottawa a few years after the Yukon challenge was followed by a long, loud party. The upshot of the celebration was the declaration by one player that he could kick the Cup clear into the Rideau Canal. And he did just that.

The next day, the sobered-up players realized what they had done and rushed back to Rideau. Luckily the canal had been frozen over and there, slightly dented but none the worse for wear, stood the Stanley Cup.

In the same era, the Cup did a brief turn as a flower pot. This time it was the Montreal team that had won it and gathered for a portrait with the prize in a local photographer's studio. After the picture was taken, the Cup was carelessly left behind. When the photographer's mother discovered it, she mistook it for a flower pot and planted geraniums. It was a while before the photographer discovered the mistake and rescued the silverware.

When the National Hockey League took over administration of the Cup, it took a little more care in handling the prize. But there were slipups on the league's part too.

In the spring of 1962, the Cup was on display in a locked showcase at Chicago Stadium. Inside, the Montreal Canadiens were in the process of being eliminated from the playoffs by the Chicago Black Hawks.

One Montreal fan squirmed in his seat until he could no longer take the punishment. He got up, walked resolutely to the trophy case where the Cup was displayed, and broke into it. He was headed out the door with the Cup on his shoulder before he was stopped. "I'm just taking the Cup back to Montreal, where it belongs," he explained.

That seemed like a perfectly logical explanation because Montreal has indeed dominated Cup play. Through 1970, the Canadiens had won it 16 times, more than any other NHL team, and other Montreal clubs such as the Maroons, Wanderers, Shamrocks and Victories won 14 Cups, giving that city a most possessive feeling about Lord Stanley's trophy.

In the first 17 years the Cup was up for grabs, Montreal teams won it 11 times. That was around the turn of the century when hockey in Canada was loosely organized with little structure beyond local teams that played the game for recreation and challenged teams from neighboring towns.

Among the early leagues operating were the Amateur Hockey Association of Canada and the Ontario Hockey Association, but teams shifted back and forth between them from year to year and there was little in the way of a structured stance for the sport.

The constant jockeying from league to league continued until 1910 when there were two major leagues competing with each other. The Canadian Hockey Association listed Ottawa, Quebec and three Montreal teams—the Shamrocks, the Nationals and All-Montreal. The National Hockey Association had teams in Cobalt, Haileybury, Renfrew and two in Montreal—the Wanderers and the Canadiens.

Teams bid furiously for the services of players, and the owners, aware that they would soon spend themselves into oblivion, combined the two leagues into one—the National Hockey Association, a seven-team league composed of Renfrew, Cobalt, Haileybury, Ottawa and three Montreal teams, the Shamrocks, the Wanderers and the Canadiens.

Meanwhile, Lester Patrick and his brother, Frank, two of the top players at that time, migrated to the West and founded the Pacific Coast Hockey League. Several other stars, including Fred "Cyclone" Taylor, Edouard "Newsy" Lalonde and Frank Nighbor, followed the Patricks west to play in the new league which had franchises in Vancouver, Victoria and New Westminster.

Detroit Red Wings' Gordie Howe, one of ice hockey's all-time great players, keeps his eye on the puck as he cuts in front of New York Rangers' Walt Tkaczuk (18) in game in Detroit in 1968.

Chicago's Bobby Hull, the Golden Jet, battles Oakland goalie Chris Worther for the puck in 1968 game in Chicago.

A season-climaxing Stanley Cup series was arranged between the champions of the PCHL and NHA, a system that continued until the Patricks' league went out of business in 1926.

Slowly, hockey evolved into the game that is familiar to fans today. In 1913, blue lines were introduced to define offsides and control action. A year later, statistics began to be kept in a more systematic manner, crediting players with assists as well as goals.

In 1914, Canada went to war and the shock waves of the conflict hit hockey too. Many players were called to serve in the armed forces and uncertain train schedules caused cancellation of some games. NHA clubs turned over entire proceeds of exhibition games to patriotic causes and a share of regular season income to the Red Cross.

By 1917, the NHA was a six-team league with the Montreal Canadiens, Montreal Wanderers, Ottawa, Toronto, Quebec and the Northern Fusiliers—an army team representing the 228th Battalion.

When the 228th was ordered overseas, it left the NHA with five teams and an unbalanced schedule. Also, there had been considerable bickering with Eddie Livingstone, the Toronto owner. On Nov. 22, the owners met at the Windsor

Hotel in Montreal to straighten out their problems. Their solution was the creation of a new circuit—the National Hockey League—with franchises granted to the Montreal Wanderers, Montreal Canadiens, Ottawa and Toronto. The Toronto franchise was contingent on the exclusion of Livingstone.

Quebec also was granted a franchise but chose not to play that first year and its players were divided among the other four teams.

Frank Calder, secretary-treasurer of the old NHA, was elected president of the new league and a schedule of 22 games running from Dec. 19 to March 10 was adopted.

Quebec's best player, Joe Malone, wound up with the Canadiens and scored five goals in his first game. He played in only 20 games that year but won the scoring championship with 44 goals—a scorching pace that never has been matched.

Malone was truly the NHL's first scoring superstar. And those early days produced their share of other outstanding players.

—Harry "Punch" Broadnet of Ottawa, who scored at least one goal in 16 consecutive games during the 1921–22 season.

—Goalie George Hainsworth of the Montreal Canadiens, who set an all-time record with 22 shutouts during the 44-game 1928–29 season.

—Boston defenseman Eddie Shore, considered the roughest player and best defender in the history of the game.

—Goalie Alex Connell of Ottawa who, in 1928–29, strung together six consecutive shutouts and a record 460 minutes, nine seconds of shutout hockey.

And there were many others, whose achievements caught the imagination of the public. Hockey was clearly catching on. After early problems, the NHL became a thriving operation.

The first reversal was the burning down of the Westmount Arena, home of the Wanderers, forcing that team to withdraw from the league in 1918. The next year, Quebec operated its franchise for a single season before shifting it to Hamilton in 1920.

In 1924, the Boston Bruins and Montreal Maroons joined the league, giving it six teams and an American member for the first time. The Bruins were an instant success and a year later, two more U.S. cities, New York and Pittsburgh, acquired teams.

By 1926, there were five U.S. teams—the New York Rangers, Pittsburgh Pirates, Boston Bruins, Chicago Black Hawks and Detroit Cougars—playing in one NHL division and four Canadian teams—the Toronto Maple Leafs, Ottawa Senators, Montreal Canadiens, Montreal Maroons and the New York Americans (formerly the Hamilton team) playing in the other.

Players were provided by the dissolution of the Pacific Coast League. Clarence Campbell, latter day president of the NHL, pointed to 1926 as the first great expansion of the league.

The Depression affected the NHL at the box-office. The Pittsburgh franchise was shifted to Philadelphia in 1930 and lasted there for only one season before disbanding. Both cities would rejoin the NHL later.

The Detroit club changed its nickname from Cougars to Falcons and then to Red Wings in an effort to inject some enthusiasm into the sagging interest in the club.

The Ottawa franchise dropped out in 1931, the same year the Pittsburgh-

Philadelphia entry quit. Later, Ottawa came back for two seasons and then shifted to St. Louis for one year before folding for good.

In 1938, the Montreal Maroons dropped out and in 1942 the New York Americans, who had tried to wake up some interest by dubbing themselves the Brooklyn Americans, also quit.

That left six teams operating—the New York Rangers, Boston Bruins, Chicago Black Hawks, Detroit Red Wings, Montreal Canadiens and Toronto Maple Leafs. From 1942 until 1967, a span of 25 years, the league retained that makeup.

After Frank Calder died in 1943, Mervyn "Red" Dutton, former player, coach and manager of the New York Americans, was named interim president of the league. In 1946, Clarence S. Campbell, an ex-referee, Rhodes scholar and noted attorney, became president.

In 1967, Campbell presided over the largest single expansion in professional sports history. The NHL doubled in size from six to 12 teams, admitting franchises in Philadelphia, Pittsburgh, Los Angeles, Oakland, Minnesota and St. Louis.

Three years later, two more teams in Buffalo and Vancouver were added, increasing the league's size to 14 teams.

The expansion step was taken only after the NHL lived through a much-needed period of stability. After the almost yearly changes in membership, the league needed that quarter century to settle down and establish its following with the fans.

No two men were more responsible for that following than Maurice Richard and Gordie Howe. Richard, a fragile youngster believed to be injury-prone in his early days, developed into a robust right winger whose scoring ability became almost legendary. He established the single-season record of 50 goals in 1944, a mark that stood until Bobby Hull came along to shatter it.

If Richard, playing for the Montreal Canadiens, was hockey's Babe Ruth, then Howe, playing for Detroit, was its Joe DiMaggio. This slope-shouldered bull came out of Canada's Western prairie land to break every career offensive record available to him. He is the longevity king of the game and in 1970 he entered his 25th season with 763 career goals, some 210 more than Richard, the No. 2 man on the all-time scoring list.

For many years, the National Hockey League's sole source of player talent was the vast amateur program which is spread throughout Canada. But recently the game has increasingly become a part of the interscholastic programs of secondary schools and colleges throughout the United States as well as Canada. Now, many boys choose to complete their educations, often financing their way through school on hockey scholarships, before trying their hand at the professional game.

There was a time when hockey players who had played the collegiate game were frowned upon by professional managers and coaches. The executives claimed that the difference in rules—most importantly the pro rule which allows hitting an opponent anywhere on the ice instead of only in the defensive zone as in college—made the change too difficult to negotiate.

But the success of several college-trained players has shattered that theory. Red Berenson of the St. Louis Blues, who tied a 25-year-old record when he scored six goals in a single game in November 1968, is a graduate of Michigan.

Chicago goalie Tony Esposito, who set a modern record with 15 shutouts during the 1969–70 season and was rookie of the year as well as the NHL's leading goalie that year, starred at Michigan Tech before turning professional.

Recognizing the widespread interest in scholastic hockey, the National Collegiate Athletic Association inaugurated an annual hockey tournament in 1948. Michigan has dominated the competition with seven titles including a stretch of five out of six.

Many players also represent their countries in the Olympic hockey competition before turning professional. Hockey has been on the Olympic program since 1920 and the competition has been dominated first by Canada and more recently by Russia.

Canada won the first four Olympic competitions and six of the first seven. Russia has taken three of the last four, missing only in 1960 when an underdog United States team took the title.

In non-Olympic years, hockey's amateur championship is determined by an annual tournament with teams competing from all over the world. Russia has dominated recent competition in this tournament, winning seven straight titles through 1970. Except for its Olympic championship in 1960, the United States' only world title came in 1933.

The Russians' great success at the game is explained by the use of a veteran team which has played together for years. The Soviet rushes are machine-like, with the players always knowing just what their teammates will do in a given situation. That knowledge comes from years of playing together and proves that hockey is really a precise game despite the occasional helter-skelter look it has to a new fan.

Bobby Orr, considered by many as potentially the greatest hockey player ever, flies through the air after scoring the overtime goal that returned the Stanley Cup to Boston after an absence of 29 years.

Austria's Tony Sailer, a 21-year-old plumber, displays his ski wizardry as he executes a leap on his way to win the men's downhill Olympic ski championship at Cortina D'Ampezzo, Italy, on Feb. 3, 1956. Combining this victory with giant and special slalom wins, he scored the first Alpine grand slam.

chapter 12

SKIING

Snow-Covered Slopes Beckon the Masses

by Mike Recht

Young Toni Sailer, a handsome Austrian, stood poised at the top of a snow-covered mountain slope at Cortina, Italy, and the entire world watched and waited breathlessly, anticipating one of those great moments in sports history. They weren't disappointed.

The dashing 21-year-old plumber sped down the hill and flashed across the finish line to win his third gold medal of the 1956 Olympic Games, and skiing had its first international hero.

This shy lad had caught the imagination of people everywhere, even those who normally hibernated during the winter months. He helped bring a glamor and a recognition to skiing similar to what Babe Ruth had brought to baseball and Arnold Palmer to golf.

Sailer never won another Olympic gold medal, but he had accomplished enough, opening the eyes of the world to a new and exciting competition, and that recognition continued to grow with the appearance of colorful skiers such as Jean Claude Killy of France, Karl Schranz of Austria, Nancy Greene of Canada and Bud Werner and Billy Kidd of the United States.

It's not that skiing was not popular before Sailer. It has been high on the sports lists in France, Austria and the Scandinavian countries since the early 1900s, and by 1920 it began to take hold in America.

Skiers today would be hard pressed to recognize this 1938 photo as Sun Valley, Idaho. The sweeping hills and mountains now host a vast modern ski complex.

Since the 1930s, it has been one of the fastest growing sports in the United States. But when Sailer rocketed into the headlines he sent both weekend fun skiing and international competitive skiing soaring to new and greater heights.

There had been many earlier important moments in ski history—the first jumping and racing competition, the first rope tow, the introduction of the sport into the Olympics, the first ski train—but the real beginning goes back some 4,500 years.

Skiing is one of the few sports that did not begin as a sport. A type of ski was found in Siberia and in Sweden dating back to 2500 B.C. when ancient man probably lashed animal bones to his feet and glided across the snow as a means of travel. Scandinavian countries led the way, using skis in war during the Battle of Oslo in 1200, and by 1500 they had introduced them to the rest of Europe.

By 1722 skis had spread to Greenland, and they are mentioned in a story on a Canadian ice carnival in 1759.

Norwegian immigrants were believed to have brought skiing to the western United States when gold was discovered in California in the late 1840s, and the miners made skis a way of life.

Using 10-to-12-foot-long skis made of barrel staves, with one stout pole, they found a new pleasure in racing that helped take the cold gloom out of winter and make the frigid weather something that could be enjoyed.

Skis also were used by doctors to reach mothers about to deliver. Kids learned to ski as soon as they could walk and traveled to school on skis. Men went to work on them, and even funerals have been held in the Old West with the mourners on skis.

From the Sierra Mountains in California during this period comes the legend of John "Snowshoe" Thomson and the U.S. mail.

The Norwegian-born Thomson trudged his way across the mountain passes to deliver the mail, using a webbed footgear similar to a tennis racket supposedly invented by the American Indians.

The first recorded ski race in the United States was in Sierra County in 1854, and one bearded miner named Isaac Steward earned the unofficial title of the father of American skiing by founding in 1867 what is believed the world's first ski club, the Alturas Showshoe Club of La Porte, Calif.

The first official ski club, however, is recognized as the Kristiania, formed in Norway in 1877. Sondre Norheim made the first officially measured jump, 30.5 meters, in Norway in 1860, and the first ski competition on record was at Grorud near Oslo in 1862.

But the world's first organized meet came in 1879 on Huseby Hill when Kristiania and Telemarken, two communities of Oslo, opposed each other.

The Nansen Ski Club of Berlin, N.H., was the first official U.S. ski club in 1882 and five years later the first U.S. ski competition was held, a jumping meet at Red Wing, Minn., by two Norwegian immigrants, the Hemmestvedt brothers, Mikkel and Torgus. Mikkel set the first U.S. record on Feb. 8 with a jump of 37 feet.

Then in the blizzard of 1888, Carl Conradson astounded city folk by skiing from Brooklyn across the Brooklyn Bridge into Manhattan, and then the King of Norway gave the sport a big boost by sponsoring a jumping meet in 1892.

Skis by then were being made of wood with better bindings and boots to offer more maneuverability. Metal skis did not reach the sport until the 1950s.

But it was two Austrians who provided the next big jump. In 1890, Mathias Zdarsky began working on a faster and easier method of teaching people to ski. His disciple, Hannes Schneider, perfected the method and opened the first popular ski school which spread the ski fever first to the rest of Europe and then to the United States in the 1920s.

In 1904 the National Ski Association of America was founded at Ishpeming, Mich., and the next year Gustave Bye turned in a U.S. record jump of 106 feet at Red Wing, still a far cry from today's leaps of more than 300 feet when the jumper soars some 70 feet above the ground for three or four seconds after racing downhill at speeds of about 65 miles per hour.

Until 1910 competition was confined mostly to jumping and cross-country racing, but then the Dartmouth Outing Club of Hanover, N.H., introduced downhill racing to North America. While cross-country racing is considered the most demanding and grueling, the slalom runs requiring the most skill, and jumping the most courage, the downhill is easily the most dangerous.

In 1911, Fred T. Harris helped start the Dartmouth Winter Carnival, and that same year he recalled his first trip up Mt. Washington in New Hampshire.

"There were 13 of us," he recalled, "and I was the only one to go up on skis. In 1912, 13 of us went up and five of us skied, and by 1913 there were 25 and 12 were skiing."

By that year, the National Ski Association, formed in 1904 with a membership

Andrea Mead Lawrence grits her teeth during a run in the combined downhill and slalom at the International Ski Meet for women at Gridnelwald, Switzerland, in 1951.

of three ski clubs, had expanded to 29 clubs. In 1924, the International Federation of Skiing officially came into being, and that same year the International Olympic Committee gave in to the demands of European countries for separate Winter Games for skiing and speed skating to go with figure skating which entered the Games in 1908.

Those first Winter Games, held in Chamonix, France, as an experiment, were so successful that they have been held every four years since, with breaks for war years, in conjunction with the Summer Olympics. It was a major breakthrough.

Norway dominated the first seven Winter Games with Thorleif Haug starting the reign by winning three gold medals in 1924 in the Nordic events composed of jumping and cross-country.

Women were allowed to compete in the 1928 Games at St. Moritz, Switzerland, where the United States had only three entrants. But in the next five years, four things happened that started the big boom in skiing in the United States.

In 1929, Katherine Peckett of Franconia, N.H., established the first U.S. ski school, importing expert European instructors.

The birth of the ski train came in 1931 at the pleading of the Appalachian Mountain Club of Boston. Some 200 members of the club traveled by train to a ski area, and with it was born the carefree fun that ever since has been attached to skiing and subsequently attracted thousands of brave souls.

By the winter of 1932, every railroad in the East was running ski trains with some of them out of New York carrying as many as 1,500 skiers to the White Mountains and the Adirondacks. It gave those city dwellers a chance to get into the fresh country air on a weekend vacation.

That same year, 1932, skiing in the United States received still greater impetus when the Winter Olympics were held at Lake Placid in New York. Thousands saw skiing for the first time and were fascinated.

Also in 1932, a Swiss engineer named Gerhard Mueller introduced the rope tow, and the first one came to North America at Shawbridge in the Laurentian Mountains in Canada. Former Dartmouth team captain Bunny Bertram brought one to the United States at Woodstock, Vt., and it was to skiing what the Model T Ford was to automobiles, the Wright brothers' airplane at Kitty Hawk to flying.

No longer did skiers have to trudge up hills, a back-breaking task, for those precious minutes of skiing.

Then in 1936, the Union Pacific railroad, under chairman of the board Averell Harriman, developed and opened at a cost of $3 million the first of the glamorous ski areas, Sun Valley in Idaho. And with it Union Pacific developed the first chair lift for still more convenience.

Following Sun Valley came such famous winter places as Aspen, Squaw Valley and Mt. Snow, and they joined the list of famous sports theaters such as Madison Square Garden, Yankee Stadium and the Rose Bowl. Smaller ski areas began springing up everywhere.

The boom was on, and in the Olympics that year the United States sent its first full team of skiers.

There was no way to estimate the number of persons skiing in the United States, but some guesses ranged to three million in the early 1940s. In 1940 sporting goods dealers called it the fastest growing participating sport in the country.

By 1964, an estimated five million belonged to ski clubs alone, and by 1970 there were more than 800 ski lifts.

Jean Claude Killy of France, a star of the 1968 Winter Olympics at Grenoble, France, is shown in action at Hindelang.

In 1939, a young Norwegian came to the United States and became this country's first ski hero. He was Torger Tokle, who in four seasons won 42 of 48 jumping tournaments and set 24 hill records, including a leap of 289 feet, an American record. But in 1945, as a member of the U.S. ski patrol force fighting in Italy during World War II, he was killed in action.

Tokle never got a chance at the Olympic gold medal as the Games were suspended for 12 years during the war, and the United States had to wait until 1948 when a housewife from Vancouver, Wash., won the country's first ski medal. Gretchen Fraser won the women's slalom, introduced with the downhill in the Olympics that year.

Then in 1952 Andrea Mead Lawrence, 19, a housewife from Rutland, Vt., beat 44 other skiers from 15 countries to win the newly-introduced giant slalom, and then became the first American to capture two gold medals by winning the slalom at Oslo.

Stein Erickson of Norway also hit the Olympic scene in 1952, winning the giant slalom. He later brought his fame and handsome looks to the United States as a teacher and became a romantic hero.

The downhill, the slalom and the giant slalom were called the Alpine events. Jumping and cross-country racing were Nordic.

The next Olympics, of course, belonged to Sailer as the U.S. men again failed to bring home their first medal. But in the year leading up to the 1960 Games, Bud Werner of the United States earned the respect of European skiers by winning a number of international races, the first U.S. man to do so. But on the eve of the 1960 Games at Squaw Valley, U.S. hopes were jolted when Werner broke a leg in training.

Billy Kidd of Stowe, Vt., competing in the International men's slalom at Hindelang, Germany, in 1964.

Penny Pitou won two silver medals and Betsy Snite one for the American girls, but by now the French and Austrians were dominating the scene with Karl Schranz of Austria and Guy Perillat.

Finally, at Innsbruck, Austria, in 1964, after Joan Hannah, Barbara Ferries and Jean Saubert won silver and bronze medals for the U.S. girls, Billy Kidd and Jim Huega gave the men their first medals, a silver and a bronze, respectively, in the slalom.

But it was during those Games that Austrian Ross Milne missed a turn, hit a tree and was killed.

Only one month later tragedy struck again when Werner and Barbi Henneberger were killed by an avalanche.

Jean Claude Killy of France replaced Sailer as the international hero. A dashing and daring figure, he won the first World Cup competition in 1967 and again in 1968—a series of international competitions throughout Europe and the United States. Then he capped it all by winning three Alpine gold medals in the 1968 Olympics at Grenoble, France.

Nancy Greene of Canada was the top woman skier during the same period, winning the women's World Cup in 1967–68 and the giant slalom at Grenoble.

In the Nordic events, Sixten Jernberg of Sweden became the all-time medal winner between 1956–64 by capturing nine, including four gold medals.

But the French and Austrians continued as kings of the hill into the 1970s with such stars as Jean-Noel Augert, Patrick Russel, Marielle Goitschel, Ingrid Lafforgue, Michele Jacot, Isabelle Mir and Francoise Macchi of France and Schranz, Olga Pall, Gertrud Gabl and Annemarie Proell of Austria.

The top U.S. skiers were Bob Cochran and sisters Marilyn and Barbara Cochran, Judy and Cathy Nagel and Kidd, who gave the men their greatest triumph at Val Gardena, Italy, in the 1970 FIS championships.

In his last amateur race before turning professional after eight grueling years of international disappointment, Kidd, taped and corseted for a bad leg and back, won the combined title to become the first U.S. man to win a world Alpine gold medal.

With skiing continuing to grow in the United States in the 1970s, more winners could be expected. But more important was the new excitement and pleasure the sport had brought to winter, the creation of the winter weekend, the winter vacation.

It became a way of life.

Uruguay defender Ubinas, left, falls attempting to block scoring shot in World Cup soccer semifinal match at Guadalajara, Mexico, in 1970. Leaping in center is Brazil's Rivelino.

chapter 13

SOCCER

The World's No. 1 Sport—It Fires Passions

by Geoffrey Miller

Geoffrey Miller, 49, is an Englishman whose speciality is soccer. He has been a member of *The AP* staff in London since 1953 and a sports writer since 1960. He has covered the most important soccer matches in Europe for the last decade and has reported on golf, tennis, track and field, rowing and cycling.

The World Cup of 1970, staged in Mexico, finally set the seal on soccer as the world's most popular sport. An estimated audience of 500 million, watching television around the globe, saw Pele lead Brazil to victory in Mexico City's Aztec Stadium.

The rapid growth of soccer (association football) is a social phenomenon. The World Cup was inaugurated only in 1930 and did not draw a fully representative entry until after World War II, yet it is now one of the world's great spectacles. It is only just over 100 years since the English pioneers drew up the rules and formed the first competitions, and they would be staggered to know how their sport has mushroomed. In terms of audiences and money it has moved almost on to the level of the movie industry. The top stars are valued at hundreds of thousands of dollars in the transfer market. The governing body of the game, FIFA (Fédération Internationale de Football Associations), with 135 member countries, can claim a sphere of influence comparable with that of the United Nations. In Britain and Scandinavia, millions fill up the pools each week hoping to forecast the games correctly and make their fortunes.

The great names of soccer are legend. Pele has appeared on Brazilian postage stamps and thus keeps company with monarchs. Every English schoolboy in the last 40 years has wanted to dribble with the ball as Stanley Matthews, who on

This is the English Football Association (FA) Cup, the most prized trophy in British soccer.

retirement was knighted by Queen Elizabeth II. Ferenc Puskas, who packed a shot at the goal like a cannonball, was the idol of two countries—his native Hungary and Spain, where he emigrated. Russians viewed Lev Yashin, the black-clad, catlike goalkeeper, as the supreme symbol of sportsmanship.

How did it all start?

Football was once played through the meadows and the village streets of England, with everybody joining in and fighting for the ball by fair means and foul. From this mob pastime two separate sports emerged. The dribbling game, in which the players used their feet and nothing else to kick the ball into the goal, became soccer; the carrying game grew into rugby—and a byproduct, American football.

The rules of soccer were first written at Cambridge University in England in 1846, but the story of the game really starts with a meeting in a London pub in 1863, at which the English Football Association (FA) was founded. It was the father-body of the game, followed by the Scottish FA 10 years later. The British developed soccer and introduced it abroad. For generations, as the game spread from continent to continent, the world regarded the British as the masters. It was a myth that lasted for the best part of a century.

It took some painful and humiliating World Cup campaigns after World War II to bring home to the British that the pupils had finally overtaken the teachers.

A game in 1866 between selections from London and Sheffield was probably the start of organized competitive soccer. But the game really began to be a part of English national life with the inauguration of the English FA Cup in 1871—a knockout tournament that became the biggest crowd-puller in English soccer. All the players were amateurs and the first winners were a squad known as the Wanderers. This team, famous in its day, won the FA Cup five times in seven years, competing against such rivals as Oxford University, the Royal Engineers regimental team and the Old Boys' Association of Eton College. It was a tiny and parochial affair compared with the World Cup of today, but in a sense it was the ancestor of the World Cup, since the world came to learn its soccer and its soccer organization from England.

In 1885 came the first legalized professionalism, and in 1888 the formation of the English League, with 12 teams competing. One of the 12, Accrington Stanley, disbanded in 1962, but the rest flourished to carry the hopes of millions of pool fillers each week during the season. They were Aston Villa, Blackburn Rovers, Bolton Wanderers, Burnley, Derby County, Everton, Notts County, Preston North End, Stoke City, West Bromwich Albion and Wolverhampton Wanderers.

These were the teams that made early soccer history and were talked about in the pubs and in British communities abroad in the '90s. Scottish soccer was dominated by two great rivals in Glasgow—Rangers, a club steeped in Protestant tradition, and Celtic, which was formed by Catholic immigrants from Ireland. To this day, when Rangers and Celtic play each other, extra police have to be called in to keep the fans of the two teams apart.

Soccer in those early days was primitive. Nets behind the goals had still to be invented. A wooden crossbar had only recently been legalized across the top of the goal instead of a length of rope. Every player tried to dribble with the ball and keep possession of it for as long as he could, and there was little attempt at passing and teamwork. But as professional soccer became established, the science of the game began to evolve.

One hundred years ago, a soccer team would line up with a goalkeeper, one fullback, one halfback and eight forwards. The forwards roamed all over the field foraging for the ball and the game was a rough free-for-all. Team formations in the modern sense came into being in the '80s. Constructive planning midfield became a strategic part of the game and the standard team formation changed—first to two backs, two halfbacks and six forwards, and then to the 2-3-5 pattern which lasted for a half-century.

Until 1914 soccer remained largely a parochial affair for the British. Those were the days when the fans talked of Jimmy Forrest of Blackburn, Johnny Goodall of Preston, "Nudger" Needham of Sheffield United, goalkeeper Sam Hardo of Aston Villa, ace marksmen Steve Bloomer of Derby, Billy Meredith of Manchester City and the fullback partnership of Bob Crompton and Jesse

Pennington, who starred for England in early internationals against Scotland, Wales and Northern Ireland. In Scotland the man in the street pinned colored rosettes in his tartan bonnet and idolized Alex Smith of the Rangers or Jimmy McMenemy of Celtic, according to whether he was Protestant or Catholic. All these men were among the first greats in soccer's Hall of Fame.

Soccer was beginning to take root abroad, but nobody in Britain took foreign soccer seriously before 1914. International games against European countries were treated as a joke. England defeated Germany 12–0 and 10–0 in two matches in 1901. It played Austria three times between 1906 and 1908 and won 6–1, 11–1 and 8–1. Matches against Latin American countries were undreamed of.

Who was the pioneer of modern soccer—the super-spectacular sport that entertains the world's millions today? Some soccer historians would say it had no pioneer, that it just evolved. But others would name Herbert Chapman, Britain's most famous team manager between the two world wars, as the man who created the modern image of the game.

Chapman was the manager of two clubs—first, Huddersfield Town and then Arsenal—and built each in turn into the finest team in the land. He was the first manager who planned a soccer team with a checkbook in his hand.

Transfer fees had been gradually mounting since the start of the century. Ever since the introduction of professionalism, players were tied to their clubs by contract. If one club wanted a player of another club, it had to buy him for an agreed fee. The player himself had to give his consent to the deal, but did not get any of the money. Transfer fees at first were nominal affairs. In 1905 Middlesbrough bought a player named Alf Common from Sunderland for £1,000—and bankers and stockbrokers raised their hands in astonishment. To pay £1,000 for a footballer! In 1970 England's World Cup star Martin Peters was transferred from West Ham United to Tottenham Hotspur for £200,000 (around $500,000) and nobody turned a hair.

In Chapman's time, transfer fees for star players were mounting towards five figures. He watched stars all over Britain, singled out those he fancied for his own team and purchased them. The team he built at Huddersfield won the English League three years running from 1924 to 1926 and was hailed as "the team

Herbert Chapman, left front, Britain's most famous team manager between the two world wars, is known as the man who created the modern image of the game of soccer. He's shown in 1932 with his Arsenal team.

of all the talents," the greatest team of all time. It included fullback Roy Goodall, who seldom allowed an opponent to get past him with the ball; Clem Stephenson, the captain, who schemed the attacks from midfield, and two famous, tricky wingers, Alec Jackson and Billy Smith.

Then Chapman took over Arsenal, the wealthiest of the London clubs, and his big-spending tactics created a legend. Paying out bonuses in all directions, Chapman built a team which was, at the time, the most famous in the world. All Europe still regarded the English as the masters, and Arsenal was the symbol of English soccer supremacy.

Arsenal under Chapman invented the "W formation," using a forward line shaped like a W, the two inside forwards David Jack and Alex James hanging back to link up with the defense and start attacks, the center-forward and two wingers acting as spearheads and strikers.

Some of the Arsenal stars of that time claimed they were the forerunners of the 4–2–4 and 4–3–3 systems of the modern age. The team would fall back on defense for long periods of the game, wing-halves Jack Crayston and Wilf Copping overlapping with fullbacks George Male and Eddie Hapgood; and then Jack or James would suddenly start an attack going, and Arsenal would score. Two goals were usually enough. The technique destroyed the old soccer philosophy that attack was the best method of defense. "Lucky old Arsenal," the Cockney fans used to say—the opposing team did all the attacking but Arsenal got the goals. In fact, it was a victory blueprint dreamed up by a master planner. Chapman died in 1934 at the height of his career, but he had laid the foundations and Arsenal went on conquering. During the '30s, the great London team won the English League five times and the English Cup twice.

All over the world English coaches were being hired to teach soccer. The fame of Arsenal resounded everywhere, along with that of a new young winger named Stanley Matthews, who was jinking his way along the touchline for Stoke City and made every opponent look foolish who tried to stop him.

But the '30s brought the first signs that England was in danger of losing its world supremacy. To defeat "the masters" was the ambition of soccer teams everywhere, and at last it began to happen. British complacency was shaken to its foundations in 1931 when Austria hammered Scotland 5–1 in Vienna—and again the following year when France, gaining revenge for a string of annual defeats, downed England 5–2 in Paris.

The World Cup was inaugurated in 1930 and South American soccer made its first big impact. But the myth of England's mastery—if it was now a myth—survived shakily through two more decades, because England at this time was not a member of FIFA and did not enter the World Cup.

The big tournament had been planned for 10 years before it got off the ground. With professionalism spreading everywhere, FIFA took the view that most countries were inadequately represented by all-amateur teams at the Olympics, and that a new open tournament was needed. The great champion of the World Cup was Jules Rimet, president of the French Football Association who became president of FIFA in 1920, and the handsome cup, mounted on a gold statuette, was named after him—the Jules Rimet Trophy.

Uruguay, winner of the gold medal at the Olympics of 1924 and 1928, was given the honor of staging the first World Cup in 1930. Uruguay duly won the tournament. It was only a partial success because some European countries were not members of FIFA and others decided it was too expensive to send teams. Only four European nations—France, Belgium, Romania and Yugoslavia—were among the 13 entries, and the way was clear for South American domination. The teams were divided into four pools and the four winners moved into the semifinals and then competed on a knockout basis. Uruguay, led by sharpshooting inside-left Cea, crushed Yugoslavia 6–1 in the semifinals and defeated Argentina 4–2 in the final. The big surprise was sprung by the United States, which fielded a team composed mostly of ex-British pros and won its pool, only to lose 6–1 to Argentina in the semifinals.

In 1934 and 1938 the World Cup shifted to Europe, and Italy won the trophy twice running. But the tournament was still not the all-embracing world competition which it was to become after World War II.

The 1934 tournament was held in Italy. Most of Europe took part, but not Uruguay, which felt it had been snubbed by the European countries four years before. Argentina, afraid of having its best players signed up by wealthy Italian clubs, sent a team below full strength.

The man behind Italy's success was team manager Vittorio Pozzo, who established an authority over his squad of a kind never seen in soccer before. He used three Argentinians of Italian extraction, arguing that they would have been eligible to fight for Italy in the war and if they could die for Italy, they could play for Italy. The Italians had a fine attacking center-half in Monti and a lively striker in Meazza, but they had to work hard to win the cup. In the semifinals they defeated Austria 1–0 on a heavy, muddy field in Milan. The final against Czechoslovakia in Rome went to 30 minutes of extra time before Schiavo scored to give Italy a 2–1 victory.

France hosted the tournament in 1938, and Italy won the cup again. Only two players, Meazza and Ferrari, remained from the victorious 1934 team, but Pozzo was still the manager and many critics considered that he had built a better side this time. It took a penalty by Meazza to send Italy into the final with a 2–1 victory over Brazil in Marseilles, but the final was a more clearcut affair. Italy downed Hungary 4–2, Colaussi and Piola scoring two goals each.

Italy thus became the holder of the cup for the longest period in the history of the tournament. It lasted from 1934, right through World War II to 1950, when the competition was resumed in Brazil. During the war, Italian soccer officials buried the trophy on a farm near Turin and hid it from the Nazis.

In Brazil in 1950, England, the so-called masters, entered for the first time and met humiliation. The English defeated Chile 2–0 but lost 1–0 to the United States—to the utter disbelief of the fans at home—and then 1–0 to Spain. In the final in the Maracana Stadium in Rio, before a crowd of 200,000, Uruguay edged Brazil 2–1. Critics picked the Brazilians as the team of the tournament, although they did not win. They had a fine marksman in Ademir, who was top scorer of the tournament with seven goals. In the final they did nearly all the attacking but failed to batter down the superb Uruguayan defense marshaled by veteran center-half Obdulio Varela.

In the 1950s the Hungarian national team exploded on the scene. The Hungarians were hailed as the greatest team of all time, yet they failed to win the World Cup.

This was the famous squad that included the goal-scoring trio of Puskas, Kocsis and Hidegkuti. Puskas packed one of the most powerful shots the world had ever seen, while Kocsis headed goals like a master. The team employed cunning decoy movements that pulled opposing defensive formations to pieces, and the three marksmen shook the goal-nets of Europe with their shooting. The Hungarians went to Wembley Stadium early in 1954 and demolished England 6–3, thus ending the unbeaten home record of the so-called masters against foreign teams. In a return match in Budapest, Hungary rubbed England's nose in the dust again and won 7–1.

After these devastating displays, Hungary was considered a certainty to win the World Cup in Switzerland in 1954, but it didn't work out that way. Instead the title went to West Germany, and credit for the victory went to the West Germans' cunning manager, Sepp Herberger.

The new pattern of competition was used for the first time—four teams in each qualifying pool, and the two top teams in each pool lining up in the quarter-finals. West Germany and Hungary played in the same pool. When the two teams came to play each other, Herberger rested half his team and fielded a half-dozen reserves. He figured he could afford to throw the game and bank on his men defeating Turkey in their last qualifying match and getting through to the quarter-finals anyway.

Ferenc Puskas, who packed a shot at goal like a cannonball, is shown in action in 1959. He was the idol of two countries—his own native Hungary and Spain, to which he migrated.

The risky tactics paid off. Hungary massacred West Germany 8–3 and Kocsis scored four of the goals. The Hungarians appeared unstoppable that day and nobody, including the Hungarian players themselves, believed that anybody could defeat them. But they reckoned without two factors—the quiet, clever scheming of Herberger, who duly saw his team through to the quarterfinals with a 7–2 victory over Turkey, and a quarterfinal clash between Hungary and Brazil that turned out to be one of the roughest, ugliest games of all time.

It went down in soccer history as the Battle of Berne. Hungary won 4–2 in pouring rain, without Puskas, who was injured, and at the cost of a heavy bruising and battering. Each team was awarded a penalty, fights broke out on the field and three men—two Brazilians and one Hungarian—were ordered off. At the end of the game the two teams swung punches at each other and continued the dispute in the dressing rooms.

The next hurdle for Hungary was a semifinal match against Uruguay—another physically exhausting battle, although this time a clean and fair one. The teams were tied 2–2 after 90 minutes and the match went to 30 minutes' extra time, in which two goals from the magic head of Kocsis took Hungary to a 4–2 triumph and into the final against West Germany.

How much had the struggles against the South Americans taken out of the Hungarians in body and spirit? Soccer fans continued to argue the point. Puskas,

The amazing Pele (King Pele to his worshippers), soars over a fallen Venezuelan player to score a goal for Brazil in a 1969 match at Rio de Janeiro.

who had missed the two previous games, turned out for Hungary, but many argued that he was unfit and should not have played. The "Galloping Major," as Puskas was called (he was a major in the Hungarian army) scored an early goal and Hungary went on to lead 2–0. But the Germans, who had been cleverly handled and had had a less strenuous campaign, lasted the pace better and came through to win 3–2 with the help of two goals by Helmut Rahn.

That great Hungarian team, which carved itself a place in soccer history, never played in the World Cup again. Two years later, after the 1956 Hungarian revolution, Puskas, Kocsis and Hidegkuti all went abroad.

And so to 1958—and to the 4–2–4 system and the start of Pele's reign. At the age of 17, Pele helped Brazil to its first World Cup triumph on the rain-soaked fields of Sweden. Positions on the field had been changing steadily over 100 years, and recently more and more men had fallen back in defense. Now Brazil lined up with four men in the back row to defend, two link men in midfield to fall back and help in defense when necessary, and four strikers in the forward line. As well as Pele, Brazil had great players in Didi and Garrincha. Pele did not play in the first two matches, but then burst on the scene with a series of scoring exploits that made him the most talked of player in the world. He scored the goal in a 1–0 victory over Wales in the quarterfinals, hammered in three more in a 5–2 semifinal over France, and then scored two in the final, in which Brazil downed Sweden 5–2.

At the end, Pele, weeping tears of emotion, was carried off the field on the shoulders of the Brazilian team. It was a famous scene in soccer history. The fans in Stockholm realized that a great new star had appeared on the soccer stage, but they did not guess that Pele would lead Brazil to two more World Cup triumphs in the next 12 years.

A Frenchman named Fontaine, who went to Sweden expecting to be a reserve, scored 13 goals—a World Cup record that still stands. England failed again, but this time the English had the world's sympathy. Earlier in the year three of their greatest stars—Roger Byrne, Duncan Edwards and Tommy Taylor—had died in the air crash at Munich which had shattered the Manchester United side. It was one of soccer's great tragedies. Besides the three English stars, five other players were killed and two more were so badly injured they never played soccer again.

Brazil went into the 1962 World Cup in Chile with its 4–2–4 system still operating smoothly and some of its finest players—Pele, Didi, Garrincha and fullback Djalma Santos—still in the lineup. The Brazilians inevitably won the tournament again despite a muscle injury to Pele, who dropped out of the competition after the second game. Brazil swept past Chile 4–2 in the semifinals and triumphed 3–1 over Czechoslovakia in the final.

England, which had taught the world how to play soccer, was well and truly out in the cold. The English had now competed in four World Cup tournaments and had never got as far as the semifinals.

Could England ever come back and take its old place as the No. 1 soccer power? Although it struggled to hold its own in the fierce arena of international soccer, British coaches returning from abroad still claimed that the English First Division, consisting of 22 teams, maintained a higher all-around standard and had a greater depth of talent than any other national league in the world. If only that talent could be tapped and organized and welded into a national team, they argued, England might reign supreme again.

And so it did. The 1966 World Cup was scheduled for England in honor of the English FA's centenary. In 1962 the FA appointed a shy, quiet-spoken former international player, Alf Ramsey, as manager of the English team and gave him complete power to pick his men and call them up for training in mid-season, prerogatives which no English team manager had enjoyed before.

Ramsey took modern soccer technique a stage further and stretched the Brazilian 4–2–4 system to 4–3–3—with three men in midfield and only three strikers. It was a fluid formation and Ramsey called on every man in his team to move up or back as the game demanded, so that the midfield line could retreat in defense and even the back-line defenders could overlap on the wings and join in the attacks.

These methods, backed up by iron discipline and supplemented by the flair of a few individual players, won the World Cup for England. The individuals were Gordon Banks, rated by most critics as the world's best goalkeeper; Bobby Moore, who captained the team from the back line and gave his men inspiring leadership, and Bobby Charlton, a survivor of the 1958 Munich air disaster, who hammered home some unforgettable goals. England played all its games at Wembley Stadium before crowds of 100,000. Some of the visiting teams complained that this gave England an unfair advantage since other teams had to move from stadium to stadium, but this did not spoil what was for English fans the greatest scenes in their long soccer history.

England defeated West Germany 4–2 in a dramatic final that went to 30 minutes' extra time. With only a few seconds of the regular 90 minutes left England led 2–1—and then Ludwig Weber swept in an equalizer for the Germans. The turf at Wembley has always been green and lush and notoriously tiring, and in the extra time both teams fought almost to a standstill.

England went to a 3–2 lead with one of the most controversial goals in history. A shot from Geoff Hurst hit the crossbar, bounced down on the line, and then out into the field of play. The referee ruled it had dropped inside the goal. With the last kick of the game Hurst scored again and became the first player to get three goals in a World Cup final.

Eusebio of Portugal, called "the Black Panther from Mozambique," scored nine goals and was the individual star of the 1966 World Cup. Brazil failed to reach the quarterfinals after Pele, roughly treated, had limped out of the tournament swearing he would never play in the World Cup again.

But in 1970 all was forgotten and Pele reigned supreme again and led Brazil to another clearcut triumph. This time, with three titles under their belts, the Brazilians won the Jules Rimet Trophy for keeps, and a new cup had to be provided for the next World Cup in Munich in 1974.

Substitutes for injured players, for many years a subject of bitter controversy, had finally been approved and was an important part in the 1970 World Cup, played in torrid conditions and in high altitude in Mexico. Each team was allowed to send in two substitutes at any time, and team managers used them as a tactical maneuver to replace tiring players who had been given a lot of running to do. These tactics helped West Germany to dethrone the champion, England, with a 3–2 victory in the quarterfinals after trailing 2–0 with 20 minutes to go. But

Russian goalie Lev Yashin makes a full-length dive in an effort to block a goal attempt in World Cup semifinal match between Russia and West Germany in Liverpool, England, July 25, 1966. West Germany won, 2–1.

European maneuvering of this kind could not stop Pele and his fellow goal-seekers, Jairzinho and Tostao. They defeated Peru 4–2 in the quarterfinals, Uruguay 3–1 in the semifinals and Italy 4–1 in the final, before a crowd of 112,000 in the Aztec Stadium.

Pele, the king of world soccer, fittingly scored one of Brazil's goals in the final. Earlier in the year he had booted home the 1,000th goal of his career and been feted as a national hero.

The pioneers who founded the English League would be astonished today to see the armies of soccer fans who travel about Europe and South America to cheer on their teams. The international club tournaments, inaugurated in the mid-1950s, have escalated and are now among the world's greatest sporting attractions. The champion team of each country wins a place in the European Cup of Champions, and the corresponding competition in South America. These cup games, played on a two-leg home-and-away basis, are the richest money-makers club sides have ever known, and supporters travel by the thousands across the two continents to watch the games.

The European Cup was dominated for the first six years by Real Madrid, an all-star team that was to Europe what Arsenal had been to England back in the 1930s. Puskas, after leaving Hungary, joined Real and took his place beside the goal ace, Alfredo di Stefano from Argentina, tactical schemer Luis de Sol and Francisco Gento, who flew along the left wing and was called the fastest soccer player of all time.

Real's fantastic reign in Europe was ended in 1961 by Benfica of Portugal, which had Eusebio as its principal striker. Real won the trophy back once. Other teams which won it were Internazionale Milan and AC Milan, which share the great San Siro Stadium in the North Italian city; Celtic of Scotland, Manchester United of England and Feyenoord of The Netherlands.

The South American title has been passed around among Penarol of Uruguay, Santos of Brazil (Pele's club) and three Argentinian teams—Independiente, Estudiantes and Racing. Since 1960 the winners of the European Cup and the South American Cup have been paired in an annual two-leg World Club Championship affair, with one game on each side of the Atlantic and the result decided on goals aggregate. Through 1970, South American teams had a slight edge with six victories against the Europeans' five.

Hundreds of thousands of dollars pour into the kitties of the clubs that win

Sir Stanley Matthews, a legend in British soccer, is carried off field by opponents after playing his last game as a professional soccer player in 1965.

these titles or reach the finals, and star players can earn $1,000 a week by helping to win the big ones. Some critics blame the big money stakes for the increased tension and mounting violence that have marred some international games in recent years.

When Celtic of Scotland and Racing of Argentina contested the World Club championship in 1967 the series went to a playoff at Montevideo in which tempers flared and six players—four from Celtic and two from Racing—were ordered off the field. Five players were sent off during the World Cup games in England in 1966. But FIFA ordered a tightening up by referees for the World Cup in Mexico in 1970 and achieved impressive results, for in that tournament not one player was sent off.

Meanwhile, the biggest money stakes were reserved for people who filled in the pools, although some of them had never watched a soccer game. An estimated 12 million Britons bet on the pools every week during the 8½-month soccer season. Most people bet a few shillings—maybe one or two dollars—each week, and the lucky ones occasionally pick up a prize of £300,000 ($720,000). The big handouts go to those who can forecast eight score-draws—that is, games ending 1–1 or 2–2 or 3–3. Sometimes there are only eight of them in the whole Saturday program of league games in England and Scotland, and if one man should pick them in advance, the result is an instant fortune. Vast armies of men and women work over the weekends, sorting and checking entries for the pools firms, which in terms of labor constitute the fourth largest industry in Britain.

It was a mystery to soccer-crazy Europeans that it took so long to start up professional soccer in the United States. The U.S. team had reached the semifinals of the first World Cup in 1930 and actually defeated England in the 1950 tournament, yet it was 1967 before the U.S. National Professional Soccer League (NPSL) was inaugurated.

In its first season the league was at war with the U.S. Football Association and was not recognized by FIFA, and European pros who signed for American clubs risked permanent suspension. The two bodies finally got together with FIFA's blessing. There were plenty of dollars behind the venture, from commercial sponsorship and television fees, and the NPSL and USFA cheerfully lost $5 million between them in 1967 in their bid to establish big time soccer in a country that lacked soccer traditions. Crack teams from Europe were imported to give exhibition games after the European season was over. But soccer crowds rarely reached 20,000 in America, compared with crowds of 60,000 and more at league games in Europe. Some European players and coaches, who went to the United States in 1967 to jump on the soccer bandwagon, returned home wondering whether the game would ever be really big there.

The North American Soccer League was reduced to six teams—Dallas, Atlanta and Washington in the southern division, Kansas City, St. Louis and Rochester, N.Y., in the northern section.

Europe has a healthy respect for sport in the United States. The first flush of enthusiasm for professional soccer in America has paled a little, but European fans still expect the United States to be a power in the future. They know from experience that when the United States takes up a sport seriously it takes a lot of stopping.

The action, thrills and enthusiasm are there, whether racing in a small boat, as are the two men at the top, or for the biggest prize of all, the America's Cup, bottom.

chapter 14

YACHTING

The America's Cup Became the Aristocrat of the Aristocratic Sport

by Sid Moody

Yachting began in America eons ago with some forgotten Indian who decided to take his canoe out one day just for the fun of it, had a squaw who thought he was crazy and who eventually traded in his birchbark for a bigger one.

Sid Moody is supervising editor of *AP Newsfeatures*. He was a feature writer there for 10 years prior to taking that post. A native of New Jersey, he joined the Newark bureau of *The AP* in 1956 after working on the *Hunterdon County Democrat* in Flemington, N.J. He has written or edited several books for *The AP*, covered the America's Cup races since 1958 and sails himself.

Not much has changed. Whether he is a millionaire in quest of the America's Cup, a husband escaping the lawn mower or a weekend Magellan whistling for wind, the American yachtsman is an amphibian who prefers life afloat to that ashore. Regardless of the cost.

The races for the Cup, alone—the oldest prize in international sport and one the United States has held uninterruptedly since 1851—have seen Vanderbilts and Morgans and Liptons and Sopwiths shell out millions after millions in pursuit of a trophy that has no bottom, looks like a pregnant pelican and was worth only 100 guineas when new, which wasn't yesterday.

In return for all his outlay, the yachtsman gets wet, cold, often hungry, lost, becalmed, disobeyed by his wife at sea and misunderstood by his friends at home. He is a perverse fellow who calls a toilet a head, a kitchen a galley and a rope a sheet. He dreams of racing to Bermuda, Hawaii, the next buoy and the size of his next yacht.

If he dreams of the America's Cup, he is probably constantly reminded of one millionaire's definition of a yacht as "a hole in the water into which you constantly pour money." The Cup is an Everest, a Holy Grail, but it is only one of countless trophies that draw Americans down to the water's edge like so many spray-soaked lemmings.

The first American yachtsman was actually Dutch. This was Adrian Block—discoverer of Block Island near which the America's Cup races are now held so long as foreign challengers keep losing them—who in 1613 in New York built what the Dutch called a jaght schip, a small fast utility vessel. Block's ship was not built for pleasure, but the name was eventually Anglicized and applied to those boats that were.

As the Colonies prospered, Americans began taking to the water for enjoyment as well as commerce, and in 1816 a Salem, Mass., shipowner launched what has been termed the first American yacht, an 83-foot hermaphrodite brig called Cleopatra's Barge.

Since yachtsmen generally are only understood by other yachtsmen, yacht clubs began springing up including, in 1844, the New York Yacht Club. It was seven years later that all the trouble started, history's longest naval battle—that for the Cup—which has sometimes been as lurid of tongue as it has been lavish of cash.

The first shot came in 1851 when the Earl of Wilton, commodore of the Royal Yacht Squadron in England, wrote John Cox Stevens, his counterpart at the infant NYYC, noting that he had heard an American yacht would be in British waters that summer. The Earl invited the Americans to drop by the club house at Cowes and added: "(I) shall be very glad to avail myself of any improvements in ship-building that the industry and skill of your nation have enabled you to elaborate."

If he only had known.

Word had drifted back to Britain of a particularly fast U.S. pilot cutter named Mary Taylor that had been designed by George Steers and launched in 1849. She was a radical departure from British design theory that called for a broad bow and tapering afterbody, as she had a knife-like bow with maximum width well aft.

Commodore Stevens decided to take the Earl up on his hospitality and commissioned Steers to build him "the fastest yacht afloat." If it wasn't, the syndicate would not pay the $30,000 yard bill. The resulting yacht, America, a 93-foot schooner, wasn't even the fastest yacht afloat in New York harbor where the sloop Maria succeeded in sailing circles around her. But the syndicate decided to take America anyway, skinning $10,000 from the price, and on June 21 set sail for Britain with two cases of Madeira "for drinking the health of Her Majesty," Queen Victoria.

America made it across to Europe in 20 days where Stevens had high hopes of making yachting pay, wagering on his own craft. But he tipped his hand prematurely in a chance encounter with the British cutter Lavrock which America won decisively but thereby congealed the sporting blood of the Old Country's sailors.

Under fire from the home press for their reluctance, the British yachtsmen finally invited America to race 14 of their boats around the Isle of Wight, the prize being what became the America's Cup. On Aug. 22, the race was held. America won. Queen Victoria asked who was second. She was told: "I regret to report there is no second."

Actually there was, the British cutter Aurora crossing the finish some eight minutes behind. The English, Canadians, Australians and lately the French have been trying to catch up ever since.

For a while the Cup stood on Stevens' mantle and at one point was almost melted down to make commemorative medals. But it was eventually presented to the NYYC along with the so-called "deed of gift" outlining procedures for future challenges. It was evident the Americans were determined to hold onto their silverware.

They accepted a challenge in 1870 from James Ashbury of England but told him he would have to ace his yacht Cambria against the whole NYYC fleet. Which he did. And lost. And was fouled, setting two precedents at one blow that were to keep the waters of the Atlantic turbulent for generations to come.

In response to criticism that they were stacking the deck unfairly, the NYYC agreed to race the challenger subsequently boat for boat. But the club reserved the right to pick its defender from one of four yachts on the day of the race to insure its entrant was the one best suited to the weather at the time.

Ashbury came back in 1871 with Livonia. And lost. And protested. And lost that, too, when the NYYC declined to rerun a race in which Ashbury claimed the defender, Columbia, had turned a mark improperly. The Englishman took it hard, claimed he had a legal right to the Cup and went home grumbling about "Yankee cunning."

The NYYC in turn declared "there are certain acts which a gentleman cannot commit" and pointedly returned three trophies Ashbury had presented the club the year before. Ashbury was not the last challenger to go away mad.

Certainly the maddest was the Earl of Dunraven whose challenge in 1895 was the Trafalgar of America's Cup history. Following the departure of the angry Ashbury there had been six more challenges—two from Canada and four from Britain—which the NYYC defenders won with dispatch and without rancor, taking 13 straight races in all.

The deed of gift had been changed in the meantime, the NYYC having agreed to confine itself to a sole defender for a challenge series. A further revision in 1887 by which the challenger was required to give the measurements of his yacht 10 months in advance of a race sent storm warnings fluttering around the Cup again. British yachtsmen protested the change gave an unfair advantage to the NYYC which could design a defender on the basis of pre-knowledge of the challenger.

After some brisk exchanges, a challenge was finally accepted from Dunraven for 1893. He lost. He challenged again in 1895. And lost.

But things had already got off to a bad start when the Royal Yacht Squadron, through which Dunraven challenged, said it didn't really want the Cup even if he won it. Which belittling of their beloved trophy miffed the NYYC mightily. Things didn't improve when the club heard that Dunraven had privately accused the Americans of secretly adding ballast to their yacht, Defender, to lengthen her waterline and hence her speed potential. Things got worse when Dunraven's Valkyrie III had a race she won taken away from her for a starting foul; got worse yet when Dunraven withdrew his yacht after the start of the third and final race in protest at the uncontrolled spectator fleet, and absolutely hit bottom after the Earl returned home and charged the Yankees with deliberate fraud by adding the ballast.

Gretel II of Australia, right, appears to be headed toward a collision with America's Cup defender, Intrepid, during tacking duel to first mark off Newport, R.I., in 1970.

The Americans were shocked, and when a former NYYC commodore appeared on the floor of the New York Stock Exchange, business was stopped for half an hour while he was cheered and Dunraven hissed. Dunraven was expelled from membership by the NYYC, and when a special committee of yachtsmen that included J. P. Morgan found no basis for the Earl's charge, it appeared Cup interest had gone with the wind.

But there are also calms after storms, peace and normalcy being returned in this instance by Sir Thomas Lipton. The British tea baron was as unsuccessful at winning the Cup as he was successful in winning the hearts of America's yachting public through his indomitable sportsmanship. Five times between

1899 and 1930 he tried. Five times he lost. He did come close in 1920, losing 3–2 to Resolute, and the second victory of Lipton's Shamrock IV in that series was the first ever by a challenger over an American defender that had not been first disabled during the race. But Lipton had restored welcomed amity to Cup races for three decades and near the end of his long life announced he had but two regrets: he had never married and had not been able to "lift the ould mug."

While Cup racing had become the premier yachting event, American sailors had been casting about in other waters. Small boat skippers were actively racing in such classes as Stars and Lightnings and inland scows. Led by Edward Burgess, who designed several Cup defenders, and Nathanael Herreshoff, the "Wizard of Bristol," R.I., American yacht design was assuming a world preeminence. Herreshoff and the NYYC drew up the Universal Rule around the turn of the century governing yacht measurement and handicapping. With improved rules came more equitable racing among boats of differing sizes and classes. Transatlantic racing had already begun shortly after the Civil War. In one such crossing in 1905 the 185-foot schooner Atlantic set a record of 12 days 4 hours 1 minute that probably will stand for all time as Atlantic-sized racers are a thing of the past.

In 1906 three yachts set out from New York to initiate the first race to Bermuda. The biennial feature, now starting from Newport, R.I., attracts up to 150 entrants. Another large fleet races from California to Hawaii every other year, the first being held in 1906, too. There are other distance races such as the Mackinacs on the Great Lakes, the midwinter Southern Ocean Racing Circuit in Florida as well as blue water races to Ensenada, Mexico, and Halifax, Canada.

But it's the America's Cup that draws the crowds, the tempers and the money. And in 1934 the spectators, at least, got their money's worth. British airplane manufacturer Tom Sopwith, who had once startled America by buzzing the statue of William Penn atop Philadelphia's City Hall, brought over the fastest challenger yet to meet Rainbow, a sloop that cost a syndicate that included four Vanderbilts "only $400,000." Cup racing by then was in J-class sloops, graceful craft about 120 feet long with masts towering more than 150 feet into the sky and which were as beautiful as any boat ever made.

Endeavor was also one of the fastest, taking the first two of the best-of-seven series that had become standard. With the Cup about to be unbolted from its long-accustomed shelf, Sherman Hoyt, in relief of Harold S. Vanderbilt, one of the greatest of Cup helmsmen, gambled on a wind shift to take the third race. The fourth race brought a protest from Sopwith and an ensuing uproar of Dunravian proportions. The protest concerned a luffing tactic and near collision which the NYYC declined to hear, claiming Sopwith, in keeping with British practice, had not flown his protest flag promptly. Rainbow went on to win four straight and the Cup, but cries of "Yankee cunning" were heard again from across the waters. American opinion was sympathetic and one home team article was entitled "Britannia rules the waves but America waives the rules."

Forgiving if not forgetting, Sopwith came back in 1937 with Endeavor II but was handily beaten by Ranger, perhaps the fastest of all Cup yachts, that was designed by Starling Burgess, son of Edward, and a young, new genius, Olin Stephens.

World War II kept the Cup on the shelf and it wasn't until 1958 that racing

Reflection of the sun sparkles on water as a number of sailboats participate in a race.

resumed, this time in 12-meter sloops, boats about 65 feet long built with the high price of boat building in mind and to a formula as complicated as Einstein's theory. Campaigning a 12 was to run upward of a million dollars for a summer's fun which, said one rueful American syndicate member, "cuts into your drinking money." That year Columbia, a Stephens design, took up where Ranger left off, badly outclassing Sceptre from Britain four straight.

In 1962 a new nation entered the lists—Australia. The challenging Gretel was generally conceded as faster than the NYYC's Weatherly and won one of the five races, surfing dramatically by the defender with spinnaker flying. But Weatherly had a resident genius at the helm, Emil "Bus" Mosbacher; a genius sailmaker, Ted Hood, and the benefit of a hard summer's campaigning against other American defense candidates on their own waters, something the challengers from overseas had chronically lacked throughout the Cup's long history.

Damon Runyon's complaint that "watching an America's Cup race is as interesting as watching the grass grow" was echoed in 1964 when Constellation swamped Britain's Sovereign 4–0 and again in 1967 when Intrepid, Stephens-designed and Mosbacher-sailed, shut out Dame Pattie from Australia.

Few lawns, however, compared to the 1970 match between Intrepid, only the second defender ever to repeat, and Gretel II from Australia. The Aussies proved they had caught up in yacht design and sailmaking in the closest and most tempestuous series since 1934 and probably the most exciting ever. They lost 4–1, but the total difference between the two yachts after 121 miles of sailing was only 6 minutes, 45 seconds.

Gretel II's victory in the fourth race was a home stretch run that caught Intrepid in the last mile and had spectators jumping up and down like horse racing fans. The Aussies had another victory reversed when the NYYC race committee upheld Intrepid's protest of a starting collision that left part of Gretel II's bow aboard the American defender.

"Why don't you get a bloody rule book?" shouted Martin Visser, an Aussie co-helmsman, to Intrepid's skipper, Bill Ficker, after the crash. A lot of critics also thought the NYYC should get an international committee to solve disputes and save itself the embarrassment of having to adjudicate protests in which its own boat was a party. There had been an earlier protest, as well, and a crewman fell overboard off Gretel II and an Intrepid tactician was helicoptered to a hospital in shock after being stung by a bee.

Ficker's cool hand and typically crisp American sailhandling preserved the victory in a neck-and-neck fifth and final race. So the Cup remained alive but not too well back on its shelf at NYYC headquarters on 44th St. in New York.

Encouraged by the closeness of the match, no fewer than seven challenges were presented to the NYYC for 1973 by yachtsmen who thought they finally could see the summit of Everest and the glint of the Holy Grail just around the next buoy.

Maybe someday, Your Majesty, America will be second.

Famed U.S. Olympic swimmers Johnny Weissmuller, left, and Duke Kahanamoku are shown in Paris at the 1924 Olympic Games.

chapter 15

SWIMMING

Teen-Age Tykes Conquer the Water

by Hubert Mizell

Hubert Mizell, 32, is a relatively new member of the AP sports team—he joined the news service in 1968—but already has distinguished himself as a craftsman and excellent feature writer. Assigned to the busy Miami bureau, he has helped cover the Super Bowl football game, the World Series, major American golf championships and auto racing. He was a writer with the *Florida Times-Union* in Jacksonville for nine years and served three years as public relations director of the Gator Bowl Association.

Bronzed, lithe Hawaiian Duke Kahanamoku knifed through crystal waters in pursuit of a world 100-meter record. Astonished timers compared watches—an incredible 1:00.4, faster than any swimmer in history.

That was 1920.

Two generations later, in 1964, another disciplined athlete sprinted the Duke's distance in a scant 59.5 seconds. This time the swimmer was Dawn Fraser, a little lady from Australia.

Progress respects no person in the world of competitive swimming. Refined to its modern variety of strokes since the birth of the 20th century, the sport seldom sees a prime performer past age 21. Seemingly untouchable records often survive for mere hours.

Swimming is an untraceably ancient happening but was omitted from the original Olympic Games. However, the Greek historian Pausanias did chronicle several instances of aquatic competition.

As far removed as 36 B.C., during the reign of Emperor Sugiu in Japan, swimming events were recorded. It was strictly a Japanese affair, however. By 1603 the island's emperor had already ordered school officials to include the sport in their curriculum.

Despite the Japanese activity, international competition did not begin to blossom until centuries later, with the formation in the 1830s of the National Swimming Association in London. The first bona fide world meet was staged in 1846 at the Robinson Baths in Sydney, Australia. When another world competition was held in 1858 at Saint-Kilda near Melbourne, Australia, the standouts were Jo Bennett of the host nation and Charles Steadman of England, winners of 100-yard races.

When the modern Olympic Games came to pass in 1896 at Athens, Greece, swimming was installed as one of the sports. Little notice was given, however, to the three events staged in the Bay of Zea near Piraeus. An 18-year-old Hungarian, Alfred Guttman, was a double winner, churning to a 1:22.2 clocking in the 100 meters and a time of 18:22.2 for 1,200 meters. Austria's Paul Newman captured the 500 at 8:12.6.

St. Louis was the Olympics' host city when the Games held the first competition in still water. Laboring in an artificial lake created for the St. Louis World's Fair, Hungary's Zoltan Halmay was a hero with triumphs in the 50-yard race with a time of 28 seconds flat and at 200 yards in 1:02.8.

It was two years before the St. Louis Games that a speedy Australian, Frederick Lane, became the first man to crack the one-minute barrier in a 100-yard race. Lane did a 59.6 in a 33⅓-yard pool at Leicester, England.

The 1886 formation of the Amateur Swimming Association was a significant boost for the sport. Among other things, the body determined just who was an amateur athlete. Many of its rules still apply, although the Fédération Internationale de Natation Amateur (FINA) came into being in 1908 as the world's governing organization for swimming.

Unlike sports where equipment advances and performing conditions cause old-timers to doubt modern feats, swimming has changed little except in the development of superior techniques both in strokes and training. Modern teachings allow slender, teen-age girls such as Debbie Meyer, Claudia Kolb, Catie Ball, Donna de Varona and Sue Pedersen to skim through the water more rapidly than musclemen of yesteryear including Weissmuller, Kahanamoku and Crabbe.

Johnny Weissmuller—later to gain fame as the movies' "Tarzan of the Apes"—clocked a record 59 seconds flat in the 100 meters during the 1924 Olympics at Paris. By 1968, handsome Don Schollander from Yale University blazed 200 yards with his two 100-yard segments done in the average time of 57.1 seconds.

The ruggedly handsome Weissmuller had the endurance that allowed him to remain unbeaten through 10 years of amateur swimming at distances from 50 yards to a quarter of a mile. His times have all been bettered. Johnny's world record time of 4:54.2 was hailed as a miracle in the 1920s, but by 1968 a cute teen-age girl named Debbie Meyer had produced a 4:31.8 in the 400 meters.

Weissmuller's forte was the crawl, an ancient stroke that carried the sport alone for centuries. The backstroke became a recognized talent in the early 1900s and was soon followed by the breaststroke and finally the butterfly.

Historians disagree on the true birth of swimming, with theories ranging from cavemen to the Ice Age to Biblical times.

Amateur competition has long been the core of international swimming with the Olympic Games the showcase of talent. There's seldom money to be made, but some standouts have catapulted into rich careers after first earning headlines in the pool. Weissmuller, a giant of a man, was voted the greatest swimmer of the 1900–50 era in an *Associated Press* mid-century poll. Before becoming reason-

Johnny Weissmuller, left, was a hero in the 1920s as he set innumerable swimming records. Forty years later, teen-age girls such as Debbie Meyer, below, would be surpassing those times with ridiculous ease. Here, Debbie is on her way to a third gold medal at the 1968 Olympic Games.

ably wealthy as Tarzan, Weissmuller won five Olympic gold medals, set 52 national swimming records and was untouched for a decade. When screen tests began around 1930, Johnny was already hauling down a fat $500 a week.

Clarence "Buster" Crabbe was a standout swimmer who parlayed muscular good looks and his aquatic ability into such movie roles as Flash Gordon and Buck Rogers. The son of a Hawaiian pineapple plantation boss, Crabbe eventually became the seventh movie Tarzan and was still around in the 1950s on television as Captain Gallant.

Best known female swimmer ever was gorgeous Esther Williams, whose true fame developed long after winning the 1939 national championship. Esther's movie career began in 1943 with a co-starring role opposite pint-sized Mickey Rooney in "Andy Hardy's Double Life."

Even a rotund Chinese emperor managed to steal swimming headlines in the 1960s. Mao Tse-tung was out of the Free World eye for some months and rumors floated that the dictator was seriously ill and perhaps even dead. Mao underlings then flooded the world with reports that the Peking chief had negotiated a fantastic distance in far under world record time, swimming upstream in a Chinese river.

It was Mao's way of proving he was very much alive, not unlike the words of Mark Twain when he stated, "Reports of my death are greatly exaggerated."

If another "greatest swimmer" poll were held today, the vote would likely be split between Weissmuller and Schollander. Debbie Meyer and Dawn Fraser would get support on the distaff side, but the premier swimmer of the past among the girls might well be Katherine Rawls. She won 33 national championships in the 1930s and was the first woman to represent her nation in the Olympics as both a swimmer and diver in 1932–36.

Individual heroes and heroines come from throughout the world, with up-to-date aces such as Mike Wenden of Australia, Hans Fassnacht of West Germany, Russia's Nikolai Pankin, America's Mark Spitz and Japan's Yasuo Takada. But, the national domination in Olympic Games has been consistently shared by the United States and Australia with an occasional Japanese reign.

Great Britain had a brief grip on heroics in the early 1900s, but the United States took command at the 1912 Olympic Games in Stockholm when Kahanamoku won the 100 meters in 1:03.4. The Duke—later a silver-haired good will symbol in his native Hawaii—was swimming's king through the Antwerp Games in 1920 where Americans dominated. With such standout women swimmers as Fanny Durack, the United States grabbed all but two events.

Twenty years after the swift Aussie, Frederick Lane, cracked 60 seconds in the 100-yard sprint, Weissmuller crushed the barrier at 100 meters with a 58.6 at Alameda, Calif. That was 1922 and a year later Johnny became the first to break five minutes in the 400-meter freestyle with a 4:57 flat.

At age 19, Weissmuller continued a muscular grasp on Olympic heroics. During those 1924 Games at Paris, he produced a 59-flat 100 meters and churned to a 5:04.2 in the 400, but a hint of the record possibilities of mid-teen swimmers was also evident. A 16-year-old Australian, Andrew Charlton, beat the 1,500-meter standard with a 20:06.6 time.

Weissmuller continued to win at age 23, however, in the 1928 Games at Amsterdam, taking the 100 meters in an even quicker 58.6.

Japan emerged as a swimming threat in those Amsterdam Games with breaststroker Yoshiyuki Tsurata winning that nation's first gold medal. Japan's power mushroomed by 1932 when the Olympics shifted to Los Angeles and the island kingdom swam away with almost every honor.

The United States managed to win only one gold in '32, a triumph in the 400-meter freestyle by Buster Crabbe in 4:48.4.

Youth again reared its head at Los Angeles with 14-year-old Kusuo Kitamura taking the 1,500-meter freestyle in 19:12.4. Kitamura stands as the youngest gold medal winner of all time.

American women managed to gain their share of the glory as the Japanese dominated the male events. Helene Madison was a double winner after having possessed all 17 world record times for females in 1931.

Weissmuller's incredible 58.6 time in the 1928 Games withstood all challenges for 10 years. Then, in 1938, an American named Peter Fick lowered the mark to 56.8. By 1970, the time was shaved to 52.2 by another in the line of great Australian swimmers, Mike Wenden.

While the 10-year life of Weissmuller's 100-meter record was unusual, it was little compared to the 20-year grip Willie den Ouden had on the women's 100-meter freestyle mark. The little Dutch girl did a 1:04.6 in 1936 and watched it stand up until the talented Dawn Fraser from Australia jetted to a 1:02 flat in 1956. Eight years later Miss Fraser's record had been personally dropped to 58.9.

Olympic Games play was canceled in 1940–44 due to World War II and when the international sports show was reborn in 1948 the Germans and Japanese were excluded as the bad guys of the conflict. Japan decided to hold its own championship and Hironoshin Furuhashi battered existing records at 400 and 1,500 meters. The FINA refused to allow them as official world marks.

Japan returned to international swimming's good graces by 1949 and immediately proceeded to dominate the U.S. championships at Los Angeles. Furuhashi toppled world records at 400, 800 and 1,500 meters and they stood as official standards through FINA.

The finest male swimmer in America during the early 1950s was not an American at all. Yale University student John Marshall, an Australian, held 19 world records at one time in 1951.

The Aussies hosted the 1956 Olympics at Melbourne and did all but drown the outside competition. The homeland's assault was paced by such superb freestylers as Miss Fraser, Murray Rose, Jon Henricks and Lorraine Crapp.

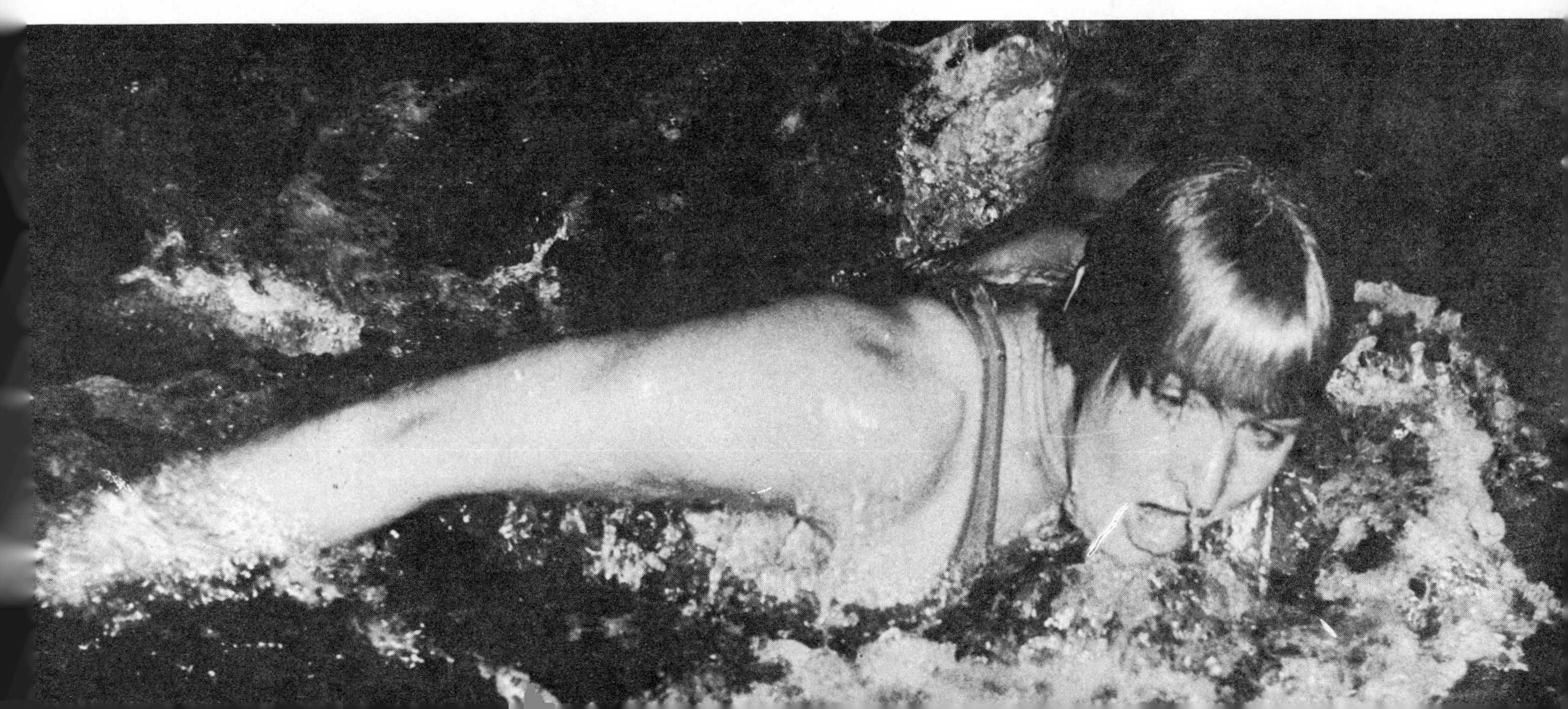

Dawn Fraser, 22, competes in Sydney in her native Australia in February 1960. At 22, she would now be considered old in international competition.

The Australian reign continued until the United States began to regain the No. 1 world position at the 1964 Olympics in Tokyo.

The speedy Schollander sparked the United States to victory, winning four gold medals. A product of the powerful Santa Clara Swim Club in California, Schollander stroked to golds in the 100 freestyle (53.4) and 400 freestyle (4:12.2).

It was an era for smashing records. In the 1960–64 period, an assault by youthful swimmers wiped the record books clean with the exception of Miss Fraser's 200 freestyle mark.

It was at the Tokyo Games that Dawn won her third consecutive gold medal in the same event, the 100-meter freestyle in a time of 59.5, an Olympic record for the Aussie great at the age of 27.

Miss Fraser's feat has been unmatched. Duke Kahanamoku was the 100-meter freestyle champion in 1912 and 1920, but his dream of three in a row was killed when World War I preempted the 1916 Olympics.

America's stronghold on swimming glory at the 1964 Games continued in 1968 at Mexico City. U.S. men took 10 titles in Mexico, including both the 400 and 1,500-meter freestyles by Mike Burton, the 200 and 400 individual medleys by

Here's an underwater view of champ swimmer Don Schollander, winner of four Olympic gold medals in Tokyo.

Pat McCormick, a 22-year-old housewife from California, executes this difficult dive at the Olympic pool in Helsinki, Finland, in 1952.

Charles Hickcox and all three relays. The American girls did as well, taking 11 golds and both relays. Debbie Meyer was best at 200, 400 and 800 meters to win three firsts. Claudia Kolb produced a double gold in the 200 and 400 individual medley events.

Most of the great swimmers go into other walks of life as they advance in age. There are only a few Weissmullers and Crabbes who can use their pool talents to earn good money. Some notable entertainment personalities who were less notable swimmers in the past were Lloyd Bridges, Fernando Lamas, Jon Hall and Vincent Edwards. The late actor Alan Ladd was once a competitive diver.

Divers are often shortchanged in news media coverage, but still manage to produce many of the world's most beautiful sports performances.

Among the best known divers was Pat McCormick, the only American to win four Olympic gold medals in diving. Gary Tobian was a standout in the 1950s, taking six straight national platform diving titles. Three-meter heroes of the past have included multiple champions Pete Deajardins (1925–28), Richard Degener (1933–36) and Al Patnik (1937–40).

Jim Henry of Bloomington, Ind., matured into perhaps the finest board man during the 1960s. He was three times the one-meter national king and also took the three-meter springboard in 1969.

Leisure time brings out the need for activity in most people. It might be a family cycling together, President Eisenhower driving a golf ball, or a man alone challenging the Canadian Rockies.

chapter 16

LEISURE SPORTS

They'd Rather Play and Pay Than Watch

by Karol Stonger

Karol Stonger, 29, a graduate of Indiana University, covered a broad span of varying assignments before she found her niche as the female sports writer of *The AP's* New York staff. After three years of general news work in Indianapolis, she transferred to New York in 1968, working on the financial and book department staffs. She moved into sports in 1970 and immediately won distinction as a feature writer.

Many of the modern day leisure time activities—recreation, sports, whatever the terminology—were born of yesterday's struggle to survive. Archery, fishing, horseback riding, fencing, sailing, snow skiing, swimming, all contributed to man's early ability to trade, to travel, to meet the enemy. When artillery replaced the bow and arrow and the saber, man turned his skills to sport. When breeding of domestic animals for slaughter replaced the need to hunt and fish, man used those skills for pleasure. When technology introduced steam- and motor-driven vehicles, man turned sailing, horseback riding and cycling into forms of friendly competition and personal enjoyment.

How man actively spends his non-working hours in sport falls into three categories—that which once was a livelihood, that which is a spinoff of science—i.e., flying, soaring, snowmobiling, automobile and motorcycle racing—and that which involves a ball or a stick and a ball—one of man's first fascinations.

It is this latter group which raises the hackles of the athletically oriented. How, they ask, can one say that baseball, basketball, football, tennis, golf, hockey, soccer are leisure time sports when for Johnny Bench, Pete Maravich, Fran Tarkenton, Arthur Ashe, Arnold Palmer, Bobby Orr and Pele they are a means of livelihood—a profession? It's simple. There's hardly an athlete who didn't first play the games in the backyard, on the street, on the empty lot or the school playground

A surfer in the shadow of a huge wave off Oahu, Hawaii, in 1970 is locked in the curl and zips along just ahead of the pounding breaker in pursuit of his favorite sport.

with Dad or the other kids on the block. And there are far more amateurs, whether they're 6 or 60, playing in their free hours than there are professionals.

The other question haunting these "true sportsmen" is how could one include bowling, table tennis, croquet, softball, pocket billiards, with the *real* sports? It's simple. All involve physical activity and prowess and all are spoken of with the verb "to play" and the noun "game."

Those words once were reserved for royalty, the wealthy, the elite in Europe, Asia and the New World. There was neither time nor money for common man to pursue such frivolity. Indeed, such pastimes were frowned upon by cultures whose creed called for work from sunup to sundown, day in and day out. But all work and no play soon gave way to a variety of pastimes in which man found he could discipline his body and his mind to accomplish many pleasurable tasks. And he sought more time and new means to pursue them. He got both and leisure time sports became a big business.

Americans alone in the first year of the decade spent more than $4 billion pursuing their sports pleasures. By 1975, the figure has been projected to top $5.5 billion and by the year 2000 some $10 billion. The growth is due in part to more time, more money, more people. The nation's population already has surpassed the 200 million mark. By 1980 it is expected to grow by 60 million and to reach 350 million by the year 2000. As the population expands the work week shrinks. At the turn of the century the average work week was 60 hours. By 1930 it had diminished to 48 hours. In the mid-1960s it was 40 hours and by the mid-1970s should be cut to 32 hours. Thus, by 1975 man in America should have 500 hours more leisure time per year than he did a decade earlier.

The growth also is due, in part, to a redirection of man's energies. Less than a half-century ago, Americans were sedentary. They listened to the radio, enjoyed organized sports as spectators, read, went to the movies. There was, of course, the active element taking up whatever those in power made vogue. President

Franklin D. Roosevelt was known for swimming, President Harry S. Truman for early morning walks, President Dwight D. Eisenhower for his game of golf. But it was President John F. Kennedy's emphasis on physical fitness that put the people on the road to active sports participation.

Television played a role, too. Sure, it was cursed for providing inane amusement for all, for nearly hypnotizing the young to the point where it became a parental substitute, a baby-sitter, a detractor of education, a promoter of inertia. But it also brought to millions of viewers college and professional sports they had heretofore been denied. And with that it brought a new interest in amateur athletics, not as spectator, but as participant sports.

Entering the 1970s, Americans were spending 10 times as much money on participant sports as on spectator events. By the end of the century, experts estimate that Americans will actively participate in 1.6 billion so-called summer sports outings while only 416 million persons will be spectators at summer outdoor sports events.

Swimming was one of man's early challenges. Unlike most other animals he was not born to swim. He had to learn by mimicking, thus the "dog paddle" which later was refined to allow man to glide smoothly through waters to escape danger, reach distant shores. In 1971, there were an estimated 35 million to 40 million swimmers in America participating for safety and sport.

After man conquered the waters he challenged the waves by surfing, a sport equaled only by snow skiing in the exhilaration it provides and the strength it requires. The Hawaiians, in the 10th century, were masters of riding the waves on which wagers surpassing any flat track betting today were placed. Succumbing to the waves could mean not only loss of man's possessions but the loss of freedom for himself and his family. Surfing dried up for nearly a hundred years after the Calvinists arrived in 1821 with the teachings that it was pagan and against God's law. Economics played a role in its return in the early 1900s—as a tourist attraction to Waikiki Beach, then to Southern California.

Long after man had found other means of transport for trade his fascination with boats continued. The challenge of the wind and water, laced with silence, lured thousands of weekend skippers to sea. Boating as a whole became the economic kingpin of the leisure sports market. It was expected to account for $1.2 billion, or more than 20 per cent, of the $5.5 billion projected to be spent annually by 1975.

A natural offshoot of motor boating is water skiing which arrived about the same time that surfing was revived. But the high cost of motor boats slowed its growth.

Archery is one of the oldest sports still being practiced. The bow and arrow has survived some 50 millenniums and by 1970 intrigued some five million persons in the United States and Canada. Nearly one-third of these bowmen practiced target archery while the other 3.5 million were field archers—accomplished in the art of hunting with a bow and arrow.

With gun in hand, man's quest for beast brought the extinction of many species and curbs were placed on the sport as a measure of preservation. Hunting has suffered a further setback as urban sprawl encroaches on wilderness areas. The number of fishermen is growing faster in the United States than is the water acreage. Although enthusiasm is expected to continue to increase their numbers, anglers may be thwarted by their own hand, and that of their fellow man, as pollution infects the waters and kills off their prey.

The saber, like the gun and the bow, was used in warfare and as the techniques of battle were refined, so was the saber, until the foil became the weapon of fencing, a sport which got its name from the British spelling of "defence." Fencing is a scientific, highly disciplined sport polished to an accomplished art by limited numbers.

Judo and karate are other sports requiring extensive skill. They first were introduced to fulfill man's desire to defend himself when he was denied weapons. The ancient Orient's jui-jitsu was the forerunner of judo, created in 1882 in Japan by Prof. Jigoro Kano. Judo, which means the "gentle way," encompasses the total man—his body, his spirit, his mind—in teaching discipline and control to overcome the enemy. Karate was conceived in Okinawa when the Japanese arrived and decreed possession of arms a capital crime in an effort to subdue opposition. It employs a combination of Yoga and Zen and a single concentrated stroke of the hand can be fatal to a man. Both are relative newcomers to the United States and are taught for sport as well as protection.

Although the painter Benjamin West is credited with popularizing ice skating in America, Sonja Henie did for figure skating what Arnold Palmer did for professional golf. Other major factors in its success were the evolution of the skates from bone to steel blades and the mechanical refrigeration which brought the skaters in from the cold. The graceful art of figure skating, called "poetry in motion" by Goethe, makes it what many consider the ideal sport for women.

So graceful was it that in 1849 an opera and a ballet were written with the method of moving about the stage meant to be on blades. But in the opera "The Prophet," first performed in Paris, and the ballet "The Skaters," which opened in Berlin, it was roller skates that propelled the performers—for practical purposes. The skates with wheels enjoyed a new-found popularity but it wasn't until the ball bearing wheel was invented in 1884, more than a century after wooden spools were put underfoot, that the craze swept America and much of the rest of the world.

Ski slopes have been calling man almost from the dawn of history. To move swiftly over snow-covered terrain was a necessity and wars even were won on skis. It wasn't until the late 18th century—in Norway—that skiing was taken up for sport. And it was well into the 20th century before it gained popularity in America. Averell Harriman, seeing European aristocracy enjoying it, brought skiing to America's "beautiful people" via the Union Pacific railroad in the 1930s and developed Sun Valley for their pleasure. Technology gave it a modern boost and a more widespread appeal—now encompassing some three million Americans—with the introduction of mechanical ski lifts, artificial snow and man-made slopes. Now not only does it provide recreation for the entire family—as does bowling and camping—but probably is rivaled only by beaches as a sports center for the nation's young singles.

Snowmobiling is a recent addition to iceboating as a motorized winter sport in America. In the nation's snowbelt, mail is delivered and police, fire and medical emergencies are answered on the vehicles which scoot along on runners and are operated in a manner similar to motorcycles. But many of the one million vehicles now in operation in the United States and Canada are finding their way into the hands of weekend sportsmen who want them for touring the frozen tundra. Others, many of which reach speeds up to 100 miles an hour, have been drafted for organized racing events over snow-covered oval tracks with competition sanctioned by the U.S. Snowmobile Association.

Sleds and toboggans may be the little folks' answer to snowmobiles and skis, but bicycles are the big people's answer to the little red wagon. The bicycle in America is just a little more than a century old, although the first two-wheeler was built by the French in 1690. Bicycles variously were called boneshakers, hobby horses and draisines. The draisine was named for Baron Karl von Drais, a German, who introduced the first fairly practical bicycle in 1816 even though it was propelled by pushing the feet along the ground much like a toddler's push bike. When it was brought to America in 1869 the bicycle was refined to the point of having pedals on the front wheel. But it wasn't until 1885 that it took on its present characteristics—chain-driven, wheels nearly 30 inches across, and rubber tires. By 1896 so popular was the vehicle for sport and transport that there were 400 manufacturers in the United States alone, among them Henry

Mike Francisco, a member of a karate club in Chicago, gives an excellent example of his art during demonstration in 1968.

Ford, the Wright brothers, Glenn Curtiss and Charles Duryea. But cycling suffered its setbacks. In the United States, cyclists were not given the right of way and often were crowded off the road by horse-drawn carriages and motor cars. They even were banned from New York City's Central Park when officials deemed them an eyesore and a public menace. Today, those same winding paths are for the exclusive use of cyclists on weekends and some weekday nights. Indeed, across America local governments have established bicycle paths or trails for the protection and pleasure of pedal pushers. Now ecologists consider the automobile the menace and are promoting bicycling as the mode of short distance travel.

The wheel, one of man's earliest practical inventions, was an offshoot of the sphere. Man probably was not long on this earth when he discovered the pleasure of kicking a sphere into a hole, striking it with a stick or hurling it through the air. Not only did it provide him with pleasure, it was a physical outlet for pent-up emotions and excess energy.

Some of the early balls were made of soft leather—or in the case of the Egyptians, fine linen—and were stuffed with reed, straw, earth, grain or cornhusks.

Football was known to exist in 2nd century China, of course not with the equipment nor the rules known today. Modern-day fans may talk about the sport's brutality or refer to an approaching game as one in which heads will roll. For primitive man that was no figure of speech. Heads did roll. Some races used the severed heads of their enemies for sport.

While football and baseball are heralded as the great American sports, basketball is the only major sport invented in the United States, and field hockey, which barely warrants a glance by today's sportsmen, is more American than most sports. It was a common game among the American Indians—the Vichita, Sioux, Nebraska tribes—who played without benefit of protective garb.

More popular among America's active youths—and spectators—is ice hockey, which came to us from Canada. There's barely a frozen pond or creek or stream or lake that avoids the scars of sticks and skates as neighborhood youths skirmish for victory in a game described as an offshoot of shinty—a game in which broomsticks were used to push stones across the ice.

Gaining in popularity in this country is soccer, the basic source of rugby and American football. Outside the United States it is the world's most popular sport and fosters a frenzy unmatched by any American sports spectacle. But the amateur is attracted to it because it is less expensive to equip, less injurious and easier to organize than football. And it provides a full 60 minutes of action for the athlete who would see only 15 minutes of play in football or be up at bat once an hour in baseball. According to one unofficial estimate amateur soccer enthusiasts have increased five-fold in less than five years to 250,000.

The fancy for the stick, found in hockey and baseball, also brought croquet and golf. Legend has it that a shepherd in Scotland passed the hours by whacking pebbles into a rabbit hole with his crook—on what now is the Royal and Ancient Golf Club of St. Andrews. Although golf was played during the Revolutionary War it didn't take on its popular aspects in America until the late 19th century.

Ladies took to the links, much to the duffers' dismay, with the demise of croquet. Croquet came to this country from Britain about the same time as golf arrived but the mallet and wicket never provided the fervor that the putter and pin did. In Britain, though, it was the national pastime of the 1850s—with championships held annually at Wimbledon. But lawn tennis took over the famed green and croquet was relegated to the back garden.

Tennis is even newer to this country than bicycling—being introduced in 1874 by Mary Ewing Outerbridge, an American vacationing in Bermuda where the game already was in vogue. So enchanted was she with it that she brought back to her Staten Island home all the necessary equipment. Soon after, the first courts cropped up. Like most new sports it was originally a game for the wealthy and it took years for the number of public courts to outnumber those behind gates of exclusive clubs and private estates.

Less demanding physically and financially is badminton which was brought to this country by soldiers stationed in England during World War I. The game, which substitutes a feathered shuttlecock, or bird, for a ball got its name in 1870 from the Duke of Beaufort's estate, Badminton, in Gloucestershire, England. It was there that the game first received recognition when it was played by the duke and several of his aristocratic friends.

Another less expensive and less demanding derivative of tennis is table tennis, also called Ping Pong when that name was copyrighted by an American manufacturer. The game is played with a hand paddle and hollow celluloid ball on a table divided by a low net. Originally it was a parlor pastime in Europe attracting such nobility as Princess Elizabeth, Nehru and King Farouk. It since has moved into the basement or family room of many an American home and is a staple of billiard halls.

Legend has it that a 16th century British pawnbroker, William Kew, invented billiards but it was the Spanish who brought it to America—to St. Augustine, Fla.—as early as 1565. No matter who first played it, it is believed to have been developed from early lawn bowling, then adapted to an indoor table.

The early days of "alley" bowling held all the evil connotations that smoky billiard halls, filled with hustlers, had later. In the 19th century, American bowling—played with nine pins—was a big gambling game and was in such disfavor that it was outlawed in many areas. Connecticut specifically outlawed nine-pin bowling. But the ban said nothing about 10 pins so another was added and the game was back in business. It ranks among the most popular of leisure sports for the entire family. Its stature was improved with its vocabulary. Bowling establishments are called bowling centers, alleys are called lanes, gutters are now channels, and pits, receptacles. While there are bars for imbibing, there are also nurseries for babies.

Sports—whether it's weekend camping in the woods, kite-flying in the meadow or playing frisbee at the beach—are so much a part of America that they probably are second only to the weather as a topic of idle conversation. The fisherman's tale of the one that got away, the hunter's brush with death, the duffer's day sans his scorecard, the yachtsman's ideal weekend sail, the bowler's perfect game are ever as important as how the Los Angeles Rams won last Sunday, how the Philadelphia 76ers were outrebounded under the baskets, or who's going to win the National League baseball pennant.

It's the diversion of the weekend sportsman from which were derived such phrases as "that's the name of the game," "be a good sport," "riding the crest of the waves," "that's not cricket," "spoilsport." The pros have rules all their own.

Eyes fixed firmly at his target, bowler Billy Hardwick shows how it's done on the bowling alleys. He won seven tournaments and $64,160 on the pro bowling tour in 1969.

chapter 17

BOWLING

A Long Jump from the German Kegel

by Tom Saladino

Tom Saladino, 33, was a teletype operator with *The AP* for seven years before switching to the New York sports department in February 1967. He has covered a variety of sports, specializing in track and field. Intent on a writing career, he took a one-year course in journalism, read numerous books on the subject and worked for a period on the *Nyack (N.Y.) News*.

Bowling has come a long way since its discovery in ancient Germany centuries ago when it was part of a religious ceremony.

It can still be considered "religion" to nearly eight million men, women and children who participate in this sport, game or recreation in the United States alone.

And professional bowling offered prize money in 1971 totaling nearly $2,000,-000 on the Professional Bowlers Association tour.

The PBA closely parallels the Professional Golfers Association in making a tour of the country and since 1962 the PBA events have been televised nationally, adding to the sport's exposure and revenues.

The PBA was organized in 1959. In 1971, the Akron, Ohio, based organization numbered virtually every top-ranking star of America's biggest participation sport.

One of the earliest stars during the 1950s was Don Carter, whom many credit with giving the game its push much the same as Arnold Palmer did for golf.

Other stars included Dick Weber, Billy Welu, Harry Smith, Ray Bluth and veterans Buzz Fazio and Steve Nagy.

The first tournament tour consisted of three tourneys in 1959 with prize money totaling $47,000. In 1960, the number grew to seven tournaments with prize money of $150,000 and by 1961 it jumped to 11 and $250,000.

In 1963 the PBA visited 38 cities, including stops in Montreal, Canada and San Juan, Puerto Rico, with prize money climbing to nearly $800,000. Since then the tour has concentrated on a flexible 33–35 city tour, with side tourneys in such places as Japan, Venezuela and Hawaii.

Thanks to Eddie Elias, an Akron attorney and Cleveland producer, pro bowling rose to the zenith as he negotiated with the television networks for such shows as "Jackpot Bowling," "Make that Spare," the BPAA All-Star and "Bestball Classic."

New stars have emerged including Jim Stefanich of Joliet, Ill., who won six championships and set a one-year official earnings mark of $67,375 in 1968. Another youngster, Billy Hardwick of Louisville, Ky., won seven tournaments and $64,160 in 1969.

The top money winner in 1970 was Mike McGrath of El Cerrito, Calif., who captured $51,149.

With the emergence of professional bowling came problems for the American Bowling Congress, which runs a 79-day tournament annually with entry lists as high as 6,238 teams.

Grumblings were heard to separate the superstars such as Carter, Welu, Bluth from everyone else in the ABC tournament.

The solution came in the form of an amendment to the ABC constitution in April of 1960 in Toledo, Ohio, with the forming of the ABC classic division and the marathon tournament.

The ABC, during the 1960s, solved virtually all of bowling's problems by forming the senior and collegiate divisions and assuming co-sponsorship and

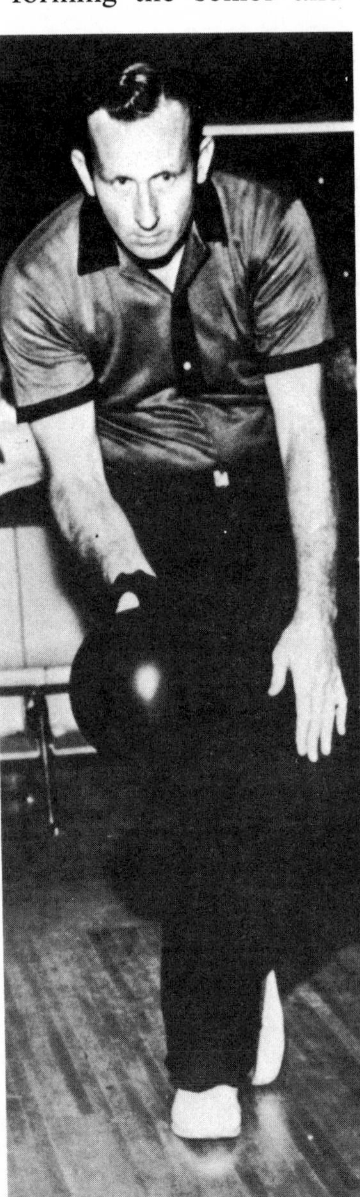

This sequence shows Don Carter, one of bowling's greatest strike artists, in action.

management of the American Junior Bowling Congress and the Woman's International Bowling Congress.

A significant step was in offering membership for the first time to bowlers competing in sanctioned and unsanctioned leagues alike. Earlier it had become optional to sanction team tourneys after years in which ABC members were not permitted to bowl in team tournaments unless they were sanctioned.

ABC membership peaked at nearly five million male members in 1964 but remains constant at well above four million today. WIBC membership is at 2.9 million now.

In 1961, ABC was granted a United States membership in the Fédération Internationale des Quilleurs, an international tournament with teams competing from all over the world. In 1963 the U.S. teams were comprised of eligible (non-professional) champions from the Regular division of the annual ABC tournament. The championships have been held in Guatemala, Venezuela, Sweden and Puerto Rico.

When no FIQ competition was scheduled, the ABC champions bowled in Canada-U.S.A. Friendship matches. In each international event, champions and high finishers from the WIBC tournament comprised the U.S. women's team. The representatives to international tourneys are picked from the All-Events Division of the ABC Intercollegiate championships.

The 1960s are credited with putting bowling over the top. Bowling centers flourished. Bowling emporiums sprouted up everywhere with the casualness of backyard barbecues. Husbands, wives, girls and their boy friends alike were rushing to bowl. Tenpins was in. Never had the American recreational scene been witness to such a phenomenon.

Men, women and children were bowling at least once a week in sanctioned leagues in league competition for periods of four to five months to as many as nine and 10 months solid.

Automation, architecture, air conditioning, the nursery, modern decor, parking lots and mixed leagues contributed to the boom.

What made the 1960s different and perhaps more exciting was that sophistication came into the game, including the refining of professionalism, the development of international competition and the last of the marathon performers.

Network television brought many of the influences to bear that in the case of pro football, baseball, basketball and golf made millionaires of athletes who used to be happy playing for the love of the game and whatever bread they could scrape together on the side.

The TV exposure made Dick Weber a household word in the '60s. Weber could look back on a 10-year period that few bowlers will ever equal. During those 120 months, he pushed his tournament prize earnings beyond the $400,000 mark. His closest pursuer was Ray Bluth, with slightly more than $250,000. Weber traveled around the world, bowling, instructing and speaking. He even launched his son on the pro bowling tour to become the first active father-son combination.

Don Carter won the ABC Masters title in 1962 and captured the All-Star tournament four times in the 1950s. Welu won it a like number of times in the 1960s—but Carter continued his mastery in the World's Invitational, winning the first three titles in 1950–51–52.

Jim Stefanich turned pro midway in the 1960s and produced a devastating effect on the play-for-pay circuit.

He won three PBA titles in 1967, then won five the following year and set his tournament earnings record. He was voted Bowler of the Year for 1968. As the decade ran out, however, the Joliet, Ill., wonder boy had leveled off and his fellow pros were tabbing Billy Hardwick as "Mr. Bowling" of the '70s. At 27, Hardwick had already won 16 PBA titles, two Bowler of the Year Awards, an All-Star championship and three bowling All-America first team berths.

Hardwick's earnings of $64,160 in 1969 were second to Stefanich's record and moved him into third place on the lifetime earnings chart.

In the amateur field, Les Zikes would probably be considered the amateur bowler of the decade. A teammate of Stefanich on the 1963 ABC champion Old Fitzgerald team of Chicago, he won the FIQ world all-events title in 1963, repeated as American zone champion in 1964 in Venezuela and starred on the U.S. team in the 1967 world tournament in Sweden. He also won titles in the Tournament of Americas and was the first to win ABC tournament championships three years running. He turned pro in 1968 and won his first tour title in the summer of 1969.

The single most explosive scoring feat of the decade was probably the 876 three-game series by Carl Wilsing of Sheboygan, Wis.

The 56-year-old machinist, who gave up the game for 13 years "because my nerves got the best of me," came within 11 pins of unseating Allie Brandt as the all-time king of league scorers. Wilsing put together games of 298, 300 and 278 in 1939, 27 years before Brandt rolled his series.

According to statistics by the Bowling Congress, their four million members averaged 153. Only 2 per cent were found to average 185 or better while Elvin Mesger of St. Louis and Sullivan, Mo., ran his record total of ABC approved 300 games to 22 and his total 800 series to 16.

The largest bowling center in the Western Hemisphere, Willow Grove Park in suburban Philadelphia, came into existence with 116 lanes but a Japanese corporation made that achievement pale by comparison, opening a center in Tokyo with 252 lanes.

The typical woman member of the WIBC averages 132 with the highest season average a 219 by Mildred Martorella of Rochester, N.Y., in 1967–68. There have been 175 perfect games in WIBC-sanctioned competition, the first by Mrs. Charles Fahning of Buffalo, N.Y., in 1929–30. Beverly Ortner of Tucson, Ariz., holds the three-game series record with an 818 in October of 1968. She also holds the four-game record of 1005.

Nearly half a million women share in $4 million in prizes, competing in the Championship Tournament of the Women's International Bowling Congress. The annual event, first held in 1916, has three average divisions so that entrants compete against others of similar bowling skills. The largest and richest WIBC tourney was held in Rochester, N.Y., in 1967 when 6,094 five-woman teams competed for $296,760 in prizes.

There are said to be more than 200,000,000 bowlers throughout the world.

The beginning of the sport is shrouded in mystery but first mention was made in the 19th century by William Pehle, a German.

Pehle relates that early-day Germans carried a club or pin, called a kegel.

It was used for any purpose and a German was never without one. He used it to strengthen his forearms or in friendly distance-throwing contests. If he were forced to fight, he used his kegel. The weapon was used in crude fencing matches and as a hammer.

In the ancient chronicles of Paderborn (Germany) it is revealed that ecclesiastics called upon the German and his kegel to prove that he was leading an honorable life. The old churches had cloisters with long runways, somewhat like the modern bowling alley.

When the time came for testing a German's religious status, the clerics required that he place his kegel topside up at the end of the runway. The parishioner was then given a reasonably round stone to roll. If he hit the kegel it proved he was leading a chaste life. If he missed he had to return periodically for further tests. The practice was abandoned in the 5th century. The clerics also carried kegels and in their spare time would practice rolling the stones at the kegels, thus the first bowling contests were started.

Soon larger stones were used and three pins were used by some and as many as 17 by others. Wooden balls then came into being, replacing the stones. Definite rules were written.

Martin Luther, an avid bowler, experimented and became convinced that nine pins was the proper number and this was the standard set for Germany.

In the Middle Ages, bowling became almost universal and very popular in Germany. It was played at baptisms and country celebrations and was an important social happening. It was almost exclusively a rich man's game. In 1518 in Breslau, Germany, an ox was awarded to the winner of the bowling contest. The German government always recognized bowling, and alleys were laid out in army barracks and in state schools. Through the 17th century it spread into the lowlands of Europe and into Austria. The alleys, however, were made of beds of clay and cinders.

Bowling at pins was introduced to the United States by the Dutch. The exact date is not known. The first actual mention was made by Washington Irving in "Rip Van Winkle" (about 1818). Irving's nonchalance about bowling indicated it long had been a game in the New York area, gaining popularity in the East in 1835–1840. Then gamblers saw the possibilities of betting on the sport. The Connecticut Legislature banned the sport.

Honorable men were disconsolate over the ban and a member devised a plan for bowling at 10 pins, rather than nine, neatly circumventing the law which prohibited nine pins.

The 10-pin plan was plotted. Scoring rules were made up and an organization to create and supervise the 10-pin bowling game came into being with the American Bowling Congress in 1895.

Bowling alleys and balls were made to conform to regulations and in 1901 the ABC conducted its first national championship tournament in Chicago with total prize money of $1,592.

Seventy years later television had given bowling its national exposure and more than $2 million in prize money—a far cry from the ancient German religious ceremony.

These men all gained fame from their performances at pool or billiard tables. Top photo shows Willie Hoppe, right, and Welker Cochran. Below, top to bottom, are Willie Mosconi, Jim Caras and Edwin Rudolph.

chapter 18

BILLIARDS

From the Pool Hall to the Parlor

by Ted Meier

E. Phillips Oppenheim was a famed English novelist noted for his spy melodramas.

In *The Great Impersonation,* published in January 1920, Oppenheim had his leading character, Sir Everand Dominey (or was it Baron Leopold von Ragastein?), say to a friend in the billiard room at Dominey Hall:

"Set them up and I will show you how I made a living for two months at Johannesburg."

The fictional incident illustrated vividly the bizarre background of the game of billiards and its various offshoots, such as pocket billiards.

In the hundreds of years the game has been played, it gained worldwide acceptance as a game of skill. It gained a place of honor in the homes of the best families.

Noted players, such as Willie Hoppe, performed before the President of the United States, and Walter Lindrum of Australia before King George V and Queen Mary at Buckingham Palace in 1931. Hoppe gave his exhibition before President Taft in the White House in 1911.

At the same time that the game gained acceptance in high circles, so-called "pool sharks" were looked down on by some who associated the sport with disreputable persons.

Oddly, the game enjoyed a revival in the 1960s after a motion picture, *The Hustler,* in which Jackie Gleason and Paul Newman portrayed the role of pool sharks. Exhibitions of trick shots on television also helped.

Pool tables also were given as prizes on afternoon TV quiz shows.

Pool tables, usually 4½-feet wide by 9-feet long and standing 31 to 32 inches above the floor, pertain usually to the game of pocket billiards which developed from the more difficult game of billiards.

The latter is played with a cue ball and two balls on a table without pockets. It is played with variations such as the three-cushion game in which the cue ball must contact three or more cushions as well as the two object balls.

In pocket billiards, there are six pockets on the table, two at each end and two in the middle. In addition to the cue ball there are 15 numbered balls. Points are scored by driving the object balls into any of the six pockets. There are variations of this, with the player calling the number of the ball he intends to put into a certain pocket.

In snooker, a variation of pocket billiards, there are 21 balls, 15 red and six colored, with a cue ball. The player alternates between the red balls, for which he does not have to call any particular pocket, and the colored balls for which he must designate a pocket. When all the red balls are gone, the remaining colored ones must be taken in numerical order.

Hoppe was one of the sports celebrities of the Golden Twenties, with Babe Ruth in baseball, Bobby Jones in golf, Jack Dempsey in boxing, and jockey Earl Sande in horse racing. He dominated billiards for 46 years, from his first title in 1906, to his retirement in 1952.

Later he gave exhibitions, his last one in Chicago, two years before his death in Miami, Fla., Feb. 1, 1959 at the age of 71.

William Frederick Hoppe was his full name, but he was known the world over as just plain "Willie" from the time he showed the home town boys at Cornwall-on-Hudson, N.Y., how to control the ivory balls in the rear of his father's barber shop.

Willie began his career by touring dirty, smoke-filled pool rooms of bygone days.

Yet, during his half century in the game, he so dignified the sport that metropolitan opera stars, ranking members of world society, kings and princes gathered to watch his wizardry with a cue.

Willie beat such established stars as Ora Morningstar and Tom Gallagher, but he first attracted worldwide attention and became the "Boy Wonder" when he defeated the great Maurice Vigneaux of France for the 18.1 balkline championship in 1906 at the age of 18.

In 18.1 balkline, the numbers refer to the distance in inches of the balklines from the rails. Anchor squares are marked out where the balklines meet the rails. Only one carom can be made in a balk area or anchor area before the balls are driven out to another area.

Vigneaux had held the world championship in balkline billiards for 25 years against all comers before his meeting at 73 years of age with the teen-aged American.

The match was held in the Palace Hotel in Paris and the partisan French audience offered odds as high as 7-to-1 against Hoppe. The odds rose to 15–1 after the first day in which Vigneaux led 130–48.

Charles M. Schwab, an American steel tycoon of the era, was in the audience and the story goes that he was persuaded "not to sell the American short." He was reported to have covered all bets and, after Hoppe upset the renowned Frenchman for the world title on the third day, he presented Hoppe with $50,000.

Hoppe ruled the balkline competition for decades, including the seldom played and difficult 71.2 in 1938, before turning to three cushions in which he won the world title in 1940 and retained it in 1941 and 1942 against his closest rivals, Welker Cochran and young Jake Schaefer.

Hoppe trained for billiard matches like a prize fighter. He did several miles of road work a day, got plenty of sleep and watched his diet. He once estimated that he had played or practiced billiards four hours a day for 50 years.

Ralph Greenleaf, who came along in the late 1920s, was the first of the champions in pocket billiards. Tall and handsome, he was a glamorous figure with a flair for showmanship. He once played the Palace on Broadway during the old vaudeville days with a routine of trick shots that earned him $2,000 a week.

Greenleaf kept his world title for years against such contenders as Erwin Rudolph, Andrew Ponzi, Onofrio Lauri and the youthful Irving Crane and Willie Mosconi.

How well Greenleaf stood up under pressure was illustrated in one tournament in which, at 125 points per game, he missed only nine called balls, nine of 1,250.

Mosconi succeeded Greenleaf as pocket billiard champion, lost it to Jimmy Caras and Irving Crane, regained it, then retired from tournament competition in 1957. He then helped to improve the image of the game with exhibitions.

In an exhibition at Springfield, Ohio, in 1954, Mosconi set a world record by running off 526 balls in a row. In a tournament game against Jimmy Moore at Kingston, N.C., on April 17, 1956, Mosconi ran out the 150 without a break to win the game 150–0.

Charlie Peterson, who toured the country for many years, was perhaps the most outstanding trick shot artist. "Show me a shot I can't make" was his famous cry and there was none he didn't pull off.

Steve Mizerak of Carteret, N.J., won the 1970 U.S. Open championship in pocket billiards with a 150–85 victory over Luther Lassiter, the defending champion from Elizabeth City, N.C.

Dorothy Wise, 55-year-old grandmother from San Francisco, won the women's title for the second straight year.

The origin of billiards is obscure. One version is that it descended from the game of lawn bowls when the players were forced inside because of rain. The first concrete evidence of the games appeared in France in the 15th century. The Spaniards brought the first billiard table to America in 1565.

The first championship game in the United States was held in Detroit in 1859. Six years later, there occurred perhaps the most celebrated incident showing the need of steady nerves in the game.

Louis Fox was playing John Derry for a $1,000 side bet in Rochester, N.Y.

Reports of the incident say a fly landed on Fox's cue ball. Fox, who had a comfortable lead, chased it away, but the fly returned and kept making dives at the cue ball. Fox was upset and missed his shot when the fly finally was shooed away for good. Derry then ran out the game to win.

Fox was said to have rushed out of Washington Hall, where the match was held, in a distraught condition. His body was found floating in a stream nearby a few days later.

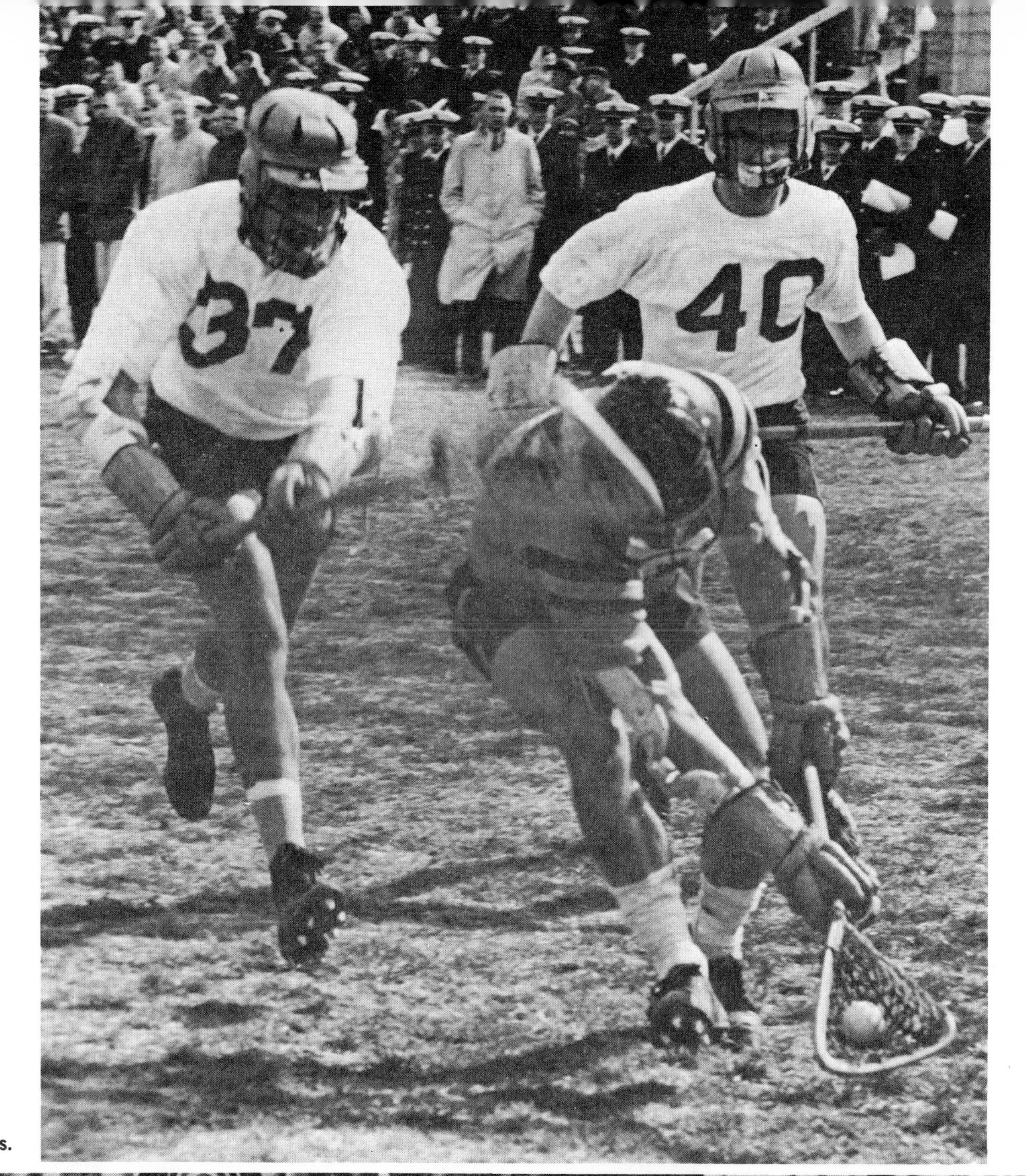

Although played primarily in colleges in the United States, lacrosse is an international game. Top, a Navy player scoops up the ball as two Rutgers players converge on him. Bottom, the Australian International team scores against the Northern California All-Stars.

chapter 19

LACROSSE

A Cross of Indian and Canadian Blood

by Ken Rappoport

Ken Rappoport, 36, has been a staffer of *The Associated Press* for eight years, working as an editor in the Philadelphia bureau before moving to New York's sports department in 1968. A Rider College graduate, he started his journalism career in 1960 with the *Dorf Feature Service* in Newark, N.J., writing sports and news stories for the *Newark Star Ledger*. He also was a general assignment reporter for the *Doylestown (Pa.) Intelligencer* for 2 1/2 years.

The sun glowered hot coal-crimson on the rooftops near Memorial Stadium at Annapolis, Md., and dipped away in a dirty haze. Symbolic near-dark dropped on the 16,000 sour and frustrated Midshipmen watching the annual Army-Navy lacrosse war.

Free-wheeling Army had crushed the Navy spirit all through that long, hot spring day—last of the regular lacrosse season—and left no doubt who was No. 1.

Final: Army 14, Navy 4.

With the sun's fast fade-out sailed Navy's fierce hope of another national championship—and, conversely, landed Army in the winner's circle.

The runaway Cadet victory gave Army a share of the glory. Army and perennial front-runner Johns Hopkins were soon thereafter selected winners of the Wingate Trophy, symbolic of national lacrosse supremacy.

It was an old story. Army, Johns Hopkins and Navy had shared the spotlight for years along with Maryland. Since 1954, one of the so-called "Big Four" of college lacrosse had either won or shared the national title.

And since 1881, when the trophy was first awarded to Harvard, Johns Hopkins had finished on top 22 times.

Hopkins' modern-day legend is due in no small part to a Goliath of the lacrosse coaching field, Bob Scott, the Blue Jays' crafty, boyishly handsome leader. Scott led the school to four national championships and was named coach of the year in 1965 and 1968.

"Great strides are being made in the sport," Scott said. "And here's great news—we have scheduled Navy in the Houston Astrodome. That's an inroad into Texas."

The Astrodome is a stylish showcase for this graceful sport, whose exponents will tell you combines the best aspects of all others: the big play, the ball whipping into the goal at 90 miles an hour, the body contact, the bruises, and the constant liquid movement.

Texas became the last outpost of the sport that now had swung full circle through the United States. East Coast-oriented, it spilled over into Midwest and Far West pockets.

Teams in the Midwest such as Ohio University, Ohio State, Michigan and Notre Dame got into the picture. Other strong-armed latecomers come from the Denver, Colo., area, notably Air Force. In California, they play a North-South All-Star game, a carbon copy of a classic born and nurtured in the East.

In the 1960s, they were developing lacrosse skills on the high school level in Long Island, N.Y., said to be the most concentrated talent of that age group in the country.

"Lacrosse has the roughness and body contact of football, the finesse of basketball with the individual dodges and set plays and the speed and color of ice hockey," said Scott. "People like to see the high-scoring games—usually 15 or 20 goals are scored. When it's played well, it's as exciting a spectator sport as there is."

This national fever for lacrosse pleases the Johns Hopkins coach immensely—for he typifies the hungry spirit of a sport born in bloodshed.

A Jesuit missionary, a bishop's insignia and an Indian bloodbath—these were the illogical components of lacrosse, probably the fastest sport on foot, and one of the most savagely rhapsodic from bloody birth to the civilized, mercurial combat of modern day warriors.

It's been called the national pastime of Canada, a blend of Indian and Icelandic legend and an educational hypo to youngsters in England's schools. Lacrosse has leaped continents, prompted euphorious acclaim from royalty and inspired American collegians.

A French cleric, Pierre François Xavier de Charlevoix, is said by some authorities to have chosen the name. Arriving in Quebec, Canada, to convert the natives to Christianity, he saw the Algonquin Indians playing a game called baggataway in 1705. He renamed it after a hooked stick with which the Indians tried to catch the ball and propel it toward the goal. The stick looked very much like a bishop's crosier, thus "lacrosse."

The game the Indians played is strikingly similar to the modern version, but some have suggested it was adopted from early Norse settlers, who brought it to Canada from Iceland. The Norse called their game knattleker.

One of the most memorable, and infamous, lacrosse games took place after the French and Indian War in 1763, just outside the British post, Ft. Michilimackinac in Canada. The game had gone only an hour, when on a prearranged signal, the ball was tossed into the fort—a ruse to get the British to open the gates.

At that moment, the Indians collected weapons from their squaws, who were on the sidelines, and rushed inside the fort to massacre the British troops.

Despite this unpleasant association, lacrosse continued to flourish. The field had to be proportioned more tightly and the game changed from a wild, disorderly affair involving literally thousands of Indians into a neatly arranged package with precise boundaries. By the 1840s, there were matches between the Indians and French Canadians.

In 1865, the Montreal Lacrosse Club was formed and the sport took a more definitive, formal shape. The game gained royal acclaim when the Prince of Wales watched a match between the Indians and Canadians in 1861. In 1867, Indians and Canadians played at Windsor Castle before Queen Victoria, who recorded the event in her journal:

"I gave both the Canadians and the Indians, each, one of my signed photographs. The game was very pretty to watch."

Dr. George W. Beers, a Montreal dentist, helped formalize the sport. Due to his work, the first definitive rules were drafted and in 1867, a convention of lacrosse aficionados formed the National Lacrosse Association. The same year, Parliament formally adopted lacrosse as Canada's national game.

Lacrosse boomed beyond Canada. The United States took the plunge in 1868, pioneered by the Mohawk Club of Troy, N.Y. It became popular in England, especially welcomed by school masters who claimed that the skill, courage and perseverance involved helped build better students.

It landed in American colleges and manufactured instant heroes for the coeds. The game was a natural, refined from its bloodthirsty beginnings, and the college crowd cheered with each graceful flick of the lacrosse stick and the jet-propelled ride of the ball.

In the latter part of the 19th century, the United States Intercollegiate Lacrosse Association actively organized and promoted the game. The association picked an annual All-American team and each year awarded the Wingate Trophy.

A traditional part of the sport has been the annual All-Star game between the North and South, started in 1940. Jimmy Brown, the pro football great from Syracuse, was one of the North All-Stars.

"He helped make a shambles of the game, he was so darn good," recalled Avery Blake, the former Penn coach now president of the Lacrosse Hall of Fame in Baltimore. "Brown was big and powerful enough to control a game all by himself. He was something."

Another pro football star, John Mackey of the Baltimore Colts, also was a big lacrosse man on campus at Syracuse. There were Lighthorse Harry Wilson and Bill Carpenter, the Lonesome End, who made names playing football at Army—but also brought stunning success to the Cadets' powerhouse lacrosse teams.

Jim Thorpe, an athlete for all seasons, put Carlisle on the map with his formidable talents—including his Herculean exploits on the lacrosse field.

Families have been a part of the lacrosse tradition. Brothers Doug and Jack Turnbull helped trigger a cache of championship gold at Johns Hopkins. Steve and Ken Dauses played Hofstra onto the front sports page. And Blake himself had a hand-me-down star in his son, Avery "Bunky" Blake, a three-time All-American at Swarthmore.

The East has produced a stellar field of lacrosse luminaries, some of whom went into club play after graduation from college: Mack Ogilbie, Carl Camulevitch, Jimmy Lewis and Bill Bilderback of Navy . . . Jim Adams of Pennsylvania . . . Joe Cowan of Johns Hopkins.

"The balance of power in the East has been maintained because it's been predominately an Eastern sport for years," explained Al Twitchell, the one-time Rutgers coach and Hall of Famer. "But it might be different with the submergence of the USILA into the National Collegiate Athletic Association."

Entering the 1970s, there was a modern lacrosse movement afoot, Twitchell said—an unprecedented national structure under NCAA auspices. Blake and Twitchell became the cheerleaders of this mod revolution. The NCAA, for the first time, agreed to decide a national champion through a system of round-robin playoffs among the nation's top regional teams.

Prior to the new setup, the national champion had been determined by a USILA committee judging comparative records.

Although the college scene predominated and produced the most ardent following, a professional league once surfaced—in the early 1930s—but didn't last too long.

"Baltimore was the only team, I think, that got paid," Blake said.

Fans dedicated to the game of lacrosse watch from the stands at College Park, Md., as Maryland and Johns Hopkins play a game won by Maryland, 9-5, in 1967. Note players wear helmets with "bird cages" and heavy gloves. Some wear shoulder pads under their light jerseys.

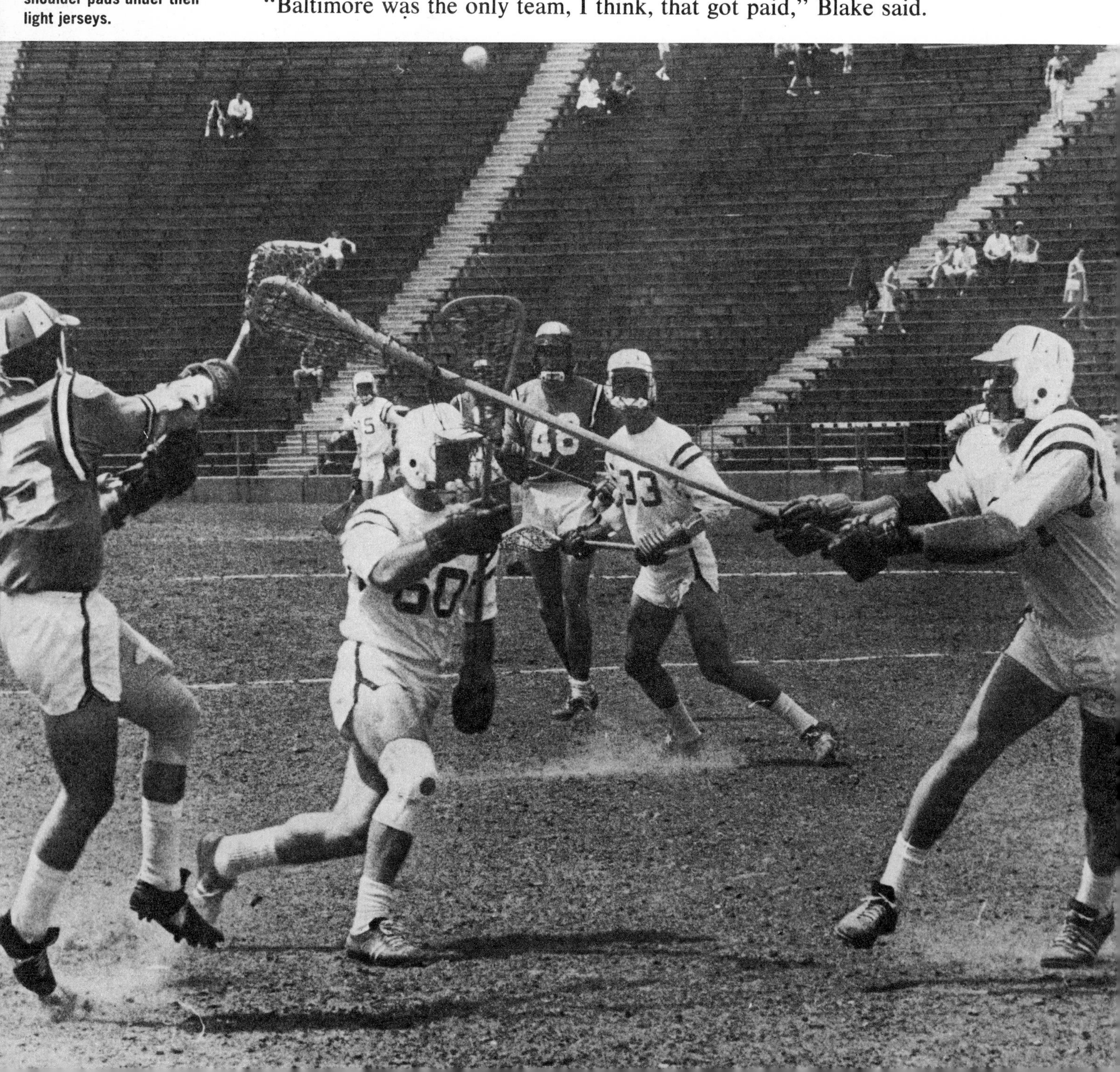

The girls, no strangers to competitive sports, go at it at lacrosse, too. Exhibiting little if any reluctance to rough play, a West Australia team member lunges across shoulder of a Victoria player to reach the ball in game in Perth in 1965.

The league, including teams in Baltimore, New York and Boston, started on a shoestring—and wound up without its collective shirt.

College-sponsored club lacrosse produced an annual North-South game every spring. The Long Island Lacrosse Club and Mount Washington, a Southern power, have dominated in recent years.

There were more than 200 colleges playing the sport on one level or another in 1970—a yardstick of its popularity.

And the tradition-breaking NCAA system to decide a national champion with a series promised greater growth for the exciting game of the Indians.

D. Lee Braun, top, was 1950's top professional shooter when he broke 96 of 100 targets in the Grand American Handicap. Mick Egan, bottom, was only 14 years old when he won the same title in 1954.

chapter 20

TRAPSHOOTING

A Shotgun and Flying Discs

by Ed Schuyler Jr.

For nine days beginning with the third week in August each year, the town of Vandalia, Ohio, is to one group of sportsmen what Louisville is to horse racing fans, what Indianapolis is to car racing buffs and what Green Bay is to football traditionalists.

Vandalia for those nine days is the site of the Grand American Tournament—the World Series of trapshooting.

During those nine days some 4,200 shooters—men, women and children—fire about $2^1/_4$ million shells at clay targets sprung from the 50-trap, mile-long firing line on the grounds of the Amateur Trapshooting Association.

They don't shoot alone. There's a daily crowd of from 18,000 to 22,000 on hand.

They don't just shoot for fun either. There are various handicap, doubles, juniors and women's championships, with the Grand American Handicap the biggest prize of all and the biggest the sport has to offer.

And there is money—a total of $494,000 in cash and $40,000 in sterling silver in 1970.

That is, there is money for the amateurs. The professionals, known as industry representatives—those who represent gun and shell companies—aren't eligible for prize money.

This unique arrangement of prize money for amateurs and none for pros came into effect after the American Trapshooting Association, which became the sport's governing body in 1900, was changed to the Amateur Trapshooting Association in 1923.

The American Trapshooting Association was controlled by makers of guns and ammunition. Then it was decided to make the association strictly a sports organization by divorcing itself from subsidies.

The pros have a place in trapshooting but strictly as representatives of their sponsors who have no control over the various tournaments.

Trapshooting can trace its origins to England while skeet shooting is strictly an American-invented sport.

The major difference between the two is that a skeet shooter calls for, by moving stations, changes in the angles at which the clay targets are fired while in trapshooting the angle of a target is not known until the trap is sprung.

Trapshooting got its beginning in 19th century England when commoners were shut off from the game preserves by the wealthy class.

Thus many hunters were forced to find a substitute sport. In 1832 a shooting club known as the High Hats was formed. It was called High Hats because members would place live birds under their hats, then, at a signal, grab their hats, put them back on their heads and then shoot at the birds.

This practice soon cut into the supply of birds, and a glass ball released from a trap was hit upon as a substitute.

The glass ball was followed, in the 1860s, by the first type of clay pigeon. Then, in the 1880s an Englishman named McCaskey developed a target made of a mixture of river silt and pitch which became known as the Blue Rock. The target was further perfected in 1885 by Walter Ligowski of Cincinnati.

Trapshooting had been introduced into the United States in the late 1870s, and enthusiasm over the sport had risen to such a degree by the early 1880s that the Interstate Association of Trapshooters was formed and the group purchased land on Long Island.

The American Trapshooting Association succeeded the Interstate in 1900 and was the governing body in this country until the Amateur Trapshooting Association took over 23 years later.

The Amateur Trapshooting Association and its Hall of Fame, opened in 1969, are housed in magnificent quarters in Vandalia. From this spot are governed the activities of more than 50,000 members.

So popular has trapshooting become in the United States that the ATA's membership shows a 20 per cent growth per year.

The three big tournaments in American trapshooting are the Ohio State Shoot which sees about 1,450 shooters competing each day, usually in the second week in June; the Gold West Grand at Reno, Nev., in the first week of May, and the Grand American.

The most prestigious title at the prestigious Grand American is that of Grand American Handicap champion.

Depending on the shooter's ability, in the Grand American Handicap, he shoots at 100 targets from 18 to 27 yards.

The 1970 Grand American Handicap winner, and therefore one of the top shooters anywhere, was Charles Harvey of Oskaloosa, Iowa.

Some past Grand American Handicap winners are proof that youth is no drawback to becoming a man in trapshooting. Daniel Paulter of Alden, N.Y., won the title in 1965 when he was about 15, and Nick Egan of Bronxville, N.Y., won the championship in 1954 at the age of 14. Each hit 99 of 100 targets from 20 yards.

Some others who gained renown in trapshooting were Dan Oilich of Reno, a North American Clay Target champion; Larry Gravestock of Wichita Falls, Tex., and Hiram Bradley. Bradley set the long-run record in 1968 by breaking 1,439 consecutive targets from the Ohio State Shoot in June to the Grand American in August.

Two of the top women shooters have been Loral I. Delaney of Anoka, Minn., and Punkin Flock of Miami.

Although 80 years old, in 1970 Carl Stutman of Peoria, Ill., still remained as one of the great skeet shooters. He was the world champion senior and in his career won a total of 17 world titles in 10 different years.

Skeet got its start in 1910 and was known as Round the Clock Shooting, the name being derived from the various stations taken by the shooters.

At the Glen Rock Kennels grounds in Andover, Mass., a small group of upland gunners used clay targets and traps to throw them as a means of obtaining wing shooting practice. The friendly rivalry among the men led to a definite program of competitive shooting which became skeet.

C. E. Davies, proprietor of the Glen Rock Kennels; his son Henry, and William H. Foster are credited with inventing skeet.

The sport is governed by the National Skeet Shooting Association, headquartered in Dallas.

Some of the great skeet shooters have been Hall of Famers Ann Hecker, Grant Ilseng and D. Lee Braun.

Dr. William Gilbert Grace of Gloucestershire (1848–1915), considered the greatest figure in cricket history, certainly looks the part. He scored a total of 54,904 runs.

chapter 21

CRICKET

Bewildering to Some with a Language All Its Own

by Geoffrey Miller

Most of the great sports have spread their wings and become worldwide. Cricket is an odd exception, for it has remained the peculiar property of England and the Commonwealth.

In England, Australia and the West Indies, when the test matches are in progress, people gobble up the cricket reports as avidly as they would read war dispatches or election results. The English, in their quiet way, pay more attention to the batting and bowling averages than to the Stock Exchange prices.

Other nations find cricket bewildering, with a language all its own. What are they to make of the batsman's strokes—square cuts, leg glances and off drives? Or the bowling deliveries, leg breaks and googlies; and those strange fielding positions—short leg, silly mid-off and the gully? Yet when the esoteric phrases have been stripped away, cricket is basically a simple game. The bowler pitches the ball and tries to hit the stumps or wickets; the batsman defends his stumps and tries to hit the ball and score runs.

Nobody really knows when the English began playing it, but it was certainly a long, long time ago because "cricket" is derived from the ancient Anglo-Saxon word "cryce," meaning a wooden stick. By the 16th century, Englishmen in every village were "playing cricket-a-wicket and making merry," to quote a commentator of the times.

In the second half of the 18th century, an age of unbridled gambling in England, it was the sport of the landed gentry, who assembled teams and challenged each other to matches for high stakes. "The Duke of Dorset's eleven against Lord Tankerville's eleven, for 1,000 guineas," said the sporting posters of the day. An element of social snobbery entered English cricket, and it took almost 200 years to get rid of it.

The Hambledon club, which flourished at that time, was the first to bring cricket honors to the common men of England. It remains the most famous cricket club of all time. It played on Broadhalfpenny Down in Hampshire and for 30 years challenged and defeated all comers, including an all-England team captained by the Duke of Dorset in an historic game in 1777. Nothing is to be seen on Broadhalfpenny Down today—just an oddly sloping field, ringed with trees, and a simple memorial stone in one corner. But the names of the Hambledon men are immortal—Richard Nyren, the captain; Aylward and Small, and Billy Beldham, known as "Silver Billy" because he played until his hair was white. Few sports can boast exponents whose fame has lived as long as theirs.

London became the center of cricket after the Marylebone Cricket Club (MCC) was founded in 1788. It played at Lord's, a ground constructed by Thomas Lord near Regent's Park, from 1813. The MCC became the rule-making body and Lord's is the game's headquarters.

Modern cricket history begins in the mid-19th century with the first inter-county games. The county clubs employed some professionals but their teams were still composed largely of the wealthy gentry. The County Championship—the basis of competitive cricket in England today, with 17 teams competing in three-day games—was inaugurated in 1873 and immediately Dr. William Gilbert Grace of Gloucestershire dominated the scene.

"W.G." (1848–1915) is the greatest figure in cricket history. Englishmen know his picture—a massive man with a profuse beard and a little colored cap—as well as Americans know the image of Abraham Lincoln. His feats were prodigious by all-time standards. He scored a total of 54,904 runs, including 126 centuries (innings of 100 runs or more). He opened the batting for England for 20 years. He scored a century in his first inter-county game, before his 16th birthday; and on his 56th birthday he scored 166 at Lord's. When he was 48, he scored 1,000 runs before the end of May, the first month of the English season, a rare feat achieved by only five other batsmen.

How would Grace have fared now, in the age of Gary Sobers? Some critics claim that amid the modern day wealth of professional talent, against improved techniques of defensive bowling and fielding, his wings would have been clipped. Others argue that he played on primitive, bumpy fields, and that on the smooth "pitches" prepared by modern scientific methods, he would have scored even more runs, not fewer. Nobody knows the answer, but it still provides a talking point for fans in the beer tent when rain stops the cricket—as it frequently does in the unpredictable English summer.

England began playing test matches against Australia in 1877, South Africa in 1888, the West Indies in 1928, New Zealand in 1930, India in 1932 and Pakistan in 1954.

Meanwhile, more and more professionals played on the county teams but the County Championship remained riddled by class distinction. Lord Hawke, who captained Yorkshire to six championship titles between 1893 and 1902, was reputed to have said: "God forbid that I should live to see professionals and amateurs using the same dressing room." (He died in 1938 and was spared the experience.) Lord Harris, pre-1914 captain of Kent, and Lord Tennyson, who led Hampshire in the 1920s, had less extreme views but were autocratic figures, addressed by their professionals as "Sir" or "Your Lordship."

Professionals were not entitled to have their initials printed before their surnames. The Hampshire team, as printed on official scorecards before 1914, included "Mr. C. B. Fry" and "Mead, C. P." Fry, one-time holder of the world broad jump record, was one of England's most gifted amateurs, famed for his batting style. Philip Mead, a professional, was one of only four batsmen to have scored more runs than W. G. Grace.

These class labels were unknown in the Commonwealth countries but took a long time to disappear in England. The MCC finally abolished all distinctions between pros and amateurs in 1962.

Between 1911 and 1929, England held an ace card in Jack Hobbs, shown here in 1922. He was rated by many as technically the most perfect cricket batsman of all time.

In recent years, South Africa and the West Indies have come into the reckoning for world supremacy, but for decades the classic encounters of cricket were the test matches between England and Australia. For nearly 90 years, the two countries have been playing each other for the "Ashes," the quaintest of all sporting trophies since they don't exist. It started as a joke. Australia came to England in 1882 and won, and some prankster had an obituary notice printed in a sports newspaper announcing the death of English cricket. The body, it said, was being cremated and the ashes taken to Australia. The two countries have been disputing the "Ashes" ever since, but it's all just a myth and no trophy changes hands.

The Australians have had a slight edge, winning 80 tests to England's 66. England was usually on top in the '80s and '90s, when W. G. Grace's bat was in full flow. Then, for a few years around the turn of the century, the Australians produced the elegant Victor Trumper and the tide flowed their way. Between 1911 and 1929, England held an ace card in Jack Hobbs, rated by many as technically the most perfect batsman of all time. Hobbs scored 12 centuries in tests against Australia and altogether in his career hit 197 centuries and 61,237 runs —both all-time world records.

In the '30s, the brilliant batting of Don Bradman swayed the series in favor of Australia. Bradman, with a hawklike eye and tremendous hitting power, once made 334 runs in a single day against England and finished his career with an incredible batting average of 99.94 per innings in test matches alone. By contrast, Walter Hammond, England's outstanding batsman in the same era, had a test average of 58.45.

Australia held the "Ashes" continuously from 1934 to 1953, helped by such great players as batsmen Stan McCabe and Neil Harvey and the devastating fast bowlers, Ray Lindwall and Keith Miller. The "Ashes" changed hands again when England finally buried its old traditions and appointed a professional, Len Hutton, as captain. This dour and patient batsman was a typical product of his county, Yorkshire, which has won the English Championship 31 times in 100 years. He led England to victory in two successive test series. Australia won the "Ashes" in 1958 under the captaincy of Richie Benaud and established a dominance that extended into the 1970s.

Hutton, in 1938, had scored 364 against Australia—a record for all test matches until Gary Sobers topped it with 365 not out for the West Indies against Pakistan in 1957. The West Indies emerged as a first class cricket power after World War II with a succession of dazzling batsmen—Everton Weekes, Frank Worrell (who died from leukemia in 1967), Clyde Walcott and Sobers. The West Indies twice conquered England in England, captained by Worrell in 1963 and Sobers in 1966. They made a historic tour of Australia in the winter of 1960–61 and played in a dramatic test match that ended in a tie—that is, with the runs total of the two teams dead level after two complete innings each. That result was unique in test history, and Australia was so excited it gave the West Indians a ticker-tape farewell through the streets of Sydney.

Cricket, one of the most peaceful of sports, has been involved in only two major international disputes.

In 1933 the England-Australia tradition was almost wrecked by a bitter row over the "leg theory" tactics of England's fast bowler Harold Larwood, who deliberately slung the ball down to a short length and made it rise into the batsman's body. The batsman's only protection was to fend it off to the leg side—that is, to his left (assuming he used a right-handed stance)—where Larwood had a ring of fieldsmen waiting to catch him out. The Australians lost the series and complained bitterly of intimidation. The quarrel was patched up two years later when they came to England and won back the "Ashes."

The other controversy was over racism and halted the test matches between England and South Africa after 80 years. Basil D'Oliveira, a South African-born mulatto who was barred from first class cricket in his own country, had emigrated to Britain and won a place in the English team. In 1968 D'Oliveira was selected for the team that was to visit South Africa for a series of test matches. The South African government ruled him unacceptable, and the MCC canceled the tour.

In 1970, the South Africans were due to visit England. The MCC was ready to forget the D'Oliveira incident and to let the tour go on, and it erected barbed wire barricades at Lord's to keep anti-apartheid demonstrators off the field. But the tour was canceled after intervention by the British government, which feared demonstrations might get out of hand.

The decision upset cricket officials. They had looked forward to a classic confrontation between England and South Africa, now reckoned the strongest batting team in the world with prolific runmakers in Grahame Pollock and Barry Richards.

In England, cricket has struggled in recent years to pay its way in the face of dwindling crowds. In a changing economy, fewer and fewer people had time to sit and watch three-day games during the week. In the late '60s, the MCC introduced one-day games on Sundays, with the accent on fast scoring, to supplement the County Championship and attract a new public and it revised an old rule that allowed stars from overseas to play for English county teams without qualifying by two years' residence.

Some of the outstanding players in the English Championship in 1970 were from overseas—Sobers, Rohan Kanhai and Clive Lloyd from the West Indies, Richards from South Africa, Graham McKenzie from Australia. It was a strange final twist to the story. England, which taught the Commonwealth to play cricket, had to import the best Commonwealth players to prop up the game at home.

Crowds filled the stands to watch England play Australia in this cricket match in England in 1953.

The running of the bulls in Pamplona is one of the most exciting aspects of the annual San Fermin Festival. Hundreds of men run ahead and after the bulls on their way from the stockyards to the arena in a mad race between man and beast.

chapter 22

BULLFIGHTING

The Latins Love It

by Fenton Wheeler and Alejandro Torres Victoria

"Bullfighting is not a sport. It was never supposed to be. It is a tragedy. A very great tragedy."

—Ernest Hemingway, in a dispatch to the *Toronto Star Weekly*, Oct. 20, 1923, after seeing his first bullfight.

John Fenton Wheeler, 45, son of an Abilene, Kan., newspaper editor and graduate of the University of Kansas, is chief of bureau in Spain and Portugal. After two years as reporter and telegraph editor of the *Topeka (Kan.) Daily Capital* and 11 years as news editor of the *Corpus Christi (Tex.) Caller-Times,* he joined *The AP* in 1964 at Columbus, Ohio. As correspondent in Havana, he was expelled at 4 a.m. with two hours notice Sept. 8, 1969. He saw his first bullfight in 1960 in Reynosa, Mexico.

Alejandro Torres Victoria, 60, had an unforgettable experience when he saw his first bullfight at the age of 12. He saw matador Valenciano Manuel Grenaro gored to death. Since then he has witnessed more than 2,400 corridas and more than 100 serious gorings. He joined *The AP* in 1928 as a messenger and remained with *The AP* through the Spanish Civil War. He has known most of the great matadors intimately.

A lady with a French poodle is on the barrera, the front row. Behind her, a Canadian couple is trying to settle their children into seats never meant for children. There are Spanish new rich, women fashionably dressed, men with cigars. They greet one another effusively.

Across the ring in the sun it is hot. Other Spanish are there, men, despite the heat, in black berets, squinting against the sun and smelling of Spanish brandy.

Below on the sand, having a hard time spitting, is Santiago Martin, "El Viti," a bullfighter.

Two men in coveralls open big wooden gates on a long, dark corridor and step back quickly. There is almost silence.

Out of the chute, head up and moving it from side to side, comes the bull, a half-ton of bred killer, hooted or cheered by the crowd for his shoulders, his horns or his presence. The tourists are quiet, forgotten.

The grace of fine matadors in action is evident here. Left, Antonio Chenel (Antonete) and right, José Gomez Ortega (Josélito) execute passes in the Madrid bullring.

This time the bull looks good, but you will never really know until he is hurt. Now he is merely foolish, dangerous and strong. Later, if he is brave, he will be cunning and deadly.

A member of the cuadrilla (team), El Viti's name stenciled on his pink and yellow cape, tries "to pass" the bull but is chased behind the barrera. Luckily, the bull skids to a stop before he damages his horns on the wood. His snorts are deep, audible several rows up.

El Viti walks into the bull's range, carrying his cape as if it were a briefcase. He is a professional, seemingly uninspired, a man without a smile who keeps the horns in sight. His distance perception is excellent and he is good with the banderillas, the harpoon sticks used nominally to tire the bull's neck muscles and get his head down so a sword can follow.

Carefully, he spreads his cape and calls the age-old challenge: "Toro. Toro."

And another bullfight—tragedy, art, sport, show business, perhaps all of them—is under way.

Before the afternoon sun is gone, six bulls will be dead, horses will be down and men may be injured, even killed. There will be blood on the sand, lots of it if the bullfighter makes a bad kill and hits the bull's lung. Or it will spurt steadily to the sand if the bull's horn finds the femoral artery in the man's thigh.

People will try to walk out as the bull raises his head for a dying bellow, or hide their faces as a man is tossed in the air and the bull waits to get him again.

Inevitably, someone will try to leave his seat to go to the bathroom. And someone else will cheer the bull. A Spanish woman will grip her husband's arm but never take her eyes from the ring. Somewhere in the crowd, Fernando Botan, a specialist in photographing gorings, will try to avoid the eyes of waiting matadors.

But the centuries-old drama will be played out to the end, obviously not as Ernest Hemingway saw it in the 1920s, the 1930s or even 1950s. Gone are the days when mammoth 1,300-pound bulls killed 20 unpadded horses in an afternoon. Today the bulls weigh 200 pounds less and the horses are padded. Certainly it is not the same as when it began, perhaps in 815, when men jousted bulls from horseback and the real bullfighters were those on the ground luring the bull toward the horse. And nothing like 1126 when men began testing whatever it is they feel destined to test by running ahead of the bulls in the streets of Pamplona.

Of the 650 officially sanctioned bullfights (corridas) in Spain in 1970, there may have been less than 50 good ones. But all contained the element—death—that has pleased and disgusted spectators since bullfighting began.

Figures tell something: 13,262 bulls killed in Spain in 1970. Of this total, 3,779 were "toros," officially approved bulls; 6,573 were "novillos," second-rate bulls not good enough for a bullfight because of age or physical defect; and 2,900 bull calves.

One man was killed in 1970—Jose Rodena Lopez, "Tarranguenito," a novice fatally gored in the leg. Full bullfighters, "matadores de toros," suffered 43 injuries, none grave. The novices—55 injuries, 10 of them classified as very grave. Cuadrilla members suffered 79 injuries, 15 of them grave.

It was not a bloody year. In 1969 there were 348 injuries and two deaths.

The most publicized injury was the goring in the neck received in the off-season in Bogotá, Colombia, by Spain's No. 1, Manuel Benitez, "El Cordobes."

Recovered in time for the Spanish season, the flamboyant 35-year-old bullfighter set a new record of 121 individual bullfights. The old record of 111 fights was held by none less than the great Juan Belmonte.

Bullfighting, of course, is more than statistics and death.

It has spread, with Spanish culture, to seven countries of Spanish America. Mexico City boasts the biggest bullring in the world—capacity 55,000 persons. But it is in Spain that the real roots and "aficion" (love of bullfights) remains. To get something from a bullfight, you should attend at least a dozen. You will need a glossary, patience and a strong stomach. You may never understand it but you may feel it.

There remain today three basic styles of bullfighting—rondena, sevillana and tremendista, the last of which can be translated as "excessive." Of the three, it is the most commonly seen.

The rondena style was begun at the end of the 17th century by Francisco Romero of the town of Ronda near Malaga. It is a serious, classical style that includes the natural pass to the left where the bullfighter opens himself up to the horns and lets the bull move by slowly offering his leg as a target. With the exception of Paco Camino, few bullfighters in Spain today follow the style or can do it consistently. Belmonte fought this way.

The sevillana style is described as the happy style of fighting, depending much on the bravery of the bull and permitting improvisation. It includes natural passes but supposedly done only with the grace of someone from Seville, or at least from Andalucia in southern Spain. To this school belonged Jose Gomez Ortega, "Joselito." The best of the modern fighters included Jose Luis Parada, Manolo Cortes and again Paco Camino.

Another style, a branch of the sevillana, called castellana, was practiced by Domingo Ortega, Lúis Miguel Dominguin, Agustin Parra, "Parrita," and Julio

Aparicio in the last 20 years. This style was practiced by El Viti, Damaso Gonzalez, Angel Teruel, Gregorio Sanchez and Andres Vazquez.

But much of this changed on the 20th of May, 1964, when a brash and scarred young man named Manuel Benitez became a full-fledged matador in the Madrid bullring. He was painfully gored as thousands watched on nationwide television.

His unorthodox style, guts and daring had caught fire. By sticking the bull's horn in his face, petting its nose and fighting the animal on his knees, El Cordobes rejuvenated bullfighting much as Cassius Clay did boxing. He filled bullrings from Caceres to Caracas. El Cordobes became No. 1 and several times a millionaire.

His closest rival was a 22-year-old cobbler's son from Linares—the town where Manuel Rodriguez, "Manolete," was killed in 1947 and sent the nation into mourning.

Sebastian Palomo, "Linares," 13 years younger than El Cordobes, fought in the tremendista style but at times with the grace of a Sevillano (from Seville). His talents were courage and quickness. He often started into a pass that would kill slower men.

For the purists, however, there was only one bullfighter in Spain in the 1960s and early 1970s—Paco Camino. His classic style was applauded during a solo benefit attended by Gen. Francisco Franco at which he killed all six bulls.

A month later Paco Camino suffered the most serious goring of the season.

Diego Puerta set the record among current matadors—20 gorings during his career.

It wasn't easy for El Cordobes. He suffered 10. Palomo Linares carried a scar from the corner of his mouth, a remembrance from a bull in Colombia.

Compared to the Joselitos, the Manoletes and the Belmontes, today's fighters earn big money. Manolete in his heyday got $3,500 an afternoon. Palomo Linares averaged $11,000 and El Cordobes about $15,000.

But their wide-open style, disdain for the crowd and clowning have increased charges they are turning bullfighting into show business.

With an estimated 25 to 30 per cent of the house being tourists who know little about bullfighting, does it matter?

Probably not. But even with spectacular performances (or show business) there has been a skid at the gate. In 1970, an estimated 7.5 million persons watched bullfights of all kinds in Spain. This, said promoters, was about 15–20 per cent less than in 1969.

Several reasons were advanced: that the superstars only fight small bulls, that the bulls' horns are shaved, that the age of the automobile had taken people from the bullring on Sunday afternoons, that people spend their money on soccer, the No. 1 sport, and, of course, the rise of television. Prices undoubtedly have been a factor. A seat on the barrera costs $13.

In past years, the two-week marathon of bullfighting in Madrid's bullring known as the San Isidro fair offered some great spectacles. But the big money stars soon began to avoid that ring. Part of the reason was the crowd, very tough, as at Yankee or Wembley Stadiums. So are Madrid bullfight critics.

"I would rather be gored in the Madrid ring than fail," said Henry Higgins, "Enrique Canadas," a young English bullfighter.

Higgins also said the bullfight promoters were too obligated and corrupt to

The horror and danger can be seen here as two of Spain's greatest matadors fall prey to their bulls. Top, Manuel Rodriguez (Manolete) is fatally injured in 1947. Bottom, Manuel Benitez (El Cordobes) somehow recovered from this goring in 1964 and continued to thrill crowds with his daring.

try an unknown, especially an Englishman. He promoted his first two fights with his own money.

To be a draw in Spain, or Latin America, an aspirant first had to be declared a full bullfighter, or matador. This was done in any of Spain's provinces by getting a matador to turn over his sword to the aspirant at the beginning of the fight. This was called taking the alternativa.

But a bullfighter doesn't really arrive until he confirms his alternativa in the Madrid bullring as El Cordobes did in 1964 or Palomo Linares did in 1970 after fighting in the provinces and South America for six years.

Madrid's bullring, with 24,000 capacity, is No. 1 in the bullfight world. Second is Seville, with 13,000, and third is in the Basque capital of Bilbao. Barcelona, with the largest seating capacity in Spain at 26,000, rates equal with Latin American bullrings.

"The Catalans around Barcelona have never understood bullfighting," says a Madrid fan.

Spanish America has begun to serve as a good draw for the top Spanish matadors during the off-season. The Latin American countries that permit bullfighting have produced some stars over the years.

Rodolfo Gaona of Mexico was a standout in the time of Joselito and Belmonte; Fermin Espinosa, "Armillita," Lorenzo Garza, Luis Castro, "El Soldado," Silberio Perez and Carlos Arruza in the time of Manolete. The newest Mexican stars include Manolo Martinez, Curro Rivera and Eloy Cavazos.

Cesar Giron of Venezuela had a brilliant career. Countrymen Curro Giron and Efrain Giron carried on the family tradition when Cesar prepared to retire in the early 1970s.

The bull charges a picador (mounted horseman) in Madrid ring. Horses are heavily padded for protection against the bull's horns. The picador's job is to drive his shaft into the bull's shoulders and weaken the muscles so that the bull will keep his head low for the matador's final thrust.

The best from Colombia in recent years has been Pepe Caceres but Jaime Gonzalez, "El Puno," emerged as a potential star. He took his alternativa in Spain in 1970.

Ecuador produced a novice of class, Fabian Mena, but Latin America never matched Spain in bulls, matadors or tradition. Or bullrings. In 1971, Spain had 346 permanent plazas de toros, more than four times the number in Spanish America.

There were 269 bull breeding ranches in Spain with names famous throughout the bullfighting world—Francisco and Eusebia Galache, the Perez Tabernero family, Lisardo Sanchez, Carlos Sanchez, Juan Pedro Domecq (of sherry fame) and Eduardo Miura and its deadly big, black bulls. Several bullfighters over the years, including El Cordobes, have not appeared against Miuras. Manolete never refused, even in the smallest ring. It was a Miura that killed him.

Spain also counted 193 accredited bullfighters, 143 of them active in 1970. But only seven fought more than 50 fights. Leading the list were El Cordobes and Palomo Linares, the two who needed money the least.

Belmonte's son, living in a luxury apartment in Madrid, said a man needed two things to become a bullfighter: "Ambition and hunger."

But it must be more than that. Luis Miguel Dominguin, who made headlines in the bullrings and with actress Ava Gardner, made plenty of money, but in 1971 tried a comeback at 44.

Palomo Linares, half that age, had the name, looks and an income five times that of the President of the United States. Yet 100 afternoons a year he continued to walk onto the sands where others left their blood, their hopes and their lives. Hardly the hungry thing to do.

At first glance, it would appear that El Cordobes has just successfully killed a rabbit. Actually, the rabbit was tossed into the ring by a fan to add to the trophies that El Cordobes earned in this 1967 bullfight in Castellon de la Plana, Spain.

Two distinctly different styles of wrestling are exhibited here. On the left, New Zealander John Da Silva, apparently in trouble, is in the process of winning the British Empire professional wrestling championship from George Gordienko of Canada. On the right, Takao Watanabe, a Japanese all-star wrestler, is about to pin Bob Nelson, a Portland, Ore., high school wrestler, in a 1968 match.

chapter 23

WRESTLING

Half Sport and Half Theater

by Ben Thomas

Ben Thomas is night supervisor of *The AP* general sports staff in New York. A native of Sarasota, Fla., he attended Henderson State College at Arkadelphia, Ark., and Louisiana State University. He began his newspaper career in Hot Springs, Ark., in 1950 and, after a hitch in the Navy and a period with the *New Orleans Times-Picayune*, he joined *The AP* in New Orleans in 1960. He wrote general news and sports before being transferred to the New York desk in 1970.

One of the most ancient and universal athletic contests is wrestling, in which two persons attempt to throw each other to the ground. Wrestling was an important sport in ancient Greece and, before that, in Egypt of the Pharaohs. The walls of many ancient tombs on the Nile show many scenes of wrestling and depict virtually all of the holds and falls known today.

Greek mythology credits the invention and original rules of the sport to the legendary Theseus, but scholars believe its beginnings antedate man's descent from the trees. Primates of all types, man included, wrestle playfully, particularly when young. Even animals, whose only common ancestor with man might be the single cell, wrestle with each other in play or sport. Man, in fact, may even have got the idea of wrestling from watching a pair of saber-toothed tiger cubs cuff one another and wrestle.

The Greeks included wrestling in the earliest Olympics and the sport, or at least a version thereof, is still an Olympic contest. Olympic-style, or Greco-Roman, wrestling, bears little resemblance, however, to the grunt-and-groan sport popularized on American television.

The popularity of wrestling in its various forms continues throughout the world today. The Japanese have sumo and judo, and jui-jitsu is an outgrowth of wrestling. The occupancy of the Japanese throne was once decided by wrestling. Two sons of the Emperor Buntoku wrestled for the right to succeed their father.

Antonino Rocca caught the camera's eye as he was caught in a cradle crab hold by Lou Thesz during match in New York in 1953.

Koreshito, the victorious son, took the name of Seiwa upon ascending the imperial throne.

Jui-jitsu combines wrestling with scientific self-defense while sumo consists mainly of pachyderm-sized men of great bulk grappling one another.

India has a form of wrestling akin to sumo and in both Japan and India there are tricks and holds which Western rules exclude as fouls.

Actually, the Greco-Roman rules applying to Olympic wrestling bear small resemblance to the wrestling practiced in ancient Greece and Rome but rather are an outgrowth of a variation developed over a century ago in France. It is extremely restricted with neither tripping nor any hold below the belt permitted. This results in the bouts consisting chiefly of struggling on the ground. Americans, nurtured on the catch-as-catch-can wrestling with the forms sanctioned by an Amateur Athletic Union and the National Collegiate Athletic Association, have little zest for Olympic wrestling. Thus America's claim to Olympic wrestling medals is nil.

Amateur wrestling in the United States has a wide sway, particularly in colleges. It, of course, doesn't attract large gates and hasn't been oversaturated by television.

Professional wrestling was one of the first television overkills in American athletics. The antics of professional wrestlers didn't help any, however. But these occurred long before the advent of television.

One historian of the sport tells of late 19th century wrestling promoters who, to attract crowds, "would have grapplers beat each other with fists, rubber hoses and the like and violate almost all the 'within ring' rules. Then they'd pitch each other out of the ring into the spectators. The concussions resulting therefrom resulted in many serious injuries and deaths."

American professional wrestling encompasses female practitioners of the sport also. And the entire scope of professional wrestling in the United States today consists a great deal of showmanship. Gorgeous George and other long-haired, pre-hippie, marvels of the sport attracted as much notice from their pre-bout activities as they did in the ring.

After the turn of the century, wrestling was a popular sport and on Labor Day 1911 spectators shelled out $155,000 to watch a match between Frank Gotch and George Hackenschmidt in Chicago. Gotch, one of the all-time greats of pro wrestling in this nation, easily won. From 1898 through 1913, Gotch had 160 professional matches and won 154. His last professional loss, in 1906, was for the world's title when he was defeated by Fred Beell after having been knocked out when his head hit a ring post. Gotch, from the cornfields of Iowa, defeated Beell in a return match later that year and then went on to win 76 matches before retiring undefeated late in 1913.

Wrestling became an intramural sport in college not long after the Revolutionary War when it was popularized on the Harvard campus. It didn't gain hold as an intercollegiate competition until after the start of the current century, however, when the Eastern Intercollegiate Wrestling Association was formed. In later years, Oklahoma State University, formerly Oklahoma A&M, has dominated collegiate wrestling. Edward Clark Gallagher, who died in 1940, brought the Aggies to the forefront of collegiate wrestling and they are still there. Gallagher's teams won 70 consecutive dual matches and 11 of 13 national titles from 1921–32.

The American freestyle form derives mainly from the Lancashire style of wrestling developed in that section of England. It was nurtured as a feature of country fairs and carnivals and Abraham Lincoln's exploits as a wrestler in pioneer days include his victory over Jack Armstrong, champion of Illinois' Sangamon County.

The Lancashire style is considered by wrestling historians to be a legitimate descendant of the ancient Greek upright wrestling combined with ground struggling, but minus the all-in freedom the Greeks permitted. It allows a great amount of action, including struggling on the mat, tripping, catching hold of legs and similar tactics.

A fall is gained when both shoulders of one wrestler touch the ground together —pinning. Most contests evolve around a best-of-three falls match.

Bill Mayer, left, of a Dallas team, battles Benny Guittarez of a team from Boca Raton, Fla., for shot in 20-goal tournament of the U.S. Polo Association in Milwaukee in 1960.

chapter 24

POLO

Tommy Hitchcock Was King

by Hubert Mizell

Polo is an aristocratic blend of soccer, hockey and equestrian skills. Its blood traditionally runs blue and advocates through the ages have included kings, queens and the most heralded of family patriarchs.

Contemporary enthusiasts are often plucked from social registers bearing such classic names as Dinwiddie Lampton III, Adalbert von Gontard Jr., and Lance Reventlow. Prince Philip of Great Britain is a noted devotee.

Despite polo's modern standing, it wasn't always executed by the most gallant of men. Iranian war lords once used it as a training exercise, playing as much for human lives as goals with as many as 100 players on each side.

Even the most astute of polo historians are hazy on the sport's birth. Significant 1st century mentions were recorded in Iran and some scholars place polo's origin as 2000 B.C. in Persia.

It was documented in 4th century Persia that one of the noted Sassanian sovereigns, Sapor II, went at age 7 to "learn the art of war and play at polo."

The sport spread slowly about Oriental nations and by the 9th century was a favorite of Harun-al-Rashid of Arabia. It was his son, Mamum, who may have stolen the thunder of Houston's Astrodome by more than 1,000 years. Mamum constructed a full-sized polo course inside a magnificent castle near Baghdad.

China had become a hotbed for polo by the 10th century, but it often became something more serious than a game. A favorite relative of Emperor T'ai Tsu was killed during a match and the angered head man ordered the remaining players beheaded.

An officer of the famed 10th Hussars of England took notice of polo activity while stationed in India and began organizing games among his men. Polo finally made its debut in Great Britain just ahead of the Franco-Prussian War in 1869.

On came the sport to the United States in 1876 under the leadership of James Gordon Bennett, publisher of the old *New York Herald.* He had seen polo played at Hurlingham Club in London and returned to America with a supply of polo mallets and balls.

Eight players on each team jammed the 300-by-160-yard field when polo came to the United States. For safety's sake, the number was trimmed to five and finally to four. A handicap system to equalize team play was the 1888 brainstorm of H. L. Herbert.

Herbert's format transformed polo into one of the world's most evenly matched sports. Every player listed with the United States Polo Association has a rating between zero and 10. The Herbert scale places most performers at zero and seldom does one rise above a five or six.

Horsemanship is a major part of the handicapping method. The ability of a player to handle his horses—how he rides and plays them—is basic to what he can accomplish on the playing field. To earn even a minimum rating in polo, a player must be a qualified horseman.

Value to his team is another giant factor since no polo purist will bow to calling the game an individual sport. "Game sense" also is considered. That is the participant's ability to think out strategy and react intelligently on the field.

Swatting a tiny ball from aboard a speeding horse isn't the easiest task. A player's talent to strike the ball solidly with his mallet and control its direction is most important to the valued handicap rating.

Many polo authorities consider the polo pony as being between 50 and 75 per cent of the game. "If your horse can't get to the ball," goes the cliché, "then you can't hit it." It is generally accepted that a good polo player can be better with a finer horse under him, but a weak player will be unimproved on the finest of animals.

The target of any polo shot is a 24-foot-wide goal. Polo's playing periods are called chukkers and consist of seven-and-one-half minutes. Americans play six chukkers, Argentina uses eight and England has stuck with four.

Players wear headgear similar to the protective helmets worn by auto race drivers, but it does not cover the ears. Riding boots are worn to a height just below the knee. Players wear riding britches, and colorful shirts bearing the number of their positions. Some wear knee pads and dull spurs and carry a whip.

The Polo Association of America was born in 1890 and finally evolved into the United States Polo Association, which is headquartered in Oak Brook, Ill. Major international play prior to 1928 was usually restricted to matches between the United States and England.

Argentina developed the sport in the 1920s and by 1928 had challenged the United States to play for the Copa de las Americas (Cup of the Americas). "Ten-Goal" Tommy Hitchcock led the Americans to a 34-32 victory in the three-match play. Hitchcock also scored 10 goals in a 1936 match when the United States won again, beating Argentina by a 30–27 score.

Polo's heroes are seldom recognized beside the Babe Ruths, Ben Hogans and Jim Thorpes of other sports, but the name of "Ten-Goal" Tommy Hitchcock was—in its time—emblazoned on America's newspaper pages.

Tommy was too young at 17 to fight for his country in World War I, but he ran away to fly with France's famed Lafayette Escadrille.

Tommy was shot down and captured behind German lines. He outwitted the enemy en route to a prison camp, however, and dragged a severely injured leg hundreds of miles back to his squadron. Hitchcock was soon fighting again for the Allies.

It was a different twist when, after his great polo career, Hitchcock went back to the wars in the early 1940s. He was 48 then, a true graybeard among the United States' fighter pilots.

Hitchcock won a battle on home soil before ever being shipped across the Atlantic to fight World War II. He championed the cause of the P-40 fighter plane, battling critics, Army generals and even the United States Congress before finally proving his point.

"Ten-Goal" Tommy never backed down from what he thought to be a worthwhile fight, whether it be atop a swift polo pony or in the cockpit of a heavily-armed war aircraft ready for battle.

Hitchcock and the P-40s were shipped east and Tommy was running his favorite war machine through final tests over a green British hillside. He took it into a power dive and never pulled up. "Ten-Goal" Tommy died in the flaming wreckage.

The news of Hitchcock's death was page one material throughout England and the United States. Deeper inside the papers, sports columnists such as Grantland Rice, Bill Corum and Arthur Daley eulogized Tommy as an immortal.

For one fatal day, his name was there with not only those of Joe DiMaggio and Tommy Harmon, but with Eisenhower's, Churchill's and Roosevelt's.

Polo throughout the world is played not so much for headlines as for personal and aristocratic satisfaction. Mostly, it's played by the rich and for the rich. But, it's also performed with even lighter notice by cowboys in pastures and kids on deserted fields.

Somewhere among them may be another budding "Ten-Goal" Tommy . . . a man who can, one way or another, put polo on the front page.

Cecil Smith, left, aboard Bonnie J and Tommy Hitchcock on Pampero are among polo's all-time greats.

Weight lifters also come in different sizes. The super-heavyweight above is J. Dube of the U.S., who won a gold medal in this competition at the World and European championships in Warsaw, Poland. Hawaii's Emerick Ishikawa, right, competed in the featherweight class in Paris in 1946.

chapter 25

WEIGHT LIFTING

Accent on Men and Muscle

by Ben Thomas

Weight lifting is one of man's oldest competitive sports. There is positive evidence that weight lifting was part of the ancient Tailtean Games conducted by the Celts in Ireland.

Man, out of necessity, always has been a weight lifter—from the days when the cavemen strained to lift huge boulders to block the entrances of their caves for protection.

The pharaohs of ancient Egypt assembled the greatest collection of weight lifters the world has ever known, but not for sports. These men were used to heave mighty stones into place for the pyramids, monuments to dead kings.

There is inconclusive evidence that the Greeks included weight lifting in their ancient competitive sports but weight lifting as we know it today originated with the Europeans. The origin is lost in antiquity but most likely some village's young man, in an effort to show off his muscular prowess to a fair lady, bragged to a rival that he could lift a great weight. The challenge was made and accepted, and, thus, a new sport and diversion probably was born.

The sport was popular after its inception in central Europe. Then it spread to Scandinavia, Egypt, Turkey and even to Japan. About 100 years ago, European settlers introduced weight lifting to America. Its appeal was limited, however, and it was not until its introduction in the modern Olympics that interest became widespread throughout the world.

At the Olympics in Athens in 1896 two weight lifting events—the dumb bell and bar bell—were included among the track and field events. There's an interesting sidelight to this first Olympic weight lifting contest. One of the judges was Greece's Prince George, a man of 6-feet-5 with the reputation of a strongman. When the prince saw that an attendant was having difficulty removing weights, he couldn't resist picking up the heaviest one and throwing it a good distance out of the way—much to the delight of the spectators.

In modern weight lifting, the three important lifts are: the two-hand or press, in which the lifter must toe a line, not move away from it, and, after lifting the weight from the floor to rest on his chest, neck, or shoulders, then lift it to the limit of his arms without bending, maintaining all the while a military-like position; the clean and jerk, or jerk, in which, with either hand or both, the lifter heaves the weight to rest against his chest, then raises it as high as possible on call from the referee; and the snatch, in which, with either hand or both, the contestant snatches up the weight and in one continuous movement, lifts it as high as possible. The lifter must hold the weight for a count of two by the referee.

There are two judges and a referee in official weight lifting contests. Records are figured by adding totals of press, snatch and clean and jerk. Weight lifting

When Russia's Vasily Alexeyev cleaned and jerked these 501-1/2 pounds in 1970, he became the first man to lift over 500 pounds in competition.

One of America's better-known heavyweight weight lifters, Paul Anderson, is shown lifting a 325-pound weight in California in 1956.

divisions parallel wrestling divisions with bantams, featherweights, lightweights, middleweights, light heavyweights and heavyweights.

Weight lifting came into its own in the Olympics in 1920 when it was separated from track and field after the sport had been standardized and given its own definite rules and procedures.

The United States won its first Olympic weight lifting gold medal in 1936, with a victory by featherweight Anthony Terlazzo.

Weight lifting, in connection with isometric and isotonic exercises, is used for conditioning by many athletes in such diverse sports as golf, horseback riding, football, and even archery.

As of early 1971, the recognized king of the weight lifters was Vasily Alexeyev, a 30-year-old Russian student from Shakyty. Alexeyev came to the fore in weight lifting circles only a year earlier and since then has chalked up at least two world records in every competition.

The Russian, billing himself as the strongest man on earth, weighs 308 pounds. In mid-February 1971, he broke three of his own world heavyweight marks in a meet in France, lifting a total of more than 1,188 pounds.

Spectators jammed craft on the Thames on March 29, 1952, as the crews of Cambridge, left, and Oxford, almost neck and neck, approached halfway mark during their 98th annual race. Oxford won by five feet after spotting their opponents a quarter of a length.

chapter 26

ROWING

Oars are the Weapons on the River

by Ken Rappoport

Each summer, a slice of English river turns into a rowing heaven.

It knifes a mile and 550 yards through tree-lined banks and finishes near a town bridge in sheltered water with nearby, brilliantly colored meadows and the shaded lawns of country houses.

Along the way, the river banks bulge with thousands of spectators and their tireless exhortations.

This is the royalty of the racing set, the pick of the rowing championships. This is the Henley Regatta.

Since its start on the Thames River when Oxford met Cambridge in 1829, it has attracted the elite of the rowing world—the cream of Europe, Australia and the United States.

Among the prize-seekers from America in the 20th century was a Philadelphia bricklayer with a tough, aggressive reputation—John B. Kelly Sr.

He was twice national amateur single sculls champion and an Olympic winner in 1920. He went to England in 1920 to compete in the Diamond Sculls, the most coveted of singles rowing titles. But he came home disappointed, barred because of strict English rules that didn't permit blue collar workers to compete.

A generation later, young John Kelly Jr. succeeded his father as national champion and went to England with unsullied hands and a motive for winning the Diamonds.

John B. Kelly Sr. imparts some advice to his son, John B. Kelly Jr., as the latter prepares to work out in a single sculls at Henley, England, in 1948. Both were Olympic champions.

He brought back the big prize.

Kelly Sr., joyfully delirious, sent the King of England a cap of kelly green as a piece of symbolic meaning.

From the beginning, man learned to build boats. Ancient canoes portrayed on rock by the Egyptians furnish proof that boat building was one of the first crafts.

The North American Indians plied the streams. By trial and error, they found ways to introduce more speed and this gave impetus to boat races among the warriors. Rowing appeared in classical times. Greek mythology is rich with it. Rowing contests also belonged to early Greek festivals, such as the Isthmian and Panathenaean Games.

The credit for reviving the sport goes to the British—just after the turn of the 18th century. They were the first in the world to adopt canoes for the specific purpose of racing. Rivers were flowing highways—and one of the greatest was the Thames through London.

The nobility who lived on the Thames had chicly-appointed barges for travel and soon promoted races between their bargemen. Water parties became royal entertainment and it's said the famous composer Handel wrote his "Water Music" for one such occasion.

Thomas Doggett, a Dublin-born actor, was the first to make an annual event of boat racing. He used to watch matches between bargemen from a vantage point of the Swan Tavern, on the Thames. His keen appreciation of the sport and a favor done for him by one of the oarsmen prompted his establishment of the first race from London Bridge to Chelsea, about 4½ miles.

Few remember his stage talents—but he is legendized in a yearly, midsummer race called "The Red Ribbon of the River." The title was symbolic of courage, for Doggett had admired the bravado of the sturdy bargemen who would defy ill weather on the Thames, pointing their crafts through often turbulent waters.

At the beginning of the 19th century, English public schools took up rowing. Eventually Oxford and Cambridge met at Henley.

All of the innovations that led to the modern racing craft were fashioned in the 19th century.

The earlier boats were heavy and built so ponderously inside that they restricted the oarsman's stroke. The first important change was the introduction of the outrigger, perfected in 1844 by Henry Clasper, an English boat builder. It gave oarsmen a freer stroke and set in motion a chain of improvements.

The boats got smaller, lighter and narrower, carried less water resistance, and therefore were faster. They were lengthened to maintain buoyancy, providing more room so the oarsman could use an uninterrupted swing.

Next significant step in the maturity of the racing boat was the building by Clasper of the first keel-less craft. It proved its superiority, with Oxford leading the way as an early college racing power.

Another history-making improvement occurred with the 1870 invention of the sliding seat in America. It enabled rowers to move backward and forward, supplying more thrust and power.

So in less than a half-century, rowing had made big strides. The time witnessed the change from a short, heavy keel boat with fixed seats to the sleek, new racer with sliding seats, the smooth exterior and no keel.

Others approached the sport scientifically, with diagrams and formulas for shaping boats worked out mathematically. Still other rowing enthusiasts doted on methods of training and physical culture.

German-born Eugene Sandow professed that physical culture was the only way to produce a champion rower. No drinking, eating heavily or smoking. All that was required, he said, was two hours of daily practice geared toward greater strength. He convinced some of the Britons, but not all.

Rowing bloomed into a popular sport in the United States in the early 19th century. A scandal diminished its luster when betting and suspicion of foul play arose. But time, and the advent of the first amateur rowing club—the New York Castle Garden Boat Club—helped rowing surface once more in America.

Enter Steve Fairbairn in the middle of the 19th century—a rowing revolutionary.

Fairbairn, an Australian, disrupted years of expert English opinion with his rowing theories. Previously, rowers assumed that a steady, flowing pull with the arms and trunk was needed for speed. But Fairbairn figured that the true basic principle was a powerful thrust of the legs, which produced a punch-like effect and gave maximum efficiency to rowers at the start of the stroke.

In his exposition, "The Fairbairn Style," he explained: "I coach for wins, not for show."

Then he went out and showed them by producing a string of winners.

Meanwhile, back in America, the golden age of sculling was born with the organization of the National Association of Amateur Oarsmen in 1872. It produced a gaggle of glory guys who entertained international attention—James Hamill, James A. Eyck, Wallace Ross, George Hosmer, Fred A. Plaisted, Walter Brown and Joshua Ward.

Amateur clubs had been the rage in the States, for after the Castle Garden bunch from New York came the Detroit Boat Club, an important member of the NAAO, and the Schuylkill Navy Boat Club on the tree-lined Schuylkill River in Philadelphia, a rowing haven for years to come.

Canada got wet, too. The 1870s were the heydays of the professional sculler and Edward Hanlan of Toronto made world rowing news by whipping the best of Canada, the United States and England for money. A winner's purse went as high as $2,000, a small fortune at that time.

When colleges and universities got into the act in America, Cornell made victory a habit. It was due to one man—Charles E. "Pop" Courtney, who gave the rowing world "the Courtney Stroke." Recognized as one of the country's top scullers, he took over at Cornell in 1883 and modified the hard catch that rowers take in their swings, shortened the stroke at the finish and developed a slow slide between strokes.

The "Bob Cook" method, big at Yale, was characterized by a hard catch, with squared shoulders, straight back, straight arms, quick hand shoot and slow slide on the recovery. Cook also was a professional sculler, as were many of the other first college coaches—Ellis Ward at Pennsylvania; Eyck at Syracuse; Richard Glendon at Annapolis and William Haines at Harvard and MIT.

Of them all, though, Courtney's success was the most phenomenal. He sent 59 crews to races at Poughkeepsie and Saratoga, and won 39 times. When he left Cornell after the turn of the century, rowing dominance shifted from East to West. Cornell and Schuylkill-bound Penn had been the aces, now Washington University took over. This was owed, in good part, to the favorable climatic conditions on the West Coast, permitting year-around rowing. The abundance of material in the Far West quickly produced winners for the Huskies, who for some time owned the Poughkeepsie Regatta, a showcase of major college talent.

Their success was also due in large measure to Hiram Conibear, a coach gifted with emotion-charged leadership, who introduced the "Washington Stroke." Conibear applied practical kinesiology—or efficient use of muscle systems—to rowing.

Conibear was responsible for bringing to the Washington campus George Pocock, the well-known boat builder. Pocock was able to set up shop in the crew buildings—and was soon turning out rowing shells by the hundreds after World War I. It's said he built 90 per cent of all the shells used by U.S. crews in the last half-century.

"There's a bit of me in every boat I build," Pocock once said. "There is no more beautiful sight than an eight-oared shell, alive with human rhythm. This is the nearest thing I know to the symphony of the soul."

Another talented aggregation was the Vesper Boat Club of Philadelphia, which provided American victories in the Olympics over formidable opponents.

Among American rowers, the elder Kelly could be termed "most valuable"

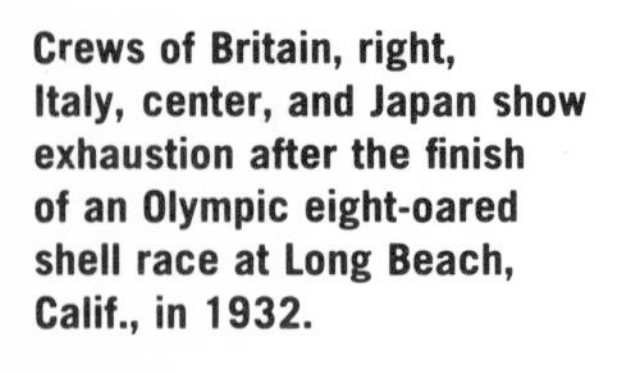

Crews of Britain, right, Italy, center, and Japan show exhaustion after the finish of an Olympic eight-oared shell race at Long Beach, Calif., in 1932.

for his versatility. In addition to winning three Olympic titles, he stroked pairs, fours and eights to victory on several occasions.

Joseph W. Burk was another top-notch talent, winning 46 single sculls races from 1937 to 1940. Included were the U.S. championship four times; the Canadian championship four times; the Diamond Sculls twice and the Philadelphia Gold Challenge Cup.

Other top rowing Americans included Paul Costello, Walter M. Hoover, William G. Miller, Joseph Angyal, Seymour Cromell and Don Spero.

England produced a flood of champion oarsmen: Guy Nickalls Sr., who won the Diamond Sculls five times and stroked pairs, fours and eights to victory at the historic Henley; F. S. Kelly, a super sculler who copped the Diamonds three times, and J. Beresford Jr., who won the Diamonds four times and added three Olympic regattas to his trophy room.

Joseph Wright Sr., of the internationally famous Argonaut Rowing Club of Canada, was a star of that country's rowing galaxy. He helped crews win at Henley, stroking pairs, fours and eights with muscular ease.

Australia produced plenty of good crews and scullers. An Australian entry won the Grand Challenge Cup at Henley and the Diamond Sculls. In single sculling, probably the most outstanding was H. R. Pearce, who won the Olympic single sculls title in 1928 and 1932.

Today, there are four races held annually that are of international interest: the Grand Challenge Cup Regatta at Henley; the Oxford-Cambridge race on the Thames between Putney and Mortlake; the Intercollegiate Regatta staged at Poughkeepsie and later Syracuse, N.Y., and the Yale-Harvard race at New London, Conn., which caps the American collegiate rowing season.

Of course, there are the Olympics every four years. Among the annals of these championship events, a sports writer captured the moment when the University of California took on a powerhouse Italian shell in the eight-oared event at the 1932 Games:

"In all the history of American rowing, there has never been a more thrilling or magnificently-fought boat race. In a herculean, driving finish, that brought a deafening roar from the throats of 80,000 spectators, the California Golden Bears cut down Italy's three-foot lead in the last 25 yards of the 2,000-meter course to slam over the finish line the victor by the exceedingly close margin of a foot."

Later, in 1956 at Melbourne, Australia, Yale was shocked in a first-round match of the eight-oars. But the favored Elis had a second chance—a repechage faceoff for losers.

Yale won that, took the semifinal and went into the finals against its early conquerors, Canada, Australia and Sweden.

Canada and Australia took the lead at the beginning of the 2,000-meter race. But Yale poured it on and pulled away at the halfway mark and jacked up its stroke to 38, then a pulsating 40-a-minute.

With 40,000 looking on, the Elis beat back Canada's bid by a slim half-a-length.

Some of the Yale oarsmen collapsed, some got sick and a few cried.

"We're the toughest crew ever put together," Capt. Tom Charlton crowed between lung-burning gasps for air. "And we beat the finest."

Spectators peer from behind a glass enclosure as they watch Paul Haber, left, in action against Bill Yambrick in the 1966 finals of the U.S. handball championships in Salt Lake City, won by Haber.

chapter 27

HANDBALL

Ancestor of Modern Tennis

by Dick Joyce

During the 1970 professional football season in the United States, fans became enamored of a 43-year-old quarterback, a veteran of more than 20 years in the game, who repeatedly came off the bench and by what sports writers termed "sundown magic" led his team, the Oakland Raiders, to victory.

His name was George Blanda. He was a phenomenon, matching the skills of young team leaders half his age.

It was only natural that Blanda should be asked the secret of his competitive longevity in a sport requiring stamina and toughness.

"Basically, I keep my legs in shape," he said simply. "During the off-season, I play handball five times a week."

Thus, this football hero was revealed as a member of a rather exclusive but little publicized club of sportsmen, business executives, ordinary laborers, secretaries and housewives who discovered physical fitness in the game of bouncing little rubber balls off walls.

An ancestor of modern tennis, handball has survived not as a big time spectator sport but as a quick conditioner which can be picked up during the lunch break or in the afternoon after work before going home to dinner.

There are said to be 8,000 handball courts in the United States alone. It is played on every continent. Its popularity is centered in the large metropolitan areas such as New York, Chicago and Los Angeles.

It reportedly was brought to the United States by Irish immigrants, who played the game on the back wall of saloons.

Most historians agree the sport originated in Ireland. It was played by the Irish as early as the 10th century, under the name of "fives"—for five fingers on the hand. It gradually spread throughout the British Isles. It became extremely popular through the 16th, 17th and 18th centuries and was part of the exercise program at English schools.

It was quite a distinction to be an outstanding "fives" player. John Cavanagh is considered the first truly famous player and was accorded fitting tribute by newspapers upon his death in 1819. "There was not only nobody equal, but nobody second to him," said one newspaper.

Phil Casey, an Irishman who settled in Brooklyn about 1882, is considered the father of handball in the United States. Much to his displeasure, he found no handball courts or no one who knew the game except his fellow Irishmen. Some of them had the foresight to bring along handballs (cork center balls wrapped in yarn and horsehide).

Casey and his friends began playing on brick walls in their neighborhood and the game caught on. Seeing, though, that the brick walls were inadequate, Casey acquired enough money to build a court. It measured 65 feet long, 25 feet wide, with a front wall 30 feet high and side walls 25 feet high.

Handball enthusiasts began flocking to Casey's court, and soon he used his profits to erect other courts. In time the sport spread to every large city in the nation.

In 1888, Bernard McQuade, another Irishman living in New York, challenged Casey to the U.S. championship. Casey defeated him easily and then whipped John Lawlor, the champion of Ireland, in a series of matches played in the United States and Cork, Ireland. Casey also pocketed a $1,000 side bet and continued to defeat all comers until his retirement in 1900 because of lack of opponents.

Because of his professionalism, Casey is not regarded as the first official handball champion. That honor goes to Michael Eagan of Jersey City, N.J., a native

Handball players Marty Decatur, Ruby Obert, Jim Jacobs and Oscar Obert, left to right, show how it's done. The Obert brothers reigned in 1970 as the U.S. Handball Association doubles champions. Decatur and Jacobs were undefeated in 10 years of play as a team.

of Galway who won the first hard ball handball tournament held under the auspices of the Amateur Athletic Union in 1897.

Up to the 1900s the game had been played with a hard ball on a court of four walls. But before long a new variation took hold in the East. It originated along the beaches of New York City in 1913 where hard sand and open walls of bathing houses furnished a perfect court for exercise and fun. Bathers discovered hitting a tennis ball with their hands against the wall made an excellent game before or after swimming. Thus what is known as one-wall handball was born in Brooklyn. It became so popular that by 1919 many courts were constructed throughout beaches near the city.

The tennis ball, however, proved unsatisfactory and a smaller, softer ball was introduced. Bleachers were erected to seat up to 3,000. By 1915 the sport spread west where four-wall courts with board floors became the fad.

The Detroit Athletic Club helped stimulate interest throughout the country by constructing several courts. In 1915 the city sponsored the first invitation four-wall tourney, won by Fritz Seivered of Cleveland. In 1919 at Detroit, the AAU held the first tourney with the new soft ball, and the game had caught on so that a Los Angeles player, William Ranft, won it.

In the meantime, handball in the East was picking up indoors. Courts were erected in school gymnasiums, YMCAs and athletic clubs, and the ball and court rules were standardized. Additional courts led to leagues formed by boat clubs, Knights of Columbus chapters and Elks Clubs. Without the handicap of rear walls, spectators could be accommodated in great numbers at championship events. This had not been possible at four-wall games. One-wall handball had arrived.

The ball is the same for both type games, weighing about 23 ounces and measuring $1^7/_8$ inches in diameter. Court dimensions differ. The one-wall game has a smaller front of 16 feet and its playing surface, usually concrete or cement, is 20 feet wide by 34 feet in length. The four-wall court is 23 feet wide and 23 feet high and 46 feet long with a back wall 10 feet high.

Mort Leve, executive secretary of the U.S. Handball Association, said the sport continued to boom across the United States because of the growing fetish for physical fitness.

Robert Kendler, a Chicago multimillionaire, founded the USHA in 1951 in opposition to the AAU, and became the sport's biggest benefactor.

Jimmy Jacobs of Chicago was the four-wall singles champion before being succeeded by Paul Haber of Milwaukee in 1966. Steve Sandler of Brooklyn won the one-wall title five years in a row through 1970. The Obert brothers of New York—Rudy, Carl and Oscar—have been outstanding doubles players.

But Haber is the only one to attain any amount of publicity. "Tennis has its bums and golf has its hustlers," says one USHA official sadly. "We've got Haber. And worst of all, he's a great player."

Haber, who won the singles title in 1966, 1967, 1969 and 1970 as well as the national doubles championship six times, constantly fell into disfavor with handball's governing body because of his free-swinging habits. In interviews, he admitted he smoked, liked to drink and spent many of his off hours in barrooms. Handball officials accused him of tarnishing the sport's image.

"I figure handball does enough to keep me in shape," Haber said. "A guy's got to live, too."

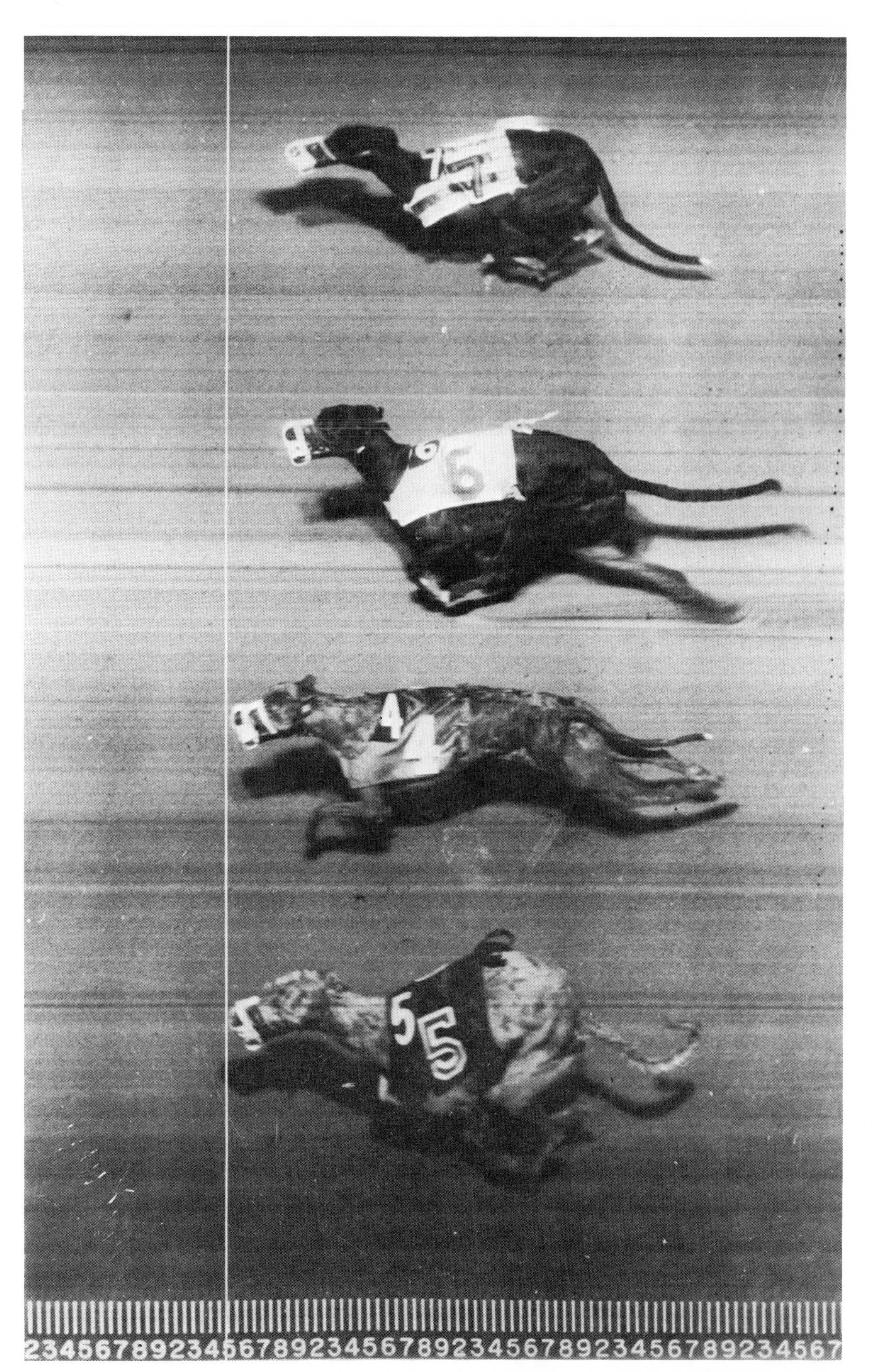

The excitement generated by dog racing can be seen in this photo finish at Pensacola, Fla. No. 5 was the winner, with No. 4 second, and Nos. 6 and 7 finishing in a dead heat for third.

chapter 28

DOG RACING

Rabbits Make the Greyhounds Run

by Ted Meier

Hundreds of years ago, greyhounds, known as very swift pursuit dogs, ran down live rabbits to provide food for their masters.

This was called coursing. From it, over the years, developed the sport of modern day greyhound racing—or just dog racing as it is generally called.

The sport, in which eight muzzled greyhounds burst from starting boxes and chase a mechanical hare around a one-quarter mile track for each race, enjoyed a phenomenal growth in the 1950s and 1960s.

This was especially true in the decade of the 1960s when dog racing skyrocketed and became one of the leading commercial spectator sports.

More than 12,000,000 persons wagered close to $700 million during 1970 in the seven states with legalized pari-mutuel betting on the sport.

This was below the attendance for the more widely known sports of horse racing, baseball, football, basketball and auto racing, but vividly pinpointed the growth of the greyhound industry.

For 1969, according to figures from the American Greyhound Track Operators Association (AGTOA), attendance in the United States was 12,006,722 and the wagering totaled $652,489,705.

Arizona, Arkansas, Colorado, Florida, Massachusetts, Oregon and South Dakota, the seven states with pari-mutuel betting, shared in $44,054,181 revenue to the states.

This compared to the 1960 attendance of 8,402,990, betting of $330,745,646 and state revenue of $22,621,916.

The tremendous growth of the sport was accented even more sharply by comparison of the 1969 data with that of 1950. In 1950, the attendance was 5,945,766, the betting $158,440,837 and state revenue $10,045,144.

In Great Britain and Australia, dog racing similarly enjoyed a boom, as did greyhound breeders in Ireland and elsewhere. The trend also was up at the Juarez and Caliente tracks in Mexico.

Florida and Massachusetts were No. 1 and No. 2 in the state parade in 1969.

Florida, led by the Flagler Kennel Club in Miami which in 1969 had attendance of more than 1,000,000 and mutuel handle of $60 million, was first in the nation with attendance of 6,335,889, betting of $354,558,893 and revenue to the state of $25,302,208.

Massachusetts, the home state of Edward J. Keelan, president of the AGTOA and also of Raynham Park, was second with attendance of 2,084,485, betting of $114,689,581 and state revenue of $11,101,166.

On the basis of mutuel handle, Colorado was third with $55,035,294, Arizona fourth at $46,019,322 and Arkansas fifth at $42,116,718. Oregon followed with $21,351,778 and South Dakota with $18,668,119.

The sport flourished on the so-called Florida Suncoast where attendance at the three tracks in the area—Tampa Greyhound Track, Derby Lane and Sarasota Kennel Club—aggregated 1,636,683 with betting of $90,439,237. This compared to the 1949 figures for the three tracks of 580,903 and $17,845,978.

The purchase of the Palm Beach, Fla., Kennel Club in September 1970 by Art Rooney, nationally-known sportsman and owner of the Pittsburgh Steelers in the National Football League, also focused attention on greyhound racing.

Rooney paid $7 million for the track which handled $27 million in bets during 1969.

Some new plants and modernization of others, with air-conditioned dining spots and closed circuit TV, helped boost dog racing. A computer system of data processing also was a factor.

"For the first time in history, the greyhound owner, trainer, breeder, handicapper and track official has immediate access to the complete record of every track dog in the nation," said Robert Niemeyer, general manager of the Greyhound Racing Record which instituted the development.

The greyhound, who usually weighs around 70 pounds, came from Mesopo-

Dog racing, which has skyrocketed to become one of the leading commercial spectator sports, usually is conducted at night. But this daylight event was arranged especially for photographers in Miami early in the '50s. The greyhounds, chasing the "rabbit," make a hurdle made of broom-like slats.

tamia or the Near East where the breed still survives as the saluki or gazelle hound.

Blessed with keen sight and great speed it was natural that these qualities should be exploited by promoters.

It is recorded that coursing became a national sport in England during the time of King Charles I and that the Duke of Norfolk, Lord Orford, originated the first known coursing club at Swaffham in 1776.

The duke was so enthusiastic about his favorite bitch, Czarina, that it led to his death. He got up from a sick bed in 1791 to watch Czarina win her 47th straight race. He was overcome by the excitement and toppled off his horse, dead.

The first dog races in the United States were held in Massachusetts during the 18th century with a breed known as whippets, a cross between the greyhound and terrier.

Greyhound racing was preferred, however, and greyhounds came to dominate.

To help quiet protests that live hares should not be used in dog racing, efforts to substitute a mechanical lure started as long ago as 1876.

It remained for Owen Patrick Smith of Oklahoma to develop a successful mechanical method which still is essentially used today. Smith's method had a mechanical hare moving around a circular track at a fast enough speed to keep ahead of the chasing greyhounds.

Smith used it for the first time at Hot Springs, S.D., in 1907. He also used it at the greyhound tracks he built at Tucson, Ariz., in 1909 and at Emeryville, Calif., in 1919 before his death in 1927.

Paul Kiscolo's Stanno was one of the leading greyhounds in 1970. He won the finals of the $50,000 Wonderland Derby at Revere, Mass., in July and, in September, took the McCormick Memorial Stakes at Taunton, Mass., by a resounding 11½ lengths in the track record time of 37:34 seconds for the three-eighths mile course.

The first five all-time leading greyhound winners in America, as listed by the Greyhound Racing Record in September 1970, were Indy Ann with 137 triumphs, L.L.'s Doug with 128, Miss Whirl with 115, Westy Whizzer with 107 and Lurcher Boy with 105.

Lurcher Boy was still active going into the 1970s and led Whit's Zip, Princess Putt, Cantina Blue, B.A.'s Silver and L.B. Dallas Girl on the list of dogs in competition.

The five leading sires for 1970 were My Friend Lou, Duke of Loup, Sought After, Venerated and Tell You Why. Poor Mick was an especially sought-after sire in England since in 12 months at stud he had sired 139 pups. Some of Poor Mick's puppies were purchased by R. C. Pflueger of New Orleans for racing in the United States.

An advertisement for Southland, at West Memphis, Ark., put the case for all the greyhound tracks. "We can't guarantee that you'll be a winner, but we can guarantee that you'll have a ball trying. We're rated 'A' for adult entertainment."

The "adult entertainment" included trying one's luck at the daily double, the quinella, the exacta or perfecta, the Big Q, the Big E and the Twin Double plus the old-fashioned betting just to win, place or show.

The Russians excel at gymnastics and the Americans are running hard to catch up. At right, Larisa Latynina of the U.S.S.R. performs at the world championships at Dormund, Germany, in 1966. Below, young Cathy Rigby of Long Beach, Calif., exhibits her form and hopes in 1968.

chapter 29

GYMNASTICS

The Russians Steal a March on America

by Mike Recht

Money or applause can often be an inspiration for athletic greatness, so it is no wonder that Russia and Japan dominate the world in gymnastics, while the United States lags far behind.

Although one of the least publicized sports in the world, gymnastics holds a place of prominence in Russia and Japan and some European countries where it receives special appreciation. In these countries the emphasis is placed on physical fitness for its own sake, rather than for any awards of money and glory it might offer.

But with baseball, football and other sports holding the upper hand with the monetary awards and public acclamation given them, gymnastics receives few headlines in the United States. Certainly the reward is not enough for the difficult hours and years of training and the grace, strength and muscular control required to be a world champion gymnast.

"Gymnastics is the basis of all sports in Russia," says Olympian Yuri Titov of the Soviet Union.

With that to go on, it is easy to understand how the Russians, since they entered the Olympic Games in gymnastics in 1952 through the 1964 Games, captured 40 of 60 possible medals, including 12 gold medals among the women, and the men won 38 of a possible 84, including 14 gold.

The powerful Russian men won the team title in 1952 and 1956 before the nimble Japanese men stepped in to win the next three titles, which the Russian women won from 1952 through 1968.

During that time, the outstanding performer of the Games was a Russian girl, Larisa Latynina, who won six gold medals, five silver and three bronze from 1956 through 1964.

The only girl to crack the Russian dominance in recent years has been pretty Vera Caslavska of Czechoslovakia, who won three gold medals in 1964 and four golds and a silver in 1968, bringing the sport into the public eye briefly.

However, the United States has not won a gymnastics medal of any kind in the Olympics since 1932, and the U.S. girls have never won any kind of medal.

The poor United States showing can be attributed to the relative lack of competitors in the country, the lack of competition by the U.S. team in international meets, not enough exposure to international judges and their method of scoring and the lack of top notch coaching because the sport receives such little emphasis.

Competition in the United States did not even begin until after the Civil War, and that was spurred by European immigrants, while gymnastics began in Europe in ancient Greece, or at least the Greeks originated the term gymnastics, which means "naked art." They believed that physical well being was a major ingredient to the complete man, and they used disciplined exercise to reach that goal.

When the Romans conquered Greece, they turned the exercise into a training for warfare. However, the advent of Christianity, with its emphasis on the soul over the body, caused gymnastics to virtually disappear for some 1,000 years.

Gymnastics as we know it today largely originated in the late 1700s and it came to mean stunts performed on apparatus such as mats, bars and trampolines.

Johann Basedow conducted the first course in gymnastics as part of a school curriculum, Gerhard Vieth published an encyclopedia on body exercise and Adolf Spiess introduced exercise to music for grace and helped make gymnastics a school subject, all in the 1700s and early 1800s.

Frederick Jahn, the father of German gymnastics, organized gymnasts into Turner Societies and introduced the side horse with pommels, the horizontal and parallel bars, jumping standards and balance beam, among others.

The Turner Societies, or turnverein (gymnastic societies), were brought to the United States by Europeans in the 1800s and gained a place in some schools by the end of the century. In 1881, the Milwaukee Turners gymnastics team competed in the national turnfest in Frankfurt, Germany, the first United States team to compete at an international level.

The YMCA played a great part in the spread of the sport in the United States and the Amateur Athletic Union took national control of gymnastics. By the start of the 1900s, foreign systems had gradually been eliminated with their stiff, formal military manner of training that took away much of the pleasure and fun.

Gymnastics made the Olympics in 1896 with several individual events, such as the vaults, side horse, horizontal bar and flying rings, along with a team title in the horizontal bars. Germany dominated. Germany also won the first team gymnastics title in 1904 after the first all-around championship was held in 1900.

Among the United States winners in those first years were Anton Heida, George Eyser, E. A. Hennig, Frank Kriz, Herman Glass, George Gulack, Dallas Bixler, Raymond Bass, George Roth and Rowland Wolfe.

In fact, the United States won five gold medals in 1932 and finished second in the team standings, but since then the men have not won any medal, and the U.S. women have never won anything since their gymnastics entrance in the Olympics in 1936, eight years after women's competition began.

However, the sport was growing, with 14 nations competing in 1920 and more competitors than ever before in the 1932 Games at Los Angeles.

Roy E. Moore was the manager of the U.S. team in 1920 and was a moving force during the next decade, organizing the selection and training of the team.

Alfred Jochim was considered the best gymnast in U.S. history. A member of the Swiss Turnverein of Hudson County, N.J., he won the AAU all-around title from 1925 through 1930, and again in 1933, while his team won the first team title in 1926, and then went unbeaten from 1928 until 1940 when the University of Illinois won the national championship.

George Wheeler of Pittsburgh and Frank Cameskey of New Jersey each won the title five times, and Clara Schroth of Philadelphia won the women's crown five times between 1945–52 after Roberta C. Ranck of Philadelphia captured the first AAU women's all-around title in 1931. The first men's champion was Earl Linderman of Camden, N.J., in 1897.

The AAU events have included the flying and still rings, free calisthenics, horizontal and parallel bars, side and long horse, tumbling, Indian clubs and rope climb, with the women adding the balance beam. The collegiate championships include free exercise and trampoline, an American innovation.

In international competition, there are six events for men—free calisthenics, long and side horse, horizontal and parallel bars and still rings—and four for women. One compulsory and one optional exercise are required with five judges grading on degree of difficulty, execution and form.

The sport underwent a major growth in the United States after World War II when the AAU ordered a revitalization of its national sports program. Despite poor facilities and lack of experienced judges, meets were conducted all over the country. Clinics and college courses also helped raise the standards.

Between 1960 and 1966, the number of high school gymnasts increased tenfold, with Illinois and California the leading states.

Internationally, the Germans, Swiss and Scandinavians dominated the sport until the Russians took over in 1948 and then in the Olympics in 1952 with their superb conditioning, strength and consistency. E. V. Tchoukarine of Russia won three gold medals and one silver in those Games.

The U.S. men could do no better than eighth among 29 teams and the women 15th of 18 in 1952. In 1968, the men were seventh of 16 and the women sixth in 14 teams, and individually the outlook did not look bright.

With baseball, football and other more profitable sports not around to provide competition, it appears that gymnastics will continue to be the realm of Russia and Japan in future international competition.

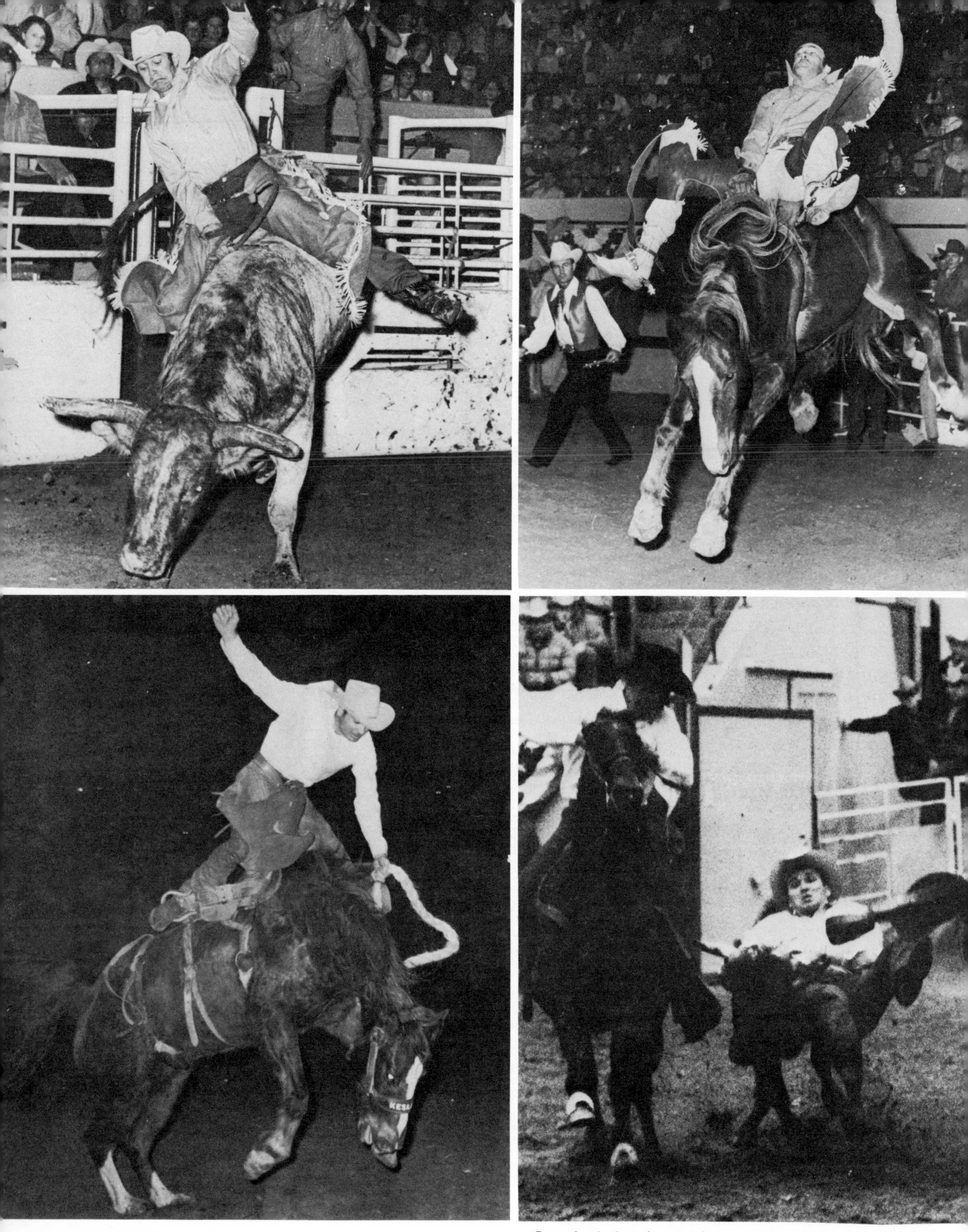

Four of rodeo's main attractions are shown here: top left, Brahma bull riding; top right, bareback bronc riding; bottom left, saddle bronc riding; and bottom right, steer wrestling.

chapter 30

RODEO

Broncs and Bulls Test the Cowboys

by Denne H. Freeman

Denne H. Freeman, 34, is Southwest sports editor of *The Associated Press*. He has covered numerous prestige events, including the Cotton Bowl and Super Bowl football games and the U. S. Open and PGA Golf Championships. He picked up his rodeo material in covering the National Rodeo Finals.

The rodeo, born in Texas after the Civil War on dusty, bone-jarring cattle drives, flourishes in America as no other sport on a year-long basis.

The Rodeo Information Foundation estimates more than 10 million persons watched contestants wrestle steers, rope calves, and ride bulls and broncs for $3.8 million in prize money in 1969.

That's a far cry from the 1870s when the stakes were held in a 10-gallon hat on some godforsaken cattle trail.

The Texas longhorn herds, which multiplied like prairie rabbits during the war, were driven by rugged, independent men who made their living in the saddle.

It was only natural that these men would challenge other outfits when they came together on the trail. But the cowboy sport might have died eventually on the plains if the railroad hadn't brought civilization.

The Western frontier townsmen went out on the plains and invited the cowboys to bring their contests into town.

The name rodeo—for roundup—stuck. In 1872 at Cheyenne, Wyo., townspeople gathered to watch some Texans ride wild stock. In 1883 at Pecos, Tex., longhorns were penned on the courthouse lawn. Lean, young waddies then used main street as the roping area. Five years later in Prescott, Ariz., citizens built a grandstand and sold tickets.

With the fencing of open range, the rodeos began to thrive. Entering the 1970s, there were 533 rodeos sanctioned by the Rodeo Cowboys Association in 40 states and four Canadian provinces from January to December.

The 74th "Daddy of 'Em All" Cheyenne Frontier Days in July 1970 drew almost 800 entries, vying for a $102,000 purse. Besides the six rodeo performances, there were street parades, Indian dances, square dances, a carnival and free chuckwagon breakfasts—a long way indeed from the curious gathering of 1872.

The rodeo is truly an extension of the frontier spirit.

Besides gambling his entry fee, a contestant takes considerable risks when he mounts a 1½-ton Brahma bull.

Commented former bull-riding champion Ron Rossen of Broadus, Mont., "It's the challenge. Money isn't the big part of riding bulls. Just thinking about a certain bull for a few days beforehand . . . it's a hell of a feeling; knowing you've got to get on him, knowing you can get hurt . . . you can get butterflies in your stomach and sweat in the palms of your hands.

"I know you can damned sure get killed."

Bull-riding is the most popular event for the spectators. A rider uses a rope which is looped around the animal's midsection. The rope has a bell. The contestant puts a gloved hand in a loop in the rope and another cowboy pulls out the slack. The bull must be ridden for eight seconds. The rider is disqualified if he touches the animal with his free hand or if he is bucked off.

Rossen, who had plastic surgery near one eye because of a 1965 bull-riding injury, gave this capsule description of how to ride one of the bucking devils: "I keep my eyes toward the horns; whichever way his head goes, usually his body will follow. You've got to have the split second instinct of knowing what he's going to do."

Rodeo's classic event is the saddle bronc riding. Judges mark the rider on how well he spurs from the horse's shoulders to the saddle's cantle in a stroke called a "lick." The rider has nothing but a rope rein in his hand. The judges give the bronc a grade from one to 25 points on how well the animal bucks.

In both saddle bronc and bareback bronc riding the animal must be ridden for eight seconds.

The bareback rigging is similar to a handle on a suitcase. The rider uses one hand and must have his spurs over the break of the shoulders when the horse's front feet touch the ground on the first jump out of the chute.

Rodeo hand Jack Roddy said bronc riders adopt such unique styles it's almost dangerous for them to ride for pleasure.

"There was one cowboy who's one of the best bareback bronc riders in the country, but we wouldn't let him ride in the parades because we were afraid he'd fall off his horse," Roddy said. "He's used to holding onto that bareback bronc rigging and riding a certain way. It's not like sittin' a horse."

Steer wrestling is a crowd pleaser.

A contestant hurls himself from a galloping horse onto the horns of a madly scrambling steer. The cowboy must stop the steer and flip it to the ground. A second man, called the hazer, rides on the opposite side of the steer to keep the animal running on a line.

Calf roping demands intricate timing and the teamwork of the contestant's

Horse and rider show the perfect form that produces prize money in rodeo bareback bucking event at Colorado State Fair at Pueblo, Colo., in 1951. Spurring high ahead of the cinch is Harry Tompkins of Texas. Horse is Sunshine.

horse. Thousands of dollars in prize money rides on fractions of seconds. A good horse "rates" the calf and closes on him quickly regardless of how the calf dodges and weaves. The horse keeps the rope taut after the cowboy is successful with his throw. The contestant downs the calf and uses a light rope called piggin' string to tie the animal. The tie must hold for six seconds.

Bull-riding, steer wrestling, bulldogging, bareback and saddle bronc riding and calf roping are the main events in the rodeo. However, there are other added attractions such as barrel racing, quarterhorse cutting, team roping, steer roping, and an occasional greased pig chase.

Rodeo contestants are among the best conditioned in sport.

Dr. Bruce F. Claussen of North Platte, Neb., who was attending physician at more than 60 rodeos, said: "The top rodeo cowboys I have met are superbly conditioned individuals. I feel this is probably the major reason for the relatively low incidence of injuries. Of course, there are significant injuries in rodeo, and many of them are quite serious. But these are few and far between considering the number of rodeos the association sanctions."

Jim Shoulders is the Babe Ruth of the rodeo. He won a record 16 world championships between 1949 and 1959. The Henryetta, Okla., product, after retirement, ran a commercial rodeo school where young would-be ropers and riders learned the trade. Shoulders also raised stock and sold them to such events as the Mesquite, Tex., Championship Rodeo, in which he had a part interest.

The 5-foot-11, 160-pound Shoulders stressed that rodeos were not Wild West shows, but a sport where competition is stiff. He broke both arms twice, both knees twice and an ankle during his career. Once a racing steer stepped in his mouth, knocking out his teeth. A free bleeder, he bled for more than a day before the blood flow was stopped.

He confessed: "It's a young man's game."

The rodeo game has changed since Shoulders' heyday. The modern performers largely are college-bred men who take a splash of soda in their Scotch.

"Used to be," said Harry Tompkins, former world title holder from Dublin, Tex., "you could have a good time. Maybe get in a fight at a rodeo. But you better not now."

Tompkins, a rodeo immortal such as Dean Oliver, Casey Tibbs and Shoulders, said the well-groomed junior businessman was probably a good thing for the rodeo circuit.

"Actually, you shouldn't be out there making a dunce of yourself in front of the public, anyway," he said.

Larry Mahan, 26, of Brooks, Ore., became king of the modern rodeo professionals. He earned $57,726 in 1969 riding wild beasts.

Mahan owned a $20,000 twin-engine plane which he flew around the circuit. He put about 450 hours a year on the plane himself. Also, he spent $5,000 a year just for commercial plane tickets. He doled out $8,000 in entry fees alone.

But Mahan, who won the four all-around cowboy titles, doubled his winnings with endorsements of sportswear, hair oil, and the like. He's made television commercials, invested in Western wear products, played the stock market and had three new cars given him every year. He proved rodeo wasn't a hick sport.

The 5-foot-8, 152-pound Mahan never smoked and took only an occasional highball. The called him "Super Saddle" because of his uncanny ability to stay aboard the rankest of the bulls and broncs.

He was named the top professional athlete in his state in 1969. "This is so great because you have recognized rodeo as a sport," he said.

Mahan lived at Frisco, Tex., on the outskirts of Dallas—the centralized location easing the strain of traveling.

New Zealand, Australia and Canada have rodeos, but the world championship—the National Finals Rodeo—is held in Oklahoma City each year.

A foreigner qualified for the finals in 1970 for the first time. He was Jimmy Dix North of Collie, West Australia, who made the rodeo World Series in bareback bronc riding.

The National Finals is the rodeo World Series but the Houston, Tex., rodeo had the biggest payoff in 1969—$91,943.

Other top paying rodeos included Cheyenne, Wyo., $88,063; Fort Worth, Tex., $79,895; Denver, Colo., $78,548; Calgary, Alta., $75,037; San Antonio,

Tex., $59,388; Salinas, Calif., $53,503; Phoenix, Ariz., $50,681; San Francisco, Calif., $47,016, and Pendleton, Ore., $46,637.

Intercollegiate rodeo had a sharp growth. The National Intercollegiate Rodeo Association started at Alpine, Tex., in 1949 and by 1971 had 88 member colleges.

"It's got to be a big business," Shoulders said. "You talk about somebody winning $50,000. People realize it's a big thing. Look at pro football back 10 years ago compared to today. It's the same for rodeo. It's a growing business."

Mahan, who even designed his own clothes, said: "I can't think of anything I'd rather do. Even if I had a job where I'd make $50,000, it wouldn't be as much fun. I enjoy it so much I feel like I can go on forever."

Bareback rider at the Montana State Fair in 1946 found the world upside down after being flipped by his bucking bronco.

Competitors in the County Cork-New York selected hurling team duck the free-swinging effort of a Cork player in match at the Polo Grounds in New York in 1954. The visiting team, the All-Ireland champs, won, 29–19.

chapter 31

HURLING

Irish Were Playing When Greeks Were Running

by Geoffrey Miller

Irishmen claim that their ancestors were playing the ancient Gaelic sport of hurling when the Greeks were running and wrestling at the first Olympiad.

There is no telling how much truth is in the legend that Cu Chulainn, one of the mighty heroes of Irish mythology, once took on 150 men at once in a hurling game and defeated them single-handed. But it is recorded as history that the kings of Tara in the 6th and 7th centuries A.D. watched the boisterous game, in which the players wielded ash clubs and smote a ball the size of a man's fist.

In other European countries a man proved his prowess by taking a lance and tilting at an opponent in armor. In Ireland he was expected to excel with the hurling stick, or caman, as well, before he could win a fair lady.

The tremendous popularity of hurling today in the Republic of Ireland, and among Irish emigrants in many other countries, is partly due to the studied revival of interest in ancient Gaelic culture since independence. An estimated 100,000 men and boys in Ireland are affiliated to the Gaelic Athletic Association, the ruling body which controls hurling, Gaelic football and handball. But the association was formed in 1884, when independence was still 40 years off, and hurling had always been played.

Basically hurling is like a highly developed form of field hockey. The curved caman, four feet long, called the hurley by Irishmen, is not unlike a hockey stick.

The ball, called the sliothar, is hard and cased in leather. In modern hurling a team consists of 15 men—a goalkeeper, three fullbacks, three halfbacks, two midfields, three half-forwards and three full forwards. A score is made by hitting the ball into the goal-net (three points) or over the crossbar and between the rugby-style posts (one point).

The sport has come a long way since the kings of Tara watched it. In those days it was contested by huge armies of players. Even in the 17th century, when Oliver Cromwell's troops were in control of Ireland, the peasants played matches with 200 men on each side, and the English commanders gambled heavily on the results. Goals, it seems, were introduced to the game in Wexford long after that. "Hurling to goals," Wexford men called it in the early 19th century.

Only once was hurling in danger of dying. That was in the great famine of the 1840s, which led to the most massive emigration in Ireland's history, and so many young men left the country that there were no teams left. But in Limerick and Galway, Kilkenny and Cork, Tipperary and Waterford, the game was too deeply rooted to come to a permanent standstill. It was in full swing again, though badly in need of organization, when the Gaelic Athletic Association (GAA) was formed in 1884.

The GAA had a small beginning, for only seven men attended the public inaugural meeting. It took shape under the patronage of Dr. Croke, Archbishop of Cashel, after whom Ireland's biggest sports stadium, Croke Park in Dublin, was named. Michael Cusack, a Dublin schoolmaster with a passion for Gaelic culture, who later became the prototype for the Citizen in James Joyce's novel, *Ulysses,* was one of the association's founders.

The first championships between Irish county teams were staged in 1887, when the game was played by 21 men on each side. The team was reduced to 17 men, and then to 15. From 1887 to 1910 each county nominated a club side, but from 1910 the title has been disputed by county selections.

It is an all-Ireland tournament and the British-governed Northern counties compete, but the South has always dominated the title. Cork and Tipperary each has won it 21 times. Cork's most famous player was Christy Ring, a corner forward who took part in seven championship triumphs. Tipperary's stars have included Jimmy Doyle, Tony Wall, Johnny Leahy and Mick Mackey—names at which every Tipperary man bows the knee. Crowds of 90,000 watch the final at Croke Park.

Hurling clubs flourish among Irish communities in England, in London principally, but also here and there in the provinces. The sport is in a healthy state in New York and is played also in other parts of the United States as well as in Australia, New Zealand and South Africa. Irish emigrants introduced it to Argentina, but it died there in the 1930s.

Since about 1950, the New York club has maintained links with the old country by playing the winners of the All-Ireland Championship each year. Hurling has remained an amateur sport, and the championship winners get no prizes, but a trip to New York has become a prized reward. English teams go to Ireland to compete in the intermediate and junior championships, but have not been admitted to the senior event.

The annual encounter in New York was temporarily suspended following two tough games between Cork, the reigning Irish champion county, and New

York in October 1970. One match finished in a fracas which resulted in Clem Foley, who had been sent over from Dublin to referee, being hospitalized. On his return home, Foley sent in a report to the GAA, which took a stern view of the affair and suspended New York from membership until 1972.

Hurling is always liable to boil over. It is a rough game, but any Irishman will tell you that it is also a highly skillful game in which lightning reflexes, anticipation, sharpness of eye and control of the sliothar can make a player a star. A great hurler can trap the ball, lift it and send it flying to a teammate or into the net with skill equal to that of Pele in controlling a soccer ball.

The period following World War II brought a threatened decline in hurling. Gaelic football showed signs of overtaking it in popularity, and clubs were hard pressed to afford the ash camans in the face of spiraling prices. The GAA launched an energetic campaign to revive the game and in 1970 claimed that hurlers were increasing in numbers again. The association has never had any subsidy from the government and has paid its way from admission money paid by spectators, building Croke Park and equipping fields throughout Ireland.

Hurling remains an Irish sport through and through. Its players and officials are subject to a curious law which has survived, despite annual efforts at the GAA congress to have it abolished. They are not allowed to play, watch or encourage soccer, rugby union, cricket or field hockey, because those games were once associated with the British garrison in the days of Ireland's subjugation.

Tipperary goalie D. O'Brien, left, and Wexford forward J. Harding converged at O'Brien's goal during hurling match at Wembley in 1961.

Rosemary Cunnington, left, and her partner, Julie Charles, are shown in action in the girls' doubles event of the All-England junior badminton championship at Wimbledon in London in 1957.

chapter 32

BADMINTON

In India They Call it Poona

by Tom Saladino

Although badminton originated in India many centuries ago, the sport, then known as poona, did not leave that country until the 1860s when English army officials carted the game home.

It wasn't introduced to the United States until the close of the 19th century.

The English army men demonstrated the game for friends and officially launched it in 1873 at a party given by the Duke of Beaufort at his country place, "Badminton," in Gloucestershire. Until then this court game—considered by many the fastest and most exhausting of court contests—had no name but it was referred to as "the game at Badminton." This became its official title.

In the ensuing years, the popularity of the sport, played with a shuttlecock—a piece of cork with feathers attached, instead of a ball—a net stretched across a 20-foot court, 5-feet high by 44-feet long and with much shorter and lighter rackets than in tennis, weighing between 4½ and 5½ ounces and approximately 26 inches long, grew in popularity. It is now considered an international sport.

Until 1887, the sport remained almost exclusively in England, under the antiquated, original rules played in India, which were contradictory and indeed confusing.

A group of Englishmen organized themselves in 1887 into the Bath Badminton Club and standardized the rules which to this day regulate the game.

In 1895 the Badminton Association (of England) was formed to take over the authority of the Bath Club and it made up the rules which now govern the sport throughout the world.

Now the sport was ready to make a move internationally.

Quickly it spread to the United States, Canada, Australia and New Zealand as well as making inroads in Europe. Until then the game was played primarily by men, but now women began to take an interest and to this day the game is played equally by both sexes.

Probably the finest of American stars was Dr. David G. Freeman of Pasadena, Calif. He was a seven-time national champion and won countless tourneys in Canada, England and other foreign countries. From 1939 until the national championships were abandoned in 1942 because of the war, and for a few years after it, he dominated the men's game. He had uncanny accuracy from any spot on the court.

Among the women, Judy Devlin dominated from 1954 until 1962. The Maryland miss captured five U.S. girls championships and in 1954 was the first woman to hold both the senior and junior titles. She won five U.S. singles titles and numerous championships abroad. In 1957 she was the women's world champion and in that same year led the U.S. women to the Uber Cup world championship over Denmark, 6–1.

Another top women player, just a step below Miss Devlin, was Margaret Varner. In the 1960s Judy Hashman took over as the top women singles player.

Championships and tournaments, however, didn't start until 1899 when the first All-England championships for men were held. Women had their initial tournament a year later. Both were considered unofficial, however, until 1904, when the first official All-England Championships were held.

Evidence of the growth of the sport in England can be traced to the mushrooming of clubs. There were a mere 300 clubs in England in 1910. By 1930 there were 500 and more than 9,000 soon after World War II.

Recently the sport made even bigger strides, picking up recruits from the tennis courts. In general, badminton is considered less strenuous than tennis but when played by experts, particularly singles matches, it is one of the fastest and most exhausting sports of all.

Canada adopted the game in 1890 and the Americans soon after. The United States, however, eventually discarded it, then picked it up again in 1929 with vigor. It was a sport that called for lightning speed, extraordinary alertness and more skill than in most court games.

International teams were soon envisioned, patterned after the Davis Cup of tennis, but nothing was launched successfully until the 1930s when the game became organized in a sufficient number of countries. By 1940, 16 countries held national championships in the sport.

In March 1939, the International Badminton Federation felt the time for international competition was at hand. However, the war delayed the competition until the 1948–49 season when the inaugural Thomas Cup matches, named for the IBF president, Sir George A. Thomas, were played.

The matches are held between amateur teams, consisting of four to six players, and the series is held every three years. Preliminary rounds are in three zones—similar to the Davis Cup—American, European and Pacific. In the first series,

Malaya won the championship, defeating Denmark 8–1. Malaya again captured the trophies in 1952 and 1955, whipping the United States 7–2 in Singapore in 1952 and Denmark 8–1 in 1955.

Badminton can be played either indoors or out, but is primarily contested out of doors. For that reason it is almost exclusively a summer sport in America, while it is played year-around in California, which has produced the most outstanding players.

Outstanding American men besides Dr. Freeman were Walter R. Kramer, Chester Goss, Donald Eversoll, Hamilton Law, Richard Yeager, William Markham, Carl Loveday, Donald Richardson, Phillip Richardson, LeRoy Erickson, Reaford Haney, William Faversham, Wayne Schell, C. Raynor Hutchinson, Clinton Stephens, Richard Mitchell, Barney McCay, Webb Kimball, Roy Lockwood, Wynn Rogers, Marten Mendez and Joseph Alston.

Other outstanding women included Mrs. Del Barkhuff, Mary E. Whittemore, Evelyn Boldrick Howard, Mrs. Roy C. Bergman, Helen Gibson, Zoe Smith Yeager, Thelma Scovil, Janet Wright, Elizabeth Anselm, Helen Zabriski Ough, Shirley Stuebgen and Ethel Marshall.

Figure skating and speed skating are at opposite ends of the skating spectrum. Sonja Henie, above, and Lidia Skoblikova each excelled in their own specialties.

chapter 33

ICE SKATING

Sonja Henie's Movies Intrigued America

by Mike Recht

Ice skating is a bit of an unusual sport, owing its popularity not so much to talent and competition but instead to theatrics and showmanship, and a pretty, blonde Norwegian girl who caught the public eye at the age of 11.

Sonja Henie had been skating for three years when she won the championship of Norway at the age of 10, and then in 1924, the first year figure skating officially became a part of the Olympic Games, she finished dead last in the Games. But it was a very impressive last.

"Future aspirants for the world title will have to reckon with Sonja Henie of Norway, already a great performer who has every gift—personality, form, strength, speed and nerve," wrote Beatrix Loughran of the United States, who was the runner-up in these Games.

Indeed, Sonja Henie in the next three decades became the most successful figure skater in history and the darling of not only Norway but of the world. She was loved, admired and cheered even in places where there was no ice skating. She was not only a great figure skater, but the first heroine of the sport, a celebrity and a movie star.

Yet while she went on to win three Olympic titles—1928, 1932 and 1936—10 world titles from 1927 through 1936, eight European crowns from 1929 through 1936 and six Norwegian championships from 1924 through 1929, it was her costumes, her flare and her personality that carried ice skating to its current height of popularity.

Until Miss Henie came along, figure skating had not gone far from the long, black costumes and bulky hats trimmed with fur worn by women skaters, and spins, splits and jumps had still not gained full acceptance.

But she dressed in short, colorful skirts that caught the fancy of the public—an older girl might not have been able to appear in such skimpy outfits during that period—and the shorter clothing allowed her to be free and do more things on the ice. And they led to more dramatic figures.

She brought a charm and style and color to skating and this "girl in white," as she was lovingly called by her fans, soon had the entire world talking. But her competitive days were just the beginning.

In 1936, after winning her third Olympic title, she turned professional, and it was then that she did even more for the sport.

First, she starred in a skating act in Paris and then this 5-foot,110-pound magnetic personality came to the United States with her act and was a tremendous success. Then Hollywood put her in an ice show, followed by her own "Hollywood Ice Revue," the forerunner of all the great and successful touring ice shows. And finally came the movies. She became the first figure skating movie star, and millions who had only read about her now were able to see her and ice skating. She made millions of dollars.

Her success also influenced many other youngsters to turn to skating, with competitive skating now followed by a lucrative financial field of professional skating.

Because of the glamor she brought to ice skating, people such as Dick Button of Englewood, N.J., perhaps the greatest male skater in history, was able to get $150,000 for turning pro in 1952 after winning five straight world titles, seven consecutive U.S. crowns and two Olympic gold medals. He skated in ice revues, carrying through his introduction of power and athletics to skating with his high jumps, speed and jump-spin combinations.

Later came Peggy Fleming, a dazzling beauty from Colorado whose delicate grace on the ice won her the 1968 Olympic title and earned her a contract to skate in ice shows and on television that approached $1 million.

At least one judge during these Olympics called her "the best skater there has ever been." Button called her "a delicate lady on the ice."

"She is not a fiery skater," he said. "She is an exquisite skater, lyrical, expressive and technically fine."

Miss Fleming practiced seven hours a day for 10 years to acquire such finesse, class and style. Her name became a household word in the United States, and she also put the United States back on top in figure skating.

The Scandinavians had dominated the sport until 1948 when Button gave the United States its first gold medal in the 1948 Olympic Games and Barbara Ann Scott of Canada won the women's title.

In 1952, it was Button again with two teammates second and fourth, while U.S. girls finished 2-4-5 behind Jeanette Altwegg of England.

In 1956, Hayes Jenkins, who blended elegance and outstanding athletic feats, Ronnie Robertson and Dave Jenkins were 1-2-3 and Tenley Albright and Carol Heiss 1-2. Four years later the winners were David Jenkins and Miss Heiss.

But then tragedy struck the U.S. team when an airplane carrying many of the top U.S. skaters, promising new ones and teachers crashed over Brussels in 1961. Eighteen young men and women en route to the world championships were killed.

The United States didn't win another medal until Miss Fleming's performance at Grenoble. Miss Fleming brought the U.S. a long way in a short time, much shorter than it took the U.S. to become a power the first time.

While Americans have made important contributions to ice skating, the sport did most of its developing in Europe, and it wasn't until Miss Henie came to the Olympic Games at Lake Placid in 1932 that Americans really took notice.

Skating started in the Scandinavian countries as a means of travel, with small bones and then wood used for blades. The Scots fashioned the first iron skate and also started the first skating club in Edinburgh in 1642. It was in Scotland that it became more of a sport than just a means of travel or winter exercise.

British soldiers were believed to have introduced skating to the United States in the 1700s, and a U.S. artist, Benjamin West, won a skating championship somewhere in Europe during the 1770s.

Another American, E. V. Bushnell of Philadelphia, gave skating a tremendous boost around 1848 when he created the first steel skate.

In 1849, the Philadelphia Skating Club was formed.

During this same period, four Englishmen formed the scientific half of figure skating, documenting all turns and discovering new ones. They were H. E. Vandervell, whose other great contribution was the extending of the blade the length of the boot and rounding it off at the back to make skating backward easier; Maxwell Witham; Montague Monier-Williams, and a man named Pidgeon.

Graceful Peggy Fleming, who was to win a gold medal in the 1968 Olympic Games at Grenoble, France, executes this difficult maneuver during a practice session.

Dick Button, shown in a practice session, won an Olympic gold medal in the 1960 Games with a fantastic display of jumps and athletic feats never before seen on the ice.

These four represented the Victorian style of skating, the stiff, formal, dignified form of doing turns and figures on the ice.

Then along came another American, Jackson Haines, the male Sonja Henie of his day. Haines was a dancer who had studied ballet, and he also was a showman, handsome and charming. He brought to skating the dramatics and grace used in dancing. He revolutionized the sport.

While Americans and the English frowned on this new and more spectacular dimension to skating, the rest of Europe loved his spins and twists and jumps that took them away from the dreary, exacting figures of before. He was particularly loved in Vienna, where he introduced in 1854 the idea of skating to waltzes.

But Haines made one other great contribution—a new skate with the blade forged on to the toe and heel plate, which could be screwed on to the sole and heel of the boot. The cumbersome straps, with their loose fit, were done away with, and the skater now had new support and reliability which enabled him to do many more intricate turns and twists.

Finally, in 1876, came the first artificial ice rink, off King's Road in London, using John Gamgee's patented process of refrigeration. He had built a small ice floor earlier, but this later one was located in a permanent building and was 40-by-24 feet. Now skating was possible in countries where the weather failed to provide outdoor ice, and it also provided better conditions.

Speed skating had been popular before the 1800s, and by the 19th century it had become the national sport of Holland.

The first international speed and figure skating competition was held in Vienna in 1871–72 between Austria and Germany, and in Vienna in 1882 an international skating contest was held in which the two categories of figure skating emerged—special figures and free skating.

The first figure skating championships of Europe were held in 1891 and in 1896 came the first world championships, under the sponsorship of the International Skating Union, formed in 1891.

In 1893, the first amateur speed skating championships took place in Amsterdam at four distances—500, 1,500, 5,000 and 10,000 meters.

Women began competing for their own world championship in 1906 after Madge Syers of England shook up the men by finishing second to Ulrich Salchow of Sweden in the world championships in 1902. The pairs skating championships began in 1908.

The United States men's and women's titles began in New Haven, Conn., in 1914, established by Irving Brokaw of New York, a skater who went to Europe to learn the Viennese method and brought it back to America.

Brokaw also brought the first ice ballet show from Berlin to the United States.

In 1908, figure skating was held as a part of the Olympics and Salchow won. The United States did not send a team until 1920, after a break for the war, and in 1922 the U.S. Figure Skating Association was formed.

Salchow won the world title 11 times before Gilles Grafstrom of Sweden took over and won the Olympic gold medal in 1920, 1924 and 1928. U.S. skaters were unable to win any gold medals, but they were improving with such skaters as Nathaniel Niles, Theresa Weld, Beatrix Loughran, Maribel Vinson and Sherwin Badger.

Speed skating reached the Olympics in 1924, and by 1932 Charles Jewtraw, John Shea and Irving Jaffee gave the United States five gold medals, although the U.S. women had not won a medal up to the 1972 Games.

The Scandinavians dominated speed skating during this period, along with figure skating, until the Russians came along in the 1960s with such stars as E. Grishin and Lydia Skoblikova, who won six gold medals in 1960, the first year women competed in speed skating in the Olympics, and 1964.

A Russian couple, Ludmilla Belousova and Oleg Protopopov, dominated the pairs event in figure skating.

Millions of spectators come to see them race and perform now, whether it's in world competition or the touring ice shows, on television or in the movies. Skating now can be found on the sports pages and in the theatrical reviews, and much of the credit still goes to that pretty little Norwegian girl who opened the eyes of the world to skating.

Members of the Wimbledon Curling Club watch as a participant throws his stone during game on Wimbledon Common. The stones, which weigh 42 pounds, are beautifully polished granite fitted with handles.

chapter 34

CURLING

You Always Need a Broom

by Geoffrey Miller

Curling, one of the most ancient sports in the world, has probably the youngest world championship. The "bonspiel" for the world title was first held in 1968, and Canada won it to start a string of triumphs.

"Bonspiel" is one of the quaint terms used by curlers in the language of their sport, along with besom, pat-lid, wicking, chipping the winner and sooping the ice. They are all old Scottish words, for Scotland is the home of the game. There is some doubt whether it actually originated in Scotland or The Netherlands. The Dutch certainly had a hand in it, because even Scots at one time called the sport "kuting," which comes from an old Dutch word "khuyten," but if you were to tell a Scottish enthusiast that this was anything but a Scottish sport you would get a fierce answer.

Nobody knows for certain how many centuries it goes back. But it is safe to say that in the 16th century, when Mary Stuart was ruling Scotland and trying to keep her head on her shoulders, Scottish lairds and their ladies were sliding round boulders across the frozen lochs and trying to hit the target.

The Scots played lawn bowling centuries ago, and possibly curling was invented as a version of bowling on ice. They usually used crude, natural boulders in those days, drilled with a hole where a player could put his thumb to give the rock a twist and make it curl as it slid across the ice, but one curling stone, bearing the date 1551 and dug up near Stirling in the early part of this century, had handles attached.

The old Scottish curling terms have persisted and are used wherever the game is played. A bonspiel is simply a tournament. The besom is the broom used for sooping (sweeping) the ice in front of the sliding stone, to make it run true. A pat-lid is a stone lying on the tee. Wicking is cannoning off another stone. Chipping the winner is striking a stone which is largely obscured from the player's view.

A traditional grand bonspiel, dating back at least 150 years, is played annually on Lake Montieth in Perthshire—strangely enough the only lake in Scotland that is called a lake and not a loch. That bonspiel originated as a contest between clubs lying north of the Forth and Clyde Canal and clubs south of it. Hundreds of clubs take part. But curling today is played mostly on indoor rinks, which have multiplied at a remarkable rate since World War II.

The ruling body of the sport is the Royal Caledonian Club, which has its headquarters in Edinburgh. It began in 1838 as the Grand Caledonian Club, but changed its name to "Royal" after Queen Victoria watched the game being played on one of her many Highland holidays. The club today has an array of vice presidents drawn from Canada, the United States, Sweden, Norway, Switzerland, France, West Germany and New Zealand—an indication of the extent to which curling has spread in popularity.

In 1970 there were an estimated 50,000 curlers in Scotland, and about one-third of them were women. This is in a country that has a population of five million. Sixteen indoor rinks are in use, extending from ancient curling centers in the Highlands to the industrial cities in the south. In the Crossmyloof Rink in Glasgow, which is open seven days a week and 12 hours a day, 4,000 curlers enjoy their sport every week.

Curling reached Canada in 1807 and the United States about 15 years later. Emigrating Scots helped to make the sport popular in both countries. In Canada it was first played on the frozen St. Lawrence River at Montreal and Quebec, and iron stones were used when the Scottish granite stones were not available. In the United States the sport first took root in Detroit, Mich., with the founding of the Orchard Lakes Club, and later flourished in Utica, Schenectady and Saranac in New York State. Canada has 140,000 affiliated curlers in addition to 40,000 high school students. In the United States women players have their own association with 65 women's clubs.

In Switzerland, many hotels have their own curling rinks and there is a newspaper devoted exclusively to the sport. The Swiss have 159 registered curling clubs. France has 50 ice rinks, with curling growing rapidly in popularity year by year, and in 1970 a tournament in Germany was contested by 14 clubs. In Norway, more young people are reported taking up curling than any other sport, except skiing.

The first recorded international match was in 1902, when Scotland challenged the United States to send a team across the Atlantic. Scots, Americans and Canadians have played against each other regularly since, but it was not until the 1960s that any attempt was made to stage a representative world bonspiel. The Scotch Cup, sponsored by the Scotch Whisky Association, was contested by Scotland, Canada and the United States, with Sweden joining in later. Then Air

Canada took over the sponsorship and the bonspiel took the name of the World Curling Championships.

The event was held at Pointe Claire, Quebec, in 1968, Perth, Scotland, in 1969 and Utica, N.Y., in 1970. The Canadians have dominated the world title thus far, and in 1970 successfully defended the crown against seven rivals—Scotland, the United States, Switzerland, Norway, France, Sweden and West Germany.

Curling is one of the world's oldest sports. Players are shown in competition on ice at St. Moritz, Switzerland.

Englishmen M. J. Perkins, left, and F. R. D. Corbett, both of Surrey, England, participate in the British Amateur Squash Rackets Championships in 1955.

chapter 35

SQUASH

It's Not a Vegetable—and Not for Sissies

by Mike Recht

Just the name of the game brings a quiet chuckle from baseball-football devotees. No, squash is not played with vegetables, and it certainly is not a game for sissies.

Squash is, in fact, perhaps the fastest and most pressing game in the world, and also a fast growing one. It has come a long way from its start in an English prison to inclusion in the Ivy League and many of the nation's most exclusive athletic clubs.

During the years from 1963 to 1970, squash is said to have expanded more than 60 per cent in the United States, with more than 2,500 courts and 500,000 players. Perhaps the main reason it has not grown more is that it is so strenuous.

"Without question, the greatest appeal is that you can get a lot of exercise in a very short time," said 51-year-old William T. Ketcham Jr., special counsel to IBM's World Trade Corp.

Ketcham was one of the many executives who continued to play the game from his college days because it offers physical fitness and competition by the half-hour. That is all the time it takes to work up a very good sweat and lose six or seven pounds.

"There aren't many strenuous games you can play during the business day and still be back at work in 1½ hours," said Robert Tritsch, an attorney.

"For me it is a form of self-renewal. It's great exercise, requiring tremendous stamina and a great desire to win," added Richard Gelb, president of Bristol-Myers.

These are the type of men who play squash at such places as the exclusive Racquet and Tennis Club on Park Ave. in New York and the very proper Princeton Club.

Most of them are former students at Ivy League schools, where the game first took hold in this country after being shipped from England. But now it seems to be stretching farther into the middle section of the country.

By 1970 many colleges throughout the country were building courts and the YMCA also was adding the sport to its program. It no longer was just a "gentleman's" game, although it still remains a very sportsmanlike, courteous game marked by self-regulation and absence of controversy.

It is not a social game, however, such as golf in which businessmen are able to talk and conduct business. There are few statistics or incidents leading to rich anecdotes, no great games to relive, no great moments to remember.

"It is too fast a game for casual humor," said Frank Pace, former chairman of General Dynamics. Gelb added: "You don't play the game for chit-chat."

Yet while most squash players probably know little about the history and heroes of the sport—contrary to baseball and football devotees—squash has perhaps the most unique beginning of any sport. It was born in a prison.

During the 1700s, on the famous Fleet Street in London, a group of bored inmates in debtor's prison were supposed to have tried their hand at banging a rubber ball against a wall with a racquet, a kind of handball with racquets, or tennis without nets.

It was a big court, played outdoors with only one wall. Robert Mackey of England, a graduate of the Fleet Street prison, was the first World Open squash champion in 1820, although the sport faded a bit during that period until 1822 when it was revived at Harrow School in England.

In 1850, Harrow students were reported to have introduced a smaller court to counter the area and the cost needed to build one, and a smaller, softer ball that was easier to keep up with on the smaller court. This ball, when it hit a wall, gave off a squishing sound, and thus the name squash.

Racquets, played on a court as big as 60-feet-by-30-feet, with walls 30-feet high, uses a polyethylene ball with a tape covering. It moves very fast, but the bigger court compensates.

Squash racquets and squash tennis are played approximately on the same size court, about 32-by-21 with lower walls, although the doubles court is larger, 45-by-25.

Squash racquets use a softer, hollow rubber ball that can produce twisting, more difficult return shots. Squash tennis first used a regular tennis ball that speeded play, but didn't offer the same dazzling shots until a netting was put around it.

Allison Danzig described the difference between racquets or squash racquets and squash tennis this way:

"In racquets and squash racquets, the player goes to the ball, the speed is in the player's legs; in tennis, the ball comes to the player, the speed is in the ball."

But because the ball does travel so fast, squash tennis has little popularity today, and now is played mostly in New York, and then only in a few places. Racquets is played more and in a greater number of places, but squash racquets is by far the most popular.

The first costly racquets court was built at Woolwich, England, in the 1840s, and the first court in the United States reportedly was built in 1850 at the Broadway Racquet Club. By then, the sport was spreading to the United States, Canada, India and South America.

The New York Racquet Club opened its court in 1875 and numbered many of the leading sportsmen of New York City. By 1918, it moved to its palatial quarters on Park Avenue, where it has remained ever since as the Racquet and Tennis Club, the headquarters for racquet and tennis devotees.

The World Open racquets championship was held at odd intervals with breaks sometimes as long as 16 years, but Clarence C. Pell is generally considered the greatest player of all time, winning 12 U.S. singles titles between 1915 and 1933. He and Stanley Mortimer also won nine doubles crowns.

The new squash racquets spread from Harrow to Rugby and Eton in England, and then to Canada. From there, the Rev. James P. Conover, master of St. Paul's School in Concord, Mass., was said to have introduced it at St. Paul's in 1882.

While the enthusiasm for squash on the part of King Edward when he was the Prince of Wales helped lend impetus to the sport in England, clubs sprang up in the United States at Harvard, Yale, Princeton and in New York. The sport spread then to the Midwest and Pacific coast, although the East remained the center.

A Central Squash Committee was formed in 1919 in the United States and then the Tennis and Racquet Association came into being in 1923 and standardized rules.

The sport caught on quickly in the colleges because it was easy to learn, did not demand hours of practice and was fun. John A. Miskey was the first U.S. champion in 1907 in a tournament held in Philadelphia, and Stanley Pearson won the title six times between 1915 and 1923.

Hashim Khan of Pakistan was considered the greatest player after entering international match play in 1944. Seven times he won the British Open, the largest tournament, the last time in 1967 at the age of 42. Only some 250 people can squeeze into that London court for the championship, while other courts hold perhaps 50. The first women's U.S. champion was Eleanora Sears of Boston in 1928.

Matches developed between countries—the Wolfe-Noel Challenge Cup between the United States and Britain began in 1933, and the Laphan Trophy, between the United States and Canada, started in 1922.

The first squash tennis champion was Dr. Alfred Stillman of Boston in 1911, although Stephen Feron, who helped create the game, was the professional champion from 1902–14. Harry F. Wolf of the New York Athletic Club dominated the sport from 1930–40, earning the title of the greatest squash tennis player.

By 1934, sporting goods dealers who sold the ball and the racquet rated squash the fourth fastest growing sport, although it slowed later with the growth of other sports.

However, in the 1960s particularly, it began to pick up steam again after the national emphasis on physical fitness. It was perfect for students who didn't have the time or talent for football, baseball and basketball in college, and for those businessmen who had to sneak in their exercise during lunch breaks.

One executive said: "It keeps your responses lively, provides a lively thinking situation and a lot of action."

This is rugby—rough, tough and muddy. Like figures caught in an artist's clay model, these are players in an Australia-England match in Sydney in 1950.

chapter 36

RUGBY

Mass Emotion at its Peak in Wales

by Geoffrey Miller

Mass emotion is a feature of most of the big spectator sports. But one does not really know what mass emotion is until he has stood on the terraces at Arms Park, Cardiff, to watch the Welsh rugby union team play an international match, and has heard 60,000 Welsh fans break spontaneously into *Land of My Fathers* as Wales surges toward victory. For the Welsh, rugby is the highest form of patriotism.

It is one of the most physical of all sports, with success depending largely on sheer brawn, but it has remained strictly amateur. The four British rugby unions—England, Wales, Scotland and Ireland—have for years refused to listen to suggestions for starting league or cup competitions for their clubs, for fear such a move might destroy the tradition of rugby as an amateur sport, played purely for enjoyment. The game, which originated in Britain, has spread throughout the world and retained its amateur character everywhere.

When the English Rugby Union celebrated its centenary in September 1970, it invited delegates from all over the world to a congress at Cambridge, and more than 50 countries responded. It was informal, because there is no world governing body. Some countries even sent delegates from more than one rugby authority. South Africa was represented by four regional unions and the United States by two—the Eastern Union and the Pacific Coast Union. Yet strangely enough, although the game is so disunited, it is played everywhere to the same pattern—15 men on a side, aiming to score tries (touchdowns) or goals (kicked between the posts and over a crossbar), with a pack of eight forwards to push forward and gain ground, four three-quarters to run with the ball and score tries, two halfbacks to link up and coordinate, and a fullback to make the last line of defense and specialize in place kicking.

Argentina and Fiji have sent touring teams to Britain in recent years and offered strong opposition to the best club sides, and there are more than 1,000 clubs in Japan. But top-class international rugby has always been dominated by the four British countries, France, Australia, New Zealand and South Africa.

Alone among sports, rugby can claim an individual inventor. He invented it, apparently, out of frustration while trying to play an all-kicking form of football. Just when and how rugby players took to using an egg-shaped ball instead of a round one is obscure, but a memorial stone at Rugby College in the English Midlands explains how the game was born:

WILLIAM WEBB ELLIS

of Rugby College, 1823.

This stone commemorates the exploit of

William Webb Ellis,

who with a fine sense of disregard for the rules of football, as played in his time, first took the ball in his arms and ran with it, thus originating the distinctive feature of the Rugby game.

A.D. 1823.

The first international match was between Scotland and England at Edinburgh in 1870, with 20 men on each side. The present 15-man team formation was adopted soon after that, and the modern scoring system—three points for a try, two more if the try is converted to a goal, three for a penalty goal or drop goal—dates basically from 1905, though it has undergone some amendment.

After 1878, England and Scotland competed annually for the Calcutta Cup, one of the handsomest of all sports trophies—a finely-worked Indian silver tapered cup with snake handles and a model elephant on the lid. England, Scotland, Ireland and Wales have competed in the International Championship since 1893. France, which took up the game early in this century, joined the championship in 1909, dropped out of it in 1931 after a bitter row with the British over alleged rough play and professionalism among French clubs, and re-entered after World War II. The event is now often called the Five Nations Tournament.

Through 1970, the championship title was won outright 16 times each by England and Wales and 14 times by Scotland. The Irish, though always famed for their fiery forward play, managed only seven titles. The French, coming into their own after World War II, won the championship five times between 1959 and 1970. On 15 occasions the crown was shared in two-way or three-way ties.

In the early days it was the Scots who dominated the international scene, with such famous players on their team as Mark Morrison and D. R. Bedell-Sivright in the pack and K. J. Macleod at fullback. The Welsh, with stars such as Gwyn Nicholls, Percy Bush and Dr. Teddy Morgan, reached the top later. They won the title six times between 1900 and 1911.

Then came England's turn to dominate. The English were champions three times in five years before World War I and again three times in five years from 1920. Some of the men who took England to the top were "Cherry" Pillman, Adrian Stoop and R. W. Paulton-Palmer before 1914, and W. W. Wakefield (Wakers, as rugger fans called him), W. J. A. Davies and C. A. Kershaw in the postwar period. It is a tradition of British rugby that players are known by their initials rather than by first names.

Pillman revolutionized forward play. He broke fast from the scrummages and ran in support of his three-quarters—and started a technique that has become a feature of the modern game. Davies and Kershaw were rated by many critics as the finest halfback pair of all time.

The luck of the Irish eluded them in rugby and they went from 1899 to 1935 without winning the championship once, although they produced their full share of great players. Eventually they triumphed under the captaincy of Karl Mullen and won the crown two years running in 1948 and 1949.

The rise of France after World War II was led first by Guy Basquet and then by Jean Prat, both honored captains. Recent French triumphs have underlined the importance of a specialized goal kicker, who can swing a whole tournament by piling up the points. When the French won the title in 1967, Guy Camberabero, one of two brothers on the team, kicked five drop goals, two penalties and four conversions and contributed 29 of his side's total of 44 points in three international games.

France won the tournament again in 1968 and Guy Camberabero again played a vital part, landing a drop goal, a penalty and a conversion in the 14–9 victory over Wales at Arms Park which silenced the Welsh hymn-singers and clinched the title for France at the end of the season. The following year, however, Wales found an answer in Keith Jarrett, who stole Guy Camberabero's thunder and kicked five conversions and two penalties. That helped to bring the Welsh their 16th title.

New Zealand, South Africa and Australia have been world powers in rugby since before World War I. Dave Gallaher led the first New Zealand touring team, the "All Blacks," to Britain in 1905. The South Africans—the "Springboks"—first challenged the British in 1906. The Australians—the "Wallabies"—first toured Britain in 1908 under a famous captain, Dr. H. M. Moran.

At various times New Zealand and South Africa have been hailed as unofficial world champions. Australia has been less successful but has often played the most popular rugby—an open, running game, more exciting to watch than the power play, based on heavy and brawny forwards, favored by the other two countries.

British fans took a long time to accept the South Africans' style. The forwards pushed relentlessly forward and the backs were used as support troops, kicking into touch to gain ground and only attacking when in comfortable striking distance of the line. B. L. Osler, South African captain in 1931, gave his men a motto: "Attack only within sight of your opponents' goalposts," in the fashion of the general who told his soldiers to hold their fire until they could see the whites of the enemy's eyes. It was not the most popular rugby, but it made the Springboks the most feared team in the world.

The four British countries, traditionally rivals at home, have linked up as the

The menacing figures of his teammates do little for Ken Kearney of New South Wales who clutches ball but is grappled by Englishman Charlie Pawsey in rugged rugby match in Sydney, Australia.

British Lions for tours of New Zealand, South Africa and Australia since 1903. The Lions have never won a series of test matches in New Zealand or South Africa, although they have conquered Australia several times.

The Lions first learned to respect the South Africans in 1903, when they toured the Union and foundered against the brilliant three-quarter play of Bob Loubser and Japie Krige. Even in 1910, when Cherry Pillman was at his peak and was inspiring the team, the Lions could manage only one victory to South Africa's two.

The Lions' best effort in South Africa was in 1955, when the series ended in a 2–2 tie. That tour included one of the most historic of all international games, the first test at Johannesburg, in which the Lions held out to win 23–22 after leading 23–14 with only three minutes to go. Chris Koch put South Africa within sight of victory by bulldozing his way through the England players to score a magnificent try. But J. H. Van der Schyff, usually noted for his deadly goal-kicking, missed a simple conversion in the tension of the final seconds. That game was watched by a crowd of 95,000, a world record.

New Zealand's supremacy on its home ground is told simply by the match records of each test series against the Lions—1–0 in 1904, 3–1 in 1930, 3–0 in

1950, 3–1 in 1959, 4–0 in 1966. Bob Scott and Don Clarke, both fullbacks, are New Zealand heroes of modern times who have helped to clip the Lions' claws.

Considering its brawny character, rugby has been kept remarkably free from arguments on and off the field. It is rare for a player to be sent off the field for dirty play. Even the tough South Africans managed to steer clear of trouble when they toured Britain in the winter of 1969–70 and ran into violent demonstrations by political groups protesting the South African government's racial policies.

The scenes were the most remarkable ever seen at British sports centers. On occasions hundreds of police battled with demonstrators who were trying to get into the stadiums. Those who did infiltrate invaded the field at given signals and held up play by sitting down or scattering nails on the turf.

The South Africans, led by a quiet and dignified captain in Dawie de Villiers, kept their cool and never got involved in a single scuffle. But the tension apparently undermined their form, for they lost to England, Scotland and Ireland and could manage only a draw with Wales.

It's rough and tough, this game of rugby, and it has its embarrassing moments, too, as this Australian player can attest. As he was tackled from the front by an opposing player in Sydney another opponent grabbed him by his stretch shorts setting up the pink cheek episode.

This woman judo expert easily flipped male counterpart to mat during demonstration before spectators and judge.

chapter 37

JUDO

The Dutch Usurp Japan's Specialty

by Kay K. Tateishi

Kanemitsu Kay Tateishi, U.S.-born, bilingual and fiftyish, learned his "ABC" in judo as a boy in Los Angeles but didn't get as far as "XYZ" because of asthma. He wore a white belt, the lowest rank and honored one and all comers taking up the bruising art of self-defense. He has been a newsman for more than three decades including stints with the wartime *Domei News Agency, Asahi Shimbun, Japan Times,* and *Time* and *Life* magazines. He has been with *The Associated Press* for the past 15 years, working as a reporter, rewrite man and editor, handling a wide range of subjects, including sports, in the Tokyo bureau.

Ever since Anton Geesink, the 6-foot-6, 240-pound Dutchman topped the Japanese at their own game of judo in 1961 and repeated in two consecutive world title matches, including the Tokyo Olympic Games, the Japanese have been smarting over the loss of their world supremacy. The Japanese had a bitter pill to swallow when Geesink's successor, Willem Ruska, also from The Netherlands, pulled off a repeat performance in the unclassified division at the fifth world judo meet in Salt Lake City.

The Japanese had strongly opposed in 1956, when the first world judo championship began, the setting up of various weight categories, confident that David was superior to Goliath in a sport that depends largely on the skillful use of the opponent's strength, weight and momentum to throw him off balance and defeat the opponent. Man for man, pound for pound, the Japanese took over when the weight divisions were decided upon for making judo, literally "the gentle way," into a world sport. But within five years, the no-weight division proved the toughest for the Japanese to conquer. Although the Japanese fielded judo athletes who were far from midgets, standing 6 feet and weighing 180 to 190 pounds, they were no match in the showdown against the mighty Dutchman.

After losing the third, fourth and fifth world judo crowns, the Japanese finally made a comeback at Mexico City in 1969 when Masatoshi Shinomaki topped Ruska, the 1967 champion.

But as if to rub salt in a wound, Geesink, owner of a string of judo academies in Holland, winner of three world titles, the 1964 Olympic championship, 11 European crowns and 26 Dutch and author of several books on judo, often said before his retirement in 1965: "The Japanese don't concentrate enough on technique. . . Physical strength is necessary for judo. A big man has a better chance of winning the match over a small man if he practices and competes under the same conditions."

The gathering of judo greats in Tokyo for the first world judo championships in 1956 fulfilled the dreams of Dr. Jigoro Kano, originator of modern day judo as a character molding sport. He consolidated the best techniques of a variety of jui-jitsu, hand-to-hand combat, said to have originated in ancient China. In 1882, Kano founded the Kodokan, the Mecca for some 400,000 judo black belts or graded judo competitors outside Japan and the world's foremost judo school.

Judo was introduced in the Western Hemisphere by 1887. In 1902 Kano sent Yoshiaki Yamashita, one of his oldest and ablest disciples, to the United States at the request of President Theodore Roosevelt. Others were sent to Europe and South America to spread the sport. Japanese immigrants to the United States and other parts of the world turned out to be good apostles for judo. Kano, himself a little man, a member of the Japanese Olympic committee, often gave demonstrations.

Until the end of World War II, Japan had nearly three million judo athletes in all schools and colleges and in some 6,000 public judo halls. But for two years

T. Sgt. Ralph Christopher supervises as a couple of youngsters engage in a judo lesson. The popularity of judo is skyrocketing among the young.

after the surrender, Gen. Douglas MacArthur's headquarters banned the sport along with kendo, Japanese fencing, and kyudo, archery. But claims that judo fostered militarism fell flat. Judo was primarily a method of self-defense without weapons in personal encounter. Its combative techniques were widely used by friend and foe alike and once judo was restored as a healthy sport it came back fast with widespread interest throughout the world.

Europe and Asia, after World War II, organized their own judo federation, as did the United States where the Amateur Athletic Union established rules and conducted tournaments. In December 1952, the World Judo Federation was inaugurated in Paris and today has an estimated membership of 1.5 million from more than 65 countries.

Judo is no simple sport. It requires extensive practice and training under competition. The judo athlete must learn a number of techniques, including the art of falling on his back so he won't suffer injury.

In a judo match, two contestants, dressed in baggy, knee-length pants and judo jackets which are kept tied with a wrap-around belt, walk to the center of a 30-square-foot straw mat. They exchange salutes, usually a bow to each other, from a standing position or from a sitting position. It is the equivalent of the opening handshake in boxing. After the formality, they move toward each other to grab the jacket lapel of the other. They tug, push, trip, pull, any one of an accepted assortment of maneuvers, in an endeavor to subdue the opponent.

To win, he must throw his adversary from a standing position known as "tachi-waza," pin him to the straw mat known as "newaza" or force him to give up with a stranglehold known as "schimewaza." A partial or not clean-cut throw is called "wazaari," with two "wazaaris" needed to win. Time limit in elimination matches of a championship tournament is 10 minutes; for the championship final 20 minutes. A referee and panel of judges officiate.

Japanese terminology in general prevails.

Although the Japanese have often been accused of holding back secrets and winning techniques in judo, several hundred aspiring judo athletes flock to Japan annually, seeking out the Kodokan or some other judo training camp, to train and compete against the experts. That was one of Geesink's secrets to success. He visited Japan on numerous occasions and trained hard, finally rising to the pinnacle of judo. "I learned my judo from the masters," Geesink said when he upset Japan's Koji Sone in Paris on Dec. 3, 1961.

The art of judo has lured women, primarily as a means of self-defense. And the Kodokan, well aware of the importance of women in sports, extended its official blessing in 1923 by setting up a women's department. Its objective: Build up feminine beauty, harmoniously develop the mind and body and create rhythmical movement and graceful action through gentleness. Japan now has some 5,000 female judo adherents of which 3,000 are members of Kodokan.

There is also a large following in other parts of the world where it is being taught to secretaries, guides, campus coeds, hostesses.

One of the ladies who gave the sport a healthy boost in the 1970s was pretty Dewi Sukarno, Japanese widow of the late President of Indonesia. She kept in physical trim by practicing judo daily at her home in Paris. She said: "These days a woman is so likely to be attacked that she ought to know how to defend herself."

Ted Williams, no stranger to the baseball diamond, is likewise no stranger to the sport of fishing. The camera caught him in 1955 as he landed a bone fish during a Florida fishing outing.

chapter 38

FISHING AND ANGLING

Thirty Million Americans Wet the Hook

by Tom Saladino

Fishing and angling are enjoyed by countless millions of people throughout the world. Over 30 million alone are counted in the United States as participants in this leisure sport and an added attraction is that many times it leads to an exciting adventure or an exotic spot on the map.

To the average fisherman it is the beauty associated with fishing which is more important than the actual catching of the fish. The person recognizing this perhaps derives the most from this relaxing sport.

If a sportsman's thoughts are of a more serious nature, he doesn't necessarily need to own a swanky yacht or travel halfway across the world to land a record catch.

Many casual anglers have snared world record fish in their own areas without the slightest notion that it would rate official listing in the International Game Fish Association world record book.

The more experience one has, the better it is. The finer the equipment, the chances increase. But the biggest single factor in this tremendously popular sport is luck—with perseverance a contributing quality.

There are more than 600 salt water record classifications, ranging from a 2,664-pound all-tackle mark for a white shark to a 3-pound, 12-ounce listing for sea bass in the 8-pound line test class.

The records are separated into two main divisions—one including over-all record catches by either men or women anglers, and another division for women anglers only. In both divisions, records are kept for 52 common species of salt water fish in seven categories based on line sizes. *Field and Stream* magazine is the official fresh water record keeper.

Angling and fishing are related sports but the serious and orthodox angler prefers to be regarded as a different breed than the fellow who is content just to catch a handful of fish.

The scientific angler is one who can make a cast and hit a designated spot anywhere from 125 to 375 feet away, whereas the ordinary fisherman is concerned in only acquiring something—usually a lot of it—for the frying pan. Also, an angler can find a great deal of satisfaction by making casts in competition—water is not even necessary—while the fisherman's joy is just catching fish.

No historian knows the identity of the first fisherman but it has been established that the first fish caught were with bare hands and that Persia was the pioneer nation to add fish to its national diet.

"Tickling" was an early method of fishing. It involved leaning over a pool in a stream where fish swam lazily and slipping one's hand under the belly of the fish and tickling it. While the fish enjoyed this pleasure, the sly human carefully opened his fingers and proceeded to snatch up the unsuspecting fellow, separating the prey from the water.

This method is still used in many countries. In the Rocky Mountain region of the United States it is still popular, especially during droughts. When the streams are almost dry, the only water is in the pools and the trout loiter in sluggish condition. The fish cannot dart away because there is nowhere to run to and thus fall victim to the "ticklers."

Another form of fishing was the spear, which came into being before the Christian era. Spears could be lost, thus fishing with them was considered not sport but a source of food.

Another form of modern line fishing was originated by the Egyptians. They used a vine to which a burr was attached. The burr swished in the waters to attract the fish. When the fish struck and swallowed the burr, they were hooked. Larger fish, which might disgorge the burr or break the vine, were pulled closer to shore before being hit and stunned with a club.

However, the Egyptians, realizing the weakness of the vines, devised a fishing line made of animal hair, which they braided. They manufactured lines of unlimited length and attached them to thornwood branches, which enabled them to cast well out from the shore.

The lines worked well but the burrs were still not helpful with larger fish, so they invented hooks made of bone with one end sharpened. Other nations took up the practice but soon substituted ivory for bone, then bronze, iron and steel. The reverse barb on fishhooks, which prevents fish from slipping off, was a modern creation.

The Persians started eating fish about 3000 B.C. Then the Assyrians followed suit. In 900 B.C. the Chinese started fishing enthusiastically and in 500 B.C., the Jews became interested. The Jews, realizing the folly of catching but one fish at a time, introduced the woven net, thus bringing about wholesale fishing and the beginning of a new enterprise.

It has never been established when the art of fly catching came into play. This method called for using an imitation bait instead of live lure. The original artificial bait was an imitation of a fly.

An Italian, Aelian, is credited with being the first to write about fly-casting around 200 A.D.

The reel was first mentioned in 1651, when Barker, an Englishman, wrote *The Art of Angling*. He wrote that it was created about 1496 A.D. but supplied no further data. Other historians agree that a crude reel was in existence in the 15th century.

In the 17th century, angling gained popularity and fly-casting contests were held in England. Soon informal angling clubs were formed, and entering the 19th century Englishmen spurned any other method of fishing.

In 1732 the first fishing club in North America was formed. It was called the Schuylkill Fishing Company, with headquarters in Philadelphia. The organization still functions today and is probably the oldest sports body of any type. It is now known as the Fish House Club.

The American Rod and Reel Association was founded in the United States more than 100 years ago, with all members pledged to fish only by fly-casting. The sport was finally given national fame in 1893 when the Chicago Fly-Casting Club was organized. It used the World's Fair that year to exploit the sport by holding the first U.S. tournament.

More tourneys followed in 1897, 1903 and 1905. At Kalamazoo, Mich., in 1906 the idea of a permanent organization took shape and the National Association of Scientific Angling Clubs was formed. In 1907 the first tournament under the NASAC was held. This strictly amateur organization still governs the fly-casting sport today. But its name has been changed to the National Association of Angling and Casting Clubs.

Small fry try their luck for the "big one" on a Sunday afternoon at William Land Park in Sacramento, Calif., in 1967.

Spectators line coastal thoroughfare near Los Angeles to watch Attilio Pavesi, a youthful Italian cyclist, finish first in the Olympic 100-kilometer road race in August 1932.

chapter 39

CYCLING

The Tour de France is the World Series

by Harvey Hudson

Harvey Hudson, who first showed an interest in bicycles in Olney, Ill., at about the age of 6, has been a member of *The Associated Press* staff in Paris since 1948. During his long overseas assignment, he has been a member of *The Associated Press* reporting teams at the Winter Olympics in Oslo in 1952 and Grenoble in 1968, and the Summer Olympics in Helsinki in 1952, Melbourne in 1956 and Rome in 1960. He has also covered such events as world cycling championships, world ski championships, world figure skating championships, boxing, tennis and golf.

In the era of trips to the moon, supersonic jet planes and automobiles that can roll at 200 miles an hour, the bicycle is sometimes brushed off as an anachronism, like the horse. But horse racing has lost none of its popularity; neither has bicycle racing in many parts of the world. And, if it makes any difference, a man on a bicycle can get from one place to another faster than a man on a horse.

Bicycle racing, with professionals as the stars, ranks as the summer national sport (soccer takes over during the winter months) in a handful of Western European nations headed by France, Italy, Belgium, Holland and Spain. Amateur cycling, which is part of the Olympic program, thrives in eastern and northern Europe, Central America and South America, Africa, Japan and Australia. Hardy cells of American riders, bucking the trend toward spectator-oriented sports, keep cycling at a bare subsistence level in the United States, but it's hard work both on and off the track.

Just as business activity slows in the United States during the World Series, France lives in a state of suspended animation for three weeks during the Tour de France marathon. As many as 100,000 picnicking fans turn out for the road races of the annual world cycling championships.

The history of bicycle racing goes back almost exactly 100 years. Before organized racing could start, inventive minds had worked for 80 years to dream up the principle of two-wheeled transportation and make the idea workable.

Cyclist is silhouetted against a scorching sun during workout for Pan American games at Winnipeg, Canada, in 1967.

Man had known the wheel for centuries before anyone thought of putting two of them in line, held together by a frame. No one knows who thought of it first. A design has survived of a crude two-wheeler built from wood in Paris shortly after the French Revolution. The rider straddled the frame with his two feet touching the ground and propelled himself forward. In 1818, a German had the idea of letting the front wheel pivot, to permit changes in direction. The English adopted this advance and built the frame of iron. Then an Englishman built a tricycle which was propelled with levers.

A big breakthrough came in 1861, when Ernest Michaux, working in his father's blacksmith shop near Paris, was struck by the idea of putting pedals on the front wheel. With this development, the front wheel was enlarged to get maximum distance from one rotation of the pedals. Later came the solid rubber tire to replace the metal band on the wheels, the idea of driving from the rear wheel, addition of the chain drive, and pneumatic tires.

Racing couldn't wait for perfection of the vehicle, however. Young sports chased each other around the alleys of the Royal Palace in Paris or the parks of

London early in the 19th century on their crude wooden two-wheelers. They vied for attention with the sack racers at village festivals. Horse racing was used as the model. Bets were made and riders were given handicaps based on past successes.

But the first big international competition was on Nov. 7, 1869, when about 100 competitors—both men and women—on bicycles, tricycles and four-wheelers set out for a 76-kilometer race over the muddy roads from Paris to Rouen. The winner, in 10 hours 40 minutes, was James Moore, an Englishman who had already distinguished himself in local races in France. The first woman to finish was Miss America, in 29th place. It turned out that Miss America was an English lass.

The awakening interest brought extravagant schemes. French and British teams exchanged visits in an effort to prove national superiority. Samuel Dealar, an American, said he was going to travel from New York to Paris by bicycle. He pedaled across the United States and up the west coast of Canada. Last heard from he was waiting for the water to freeze in the Bering Strait so he could make it across to Siberia. That was in 1870.

The bicycle's superiority over the horse was proved—to the satisfaction of the cyclists—in 1875. The controversy was set off by a Lt. Zubowitz, a Hungarian, who rode his favorite mare from Vienna to Paris in 15 days and was hailed as a hero for the exploit. Two French cyclists set out to prove they could do better. One of them arrived in Vienna 12 days and 15 hours later. The other had to give up because his bicycle broke down within 24 hours of Vienna.

Six-day bicycle races on indoor tracks started about this time. Cyclists and horses ran on different tracks at the Agricultural Hall in London. Charles Terront, a Frenchman, won the six-day races in Boston and Chicago in 1879.

As cycling grew in popularity, federations were formed to set and enforce the rules and keep the records for both track and road racing.

Track racing is over enclosed circuits in stadiums and is usually broken down into sprints, pursuit races, motor-paced, relays or combinations of these specialties. The sprint races are timed on the last 100 meters as paired riders complete one lap of the track. In pursuit races, the riders start from opposite sides of the track and are timed for set distances, as for three kilometers or five kilometers. In motor-paced races, the riders pedal behind trainers on motor bikes who break the wind and set the pace. Six-day races, once extremely popular in the United States and Europe with teams of two riders relaying each other over the full 24 hours, have almost disappeared.

Road races, over open highways, may be point-to-point competitions in a single day, or multiple-stage grinds that extend over several days or weeks.

Although the big classics of the point-to-point races—Liége-Bastogne-Liége in Belgium, Bordeaux-Paris in France and Milan-San Remo in Italy are examples—can contribute to a cyclist's fame, the big payoff comes from victories in the famous multi-stage endurance races such as the Tour de France, Tour of Italy or Tour of Spain.

The Tour de France is the summit of the tours. It is the oldest and hardest. A victory in the Tour de France is the most coveted prize in cycling. Because of the success of this original, the Tour de France has had many imitators. Almost any country with enough cyclists to form a quorum now has its own tour. Once there was even a Tour of Monaco, with the cyclists pedaling several times around the hilly terrain of the 370-acre principality between lunch and dinner.

The Tour de France was the brainchild of Henri Desgranges, publisher of the newspaper *L'Auto,* who organized the first edition in 1903. The Tour was divided into six stages, each averaging about 250 miles. The winner was Maurice Garin of France, who averaged about 15 miles an hour over the dirt roads. Except for breaks during wars, the Tour de France has been an annual fixture since then.

It has aroused passions, stirred hatreds, consecrated champions and seen its share of tragedies. Where cycling was once a minor attraction at local festivals, the Tour de France became the whole festival, moving its county fair atmosphere around the country for one-night stands.

Crowds gather along the roadside in sunny weather or rain or cold to watch the riders, crouched low over their bicycles to cut wind resistance, flash past. More crowds gather at the finish line, which is set in a stadium where possible. Carnival spirit reigns at night in the towns designated for stopovers. Radio stations carry progress reports during the day, and television relays the finish each day. The Tour has become as much a part of France as the vineyards of Burgundy.

The Tour barely survived one of its gravest crises in 1904. In Nîmes, supporters of a local rider who had been disqualified blocked the road and scattered tacks. Between Lyon and Marseille, the riders were attacked. At a mountain pass, spectators let their favorites pass and barred the road to the others. Four months after the Tour ended, the first four finishers were disqualified for cheating. Desgranges, the organizer, declared the Tour dead, a victim of its own success. But he changed his mind by the summer of 1905, and the third edition cut out nighttime runs and put some of the finishes outside towns to avoid crowds.

By 1950, the Tour de France was a smooth running organization but the passions were unchanged. That was the year when Gino Bartali of Italy, a two-time winner in 1939 and 1948, got the fright of his life. As Bartali tells it, he and Jean Robic of France accidentally collided and fell together during a run through the Pyrenees Mountains. Then, he said, spectators attacked him with fists and sticks. Bartali went on to win the day's leg but that night he announced he was pulling out of the Tour and he took the whole Italian team home with him. "I'm afraid," he said. "I don't want to die on the roads of France. A wife and two children are waiting for me at home."

Bartali and Fausto Coppi were Italy's two greatest modern stars. Bartali won the Tour de France twice and the Tour of Italy twice. He might have added appreciably to this list if World War II had not come when he was at his peak. Coppi, the campionissimo or supreme champion, won the Tour de France twice and the Tour of Italy twice. During his career which extended from 1940 to 1960, he also won two world pursuit championships, one world road racing championship, a number of classics and held the record for one hour of cycling for 14 years.

Philippe Thys of Belgium won the Tour de France three times, in 1913, 1914 and 1920. But Louison Bobet of France was the first to win three in a row. Bobet did it in 1953, 1954 and 1955, and won the world road racing title as well in 1954.

Then came Jacques Anquetil of France who beat the records of all his predecessors. Anquetil won the Tour de France five times—in 1957, 1961, 1962, 1963 and 1964. He had one victory in the Tour of Italy and one in the Tour of Spain. He was the first man to win each of the three big marathons. Anquetil twice bettered the record for one hour of cycling before he retired, at the ages of 21 and 33. The second record was never recognized because Anquetil failed to take an anti-dope test, but it didn't matter since the mark was beaten a few days later.

A new star moved in during the mid-1960s and threatened to pulverize all previous performances. Eddy Merckx of Belgium won the amateur world road racing championship in 1964, the professional road racing title in 1967, the Tour de France in 1969 and 1970 and the Tour of Italy in 1968 and 1970. Coppi, Anquetil and Merckx became the only riders who have won the Tour of Italy and the Tour de France in the same year.

Merckx outclassed his rivals in every element of cycling—in the mountains, on the flat, in sprints—and apparently was capable of pulling away from the field whenever he so decided. Other riders contended Merckx wanted to dominate everything and leave them only the crumbs. Merckx was reputed to have earned $400,000 in 1969. His fees for exhibitions ran over $2,000. Organizers complained that after they paid Merckx there was little money left to pay other riders. Merckx refused to be worried by such talk. He said laconically: "Every time I can, I win. My job is winning races and if the competition isn't what it should be, I'm not responsible."

Canadian cyclists get in some training before competing in a world championship event in 1969 in Czechoslovakia.

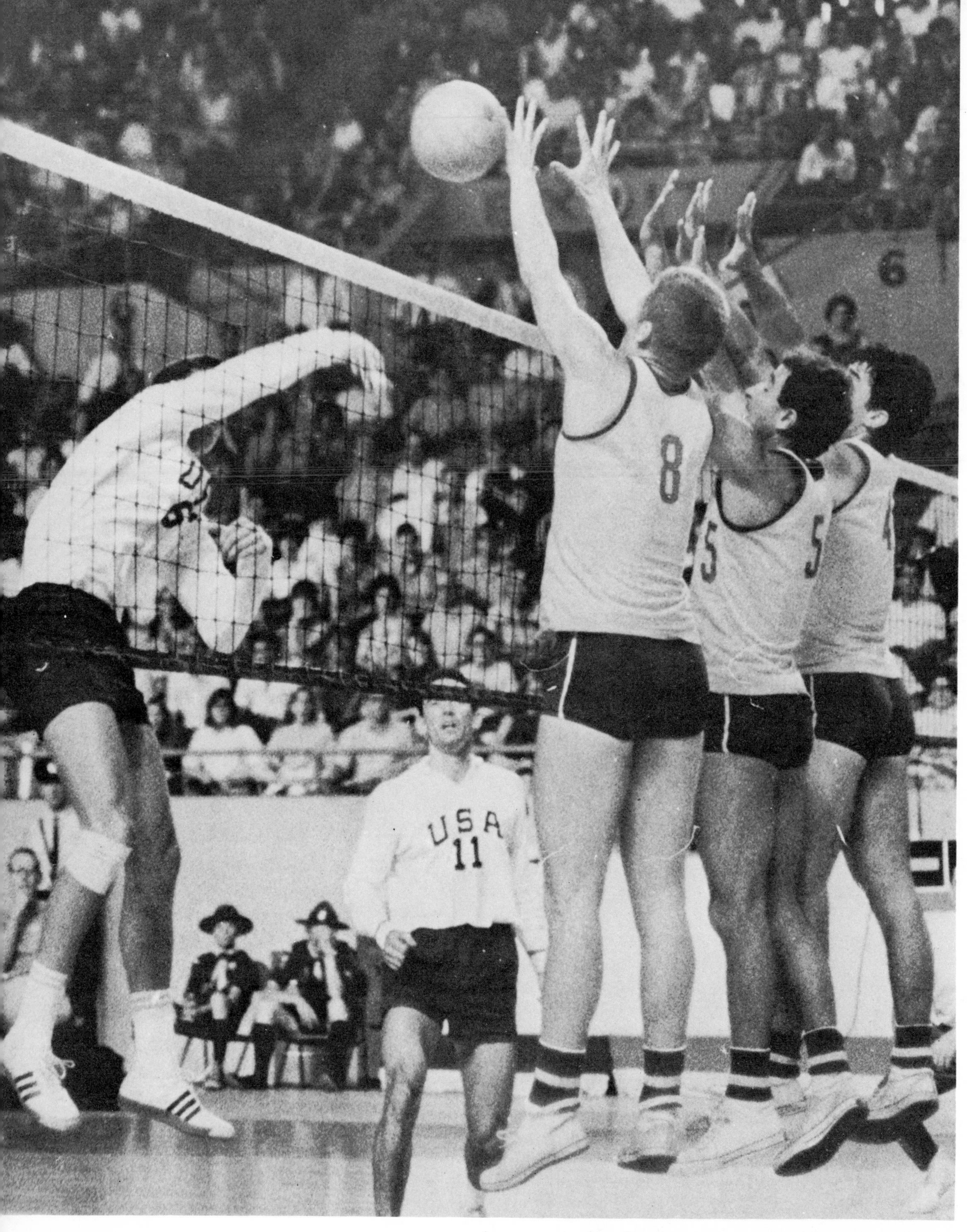

A trio of Brazilian male volleyball players go up in unison to ward off scoring attempt by a U.S. team player in the 1967 Pan American games in Winnipeg, Canada.

chapter 40

VOLLEYBALL

Its Code of Ethics is the Strictest

by Ken Rappoport

In most sports, it is the aim of the competitors to try to gain every edge. Thus, friendly games are often turned into miniature wars in which passions run deep. Tempers flare, the combat becomes fierce. Game officials become targets of abuse. Spectators frequently join in the frenzy, sometimes, in such sports as soccer, pouring out onto the field to threaten players and officials.

A sport which for some strange reason has managed to avoid this infection of mad hysteria is volleyball. Although a team sport requiring speed, skill and movement, it has made gracious behavior an ingredient of the game.

Good conduct among players, officials and even spectators has been a mandated trademark since the pastime was invented by a YMCA instructor, William G. Morgan, in 1895.

Randy Sandefur, volleyball coach at California State College at Long Beach, underlined the sportsmanship qualities when he said:

"It's considered in very poor taste for spectators to boo or razz officials or players. In addition, players themselves are closely regulated by rules in terms of demonstrating distasteful behavior like speaking to the officials, or berating or antagonizing an opponent."

Only the captain may whisper in the official's ear for a rules interpretation. Players are warned or penalized if they show displays of anger, or if they swear.

"This spirit of gentlemanly conduct is so prevalent," said Sandefur, "that spectators have been known to react critically to unsportsmanlike outbursts. The environment of friendly competition in volleyball is truly impressive."

The gentlemanly courtesies are one aspect of this sport. The spirit is another.

Teams train for months, many of the days long agonized hours of endurance involving running, jumping, diving, rolling and split-second reflexes. Players are exposed to bruises and burns by continually diving or leaping in exaggerated motions to keep the little round ball from touching the floor.

That's not exactly what Morgan had in mind when he invented the game called minonette at Holyoke, Mass.

Actually, all Morgan wanted was a recreational outlet for his noonday businessmen's class. So he yanked the rubber bladder out of a basketball, draped a 6½-foot lawn tennis net over the YMCA gymnasium floor, and told everyone to have a ball.

Morgan decided it would be as much fun to knock the missile over a net as it would through a basket. His brainchild incorporated the basic element of tennis, basketball and handball.

But it wasn't an overnight hit.

People watched it and didn't show much interest. The general feeling was that basketball or handball was sufficient for indoor sports. So volleyball for some time was confined to Holyoke and surrounding areas.

However, time and Morgan's enthusiasm took care of that. The word was spread and YMCAs soon presented volleyball in Springfield, Mass., and other New England cities.

Dr. A. T. Halsted of Springfield's YMCA logically considered the character of the game and reasoned, why not volleyball instead of minonette? Thus the name was changed officially and rules established in 1896, laying groundwork for a sport that would captivate continents as both a competitive and recreational activity.

Volleyball went from indoors to outdoors, signaling its greatest growth after the start of the 20th century. It was a time when the public playground movement got off the ground in America's cities, so it was natural that youngsters were chiefly the pioneers of this movement.

Volleyball became big because all one needed was a net and a ball—and it didn't matter where you played. Courts were laid out on playgrounds, beaches, at summer resorts and in backyards.

The number of courts had to be increased to accommodate the mass movement. Girls and boys together provided the friendly competition—and as municipal authorities installed playgrounds, none was complete without a volleyball court.

A delicate balance of recreational and team competition developed. The Physical Directors' Society of the YMCA fixed rules during its annual conventions and by 1922 the game had progressed to such a stage that a national tourney was arranged. The Pittsburgh, Pa., YMCA was the first champion. The majority of development in the sport took place between 1900 and 1925. The net was raised to its present eight feet, the court established at 30-by-60 feet and the winning score set at 15 points.

The YMCA rules committee reorganized in 1928 to become the U.S. Volleyball Association and its close alignment with the International Volleyball Federa-

The game is volleyball and these Mexico girl team members react to having failed to get ball over the net, resulting in a score for a Peru team in Winnipeg, Canada, in 1967.

tion in later years helped sophisticate the game. It took 35 years from the first slap of the ball at that Holyoke gym to get a rules committee, despite its amazing growth in the later years. Dr. George J. Fisher of New York was the group's first president and he served for 24 years.

The organization divided the country into 13 regions, triggering a flood of state and regional championships, followed by a national tournament.

Trophies dotted dens in various American homes—the C. C. Robbins Trophy, donated in 1928 for the best YMCA veterans' team, and the U.S. Volleyball Trophy, served up in 1929 by Herbert L. Pratt to winners of the U.S. Open championships.

American soldiers did more to translate the sport into a foreign language than any other force. Anywhere the doughboys went in the second world war, they played volleyball during rest periods—whether on the shifting sands of a South Seas beach or a cold grass patch somewhere in foggy London.

Prior to World War II, some foreign countries had adopted volleyball, but the sight of an American soldier at play helped shove its popularity to new heights.

It was estimated that the army of volleyball players after the war exploded over the five-million mark. Youngsters in their teens to 50-year-olds joined the movement and it became a popular American diversion.

But the seed was scattered in Europe.

It came to fruition in 1947 with the organization of the International Volleyball Federation, headquartered in Paris. It appeared the Europeans were deadly serious about making it stick.

"The difference between volleyball in America and volleyball in Europe is that we invented a recreational activity, and they made it into a sport," explained Sandefur. "The Europeans modified it and made it into a big game along with soccer. The average person in Europe knows volleyball like the average American knows baseball."

Americans invented it and Europeans added the finesse. Americans listened and learned and advanced their own play with increasingly intricate patterns of offense and defense. More recently the USVBA more closely aligned its rules with the international group, which now controls play in 62 countries.

Volleyball soon flourished beyond Morgan's original intent.

Millions were playing it in the United States so that by 1952 the USVBA national tournament included a staggering total of divisions. Among them were the collegiate, women's open, armed forces, YMCA, men's open and senior men over 35. The Army, Navy and Air Force consistently fielded fine teams in national championship play.

The vast competition was logical.

"One of the great virtues of volleyball is its universal appeal," said Sandefur. "It is for the young and old, for boys and girls and for the athletes as well as the businessman and the housewife. The game can be pursued with the ambitions and desires of an Olympic competitor or merely for relaxation, recreational enjoyment or physical exercise."

Although the International Olympic Committee reorganized volleyball as an Olympic sport in 1957, it actually wasn't introduced into Olympic competition until 1964—when both men and women played. After all, girls had actually been the most enthusiastic of the early players and the game has never lost favor with the fair sex.

But by 1964, it was too late for the United States to do anything about matching the foreign muscle.

The Iron Curtain owned international glory with Russia, East Germany, Bulgaria and Poland showing the way. Japan, too, was coming into its own with a quick, deceptive style of play that broadly contrasted with the Iron Curtain power clubs.

For all intents and purposes, the United States was still a spectator outside its own borders.

But America had a few moments on center stage, after staggering in the Pan American Games in 1955. U.S. men and women took home trophies after impressive victories at the Pan Am competitions in Winnipeg, Canada, in 1967. And the Americans reached their pinnacle with an unprecedented match victory over the world champion Russians in the 1968 Olympic Games at Mexico City.

But they still didn't finish among the team leaders.

When North Americans first visited the Pan Am Games, few recognized the volleyball competition. From a pleasant, backyard exercise, it had turned into excruciating warfare executed with practiced finesse and serious strategy.

Yet the recreational mood still lingered in America, despite the official takeover by the National Collegiate Athletic Association.

UCLA was crowned the first national champion in 1970 under the new NCAA auspices.

"The NCAA made it a sport and added to its prestige and has already opened the door for more growth in America," said Sandefur, "but it's doubtful that it will ever reach European stature."

High schools and colleges play it, and more institutions are adding volleyball to their competitive programs. California, understandably because of its climate, has produced a cache of championships—most of the talent gathered from the state's warm, southern beaches. Teams from Los Angeles, San Diego and Newport have won national recognition.

Volleyball only began as psychotherapy for nervous businessmen, but numbered 50 million among its enthusiastic worldwide followers entering the 1970s.

Around the world, field hockey maintains an enthusiastic following. Here Australian Sue Robertson, a goalie, plays in Brisbane and India's Jershan Singh and Holland's Van Gooswilligen battle for the ball during a match at Amstelveen, Holland.

chapter 41

FIELD HOCKEY

The Credit Goes to Miss Applebee

by Ken Rappoport

In the first year of the 20th century, on a warm August afternoon, some women of America got their first glimpse of field hockey—and liked it.

Constance M. Applebee, of the British College of Physical Education, was discussing the relative athletic merits of English and American women to a group at Harvard.

"An English woman cannot be judged athletically until she performs in field hockey," she said, then waited for some response.

All she got was a collective stare.

It appeared this group had never seen the sport.

"Why, then," said the vivacious Miss Applebee, "I must show you."

She did.

Using a collection of ice hockey sticks, shinny sticks and a baseball, Miss Applebee took everyone out to a field. She drew chalk boundaries and demonstrated.

One of the visiting instructors from Vassar, a Miss Ballantine, saw the instant possibilities. She invited Miss Applebee to come to the famous girls' school to teach the sport.

It was her first stop among many female institutions, including Wellesley, Smith, Mount Holyoke and Bryn Mawr. And it opened a new horizon for American girls.

Despite the physical characteristics of the female, field hockey is a woman's as well as a man's game—the aristocracy of women's sports, in fact. Played by women, coached by women and officiated by women.

The men have their day, but the sport has never lost favor with the fair sex and is a national sport for them in some countries.

Perhaps one of the reasons was its uniqueness among the world's ancient diversions. It was one of the few that didn't require the death of an opponent as a signal of victory. The fact that it didn't grow out of life-and-death circumstances was a distinctly civilized step toward present-day athletics.

It's also the type of game that sets its own pace, so girls have no trouble adjusting for speed, accuracy and endurance.

It's said to be the oldest game played with a stick and a ball. Rooted in Persia about 4,000 years ago, the Greeks also played a game with a stick and a ball which resembled hockey. Other ancient athletes once rolled pebbles at a fixed object, another forerunner of the modern game.

The French refined it centuries later with a sport called hoquet, their word for a shepherd's stick. It was played occasionally in the Middle Ages, slowly cutting its way across the English Channel to Great Britain. The Anglicized version translated the name to hockey.

It was in and out of favor in Europe and at one time outlawed in England along with every other sport except archery. The English had practical reasons, pointing out that archery was the only sport that could be transformed into a war weapon.

But in 1850 it appeared again and worked its magical, competitive force through England's schools.

The English had refined the crude French game and set down ground rules in 1875. Eight years later, the Wimbledon Hockey Club was formed and members formulated new regulations that made it a more exciting, swiftly-paced game. They tightened the rules, sharpened the game and it bounded back onto the continent with revitalized interest. The rest of Europe, though, still lagged behind England's leadership.

Because it could be played as fast or as rough as the individual teams allowed, women flooded England's hockey fields and surprisingly showed as much interest as the men. Their instant fervor made it England's national sport for women in 1887. The men continued to look on in amazement while the so-called weaker sex matched their mates in competitive spirit.

The English ladies were out to enlighten the American women, too. They sailed the Atlantic and landed in New York in the 1890s to form the Livingston Hockey Association of Staten Island, N.Y. But, the American gals showed little interest in this outdoor activity and shut their minds to it, in the process shutting out the visitors. The club died a quick, painless death.

Less than a decade later, Miss Applebee got the response the former English pioneer women were seeking. This time, it provided instant popularity.

It was practically the exclusive property of women and girls in colleges and schools. The fashionable Atlantic Seaboard set started the vogue, the rest of the country followed.

People stopped asking: What's a nice girl from Vassar doing in a sport like this? Miss Applebee was the darling of the hockey Houdinis and girls stopped crocheting to listen and learn. She toured colleges, blazing a trail for other instructors to follow.

Louise Roberts followed. An English coach at Rosemary Hall School for girls at Greenwich, Conn., she interested Henry Greer of Rye, N.Y., in the sport. He didn't know it at the time, but he was to coach American Olympic teams in years to come.

Miss Roberts also later became Mrs. Greer, something he didn't know at the time either.

While Roberts was trying to help American men catch up with their European counterparts, who had been playing Olympic field hockey since 1900, the game continued to bloom among American females. A group formed the U.S. Field Hockey Association and toured England in 1920.

Meanwhile, Great Britain's muscular males owned the Olympics. There was no team champion decided in the 1900 event at Paris, but the British won in 1908 and 1920 when it was held on a championship basis.

During the latter part of the 19th century and the first part of the 20th, Britain's influence extended to other regions of the world besides America. British army officers introduced field hockey in India, and it soon became the national sport of that country—witnessed by passionate millions.

It was this influence that soon showed its power on an international scope. India won the field hockey championship at the 1928 Olympics and unbelievably held the title through 1960, consistently producing the greatest men's teams in the world.

While the foreign powers continued to hold the spotlight, America's males were sputtering. Greer worked hard to organize men's competition, but it was a long, slow process.

Greer's efforts bore fruit on Oct. 28, 1928—when the first regular match between men's teams took place at the Germantown Cricket Club in Philadelphia. Westchester Club of Rye, N.Y., beat Germantown 2–1, inspiring the start of years of organized competition among teams on the Atlantic Seaboard.

The United States, pointing toward international recognition, finally had an official men's group in 1930: the Field Hockey Association of America. This association quickly affiliated with the American Olympic Association and the Fédération Internationale de Hockey, the international ruling body.

America at last jumped into the Olympic competition in the 1932 Games at Los Angeles and the local "greenhorns" actually surprised a few people.

They came in third and scored a goal on the great Indian team. On the other hand, sports writers were so impressed with India's athletes, they voted their showing in the Olympics the most outstanding exhibition of skill in any of the sports.

The Indians' blazing, sure-handed play was due in part to their own inventiveness. They had shortened the toe of their stick, so a player could reverse the stick without relaxing his grip, thus attaining remarkable control. This slight refinement brought greater flexibility to play and it was adopted by most European countries in hopes of wresting the title from the fabulous Indian aggregation.

It didn't help in the 1936 Olympics at Berlin, when India easily regained its supremacy. The United States, however, continued to show improvement.

Competitors in a field hockey match are shown in action in Sydney, Australia. The game, in its simplest form, is much like ice hockey.

The rest of the world showed some interest, too. Also participating in the 1936 Games were Japan, Hungary, Afghanistan, Denmark, Holland, France, Belgium and Switzerland.

Field hockey held international interest despite the four-year lulls between Olympic competition. Once again, the women in America took the leadership, trail-blazing the world with a touring group that included stopovers in England, Denmark, British Isles, Australia, British Guiana, Scotland, South Africa and The Netherlands, not to mention the remote areas of their own country. The International Federation of Women's Hockey Association was organized with a membership of eight countries "to further the best interests of the game among women of all nations." They held conferences in Geneva, Copenhagen and Philadelphia.

The magic names began to appear among America's talented women players—Anne B. Townsend, considered by some to be the greatest of her countrywomen; Frances Elliot; Betty Shellenberger and Betty Rickey. Miss Townsend was president of the U.S. Field Hockey Association and captained 15 American teams in international competition.

Women drew fans the world over. In an international match between England and Ireland in 1951, a record crowd of 30,000 rocked London's Wembley Stadium. But that huge success was topped by 45,000 fanatical followers who saw England's women whip Scotland 9–2 the next year.

In the men's world, visiting countries multiplied at the Olympics. Seventeen showed up in London in the 1948 affair when India stopped Great Britain 4–0 in the finals.

India's rule was wrecked by neighborhood foe Pakistan in the 1964 Olympics in Tokyo. The nearby upstarts took a nerve-wracking 1–0 victory, giving some hope to the rest of the world's also-rans.

But India had built a model of perfection, hard to match. The style-setting Hercules of hockey had developed a feature of short, trolled passes as opposed to the Europeans' tendency of slamming the ball around the field.

International celebrities spawned in India's star-studded galaxy included players named Pinninger and Dhyan Chand. The rest of the world attempted to track down the swift-moving Indians with brilliance of its own, including Shoveler of England, Haag and Weiss of Germany, Van den Berg and Esser of The Netherlands, and Mike O'Brien and Kurt Orban of America.

Today, England, The Netherlands, Germany and Pakistan challenge the Indian royalty.

The British taught the Indians—and now the student is at the head of the class.

Roldan of Mexico, left, and Vicol of Romania, are shown in action in the 1960 Olympics in Rome.

chapter 42

FENCING

The Yanks are Good Only in the Movies

by Ken Rappoport

Ready to strike like a hair-trigger spring, the hero stands poised and stick-straight on the leaf of the balustrade. His lithe figure, against the castle's garish drapes, dashes into action.

He dances toward the villain, his sword moving like a scalpel. Down the stone stairs, across the great dining hall, over tables and chairs.

Thrust, parry, thrust. His sword gouges the air, then suddenly strikes home in the villain, accompanied by the crashing finality of cymbals and drums in the background.

The lights come on, the curtain drops, the audience gets up and saunters out.

Another Hollywood production and the inevitable ending. How often has one witnessed this deathless scene?

The translation from the movie screen into real life, however, was a little different for Cornell Wilde, an accomplished fencer among movie actors.

He met his match in a woman.

During a rest period on a Hollywood spectacular, Wilde was introduced to an extra who challenged him to a duel. She beat him with clinical ease, but he felt better about it after he found out who she was.

Wilde was later introduced formally to Helene Mayer, a classy German fraulein ranked as one of the world's greatest female fencers.

It really wasn't fair, but Wilde learned a lesson that stuck: always be on guard.

Unfortunately, it was different 5,000 years ago when swordplay was originated in Japan. The loser didn't live to get a second chance.

It was deadly combat then, a type of fencing called kendo in which the Japanese whaled away at each other with two-handed bamboo sticks. One of the oldest known swords is the short sword of Saragon the First King of Ur, dating the pioneer weapon long before the Christian era.

One of the world's most treasured blades is the Divine Sword, currently enshrined in a Japanese museum. It was said to have been brandished by Prince Yamato Takeruno Mikoto, who used it to cut down blazing grass and whirled it at enemies in eastern Japan.

As a weapon of war, the sword bloodied many battlefields, and appeared mythically and magically in legend and poetry.

But because the blade was bronze and could not hold a sharp edge, it was not in general use until the 12th or 13th centuries A.D., when duels were the accepted means of settling disputes. It was, in fact, the vogue.

A gentleman's honor to be decided, a lady's hand, a parcel of land . . . these were all dealt with at The Duel. A face slapped by a glove, the meeting at daybreak near a quiet embankment. . . .

It was savage, but considered the only civilized way of settling things. Out of this warfare, the sport of fencing was given its first pointed direction, for men had studied long hours to master the life-and-death trickery of swordplay. Surprisingly, even today dueling is used in some instances to settle disputes—although the bout is halted at the first sign of blood.

Several European countries claim they invented the sport. About the middle of the 14th century, the Germans decided a sword needn't be always flashed in anger. They pioneered the Marxbruder (Fencing) Guild of Lowenburg, using a heavy-handed weapon 32 to 36 inches long. This clumsy bludgeon without a hand guard contrasted widely with the sliver-like weapons linked with modern fencing and more closely associated with Spain, Italy and France. A Spanish army captain who lived in the 16th century, Gonzalvo Cordova, refined the weapon with a hand guard, then the growth of fencing exploded after gunpowder silenced the bow and arrow as a major weapon of war.

Europe's upper class shed its armored suits as soon as the bullets started flying, appealing to commoners to teach them more about this newfangled weapon. They did, and schools for fencing sprang up over Europe. The aristocracy was in the students' role and the teachers were commoners who had previously earned their livelihood by putting on fencing exhibitions.

Swordplay became a continental identification. People wrote about the intricacies of the sport and the words were gobbled up in the big cities. Italian Achille Marozzo is credited with writing the first booklet in 1536, and what is said to be the first treatise of its kind in England was Silver's *Brief Introductions on My Paradoxes of Defense* in 1599.

Contributions came in from all over Europe. The French added a typical, romantic dash by giving names to the various movements. In 1570, fencing devotee Henri Saint-Didier called them disengage, coupé, double, redoublement and priz-de-fer, and many of these precision strikes stick to this day.

Of course, where would modern fencing be without "touché" and "en garde?"

In 1680, Count Koenigsmarken added Poland's offering, a radical departure to the blade's appearance. The weapon was fashioned with a wide upper half, tapered severely in a triangular mode and hollowed on all three sides. The French, for no logical reason, called it "colichemarder," and the name lasted the centuries. The epee and saber of modern use are related in fashion to the Koenigsmarken design.

France provided the world with one of the greatest swordsmen of the early era—Chevalier de Saint Georges, a half-breed from Guadalupe. Italy contributed a gallant, dashing fellow named Di Grassi, and England had a transplanted Frenchman, Chevalier de'Eon de Beaumont, in the late 18th century.

"Fencing is the mirror of the soul," said one Italian great.

It also reflected the mirror of love, for many a lady's heart was enthralled by sword-toting gallants.

Fencing fever boiled over the Atlantic to the United States, where duels to avenge honor atrophied after the Civil War, and the sport took root and flight. Modern fencing was subject to a few, conventional rules, but otherwise differed little from the fundamental techniques of the early days. Prior to the 18th century, movement was rigidly restricted because of the danger of injury to the face. Now there were wire-mesh masks and lighter, more flexible weapons.

The foil, fashioned after a short dress sword, had a blunt point. Rules stated touches must be made with the point targeting the trunk of the body from the collar to the groin lines. The epee, a replica of the dueling sword, had a rigid, triangular blade with a large bell guard. The point was covered with a small cone and touches could be scored on any part of the body. The saber, a thin, triangular blade with a dull cutting edge along the front line and part of the back edge, had a blunt point and valid touches landed on the body above the waist.

The Amateur Athletic Union supervised the sport's baby years in America. Then in 1891, active fencers established a bigger group under the leadership of Dr. Graeme M. Hammond. Thus the Amateur Fencers League of America became the governing body of the country.

Its headquarters were in New York, but the AFLA flowed across the country into dozens of substations and later became affiliated with the Amateur Athletic Union, the U.S. Olympic Association and the Fédération Internationale d'Escrime, the sport's international governing body.

Fencing was really getting started in America, instigated by transient Europeans and furthered by local devotees. It became apparent one needn't be a spry youngster to participate. In fact, experience, mental poise and maturity together with a delicate sense of timing were so important that it helped to be older. According to the experts, great fencers reached their peak between the ages of 28 and 35 and the average competitive life covered 25 years. Baron De Coubertin, founder of the modern Olympics, was a fencer who had frequent workouts in his 70s.

The first modern Olympics in 1896 featured fencing. The Europeans, taking it very seriously, brought a wealth of talent and experience to it. The Americans concentrated on track and field and therefore lost their collective shirts in fencing.

They were cut to ribbons by E. Gravelotte, one of the great early fencers from France who won both the foil and epee championships, and by a Greek flash, I. Georgiadhis, who took the saber.

The Olympics were a spectacular showcase for the best. A Cuban living in

Paris, Ramon Fonst, soon became one of the greatest modern swordsmen, flashing his extraordinary talents in the 1900 and 1904 Olympics. His one-man show in the 1904 Games, where he won the foil and the epee and led his mates to a Cuban victory in the first fencing team competition, established his immortality among fencers.

The 1908 Olympics heralded the beginning of Hungarian domination in the saber event. Italian fencing master Italo Santelli actually gave them their start years before when he coached saber in Budapest and created a style to match the character and competitive fervor of the Hungarian people. Hungarians have won most of the saber titles since and a trove of national championships wherever they've emigrated.

After the 1908 Games, many countries met on an international level, hypoing interest into the sport for future Olympics.

The first world war shut off international competition, but fencing neverthe-

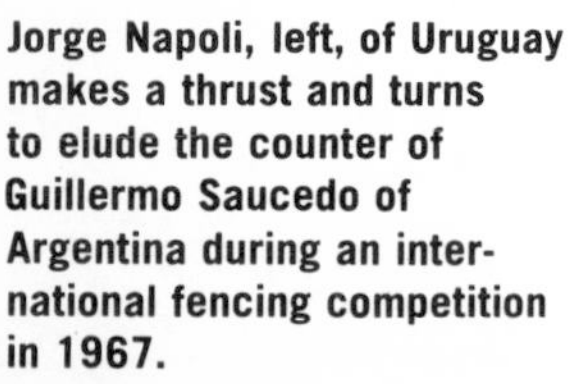

Jorge Napoli, left, of Uruguay makes a thrust and turns to elude the counter of Guillermo Saucedo of Argentina during an international fencing competition in 1967.

less grew within countries because of recreational military competitions. It reared again in the postwar Inter-Allied Games, pitting amateurs and professionals, and fencers then brought sharpened techniques into the 1920 Olympics. Seventeen countries were present, reflecting fresh interest and improved styles. Other stylists appeared among the treasured French and Italians, inspiring public applause.

Italy's Nedo Nadi and France's Lucien Gaudin were seriously being considered among the all-time best along with Cuba's Fonst.

Like Hungary, America owed its start in fencing to imported teaching. Louis Vauthier, a graduate of a French physical training school, coached at the New York Fencers Club, then went to West Point. He manipulated a number of individual and national champions while inspiring title-winning teams at Army. The Cadets dominated colleges for years, winning the national title 10 out of 14 years, and placing second the remaining four.

Women began competing on an international level in the 1924 Olympics. In the next Games four years later, Germany's Helene Mayer began her assault on the field. She was dubbed queen of fencing, and for good reason. She won a world title, settled in the United States and captured eight national championships through 1946.

Global interest leaped with the beginning of the World Fencing Championships, open championships between amateurs and professionals, in addition to the national events in many countries. Each country had its fencing god or goddess. Ilona Elek of Hungary won three world women's titles, as well as a gold medal in the 1948 Olympics. Mexico's Haro Oliva, a swaggering army officer, became the Western Hemisphere's greatest fencer since Fonst. And the United States had one—and lost him—when George Clanan was killed in a dirigible disaster, dealing a blow to the country's hopes for fencing recognition.

In Helsinki, Finland, 32 nations had entries in the 1952 Olympics. But none was as good as Italy, Hungary and France—the countries where fencing was king. The Big Three swept the gold medals.

New techniques came, but the same old countries headed the list—Italy, Hungary, Germany and Russia sharing top honors in the 1960 games. America lagged painfully behind, even though its schools were brushing up on the European game. The United States boasted over 600 colleges participating, over 400,000 fencers and expanding interest, but still had no international fame.

The sport swung full circle to Japan for the 1964 Olympics. Fencing teams visited the Imperial Palace in Tokyo and witnessed exhibitions of kendo, the ancient death-dealing matches.

There was no blood spilled this time, but war whoops of the make-believe warriors might have inspired a chill here and there.

From bamboo stick to foil, epee and saber—it was a work of art.

"Fencing combines the techniques of the golfer, the explosive energy of the sprinter and the split-second decisions demanded of the boxer," once said American fencing devotee Roy S. Tinney. "It's an education, with a lure peculiarly its own."

Kjell Johannsen, left, of Sweden, with teammate Hans Alser behind him, makes a forehand return in finals of men's doubles play at the 30th World Table Tennis championships in Frankfurt, Germany, in 1969. They defeated a Japanese team for the title.

chapter 43

TABLE TENNIS

Ping Pong Pierces the Bamboo Curtain

by Ed Schuyler Jr.

Table tennis, or, using its more popular commercial name, Ping Pong, has been a midget among giants in the Western sports world for better than half a century, struggling vainly for recognition, forced to be content with inches of space in an age of burgeoning headlines.

Then came April 10, 1971.

On that day, fifteen members of an American table tennis party which had been competing in the World Championships at Nagoya, Japan, crossed the border into Communist China—as invited guests of the Chinese.

It marked the first time since the mid-1950s that such a group had been permitted to penetrate the Bamboo Curtain and get a look at the Red Communist monster inside his own lair.

The impact was like a thunderclap—politically and socially.

The Americans were greeted in Peking by a smiling, witty Premier Chou En-lai, who said the visit "had opened a new page in relations of the Chinese and American people."

In Washington, President Nixon responded by announcing a relaxation of the embargo on trade with Communist China and a series of unilateral moves to improve relations between the two countries.

Graham B. Steenhoven of Detroit, president of the U.S. Table Tennis Association, announced plans for a reciprocal visit by Chinese Ping Pongers to the United States.

For two weeks the front pages of the nation's newspapers and the screens of the television networks were saturated with the activities of the American table tennis group—inside Mainland China and on the return home.

There was a picture of Mao Tse-tung holding a Ping Pong paddle.

Headlines were intriguing:

"Celluloid Ball Pierces Bamboo Curtain."

"Ping-Pong Diplomacy."

"Peking Pongers to Visit U.S."

The obscure table tennis breed found themselves possessed with a new and more important stature. Researchers began delving into the history of the game.

Conservative commuters argued the merits of dimpled rubber paddles and the Chinese two-finger pencil grip.

No sport and no sport spectacle—football's Super Bowl, baseball's World Series, racing's Kentucky Derby, boxing's Fight of the Century between Joe Frazier and Muhammad Ali — ever received such exposure from the news media.

Table tennis finally had come alive.

The sport in which the Orientals finally became the masters—Chinese men wresting the world crown from Japan in 1971 at Nagoya but the Japanese women retaining their title—ironically was first the pastime of the bourgeois. It was the favorite game of aristocrats in the 1890s, played at parties on the dining room table or on the floor with a net stretched between two chairs.

A big table tennis boom occurred after the second world war in the United States and Europe.

The U.S. team that competed in the 1947 world championships in Paris consisted of some of the greatest American players, such as Richard Miles and Sol Schiff of New York.

The Americans failed to win any world titles in 1947, all of them going to Europeans. Gradually European domination dwindled until most of the top players were from Japan and Communist China. However, as the sport left the 1960s for the '70s, the Europeans again were showing signs of moving to the front.

Some of the great players in the world as the '70s opened were men's singles champion Itoh of Japan, Chuang Tse-tung and Li Ching-kuang of Communist China, Denis Neale and Chester Barnes of England and world doubles kings Hans Alser and Kjell Johannsen of Sweden.

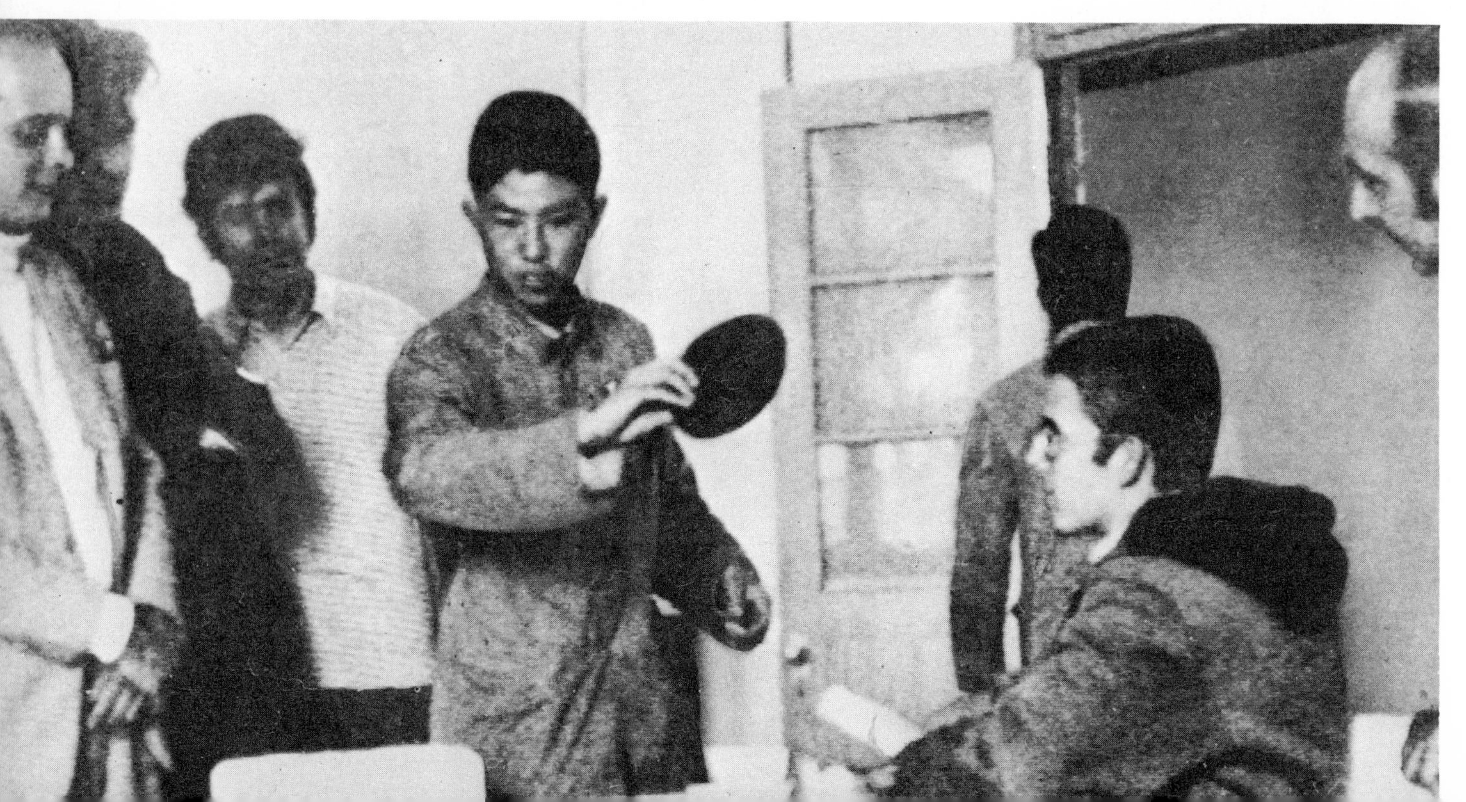

Everybody plays table tennis in China, or so it seems. Here a young man demonstrates his technique for the touring U.S. table tennis team.

The 1970 U.S. men's champion was Dal Joon Lee of Cleveland, while other top players included John Tannehill of Middleport, Ohio, and Errol Resek of New York.

Heading the women's singles players were English-born Irene Ogus of San Francisco, Patty Martinez Cash of San Diego and Wendy Hicks of Santa Barbara, Calif.

Table tennis was a late bloomer as far as worldwide sports are concerned. In fact, there are conflicting stories as to how it originated.

Some say it was started by a British army officer in India. Others say it was begun by a British army officer in South Africa. Still others claim it originated in England in the 19th century.

Then there is the version that the game of table tennis was born in New England in the 1890s.

Whatever its origin, it is known that a Salem, Mass., sports equipment manufacturer, Parker Brothers, developed a game in the 1890s that it called indoor tennis. The game, played with a knitted web, met with mild acceptance in the United States and the firm exported indoor tennis equipment to its English agent, Hamley Brothers in London.

The game caught on in Great Britain.

Hamley Brothers later came across a new ball for the game, one made of celluloid. It is not known just how the ball came into existence.

Next the Hamleys gave the game a new name, Ping Pong—for the ping sound of the bat hitting the ball and the pong sound of the ball striking the table. The name was patented by Parker Brothers of Salem.

The sport gained popularity in Europe, but it was not greeted with enthusiasm upon its reintroduction into the United States in 1900 although it began to spread two years later. However, it soon lost favor, being considered a craze, and interest in it also fell off in Europe.

Then, in 1921 several European countries revived the sport, and five years later in Berlin the International Table Tennis Association was organized. This organization standardized rules and equipment.

A table tennis revival started in the United States in 1927, and three years later the American Ping Pong Association was formed. It held a national tournament in 1931, with only Parker Brothers' equipment allowed.

Other manufacturers, awakening to the value of the sport as a parlor game, began calling their equipment table tennis equipment and there soon was formed the United States Table Tennis Association.

A fight developed between the U.S. Table Tennis Association and the Ping Pong Association as to who would control the sport, a fight that ended in a merger, with the new group using the name U.S. Table Tennis Association and aligning with the international governing body.

Table tennis grew in the United States until, as with such sports as swimming and track and field, it became organized not just on the adult level but also on an ambitious age-group scale.

There are groupings for boys and girls 17 years old and under, 15 and under and 13 and under. There also are boys and girls doubles categories.

Table tennis, as in golf, has competitions for seniors and, as in bowling and tennis, for mixed doubles.

All is not well in this Olympic pentathlon event at the 1932 Games in Los Angeles. Imre Petnehazy of Hungary reaches for safety as he is thrown from his mount in the 5,000-meter cross-country equestrian event.

chapter 44

EQUESTRIAN

Horses Take to the Stage

by Ken Rappoport

The rain poured in lumps for days.

It looked as if the equestrian event at the 1964 Olympics was all washed up.

The relentless drenching soaked the Karuizawa facilities at Tokyo, transforming the day's endurance courses into the proverbial muddy swimming hole.

It was the day of the most demanding tests, as well—the two-mile steeplechase event and the four-mile cross-country.

England's Michael Bullen climbed on Sea Breeze, a horse with the appropriate name for the weather.

Bullen, soaked and riding on a rain-slick saddle, slipped at the second jump and dislocated his shoulder. But horse and rider carried on in the best stiff-upper-lip tradition.

Later, Bullen rode Sea Breeze in the four-mile cross-country with its 31 big jumps. But pain forced him partially to lose control on the 25th obstacle, a jump across a ditch.

They tried three times and failed to make the leap.

Bullen and Sea Breeze pulled into reverse, skittering blindly backwards into a ditch. They were eliminated.

Germany went on to win the team competition, adding more Olympic gold to its burgeoning trophy room.

Another Olympiad and another European victory. It was getting to be second nature, Sweden and Germany swapping team titles with an occasional shot of anger fired from the French and Russian fronts.

But from the turn of the 20th century, it had become a cold fact of Olympic life: Nobody, well, hardly anybody, beat the Europeans at their own game.

It was an Italian named Pignatelli who founded the first equestrian school some 300 years earlier. Long before that, the Greeks had equestrians in their Olympics. And horses were an integral part of the life of the continent's royalty.

Even today, Russia leads the world in the number of species of horses.

Some looked to the United States to provide a dark horse challenger to wrest the crown from the European powerhouses. But except for a few stabs of brilliance, America was hardly in the race.

While European equestrians pounded indefatigably toward entry in the modern Olympics, Americans were in a brash, party mood on their side of the Atlantic.

The National Horse Show raised the curtain on equestrian sports in America, but it was turned into little more than a fashion fair as high society seized it as a showcase for its finery.

The opening of the horse show in New York's Madison Square Garden in the 1890s had more glitter and glamor than a fancy dress ball—and the "commoners" choked the promenades to glimpse the swells, enthroned in dazzling array in the expensive seats.

Tons of horseflesh loped through the spotlights and sawdust, but who cared?

In Europe, meanwhile, equestrian devotees finally pushed through a minor victory. Their appeals got horses into the 1900 and 1908 Olympics, in the polo event. The high-riding British army of India won both years.

Their feet in the door with polo, the horse show gadflies at last landed in the fifth modern Olympics, in 1912 at Stockholm. The competition included Sweden, Germany, Belgium, Denmark, Great Britain, France and Russia.

Host Sweden was most inhospitable, taking the team title. It was the first of a run of Olympic gold medals for the fabulous Swedes.

Any hopes of America trying to track down the stylish Europeans was further dimmed with the elimination of the cavalry as the elite corps of the U.S. Army. The next time the Olympics were held in 1920, Sweden's crack aggregation was again in the winner's circle.

Eighteen countries charged into the 1924 Olympics in Paris with the same inevitable ending. The Swedes were just too tough for the field. The United States, despite the flourishing horse shows on the home front, could only manage a 10th-place tie with France, another World War I equestrian reject.

Civilians broke into the Olympics after dedicated years in national competition. A number of them joined the 1928 event, with a promise of more to come.

The horse show continued as an entertainment feature in America, as the splendid stallions were wheeled around the country to compete in year-around warm climes for cash, ribbons or cups. Out of the fast competition, a brilliant star exploded among the United States' premier horsewomen—Helen K. Crabtree. She trained 17 world champions, became Horsewoman of the Year, and built a reputation as one of the world's top equitation instructors.

Horse shows continued to be a rich man's toy, since the prize very often was less than maintenance costs.

Some horses, of course, made money for their owners.

The prize-winning Gold Digger, an American beauty, sold for $10,000—more than repaying his original cost and maintenance. One of the most legendary show horses of all time was another gilt-edged American prancer—Sweetheart-On-Parade.

She won the Grand National championship for five-gaited horses twice—1931 and 1932—in an apparent climax to a meteoric career.

But, as it turned out, it wasn't the last hurrah at all.

Her owner, Mrs. H. P. Roth, brought her back and entered her in the mares' division of the Board of Governors stake in Kansas City, Oct. 24, 1935. Even though a bit old, Sweetheart had enough style to beat the field and earn $500 first prize. It was a big hit for the romantics.

With all the horse show popularity in America, the United States decided to shoot for international applause. The Americans, therefore, began preparations for the 1932 Olympics in 1929. Twelve riders and 40 horses were transplanted in Fort Rosecrans, Calif.—the finest supplied from the U.S. Cavalry.

The three years hard work paid off.

The result was never in doubt as the United States won its first world title in 1932.

Kelso, Horse of the Year for five years and winner of $1,893,362 during his racing career, is shown in 1968 demonstrating jumping abilities at the opening night of the National Horse Show in New York's Madison Square Garden. Riding Kelso was Mike Plumb of the U.S. equestrian team.

West German rider Lutz Merkel urges his mount, Sperber, over barrier at New York's Madison Square Garden in international jumping competition at the National Horse Show in 1970.

The military-oriented 1936 show at Berlin was won by Germany, but the soon-to-happen second world war threatened to deliver another undermining blow to Olympic equestrians. The cavalry was further de-emphasized in war strategy. It was significant from an Olympic standpoint, since national teams were still usually composed of army personnel.

The Olympics survived the Big War, and in 1948 the teams came together in battle-scarred London. It was the only other year producing an American team champion and the competitions included classic events that were standardized for future shows.

Among them: dressage—essentially an exhibition of the art of riding displaying balance, suppleness and ease of control; complete riding competition—a searching series of tests of practical riding that included endurance and obstacle courses; and Prix des Nations—jumps over obstacles formidable in height and arrangement.

The Western Hemisphere boasted another fine outfit along with the United States in that '48 spectacular—the Mexico riding team. The gallant Mexicans brought home the gold for winning the Prix des Nations.

Meanwhile, the grandiose New York shows were just getting into the swing of things after a World War II layoff. They were, once again, the social hit of the season—with healthy slices of fanfare and grandeur forked in for good measure.

They also dealt out a potpourri of horseflesh amidst a staggering number of categories—hackneys, harness, thoroughbred jumpers, interbred hunter horses . . . and the list went on. The most popular event, though, was the competition for the military, in which the greatest world horsemen met the best American riders in a series of daredevil jumps.

The American Horse Shows Association, which had taken over the reins from the founding group, now reported 2,982 individual members and 258 individual shows under its jurisdiction.

Despite this apparent popularity, and America's fine performance in the 1948 Olympics, the nation's equestrian future appeared cloudy. The abandonment of polo and equestrian sports by the U.S. Army had left a gap.

A group of sportsmen undertook to correct this deficiency by organizing the International Competitions Corp. in New York. Col. John W. Wofford, former member of a U.S. Olympic team, spearheaded the group. The corporation raised funds and in 1950 selected a team to represent the U.S. at the Pennsylvania Horse Show in Harrisburg, the National Horse Show at New York and the Royal Winter Fair at Toronto.

The corporation leased veteran horses from the defunct Army Horse Show team, trained hard and hoped to make a fight of it in the 1952 Olympics. But it was once again Sweden's show.

Thirty-one nations sent contestants and over 25,000 horse lovers were on hand for the impressive opening ceremonies at the 1956 Olympics in Melbourne, Australia. Germany won this time.

The affair was splashier than ever in 1960. It was, for a change, Australia's turn to serve notice on the world. Lawrence Morgan, a 45-year-old rancher, made it all come true for the Aussies, winning the three-day individual contest as well as leading the country to the team championship.

The flashy Australian was among the gems on display, matching his gaudy brilliance with other legendary international names through the years, such as Tommaso Lequio of Italy, F. Ventura of Czechoslovakia, Pierre Jonquieres D'Oriola of France, Henri Chammartin of Switzerland and Frank Chapot of the United States.

After Germany's 1964 Olympic laurels, Russia galloped off with the 1968 team event in the rarefied air of Mexico City.

The competitive Olympic fever, sky-high in that sun-baked Mexican aura, had brought out the best of the skilled Russian horsemen.

It was a distinctly Russian triumph, but more instinctively, European.

INDEX